ISBN 978-1-330-11185-7
PIBN 10028575

English
Français
Deutsche
Italiano
Español
Português

www.forgottenbooks.com

Mythology Photography **Fiction**
Fishing Christianity **Art** Cooking
Essays Buddhism Freemasonry
Medicine **Biology** Music **Ancient
Egypt** Evolution Carpentry Physics
Dance Geology **Mathematics** Fitness
Shakespeare **Folklore** Yoga Marketing
Confidence Immortality Biographies
Poetry **Psychology** Witchcraft
Electronics Chemistry History **Law**
Accounting **Philosophy** Anthropology
Alchemy Drama Quantum Mechanics
Atheism Sexual Health **Ancient History**
Entrepreneurship Languages Sport
Paleontology Needlework Islam
Metaphysics Investment Archaeology
Parenting Statistics Criminology
Motivational

OUTLINES

OF

PRIMITIVE BELIE

AMONG THE INDO-EUROPEAN RACES

BY

CHARLES FRANCIS KEARY, M.A., F.S.A.

OF THE BRITISH MUSEUM

NEW YORK

CHARLES SCRIBNER'S SONS

TO

A. M. K.

AND

E. H. K.

.

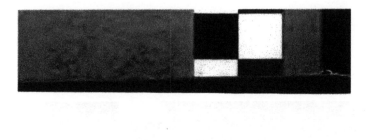

PREFACE.

THERE are two roads along which students are now travelling towards (we may reasonably hope) the same goal of fuller knowledge touching Prehistoric Belief. One way is that of Comparative Mythology, which has become so favourite a pursuit with the present generation. In this method the myth is taken for the centre-point of the enquiry, and—just as a specimen in natural history may be—it is traced through all the varieties and sub-species that are to be discovered in various lands. The other method, which is an historical rather than a scientific one, may be called the study of the History of Belief. In it our eyes are for the time being fixed upon a single race of men; and it is the relationship of these people to the world by which they are surrounded that we seek to know. The following outlines of early Aryan belief belong to the class of studies, which are distinctly historical in character. They are not designed to establish any new theory of the origin of belief among mankind; nor are they meant to deal with theories which relate to creeds other than the Indo-European. They are essentially a record of facts;

for the facts of early Aryan belief are of a kind as
surely ascertainable as the laws of marriage or of
primitive society among the Aryan races.   That the
pictures which are here held up are blurred and im-
perfect I am well aware.   But some indulgence may
be claimed for what are, owing to the necessities of
the case and to the incompleteness of our present
knowledge, mosaics and not paintings.

The active discussion which has of late arisen
over some of the secondary questions of Indo-European mythology has tended to obscure our actual
attainments in this field of enquiry.   This must necessarily have been the case with the general reader,
who cannot be expected to keep the science constantly
in view nor to register its slow advance.   By such a
reader a whole system of mythological interpretation
is supposed to stand or fall upon the question
whether certain stories can be proved to have sprung
out of 'sun myths,' or certain other tales to have
been called into existence through an 'abuse of
language.'   But still more has this discussion tended
to throw into the background the historical method
of enquiry into the early history of belief, and to
hide altogether the results which it has reached.
To this field of research some matters of high importance in comparative mythology are only of
secondary consequence, and therefore some difficulties
which have stood in the way of the one study do not
impede the other.   One of the subjects, for instance,
which has been most eagerly debated among mytho-

logists is the question as to what are and where we are to look for the originals, the actual first forms of those tales which go to make up any system of mythology; and it is upon the answer which should be given to that question that schools are at present most divided. The difficulty does not press with the same insistence upon him who seeks merely to get a clear notion of belief in some of its particular phases. He can find out who are the beings that people the myth system upon which he is engaged, and what are the stories related of them, without troubling himself to discover whether the same stories were once told concerning beings of another order. It is with the members of the Aryan pantheon as it is with such half-mythic beings as the Charles of the Carlovingian or the Arthur of the Arthurian romance. The tales told of the two may have wonderful points of resemblance, but we can distinguish between the legend of the Frankish emperor and the legend of the British king. Or, again, that which is recounted of Charles and Arthur may with variations have been told of Red Indian heroes or of Zulu gods; but this does not affect the fact that for the particular times and places under consideration the stories attach to Charles and his paladins or to Arthur and his knights. We are not compelled to trace the myths to their remotest origin to understand the nature of the two legends.

There can, in truth, be little doubt that in some crude form most of the myths of the Indo-European system existed among human beings at a date much earlier than the era in which we first distinguish the Aryan races. I hardly suppose that the most ardent hunter after histories which tell of the loves of the Sun and the Dawn would maintain that it was from the observation of the Sun and of the Dawn that mankind first gained its idea of two lovers. The tales come to attach themselves to those mythic beings whom at any particular stage of culture the people have most in their thoughts. What was once related of a tree or of an animal may come to be told of the sun and of the earth. Wherefore it is only after a complete study of the belief in question that we can form a judgment as to the nature of the existences to which such tales are likely to relate. When we have settled this point we can compare the myths of systems which belong to the same stage of thought, with a reasonable assurance that like stories will attach to like individualities.

Now concerning the creed of the primitive Aryas: Comparative Mythology has made it possible for us to reconstruct this in outline for a time which precedes the historical age. The process whereby we arrive at our knowledge in this case is precisely the process whereby we gain almost all the knowledge which we possess concerning the prehistoric life of the Aryas, their laws of marriage, their social conditions, their advance in arts or in agriculture. As to the principal result of this enquiry all, or almost all, who have entered upon it are agreed. It has been established that this primitive Aryan creed rested upon a worship of external phenomena, such as the sky, the earth, the sea, the storm, the wind, the sun—that is to say, of phenomena which were appreciable by the senses, but were at the same time in a large proportion either abstractions or generalisations. It is this form of creed which I have throughout the present volume distinguished as Nature Worship, and of necessity it is the one with which we shall be almost exclusively concerned.

Therefore, seeing that concerning the character of this early Aryan belief all those are agreed who have made a critical study of the Indo-European mythologies, it is obvious that it stands in quite a different category from the disputed questions of comparative mythology. To me individually, after a study of certain among the Indo-European systems, the presence of this nature worship at the root of them seems incontrovertible. But, what is of infinitely more importance, I find that the specialists in every field—Vedic, Persian, Greek, Roman, Teutonic, Celtic—have believed themselves to discover this nature worship at the back of the historic creeds they knew so well; and I cannot persuade myself that all their judgments are mistaken, or that there should be such a coincidence of error coming from so many different sides.

For, whether we ask Vedic scholars, as Benfey, Max Müller, Kuhn, Roth, Bréal, Grassmann, Gubernatis, Bergaigne, students of Greek mythology, as Welcker, Preller, Maury, of German, as Grimm, Simrock, we find that those who are first in each of the several branches of research, or those who have studied them all, are alike agreed upon this particular question. However in minor matters they may differ, upon this matter their judgment is uniform. This at least must be *res judicata*, a question no longer admitting of dispute.

The sources of our information touching the prehistoric beliefs of the Indo-Europeans are sufficiently well known not to need a recapitulation here. The most important which I have made use of in this volume may be roughly divided into four classes. (1) The Vedas, and chiefly the *R*ig Veda; (2) the Greek literature of mythology, especially the prehistoric poets, Homer and Hesiod; (3) the Icelandic Eddas and Sagas; (4) mediæval legends and epics, together with modern popular tales and traditions, almost all of which preserve some relics of ancient heathenism. In the case of the Vedas I have been obliged to avail myself of translations. Of the *R*ig Veda there now exist two almost complete translations into German, those of H. Grassmann and Ludwig. The beautiful metrical rendering of H. Grassmann is the one to which I have been most indebted.

C. F. K.

LONDON, 1882.

CONTENTS.

CHAPTER I.

NATURE OF BELIEF AS HERE DEALT WITH.

§ 1. *Limits of the Enquiry.*

§ 2. *Early Phases of Belief.*

CHAPTER II.

THE EARLY GROWTH OF BELIEF.

CHAPTER VIII.

THE SHADOW OF DEATH.

CHAPTER IX.

THE EARTHLY PARADISE.

Effect of Christianity in changing men's belief concerning the other world—The Earthly Paradise, however, continued to exist rather in spite of than through its influence—Prejudice in favour

CHAPTER X.

HEATHENISM IN THE MIDDLE AGES.

The heathenism of Northern Europe cannot be studied in heathen
literature or heathen times alone—It is therefore desirable to
give a glance at some of its lingering effects in the Middle Ages,
though this can be no more than a glance—The Middle Ages
ages of mythology rather than of history—The age of the Teutonic
conquests in Roman territory was that which gave birth to the
great German epic, the Nibelungen—The germ of the story to be
traced in the second part of Beowulf, in the Völsung Saga, and
in the Nibelungen-Lied—This germ is the slaying of a dragon
(worm), and thereby winning a hoard of gold—Afterwards overlaid with the story of the loves and jealousies of Brynhild
(Brunhild) and Godrûn (Kriemhild)—In the histories of Sigurd
and Siegfried are combined the characteristic elements in the
histories of Thorr and Balder—The low morality of the Nibelungen due to the special era in which it had its birth—The fatal
enchantment of wealth which fell upon the victorious Germans—
Rustic mythologies which probably existed contemporaneously
with this great epic—The vitality of folk lore—Heroic myth of
Arthur—The Legends of the Saints—Relics of popular mythology in them—The Beast Epic—'Reineke Fuchs'—The inaugu-
ration of the Middle Ages by the crowning of Charles the Great as
Emperor—The establishment of German influence upon mediæval
thought was symbolised by the same event—The 'Chansons de
Geste'—Points of likeness between Charlemagne and Odhinn—
Reappearance of the Valkyriur—Berchta—Roland compared to
Thorr—To Siegfried—To Heimdal—His horn—Ragnarök and
Roncesvalles—The last home of German heathenism now the

CONTENTS.   xxi

OUTLINES OF PRIMITIVE BELIEF.

CHAPTER I.

NATURE OF BELIEF AS HERE DEALT WITH.

§ 1. *Limits of the Enquiry.*

THE world around us is what we believe it is, and nothing more; wherefore the history of belief, so long as the belief be genuine, is real history, and can be studied by merely historical methods. This kind of enquiry can be made independent of any theory of the origin or nature of belief, just as much as history, a record of events, may be made independent of the science of history. Of late years, however, this historical way of regarding belief has been almost lost sight of, and mythology, since it became *comparative*, has concerned itself almost exclusively with a scientific enquiry into the genesis of myths. It has, as must be confessed by those who have followed its researches, been, at the expense of some extravagances here and there, fruitful in great results. It has so changed our whole outlook over the field of religion and of legendary beliefs, that we have hardly yet been able to recognise the change. Perhaps with some of us it has been that we have been so affected by the new spirit that we can scarcely, even by an effort of imagination, realise a tone of thought upon these matters such as was universally current but a few years ago; albeit that tone of thought and method of interpretation still breathe in our

B

classical dictionaries, and in those other 'standard authors' who are considered good enough to instruct the mind of youth. Now that the researches of comparative mythologists have so far cleared the ground, we are in a position to retrace our steps a little; to return once more to the historical method, only in a far different spirit and with a far clearer outlook; to take up again in a wider field the kind of enquiry which once busied itself with single religious systems and never looked beyond them.

There was once a time when the legendary beliefs of nations were in histories related side by side with the actual experiences of those peoples, as if both were of equal reality and had an interest of the same kind. A little later on historians tried to place all the mythologies in a crucible of criticism, and hoped to extract from them some golden grains of actual fact. Now we know that both these methods are wrong. We have learned that myths have quite a different canon of interpretation from the events of history; that they tell of a quite different order of facts; that the one cannot be rendered in terms of the other. But we know also, or if we do not, it is time that we should recognise the truth, that myths, or better still that *beliefs*, have a history of their own quite as important as any history of events. To interpret belief under this aspect is the object of the following pages. And though this labour differs essentially from labours in comparative mythology, still it is a task to which comparative mythology must ever be a lamp and guide.

I would not have these chapters considered simply as essays in the science of comparative mythology. They are not essentially enquiries *how* and *why* beliefs have come to be what they are, but *what* they have come to be. It is only because the ground has been broken by scientific study that we are able to glean from it historic facts; yet still the method and aims of the historian are altogether different from those of the scientist. The qualifications for the pursuits of the one do not promise success to the other.

But the History of Belief, in its early mythologic stage, is a new study, and is, therefore, without those canons of criticism which past generations of students have bequeathed to the modern historian in other fields. For this reason, and because in dealing with ages so primitive we are at once brought face to face with psycho-. logical problems applicable to the whole human race, it is needful for me to preface the other chapters of this book with one of a scientific kind, in order, if possible, to make clear the principles which have guided me in the narrative parts which follow. Let those who have no relish for psychological questions pass by this chapter if they will.

There is one very simple proposition which applies to all fields of historical enquiry, and which surely in no other field than this would have been called in question. It is that, when we are studying the beliefs of a people whose language and literature we know, it is to this language and literature that we must turn for the history of their thoughts. My investigation, for example, being narrowed altogether within the circle of the Indo-European creeds, I am not compelled to defend the results at which I shall arrive against arguments and facts drawn from other fields of enquiry, from other languages and other literatures. I read one theory of the origin and growth of Egyptian religion or of Semitic beliefs; quite another theory, perhaps, of the birth of the creeds of South Africa or of Australia. Am I convicted of error .if my results do not square with these? I do not think so. Nor will I say that what I have discovered, or believe myself to have found, in the history of Indo-European thought, is binding upon all other investigators. The student in any one field no doubt thinks that he has discovered the key to all truth. One writer will say that our history begins with too low a conception of man's faculties; another that the conception is too high. It may be—I do not say. it is—too low for the Semitic race; it may be too high for the Negritic race. But that does not prove that, for the Indo-European races, the estimate is unjust. In future, therefore, when anything is said of primitive man, let it be understood that the primitive man spoken of is he who in time developes into an Aryan. He is the first among the proto-Aryans. He is no chance primeval being, but has, let us say, the *potentiality* of Aryan culture about him.

In the case of this special people, when we desire to pry into their primitive thoughts, we are not compelled to proceed by guess work or vague analogies, but can call up two voices to speak to us of their past. The first voice is what we may call their literature, widening the use of that word somewhat to include religious or mythological poems, Vedic hymns, Greek epics, Icelandic lays, which, ages before they became in strict sense a *literature*, had been handed down by oral tradition from bard to bard. These poems are the conscious expression of men's thoughts in prehistoric days. The other voice, not less mighty for the revelation of truth, may be called the unconscious expression of the same men's thoughts; a kind of thinking aloud. This comes from the history of their language, whose slow development has of recent years been laid bare by the researches of Comparative Philology. This is our best and truest guide; it is the lamp unto the feet and the light unto the path of all future explorers in the tangled ways of psychology. It is an undesigned testimony which cannot lie; without it the study of mythology is like surgery divorced from anatomy, or astronomy bereft of mathematics. It shows us not only facts which would otherwise be hidden, but, by its own great achievements, it points out to us the method of enquiry which can alone yield results.

According to Mr. Herbert Spencer, religion may be defined as an ' *à priori* theory of the universe; ' and there is, the writer tells us, a subsidiary and unessential element in religion, namely, the moral teaching, ' which is in all cases a supplementary growth.' ' Leaving out,' he says,

matters, it must be a stumbling-block throughout the whole range of the moral faculties.

As regards an ideal life—those aims, I mean, which, for the satisfaction which they give to our aspirations, may be put forward as a full and sufficient reason for life itself—this ideal and these aims seem to be threefold, and to spring out of three separate instincts which man and beast have in common. The difference, however, between man and the lower animals lies in this, that the instincts of animals are in what science calls a position of stable equilibrium; if you move them, so soon as the emotion is passed they return to the state they were in before. But man by each emotion is pushed towards something better, and never remains constant to the position he holds. His instincts develope into passions, into ideals of life, and the grosser parts of them fall away. Now the three instincts which seem to have chiefly worked to push man forward on his path are these. First there is the sexual instinct, which we know both in its brute form and also (happily) in that ideal state which in modern times and in

c 2

Christian countries it has been able to reach. Next there
is the gregarious tendency, which makes men and animals
collect together in bands, for purposes of mutual help, and
which, still advancing, raises men up to a perfect love of
country or of humanity. Last of all there is this still
more subtle instinct of Belief, which lies at the root not
of religion only, but of all imaginative creation, for all
poetry and art (as the actual history of poetry and art
abundantly testifies) have their roots in wonder and in
worship. This faculty, too, is perhaps shared by the beasts
in some measure. Even animals have a certain capacity
for looking upward: as Bacon says, the beasts look up
to man, as man to God. But their eyes are, we know,
commonly bent down to earth; and if the instinct of
belief is shared by beasts, it is so in but a small degree.

It is essential to belief that it should *believe*, not *make
believe*. And this furnishes a certain distinction between
the history of belief and· the history of art. and poetry,
which, in the lighter kinds, are often engaged rather with
fancy than conviction; though, in truth, these are far
less often so engaged than some would suppose. Sidney,
in his 'Apologie for Poetrie,' gives graceful expression to a
common but untrue opinion touching poetic creation, supposing it to consist in mere fancy, and to be quite independent of a belief in the reality of its creations. 'There is no
other art,' he says, 'but this delivered to mankind that hath
not the works of nature for his principal object, without
which they could not consist, and on which they so depend
as they become actors and players, as it were, of what
nature will have set forth.' And then he goes on to claim
that ' only the poet, disdaining to be tied by any such
subjection, lifted up with the vigour of his own invention,
doth grow in effect another nature, in making things
either better than nature bringeth forth, or quite new
forms such as never were in nature, as the *Heroes, Demi-
gods, Cyclops, Chimeras, Furies,* and such like: so as he
goeth hand in hand with nature, not enclosed within the

narrow warrant of her gifts, but freely ranging only within the zodiac of his own wit.'

The view itself is false: the warrant of nature's gifts, be it narrow or not, has been wide enough for man; and the instances which Sidney has chosen to support his view only confirm the contrary. The Cyclops is a personification of the stormy sky; his one eye is the sun looking red and angry through the clouds, as we so often see it at the end of a tempestuous day.[1] The Chimæra is herself the cloud which drops rain as the goat drops milk.[2] The Furies (Erinyes) are descended from the Vedic Saranyû, the dawn.[3] Beings like these are the first fruits of man's poetic faculty in its commerce with nature. But they are not spun out from his imagination independently of such prompting: they are in the most literal way the actors and players of what nature will have set forth. And it is with such creations, with beings whose character is determined for them to a great extent by the phenomena which they personify, that the student in the history of Belief has first to do. It is long before he need be concerned with a god or a supernatural being who is a pure abstraction: he first gains acquaintance with those simpler divine ones of primitive days who are gods of the sunshine and the storm, of the earth glad in its greenery or stripped bare by wintry decay, of the countless laughing waves of the sea, of the wind which bloweth where it listeth.

Before abandoning this discussion over the definition

---

[1] The Cyclops is not, as some mythologists loosely say, a personification of the storm; for 'the storm' as so used is an abstraction, whereas the thing personified in this and the other cases is some actual phenomenon of nature. Therefore each one of the Cyclops must be thought of first of all as the stormy sky. Afterwards they become separated into different parts of the phenomenon of the storm: one is the roll ($\beta\rho\acute{o}\nu\tau\eta s$), another is the flash ($\sigma\tau\epsilon\rho\acute{o}\pi\eta s$), a third the bright whiteness of sheet lightning ($\grave{a}\rho\gamma\acute{\eta}s$).

[2] $\chi\acute{\iota}\mu a\iota\rho a$, a she goat, is derived from $\chi\epsilon\~\iota\mu a$, winter (also storm), $\chi\acute{\iota}\mu a\iota\rho a$ being a winterling, i.e. yearling.

[3] There is some dispute over the real nature of the Erinys. In another chapter I have sought to reconcile the opinions of Kuhn and Max Müller on Saranyû (Ch. III.) See also below, p. 28

of belief, it may be as well to compare it with those other
definitions of religion which we noted just now. It does
not, it must be confessed, quite square itself with these;
certainly not quite with those two sharply contrasted ones,
Mr. Herbert Spencer's and Mr. Matthew Arnold's. Mr.
Herbert Spencer's definition in full is this:—

'Leaving out the accompanying moral code, which is
in all cases a supplementary growth, a religious creed
is definable as an à *priori* theory of the universe. The
surrounding facts being given, some form of agency is
alleged which, in the opinion of those alleging it, accounts
for these facts. . . . However widely different speculators
may disagree in the solution which they give of the same
problem, yet by implication they all agree there is a
problem to be solved. Here, then, is an element which all
creeds have in common. Religions diametrically opposed
in their overt dogmas are yet perfectly at one in their
conviction that the existence of the world with all it contains and all that surrounds it is a mystery ever pressing
for interpretation. On this point, if on no other, there is
entire unanimity.'

How stands our instinct of belief in relation to that
something which is made up of a conviction that the
world with all it contains and all that surrounds it is a
mystery ever pressing for interpretation? Evidently the
mystery which hangs around their origin and extent is a
great element in the fear with which most parts of nature
are regarded by primitive man; and fear is, I suppose, of
all the inward feelings which man acquires consciousness
of, the most primitive. The history of words bears witness
to this fact. Other metaphysical words, such as *right*,
courage, show how, at a comparatively late time, the
abstract notions have worked their way out of physical
sensations. But the only physical root connected with
fear is the visible effect of it, trembling and failing of the
limbs. We are justified in arguing from the evidences
of language that neither *sense of right* nor *courage* were

primitive elements in human experience, but that fear was so. No doubt, then, but that this mighty affection of the mind, which in time softened down into awe and worship, has been among the earliest and chiefest of the emotions which have contributed to the shaping of belief. The sense of the unknown concerning the origin of things is necessarily a concurrent cause of the fear which they inspire. The sense of the unknown must, therefore, be a great feature in all primitive creeds.

By these considerations we seem to be led *towards* Mr. Spencer's conclusions, but we are not brought to them. For it is not the sense of the unknown as an instinct or an emotion which in fact, according to this writer, has contibuted to the formation of creeds. According to him it is not the mere feeling of mystery which is paramount in belief, but the desire to explain away that mystery. For him religion is before all else a Theory of the Universe. Now such an assertion cannot pass unchallenged, unless religion be a thing having no foundation in Belief.

Belief comes into existence when man is not reasonable enough to have a theory about anything, while he is still mainly a *feeling* animal, possessing only some adumbrations or instincts of thought. It is not possible that, for man in such a condition, either his belief or his religion could be the kind of theorising which Mr. Spencer supposes it. Out of Mr. Spencer's definition of religion proceeds directly his theory of the origin of religion. All worship began, he says, in the worship of ancestors. The ghosts of dead men were the first objects of religious belief. It is no doubt natural that, starting with the definition which he gives, the philosopher should have been led to the conclusion which he has arrived at concerning the origin of religion. We can understand pretty well that if man had before all things else desired a theory of the universe, a theory of the origin of the sunshine and the rain, had he been scientifically minded and given to reasoning from the analogy of outward experience, he might have been led to think that these phenomena were caused by human agents. His natural conclusion, proceeding on such grounds, would be that other beings like mankind were at work up there in the heaven and among the clouds. Man is the only agent detected in the process of acting and intending: reasonable analogy would suggest that man, though invisible, was the author of other acts even when remote from our earthly sphere. This is just what Mr. Herbert Spencer thinks the primitive savage did believe. The men who sent the rain and sunshine were only different from the men on earth in the fact that their sphere was different; their power, perhaps, was more extended. This different sphere and wider power were reached through the portal of death. All agents in the world not human, or at least not mortal, were the dead ancestors of the tribe. Hence the worship of ancestors is, according to our author, the origin of all religion.

All this is consistent with Mr. Spencer's definition of religion; but it is not, I venture to think, consistent with the facts. Such might well have been the form of primitive belief, had man started with his *theory of the universe*, and tried to reason of the origin of all things from the knowledge he possessed. But man is not so reasonable a being at the outset, and this truth the history of language shows us well. Man's instincts far outweigh his reasonings, and religion is the child of instinct, not of logic. It is, I venture to think, because Mr. Spencer has neglected the teaching of comparative philology upon this point that he has been led to the conclusions he has reached. The abstract words which express a power of reasoning are among the last which attain their place in a language; the intermediate ones are those which tell of the *instinctive* recognition of an abstract side to physical sensation. Man's first belief and worship were things very different from a 'theory of the universe;' and these being so much more instinctive than reasonable, it fell out that at first the physical parts of nature were worshipped essentially for themselves. It was at the first the very essence of the divine thing that it was not human. We shall see in the early history of belief how necessary is this condition of the non-humanity of the nature gods.[1]

Nor, again, could Mr. Matthew Arnold's definition of religion be made to serve us for a definition of belief. That was, it will be remembered, that religion was ' morality touched by emotion.' Such a definition is very far from holding good for the instinct which we are considering. For a long time belief has so little to say to morality, that throughout the chapters of this volume we shall scarcely ever have to contemplate religion in its distinctly moral aspect. When a belief has become anthropomorphic, and the nature god has changed into a divinity like unto man in character, then the laws of being which apply to human actions become his laws also. The gods, then, should grow, and do for the most part, into ideals of human nature, and the worship of them becomes, in effect, a worship of goodness. This, however, only takes place after a great lapse of time. *God*, when the word was first used, was not synonymous with *good.* The

---

[1] Nothing but Mr. Herbert Spencer's great name, and the value of his researches in other fields (and perhaps some unsuspected influence of the *odium anti-theologicum*), could have made his theory of the origin of religion, and his arguments in support of his theory, so eagerly accepted as they have been by a large number of intelligent students and thinkers. It is natural for many persons to like even to be 'damned with Tully.' But, in truth, Mr. Spencer's researches in other fields do not give him the weight of a special authority in this one. There is but one key to psychology of this kind, and that is philology; and to this the philosopher has never turned any special attention. Physiology, and even ethnology, are guides far less safe than the undesigned testimony given by the history of words. Accordingly, as he is really treading in a sphere which is unfamiliar, Mr. Spencer's footsteps are here far less firm than in other places. Mr. Spencer, upon any other subject, would hardly use the ' totem theory' in the way he does to support his views. The totem is the name of the dead ancestor who is supposed to have become the ruler of any special part of nature. Mr. Spencer accounts for the *apparent* fact that men do actually worship the *cloud* and *sea* and *sky* by supposing that some ancestor had received as a totem the name of ' cloud ' or ' sea ' or ' sky.' Surely by such a wide method of supposing ' anything may be made of anything,' to use a happy phrase of Mr. Matthew Arnold. (See *Sociology*, p. 385 sqq.)

idea of the divinity has ever responded to the instinct of
worship, and that worship was given first of all to *things*
which impressed the senses. While the *things* of nature were
still the gods, the moral law could scarcely apply to them.
Whatever Butler may argue to the contrary, there is no
direct moral lesson in nature's works. She brings to
death, she brings to life; and that is all we see in her. The
essence of primitive belief lies in the same outward world
and in its changes; not in any likeness to humanity, but in
their very difference from it, lie the wonder and the charm
of these external things. I will not say that there is no
hidden teaching in this kind of nature worship. It is true
enough that all things which excite the wonder or the
awe of man, whatever quickens his perception of inward
and spiritual things, all that awakens his thought and
imagination, are his masters. When fear shall in time
have changed into awe, and wonder into worship, then
man will have passed beyond the region of Nature to a
spiritual nature, and what is great outwardly will have
given place to what is great in virtue. But such a consummation is not at the beginning.

We may, indeed, to a certain extent, conciliate Mr.
Arnold's definition of religion in this way. We may agree
to consider as religious only those beliefs in which the
moral element has become clearly established. Professor
de Gubernatis intends some such distinction when, in his
lectures on the Vedic mythology,[1] he separates what he
calls the mythologic and the religious periods of the Vedic
creed. The first period is that in which the divinities
worshipped were strictly nature gods, the second stage
begins when the god is something more than a mere visible
appearance. He may still be worshipped in phenomena;
but he is separated from them in the thought of his
votaries, and can be contemplated as one apart, living in
and by himself. The visible world, the heavens, or the
cloud, or the sunshine, is deemed only his dwelling-place

[1] *Letture sopra la Mitologia Vedica*, pp. 28, 29.

or his enfolding garment. And because the god has now become an abstraction, and can be worshipped as such, Professor de Gubernatis calls this condition of a creed its religious phase: the earlier phase he calls the mythological one. A distinction like this is without doubt somewhat in accordance with Mr. Matthew Arnold's definition of religion; but it does not really go hand in hand with it. For still the chief feeling in the mind, either during the first stage of belief or the second, is not morality 'touched by emotion,' or otherwise; still the mainspring is the instinct, and morality, when it enters, comes in by the way.

We may have occasion hereafter sometimes to make use of that distinction which Professor de Gubernatis has drawn between the mythological and the religious phases of belief; meaning by the first the period during which the gods are essentially material things with a nature remote from human nature, and by the second the period during which they are essentially idealised beings with natures more or less in conformity with ours. But in giving these names I never mean it to be thought that either religion is totally excluded from the earlier (the mythic) age, or myth excluded from the religious age. There is always mythology alongside of the more religious kind of worship, and religion growing up beside mythology. Only at first there is a preponderance of myth-making, and later on a preponderance of the religious feeling. While the gods are purely of nature's belongings it is easy to see that it will be a time for the growth of stories concerning them. The myths are, be it ever remembered, the creatures of real belief, not of mere fancy, as Sidney would have them be. The conception of the Cyclops was founded on what men had seen; and the myth of the Cyclops could only grow in natural wise, so long as men really believed that the stormy sky was a being and the sun his eye. When the Cyclops had become a mere one-eyed giant, then all new tales told of

him would be but inventions, and would deserve a much
lower place in the history of belief. When the gods have
become like men, and have lost all memory of the phenomena out of which they sprang, they have laid aside the
individuality of their characters; henceforward they will
tend more and more towards uniformity of nature; and
this uniform nature will more and more adapt itself to a
godlike *ideal.* Thus the influence of moral ideas will
become paramount while the influence of the experience
of outward nature fades away.

Of the growth of morality in belief, and of the way in
which it may develope along with the contemplation of mere
external phenomena, we have an excellent example in one
among those mythic beings which Sidney enumerates.
All the three—the Cyclops, the Chimæra, the Furies—are
fearful creations; but the first two draw all their terror
directly from the things which they personify; they are
fearful because the storm itself is fearful. No natural
dread surrounds Erinys, who is the Dawn; [1] her terrible-
ness arises solely from a moral character which the Dawn
is led to take upon her. She is the detector of crimes; at
first in the merely passive way in which we say that all
crimes will some day come to light, afterwards in a more
active sense. In time the Erinyes become altogether
moral beings, and purely abstract ones, 'the honoured
ancient deities, supporters of the throne of Justice, dear
to Zeus,' whom Æschylus knows. Yet all this moral character springs out of their natural character. They become
the detectors of crimes solely because the daylight must
be a detector of crimes.

These three examples are fairly typical of the whole
range of beings who play the mythic dramas of a people.
Though all must have had a beginning in outward nature,

---

[1] This is Max Müller's explanation of the origin of the Erinyes (*Chips,*
ii. 153); and it seems to me a valid one, despite the criticisms of Welcker
(*Griech. Götterl.* iii. p. 75, &c.) and the different origin found for Saramyû
by Kuhn (*Zeitsch. für vorg. Sp.* i. 439). Gubernatis makes some suggestions
which tend to reconcile these discrepancies (*Mitol. Ved.* p. 156).

some (as the Greek furies do) will have strayed far, others less far from it. Some will keep the whole nature which belongs to outward things, some will half clothe themselves with a human personality. But never in early times shall we have a god unlinked to external phenomena. Wherefore if we read of some primitive race retiring to worship in its rocky fastnesses or woody solitudes, as Tacitus says the Germans retired to their forest haunts and worshipped an Unseen Presence there, we must not think of them going to meditate upon the riches and goodness, nor yet upon the power and wonder, of God. The presence made known to them may be an unseen, it is certainly not an unfelt one; it is in the breath of the wind or in the murmuring of the stream; it is in the storm or in the whirlwind, but it is not yet in the voice of the heart. The sensations of this external nature stir man's imagination, they raise his awe; and this stirring of the inner senses constitutes his worship. And let those doubt that religion may have had such beginnings who have never listened to the voices which arise from the solitudes of nature; those who have never known the brightness of sunny fields and streams, the sad solemnity of forests, and the majesty of mountains or of the sea.

§ 2. Early Phases of Belief.

Thus much to show the mere existence and the essential character of this faculty of Belief. We have now to say something concerning the phases of it. Here the history of language will still be our guide. What we have at present learned of the parallel histories of religion and of language is this: That, as at first *all words* expressed only the ideas of definite material objects, but many of these words which had once a purely material significance came in time to have a purely moral or metaphysical significance, so throughout all the natural world, though men at first gained from it only ideas of outward sensation, these in time changed, and metaphysical and moral ideas came to

take their place. In the case of words the change from
the physical to the metaphysical use was not, we may be
sure, made at a bound. *Stretched* did not suddenly come
to mean *right*, nor *heap* to mean *truth*.

Now one stage in that slow process of change we can
certainly detect. The first step was made when the name
for an individual thing had expanded its meaning to take
in a *class* of things. When words, from being individual,
or what we now call *proper* names, had grown to be generic
terms, they had already become half abstractions, for they
had become names for aggregates of qualities and not for
individual things. I took just now *stretched* as the example
of a word in its most material form; but in reality a word
was in its most material form only so long as it was not
an adjective, but expressed some single object. If we could
imagine for a moment the word *straight* or *stretched* as the
name, not of *any* string, but of some particular string,
then we should have a word in its most primitive possible
condition. The next stage would be when the same word
was used to express a *class* of objects—in this case all
strings which had been stretched. The stage which would
immediately follow would be that the word should come
to be an adjective (an attribute), and no longer an individual name. We have every reason to suppose that the
process of the human thought, exemplified by the history
of words, is traceable equally well in the development of
belief; whence it would follow that belief too has passed
from individual objects to groups of things, and thence
has fastened upon some attribute, still physical, but no
longer apprehensible by all the senses, which belonged to
the whole class. In a word, religion began with fetichism,
with the worship, we will suppose, of an individual tree;
it passed on to the worship of many trees, of the grove of
trees, and it soon proceeded thence to a worship of some
invisible belonging of the grove. This might be the sacred
silence which seems to reign in the wood, or the storm
which rushes through it, or any of the dim, mysterious

forest sounds. From the visible and tangible things of earth religion looked farther away to the heavenly bodies, or to the sky itself. And then at last it emerged from the nature-worshipping stage, and the voice of God, which was heard once in the whirlwind, was now heard only in the still small voice within.

With the last phase of all we shall in these chapters have nothing to do; nothing directly, at all events. It scarcely needs to be said that no one of the three phases of belief which I have described is to be found in its purity among any of the peoples whose religious career we are going to study. Each phase is found mingled with some other. All the Indo-European races have arrived at some point in the third condition of development; that is to say, all have achieved some idea of an abstract god, who is separate from phenomena. But few or none of them have completely left behind any of the other two conditions of belief. Wherefore it lies in our hands which phase we choose to study. The strata of belief are like the geological strata; primitive ones may be discovered sometimes quite near the surface; the nature of the former are no more to be told by measuring their distance from us in time than that of the latter by any measurement from the surface of the earth. It is the character and not the actual time of the formation which allows us to call it primitive; and both the first two phases of belief, both pure fetichism and that which, to distinguish it from fetichism, we may call *nature worship*, both, wherever they are encountered, may fairly be called phases of primitive belief.

The same kind of difficulty over the meaning of a word which has obscured discussion upon the nature of religion itself has been stirred up, in a minor degree, about the word fetich; and here with less excuse, for this word carries with it no strength of old association. It was never during the days of its early use applied with scientific exactness, and it was first employed at a time when the study of belief had, in any effective way, hardly begun. If, therefore, we were to wrest the word a little from its first application, in order to make it serve us in a scientific sense, there would be no great harm.

Mr. Max Müller has, with many strong arguments, called in question the very general assumption—systematised somewhat in the hands of Comte—that fetichism lies at the root of all religion. His arguments have certainly been sufficient to make us reconsider our use of the word fetichism, and in future to define it more exactly; but I do not think they have really shaken the position which Comte has taken up on this point. It is one thing to show that the great positive philosopher has not used ' fetichism' in its etymological significance, or even that he has not always attached to the term the same meaning, and that others who followed him have been yet more vague in the use of the word; it is another thing to show that there has been no primitive belief clinging to the worship of visible external things.

Fetich (*feitiço*) was, it is known, the general name by which the Portuguese sailors in African seas called the charms and talismans they wore—their beads, or crosses, or images in lead or wood. Seeing that the native Africans likewise had their cherished amulets (their *gri-gris*), deemed by them sacred and magically powerful, the Portuguese called these by the same name of fetich. Then, in 1760, came De Brosses, with his book on ' Les Dieux fétiches,' proposing this condition of belief as an initial state of religion. His term as well as his views were adopted, and fetichism assumed a fixed place in the history of religion.

Neither the *feitiço* of the Portuguese mariner, nor any Christian amulet or relic, is distinctive of a primitive phase of belief; and if it were a mere question of etymology this would be enough to show that ' fetichism' did not correctly describe the phase of belief which we do intend to

fetich, but in his conception of this Something behind.

It is superstitious, no doubt, to believe that an image may move, may sigh and groan, but it is not primitive fetichism; for the very sighing and groaning are noted as miraculous, and that they are so thought shows a knowledge that the thing is after all but dead matter. There would be nothing wonderful in the movement of an image possessed of vitality, and yet the belief in the possibility of such a vital image would savour far more of the earliest phases of thought. Even the Italian peasant woman who beats her idol does not so, I imagine, with the intention of hurting *it*, but with the dim belief that she can, through it, hurt some other being who seems to have played her false. The life of this being is, in some way, bound up with his likeness, but the saint and the image are not one.

In the same spirit of superstition did persons, in the Middle Ages, make likenesses in wax of some enemy, say incantations over it, pierce it with pins, set it to melt before the fire, in the firm conviction that they were wreaking their vengeance upon him when far away. All this is, if you will, the grossest superstition; it implies a very low conception of the supernal powers; but it is not an example of fetichism in its really primitive form. That many persons, Comte included, have spoken of this kind of superstition as belonging to the earliest phase of belief has greatly tended to confuse men's ideas of what fetichism is to be taken to mean, and has led others justly to question—as Professor Max Müller has done—whether fetichism is so primitive as it is said to be.

Others again have confounded fetichism with magic, and so have come to speak of all religion as founded upon magic rites. This too I conceive to be an error. No belief can go so far as to think that *everything* possesses *magical* power; this would be the very bull of credulity, comparable to that extreme doctrine of (Irish) republicanism, that one man is as good as another and better too. But if all things are not alike magical, whence arises the superiority of one thing over another in this respect? Does the magic power rest with the thing itself? If this is so, what distinguishes magic from a rude form of natural science? It may be a mistake to imagine, for example, that a piece of salt or a lion's tail can cure a fever, but the mistake is scarcely in itself a superstition. And why should the piece of salt be chosen as the repository of this strange power, and not rather a piece from the bark of a tree of the Cinchona tribe which really possesses it? Is it not evident that the superstition of magic arises from the belief that their potencies are *arbitrarily* implanted in certain selected objects? And the very word 'arbitrarily' implies the recognition of a power outside the object. Without such a tacit belief in a power behind the phenomenon magic would be nothing else than a rude experimental *science*. The modern and more cultured magician pronounces his charm over the thing he designs to use; he never imagines that the magical qualities are inherent in the thing, but always that they come through the agency of the incantation—that is to say, from a supernal being, be he but the Devil. The unscientific character of his belief lies just in this: that he looks for the attributes of a substance elsewhere than in the substance itself. If fetichism were a superstition of this kind, we should have to look beyond the fetich-worshipper's views concerning

the material things to his views about the power which
sent the magic. Only when we had discovered these, could
we tell what place the savage had attained in the stages
of religious development.

To sum up in one example the whole difference between
early fetichism and late superstition: The Portuguese
sailor prays to his fetich to save him from shipwreck, because he believes that he is somehow thus influencing an
Unseen Being who has power over the winds and over
the waves. The African, too, has a notion of such an Unseen Being when he prays to his *gri-gri* to save him from
the storm. Had he no such notion he would pray to the
winds and waves themselves not to drown him.

De Brosses' fetiches are of the late or magical kind.
Anything, according to this writer, *may* be a fetich—a lion's
tail, a piece of salt, a stone, a plant, or an animal. And
yet, as we have shown, *everything* cannot be a fetich. The
worship paid to the lion's tail, to the piece of salt, to the
flower, or what not, implies, though it does not outwardly
express, a belief in something beyond the visible things.
Therefore it would be very unsafe to assert that the African
gives us an example of the earliest conditions of religious
growth. Nevertheless that primitive fetichism *has* existed
we cannot doubt.

If the facts which we gathered from the history of
words, and arrayed in the first part of this chapter, go for
anything, there must have been a time when man was in-
capable of conceiving supernal forces, such as are required
for the magical kind of fetichism; for his whole thoughts
were centred in the actual. Now it must be that many of
the qualities which objects of the material world were in
primitive times thought to possess had been reflected back
upon them from the feelings which those objects stirred in
the beholder. We saw a while ago how this was continually the case. The high thing was endowed with moral
qualities, because looking upward aroused some moral
thoughts. In a general way all material things share in a

certain vitality, which is shed upon them by the subject; [1]
in a more particular sense certain objects are selected for
worship on account of the special emotions which they
excite. All worship of the fetich must have arisen out
of that subtle connection between things and thoughts of
which we have already said so much; a thing which was
great and *high* was on that account alone admirable, calling
out from man a faint fore-note of the moral sense. The
very fact that there was as yet nothing but material nature,
and no thought or emotion recognisable in itself alone,
tended to surround all the world of sense with a thin
atmosphere of thought and emotion; an instinct of belief
attached itself to these outward things. The seeds of
future poetry and ethic were being carried on the wings
of sensation, but had not yet settled and taken root.

It is to signify this condition of thought that we can
alone fairly use the word 'fetichism,' if we intend it to
express an early stage of belief. This fetichism, which is
really primitive, owns no thought beyond the material
object. Here the fetich was not the means of concentrating
the mind upon an internal idea of God; because man, in
the days when religion first began, had no idea of God at
all. God is a notion of the most abstract character, and
our race, we well know, did not start upon its career furnished with a stock of abstract ideas. Man did not say
to himself, 'That mountain or that river shall symbolise
my idea of God;' still less did he say, 'These things are
the abode of God;' he only made the objects themselves
into gods by worshipping them.

Although in this condition of thought nothing was
wholly divine, and yet everything was in a fashion divine—
for a voice spoke to man out of each object of sense—it
not the less necessarily followed that worship, to any ob-
servable extent, could only attach itself to certain conspicuous objects, which should in time develope into what

---

[1] It is this capacity of reflecting vitality on immaterial things which
Mr. Tylor calls animism,—*Primitive Culture*, passim.

we may fairly call gods. It is not in the case of this kind
of fetichism as it is in the case of the magical fetichism,
where any object, however insignificant, *may* be the re-
ceptacle of potency from without. Here the worship must
be proportionate to the impressiveness of the thing; we
may even say that it must be proportionate to the *greatness* or the *height* of the thing. In truth, it would seem
that the great fetich gods of the early world were three,
and three only—the *tree*, the *mountain*, and the *river*.[1]
Lesser fetiches took their holiness from the greater—the
stone from the mountain, the branch or the block of wood
from the tree. But such lesser fetiches were not worshipped in the prime of fetichism. They are in almost
every case where they are to be met with the survivals
from an earlier belief.

Names, we know, from being individual become generic.
The first word for river must have indicated some particular stream; later on it came to imply all those qualities which rivers have in common, and with the benefit of
a wider scope for language man lost a certain distinctness
and picturesqueness in it. The word tree, when for us it
meant only the single tree outside a nursery window, was
in a fashion far more expressive than it has since been.
While the generalising process of language goes on, it
leads to a gradual detachment of their attributes from the
individual things, and the formation of these attributes or
adjectives into a class of ideas by themselves. The mind
learns to separate the brightness and the swiftness of flowing water from any one example of these qualities, and
the result is that we get the conception of the attributes
brightness and swiftness by themselves. The same change
took place in belief. The holiness which once belonged
to a single object was distributed over the aggregate of
existences of the same kind, and the idea 'holiness' was

---

[1] The *sea*, as will be presently more fully explained, is by primitive man
reckoned in the class of rivers.

thus abstracted in a certain degree from the particular
holy thing—in a certain degree, but not entirely. The
tree, for example, became less personally sacred than surrounded by an atmosphere of sacredness; and this sanctity
now belonged, not to one tree, but to the whole grove of
trees. The general idea in this way replaced the individual one; and in the course of time the sense of holiness
was transferred to other belongings of the grove far less
tangible and real than the trees. As I have suggested
above, the sacred silence, the murmuring of streams, the
rushing of the wind, may constitute the next hierarchy of
gods.

The stage of belief, when no worship was bestowed upon
pure ideals—that is to say, upon *qualities*—we may call the
second stage in the development of belief. It is a phase
which was far from having been quite abandoned even in
the historical ages of most among the Indo-European folk,
and which has, in consequence, more often come under
the notice of casual observers than has fetichism. We
often enough come across traces of the worship of trees
in the creeds of Aryan races; but we still more frequently
hear the grove spoken of as having preceded the temple.
'Trees,' says Pliny, 'were the first temples. Even at
this day the simple rustic, of ancient custom, dedicates his
noblest tree to God. And the statues of gold and ivory
are not more honoured than the *sacred silence* which reigns
about the grove.'[1] It was the same *sacred silence* of the
grove which, according to Tacitus, the Germans worshipped in their forest fastnesses. Aristophanes, in a
revolt against the image worship and the superstition of
his day, proposes half seriously to revert to such earlier
customs as that of worship in the grove; he calls upon the
Athenians to leave their closed shrines and to sacrifice in
the open air, and in place of the temple, with its golden
doors, to dedicate the olive tree to new gods.[2]

Such a state of feeling as this was, when it arose, a

[1] *H. N.* xii. 2.   [2] *Aves.*

decided advance upon the gross conceptions of fetichism. Then, on every side, the more material things were loosening their hold upon men's imagination and falling from their former place, and worship was transferred to things either more abstract or more remote from common experience, things which were wide, far-reaching, or heavenly. Instead of the tree, the mountain, and the river, man chose for his gods the earth, the storm, the sky, the sun, the sea.[1] Men were well upon the road towards a personal divinity—that is to say, to the deification of qualities or attributes. The idea of personality (and by personality I mean all which constitutes the inner being, the *I*), the idea of personality apart from matter must have been growing more distinct when men could attribute personality to such an abstract phenomenon as the sky.

It is of the existence of this second stage in the development of belief that Comparative Philology furnishes us with such decisive proofs and such interesting examples. And as it is chiefly with beliefs in this stage that the chapters of this volume are concerned, and as the nature of the general testimony to the existence of this special phase of belief which is afforded by language can so easily be shown, it will be well if we turn aside an instant from an historical enquiry in order to glance at the *method* of Comparative Philology when dealing with questions such as these.

We know, of course, nothing directly of our Aryan ancestors themselves, but we know the various tongues which have descended from their primitive speech—the Sanskrit, the Zend, the Greek, the Latin, the Teutonic,

---

[1] It is, of course, obvious that the phenomena here enumerated do not all show an equal remoteness from fetichism, nor an abstraction of the same sort. The earth, taken as a whole, is a general notion of a very wide kind; but, as it is actually considered in mythology, it is perhaps the nearest to a fetich god of all the five phenomena given above. It always tends to coincide with some particular *bit* of the earth, some individual mountain or valley. The sea begins by being a mere river fetich, but when men have learnt something of its boundless extent it becomes distinctly an abstract idea.

the Celtic, the Slavonian—and which all stand in a relationship more or less intimate with it. By examining the relationship which exists between words of the same meaning in different Indo-European languages, we draw one most valuable conclusion touching the life of these ancient Aryas. If the names of anything in the children languages all appear to have sprung from one root, we argue that the *thing* was known to the Aryan progenitors, and by them endowed with a name which is the parent of the names which have come down to us. If the Aryas had not known the thing, they could not have given it a name; and conversely, if they have not given it a name they could not have known the thing. Once more: if the name existed among the Aryas it will be found again (somewhat changed, no doubt) among their children; conversely, if the same word does not pervade the children languages it has not pre-existed in the parent one. These are the general principles on which we build up the sum of our knowledge of prehistoric times. When, for example, we find such a word as the Sanskrit *gó* (cow) corresponding by proper laws of change [1] to names for the same animal in Greek, Latin, Persian, German, &c., we argue that the ancient Aryas were acquainted with horned cattle. The words in the offshoot languages point back to a *word* not unlike them in the parent tongue; and as the word has continued to denominate the same *thing* to the children, it must have denominated the thing (viz. horned cattle) to the parents.

Further than this, if we want to get the nearest approximation to the lost Aryan word [2] we turn first to the Sanskrit to give it us; because we both know historically that Sanskrit is the oldest among the brother languages and likewise find, upon examination, that Sanskrit can

---

[1] Skr. gô (gaus), Zend gaô, Gr. βοῦς, Lat. bos, Germ. kuh, Eng. cow, Irish bô, Slavonic gov-iado (ox).

[2] It has been already said that proto-Aryan is a better word to express the lost speech of our ancestors than Aryan, though, for the sake of shortness and simplicity, the latter will be for the future employed.

generally show us *how* a word acquired its meaning, when the other tongues are silent upon this matter. Our word *daughter* is a good instance in point. It corresponds to the Sanskrit *duhitar*, the Persian *dóchtar*, the Greek θυγάτηρ,[1] &c.; and so we come to the same conclusion about *daughter* which we arrived at concerning horned-cattle, namely, that the old Aryas had a word from which ours is a descendant. But, in this instance, we have a clear proof that, among the various forms which have come down to us, that preserved in the Sanskrit is the oldest, because in that only can we see how the word was formed. We connect *duhitar* with a verb *duh*, to milk, and recognise the origin of our 'daughter' to have been 'the milker'—the milkmaid of the family.

Now let us apply the same method of research to mythology. We find a Zeus, chief god among the Greeks, a Jupiter[2] among the Romans; we have a Zio (Tiv or Tyr), an important divinity with the Teutons, and a Dyâus with the old Indians. All these words are from the same root; and as we reasoned in the case of *gó*, so must we reason now—namely, that the root of these words was the name of an Aryan divinity. As, moreover, this name is the most widespread of all the mythical names in the Indo-European family, we are justified in assuming that the lost parent-word betokened a chief, if not *the* chief, Aryan god. We might call him Dyâus, because Dyâus, we conjecture, most nearly replaces the lost name. But more than this. As was the case with *duhitar* among all the words for daughter, so Dyâus, among all similar names, is the only one whose origin can be accounted for. **Dyâus means *sky*.**[3] No doubt

---

[1] For θυχάτηρ, by change of aspirates.

[2] From Dyâus-pitar, father Dyâus, gen. Jovis, dat. Jovi (Διουϝει Mommsen, *Unterital. Dial*, p. 191).

[3] The *bright sky* especially, as it is connected with the word *dir*, to shine. Most philologists, yielding to their too common habit of treating the abstraction or generalisation (adjective or verb) as the parent of all the concrete words of the same class, have spoken of Dyâus (Dyó) as *derived*

therefore but that the lost proto-Dyâus was also the sky.
Nay, if any further proof of this were needed, Zeus and
Jupiter, though their *names* no longer recalled the heavens,[1]
nevertheless largely did recall the sky in their *natures*.
And how could this have been unless the god from whom
they sprang had possessed the properties and the powers of
a sky god in a more eminent degree than they?   In
truth, the old Aryan god *was* the sky.   Whenever the
Aryan used the name of this his divinity, the sky must at
the same time have been present in his thoughts, and in
the most literal sense he worshipped that portion of nature
as a god.   Doubtless the old Aryas worshipped other
phenomena likewise; but these too they adored under
their physical names and not as separate entities.

When we have not the direct help of etymology, as in
the case of Dyâus, to determine the original nature of a
divine being, we have the help—scarcely less valuable if
rightly used—of comparative mythology.   In the various
pantheons which spring from one parent creed we find
the same gods recurring in slightly different guises; and
here and there they betray the substance on which their
being is grounded.

It is not difficult to see that the clothing of these
things with human form is the last stage of the three
initial ones in the history of belief, and that anthropo-
morphism, when it has once arisen, can never degenerate
into nature worship.   If Zeus or Odhinn is once conceived
clearly as an unseen being, as some one sitting apart in
Olympus or in Asgard, there is little danger that he will
come to be confounded with the visible storm.   He may
be the storm-sender, but he cannot be the actual phenomenon which he rules.   Yet even such gods as Zeus and
Odhinn drop here and there a token to show that they

---

from the root *div*, to shine.   It would be quite as reasonable to speak of
div derived from *dyô*.   Probably, however, neither comes directly from the
other, both from a lost parent-word which may also have meant sky.

[1] Or only occasionally, as in the phrase 'sub Jove.'

were once not unseen beings, but visible things, bound
within the limits which included their special phenomena.
The indication in this or the other instance may be slight;
it accumulates, as we find a hundred examples; and when,
following the creed back to its more primitive forms, or
comparing it with some kindred system which is less
advanced, we see the god, whose personality at one time
seemed so clear, fading gradually away till he dissolves in
air, or cloud, or rain, or sunshine, the inference with respect
to the total genesis of belief grows so exacting that we
cannot choose but receive it.

If it be true—and who will deny it?—that no idea can
be clearly grasped unless there be a word to express it, we
must confess that the Aryas, in the condition in which we
now suppose them, were still without a god. The word
which expressed the thing they worshipped meant also the
sky, or it meant the wind, or the sea, or the earth. When
they saw these things they worshipped; when the phenomena were absent they were forgotten. For the memories
of savages are short; their emotions are very transitory,
and are almost always under the immediate influence of
outward sensations. Even in later times, when the god
is a personality and has a name of his own, so long as he
is associated with phenomena, he will suffer the same
kind of alternate reverence and neglect. Gubernatis
notices concerning Indra, the storm god, that in some of
the Vedic hymns he is only reverenced when he is active;
when he is inactive he is scarcely thought of.[1]

As one by one the phenomena pass in review each one
while it is present seems to be *the* god, and is worshipped
with all the ardour of which the suppliant is capable.
When we read the votary's prayers to any part of nature,
we might fancy he worshipped no other part. But this is
not the case. The explanation of this seeming changeable-
ness from god to god lies in the shortness of the savage's
memory and the difficulty which he finds in realising any-

---

[1] *Letture sopra la Mittologia Vedica*, p. 28.

thing but his present sensation. The sun is at one moment his only god; but it sinks to rest, and now he prays to the heaven, studded with its thousand stars. Again these are overclouded, and from the clouds issues the blinding flash or the awful roll of thunder; and then the pure sky is forgotten and he prays to the lightning and the storm. A stage of belief such as this, when each divinity seems for the time to stand by himself and to be prayed to alone, has been called by Mr. Max Müller *henotheism*.[1] The cause of henotheism, then, lies in the worship of actual physical phenomena. The same nature origin of the gods affords a satisfactory explanation of *polytheism*; and polytheism is a state of belief not so easily accounted for as some suppose.

The belief in one god is a thing not difficult to understand; for—whether it be true or false—it is a belief of which we have a hundred examples around us. The god-idea is a distinct creation of the human mind: it is a conception in itself. The very essence of this conception is the difference between god and man. But to what instinct does the belief in many gods respond? The difference between god and god cannot be an observed difference, as that between tree and tree or between man and man. The general terms *tree* and *man* express an aggregate of qualities found to be common to a great number of different objects, as these objects come within the range of our experience. But god is not a general term of this class. The god-idea does not include anything which is a part of outward experience. If there *were* a great many different gods, our knowledge of them would not be of an external, experimental kind. Our abstract word 'god' would not have been obtained by means of a generalisation of the qualities which the *polloi theoi* had in common, in the same way that 'tree' is a generalisa-

---

[1] 'If we must have a general name for the earliest form of religion among the Vedic Indians, it can be neither *monotheism* nor *polytheism*, but only *henotheism*.'—*Hibbert Lectures*, p. 260.

tion of the qualities of many trees. On the contrary, the
many gods would owe their common name to the fact that
they shared in some inward quality which we had previously determined was essential to divinity. But to what
in this case would the *polloi theoi* owe the *difference* of
their natures? Why should Zeus be unlike Hermes, and
why Apollo different from both? The explanation once
universally given, and even now thought ' generally sufficient,' is that the characters of the gods are the result of
mere invention, and in fact the children of fancy. But
such a notion is, as we have before agreed, inconsistent
with the seriousness of true belief. It was the explanation
which Sidney gave of the birth of the Chimæra and of
the Furies; and if the explanation was insufficient for
the beings which people the outer circles of mythology,
far less sufficient is it for those who occupy the central
place in a creed.

When, however, we realise that the gods were once
confounded with natural phenomena, all difficulty in
accounting for their characters is taken away. Apollo is
not like Hermes, because the sun is not like the wind.
Just so long as the natures of both are connected with outward nature will their characters remain apart, and yet
the belief in both remain real. When they become altogether abstract conceptions, either the two will merge in
one or one of them will lose his divine character. He will
then become a subject for fancy and for the invention of
poets ; he will no longer be an object of worship.

This nature-worshipping stage of belief, then, is, so
long as it remains pure, the stage of the most pure and
unmixed polytheism. So long, and only so long, as the
name of the god and the name of the element, the portion
of nature, are one; so long as the being is thus identified
with earth, or sky, or sea; and so long as no being is worshipped under a name which has ceased to be the expression of an outward thing—the polytheistic belief remains;
for while this state continues it is impossible that the

deity of one element can have control over the god of
another, seeing that each is, of necessity, confined to his
own province.

Evidently the nature-worshipping stage of belief is a
change and an advance upon fetichism. The more the
deity is raised above the level of common things, the more
great and high does he become; and becoming thus
greater, the more does he tend to absorb into himself the
thoughts of the worshipper. He approaches so much the
nearer to an abstract god.

The third and last stage in early religious development
is the anthropomorphic stage, which links nature worship
on to monotheism. We have seen how, while the nature
worship remained, the creed was purely polytheistic; how,
as the sea could have no control over the sky, nor the sky
over the earth, the gods who represented these things
must remain apart. But in time the change does come.
Then Zeus and Zio no more recall to those who use their
sacred names the overspreading heaven; all they suggest
is the idea of beings having, in some way, the character
of the sky, in an obscure and mystic way not obvious to
the sense of the worshipper. Zeus and Zio have grown
into proper names, designations of *persons* and not of
things; and the gods stand out as clear and as thinkable,
in virtue of this name, as any absent friend may be. The
Aryans have made an immense step forward when they
have arrived at this point.

Through the natural changes which time works in
every mythic system may be traced this process of finding
a name for that aggregation of ideas which is gradually
settling into what we understand by the word *god*. With
the Greeks and Romans Dyâus remained the chief god,
because in his changed names, Zeus and Jupiter, he no
longer represented the sky; in India, on the contrary,
because Dyâus did recall some natural appearance he
ceased to be the chief divinity, and his place was supplied

by Indra, for Indra's name has not a direct physical meaning.[1]

Had the Indians and the Greeks continued always in the same spiritual condition the name of their highest god might indeed have changed—such changes are in the nature of mythology—but no change would have been effective to abstract their thoughts from the phenomena of sense. The alterations would have been in a direction the very opposite to that which they actually took. Dyâus would have remained the chief god of the Indians, and another old Aryan god, Varuna (in the form *Ouranos*), would have become the chief god of the Greeks; because Dyâus and Ouranos, in Sanskrit and Greek, still stood for the *sky.*

Suppose Dyâus, then, to have become a proper name. We have not yet seen how it grows to be a generic one. This last consummation cannot be far off. When a phenomenon, a *thing,* is changed into a *person,* and baptised with an appellation of its own, the tendency will arise to call other phenomena of nature by the same name. We shall have a sea Zeus, an earth Zeus, while men will mean thereby only what we understand by the words sea god, earth god. We do see survivals of such a method of nomenclature in the pantheons of Greece and Rome—in such a name, for example, as Zeus Chthonios, which is really synonymous with Hades, and designates a different personage from the Zeus Olympios; in the Zeno-poseidôn, of whom we have some traces,[2] and in the use by the Latins of the word Junones as a synonym for goddesses. An example of the same kind is the association of Indra's name with almost all the other gods of the Veda—e.g. Indragni, Indrasomo, Indravayu, Indravaruno. These must mean merely God Agni, God Soma, &c. But of course the essential part of the process had been com-

---

[1] For the suggested etymologies of the word *Indra* see Ch. III.

[2] Athenæus, ii. 42. Cf. also the Ζεὺς Μηλώσιος ôf Paros and Corcyra; Bœckh, *Corpus In. Gr.* ii. 1870, 2418; and Maury, *Rel. de la Grèœ,* i. 53.

pleted before any one of the Aryan creeds had emerged into the light. Yet as Dyâus, Zeus, Jupiter, θεός, deus, Sanskrit deva, Persian div [1] (deus), are all from the same root, we can scarcely doubt that as the personal names Zeus and Jupiter were derived from the sky god, so were likewise the abstract or general terms θεός, deus, 'god.'

It is just as if at first the Aryas said 'sky, sky' to the object of their adoration; then changing the word a little, they *called* their god Skoi, and, lastly, invented a third abstract word, *skey*, for *a* god. I assume that Skoi was invented before *skey*, Zeus before *theos*, because this seems the most conformable to the natural process of thought. It must be said, however, that comparative philology gives us no information upon this point. The mere absence of any certain indication tells us this much only, that the one change came treading close upon the heels of the other.

With the growth of the personal god sprang up the distinctly ethic parts of the creed—those moral laws which, as Mr. Spencer says, are subsequent to the beginning of worship. There is little moral teaching in the works of nature : the thunder and the lightning are not bound by the laws which bind us; the wind bloweth where it listeth; and it is wasted breath to cavil at the doings of these things. The character, therefore, of the early gods is discovered by observing what they are, not by considering what they should be.

> I am that I am, and they that level
> At my abuses reckon up their own.

But when the god has clothed himself in human guise he has taken therewith the responsibilities of human nature; he must, in the end, conform to one code of right and wrong. It will be long, no doubt, before he does this.

[1] The fact that the Persian *div* means devil is a matter of no consequence here. The change of meaning, in fact, came chiefly accidentally. That at least is Darmêsteter's view (*Avesta*, Introd.) Others attribute it to the reforming spirit of Zoroastrianism.

Zeus cannot, if he would, shake off his former nature. His shameless amours were innocent when he was, in very fact, the heaven which impregnates all nature by its fertilising rains. All the race of men are sons of heaven and earth, so all are born of Zeus. Earth has many names, being not uniform, but different in different places; so Zeus has many wives.

No religion which we shall encounter among the Aryan folk has stopped short before it reached this third stage, that of practical monotheism. Each one, that is to say, has got its *general name* for god. But phases of belief are not to be measured by the mere lapse of time, no more than geological strata are to be measured by their distance from the centre of the earth. Some primitive formation may lie quite near the surface, side by side with another formation which is of yesterday. Wherefore along with quite modern notions on religious matters we may trace the forms of primitive belief. It is in our own hand which parts of the science we choose to make our study.

We shall find examples sufficient of all the early phases of religious growth in the creeds of the Aryan peoples; and, what is better, we may study these phases not as petrified remains, but in a continual process of growth and change. Just as in Highland or in Irish cottages, among the fishermen's huts of Brittany, or in the Russian *mir*, or among the peasants of Greece, we may listen to stories whose prototypes were told long centuries agone upon the banks of the Oxus and the Jaxartes by the remote fore-elders of our race, so among the same people of to-day we shall detect the signs of a creed which the more enlightened among those far-off Aryas were already beginning to leave behind. The countryman who comes to his well-dressing, or dances round his may-pole, pays ancestral vows to the power of tree and stream. He cherishes his piece of wood or scrap of linen as zealously as the African his gri-gri, though he may call the one a piece of the true Cross and the other a fragment of the

linen napkin; he worships his misshapen images and his
Black Virgin in the same spirit whereby the ancient Greek
held sacred his Black Dêmêtêr, his Ephesian Artemis, and
thought them more worthy of honour than the finest examples of Greek art. Such an one as he is our best friend
when we want to tread in the ways of a past belief. As
we see in his mind the alternations between superstition
and something higher than superstition, so we believe that
in him the race renews its ancient conflict, its struggles
and questionings, before the slow advance of thought; and
if his better instincts gain the day, then the victory of all
humanity is won once more.

There is one other point which we must touch upon in
enumerating the motive causes of belief—touch upon, but
no more. All beliefs have had their origin in sensation,
but those sensations have been most efficient which have
called forth most of the inward response, which have given
rise to the strongest *emotion*. Emotion, in truth, is so
much at the root of all worship that a kind of emotional
worship (or ritual) seems often to precede any definite form
of creed. Men worship they know not what. The current
of human thought and feeling does not run smoothly;
men are subject to moments of ecstasy when, without
knowing why, they obey an influence from outside them
which they cannot gauge. Tennent, in his description of
that degraded race of Ceylon the Veddahs,[1] after telling
us that they have no knowledge of a god nor of a future
state, no idols nor temples, yet goes on to give an account
of a ceremony practised among them which, in the proper

---

[1] Tennent's *Ceylon*, ii. 437. The Veddahs, when Tennent saw them,
were divided into three different classes, the rock Veddahs, the village
Veddahs, and the coast Veddahs, of whom the first only presented something
like an image of primitive life. They, as the name implies, lived in caves
or beneath trees, never in houses. I do not know whether they were really
so primitive a race as he supposes—whether, I mean, their culture may not
have declined. This is always the point difficult to decide about savage
races.

sense of the word, we may call religious. It was a wild
dance executed by one who professed to drive out disease,
and who must have thought by this performance to gain
some supernatural power or a kind of inspiration. 'The
dance,' says Sir E. Tennent, 'is executed in front of an
offering of something eatable placed on a tripod on sticks.
The dancer has his head and girdle decorated with green
leaves. At first he shuffles with his feet to a plaintive
air, but by degrees he works himself into a state of great
excitement and action, accompanied by moans and screams,
and during this paroxysm he professes to be inspired with
instruction for the curing of the patient.' The description
of the Veddah dance might be transcribed for that of any
Oriental darweesh or fakeer; it would not be much misplaced if it were applied to the orgies of the Bacchantes
or the worshippers of the Phrygian Mother Goddess.
When the belief in any dogmatic creed—that is, in any
theory of the world and of God and man—seems to be
breaking up, men return as if by natural instinct to these
wild forms of worship, which are earlier than any dogma.
So in Greece the rites of Eleusis, and the mystic worship
of Isis in Rome, outlived the genuine belief in the Greek
and Roman divinities; and when men felt the creed of
mediæval Christendom trembling beneath their feet, they
too broke out into like orgies of emotion. Such were those
which swept over Europe in the fourteenth century, the
processions of penitents, of flagellants, and the strange
Dance of Death.

All this shows how much worship is an affair of instinct. Certain excitements are more especially allied to
strong emotion; and foremost among all these we must
place the incitement of love and wine; wherefore we need
not be surprised if these indulgences play a great part in
every primitive creed. Indeed, as ecstasies are earlier
than pantheons—though not, I suppose, earlier than any
sense of supernatural existence—it might seem as if
Phallic and Bacchic worship were more essential than any ·

other part of the early religion.   What are degrading uses for a people at all advanced in culture are not so for the lowest of mankind; and, were the subject suitable for discussion here, it would be easy to show that these indulgences, as they are the main authors of a formulated worship, and so one may say of religion, are likewise great instigators to the growth of morality.   'Iερός, holy, is from a root which means to agitate; and if Erôs be, as some say, the same with Hermês, he is a god of agitation, of rapid motion, as well as of love.   The saying of a Papuan Islander (quoted by Mr. Spencer) suggests the origin of the worship of the vine.   When spoken to concerning God he replied, 'Then this god is certainly your arrack, for I never feel so happy as when I have had my fill of that.'

Wherefore all through the history of belief we shall find one or both of these two gods—the god of love or the god of wine—possessing a mighty power.   For one class of people and for one climate the one indulgence, for other sorts the other.   Aphroditê for the southern Greeks and the Greeks of the islands, and for the Asiatic people of warm Semitic blood.   Dionysus for Thrace and the shepherds of the north, and chiefly too for the Aryan Indian [1] and Persian.[2]   Wine for the German,[3] love for the Celt.[4] 'For beauty and amorousness, the sons of Gaedhil.'

This part of the history of religion needs only to be hinted at here.   It is not a subject suitable for a popular treatise.   Moreover, it has little direct bearing upon the subjects of the following chapters, which are not, as a rule, concerned with creeds in their emotional aspect.

[1] The place which is occupied in the Vedic ritual by the intoxicating plant soma is a sufficient proof of this.
[2] Herod. i. 131.
[3] See Tacitus, Germ. 22. The custom of deliberating when drunk, common to Persians and Germans, arose no doubt from a belief in the inspiration of the vine.
[4] Cf. Diodorus Sic. v.; Strabo, iv.; Athen. xiii. 8.

house. But in this case the ancient forms of building had become overlaid with other uses : the tree trunk no longer stood simple and bare ; it was hidden in brass, and polished smooth like a pillar.

All this is mere prosaic fact; but soon we pass on to the region of belief and mythology. The Norseman on the image of his own house fashioned his picture of the entire world. The earth, with the heaven for a roof, was, to him, but a mighty chamber, and likewise had its great supporting tree, passing through the midst and branching far upward among the clouds. This was the mythical ash called *Yggdrasill*, Odhinn's ash. ' It is of all trees the greatest and the best. Its branches spread over all this world of ours and over heaven. Three roots sustain it, and wide apart they stand ; for one is among the Æsir (the gods), and another among the Hrimthursar (frost giants), where once lay the chasm of chasms ; the third is above Nifl-hel (Mist-hell).' So speaks the younger Edda ; [1] and the elder in still more beautiful language, but to the same effect :—

> I know an ash standing Yggdrasill hight,
> A lofty tree laved with limpid water ;
> Thence come the dews into the dales that fall ;
> Green stands it ever over Fate's fountain. [2]

Deep down are the roots of Yggdrasill in gloomy Nifl-hel, the Northern Tartarus ; and yet from under these roots wells up the fountain of life. In obedience, no doubt, to the same original belief in an earth-supporting tree do we read in classical mythology of the mystical oak (φηγός) of Dodona, which had its roots in Tartarus,[3] while

---

[1] Edda Snorra, D. 15. On the worship of trees by the Scandinavians see the passage quoted from Adam of Bremen in Ch. VII. And compare with that (for other heathen people) what is said in Zonoras, *Annal.* 3 ; Leon Isaur. 82.

[2] Völuspá, 19. On the Teutonic earth tree see Kuhn, *Herabk. des Feuers*, 118-137 ; Windischmann, *Zor. St.* 165-177 ; Mannhardt, *Germ. Myth.* 541-671 ; and Kuhn's *Zeitschr. f. verg. Sp.* xv. 93 sqq.

[3] Schol. ad Virg. *Georg.* ii. 291.

at the roots of this same tree there was likewise a magic
fountain, which by its murmurings gave forth the
oracles of Zeus. Yggdrasill stood ever green over Fate's
fountain; this oak of Dodona never changed nor shed its
leaves.

In such cases as these, because the people have
advanced far from primitive thought, mythology and
experience, the real and the ideal, are kept separate.
But to savage men it may well seem that the tree which
is his home does touch the sky and hold it up. The
Maoris have a tale how that the earth and sky were once
so closely embracing that the children whom· they had
begotten found no room to live; how those took counsel
together by what means they might separate their two
parents, and how the first tree—Tanemahuta,[1] the father
of trees—accomplished this feat by pressing continually
upwards, until with great pain he had rent apart the sky
and earth. An idea like this is the origin of the mythical
earth tree.

It has often been noted how man, alone among all the
animals, has the power of gazing upward to heaven, while
the rest of moving things have their faces bent ever
towards the earth. This faculty—like our sense of
morality, our sense of God—came to us not all at once,
but gradually through lapse of time. Savages are said
scarcely ever to raise their eyes, and their heads are
naturally ·inclined with a downward gaze, so that it must
be an effort for them to look at the sky and the heavenly
bodies. Primeval man lived upon roots and berries, or on
the lesser animals and the vermin which he gathered from
the soil, and so habit as well as nature kept his eyes
fixed upon the ground. We need not therefore wonder if,
in their half-glances upward, our forefathers had not
leisure to observe that the tree-top was not really close
against the sky, and that what childish ignorance still

---

[1] Sir George Grey, *Polynesian Myth.* pp. 1-4.

fancies [1] was more certainly believed by them. They may well have deemed that the upper branches hid themselves in infinitely remote ethereal regions. If it be true that ' high ' is the word most expressive of moral perfection, we are not at liberty to doubt that with such upward gazes as primitive man could take there went a dim sense of elevation of mind and character, high instincts which his mortal nature could only half understand.

Man abode on the ground, beneath the tree-shade, or in the tree's lower branches; the denizens of the upper regions were the birds. These last must therefore, very early in the history of belief, have seemed wonderfully sacred and wise. Before man had advanced far enough to worship the heaven itself or the heavenly bodies, while he was still bound to a narrow phase of belief, birds became expressive to his mind of height, and of intimacy with those far-off branches of the tree or with that unsearched mountain summit which were then his heaven. Later on, when the gods had become celestial, and, leaving the earth, had gone to dwell in the heaven itself, the birds still were seen flying thither. The worship of birds as divine existences, therefore, belongs of right to men of the prime, before statues were carved or shrines were built. ' No need to raise for them temples of stone nor doorways with golden doors; for they in fruit trees and dark oak shall dwell, and in the olive tree receive our vows.' [2]

When the birds ceased to be *divinities* they remained still the best *diviners*, for they, it was thought, shared most intimately in the counsels of the gods, and were the

---

[1]　　　I remember, I remember
　　　The fir trees dark and high:
　　I used to think their slender tops
　　　Were close against the sky.

　　It was a childish ignorance ;
　　　But now 'tis little joy
　　To know I'm further off from heaven
　　　Than when I was a boy.—HOOD.

[2] Aristoph. *Aves*, 615, &c.

most trustworthy of omens.   Each of the greater gods
among the Greeks had his own special bird, which he sent
on missions of a prophetic nature.   From Zeus came an
eagle, from Apollo a hawk, and from Athene a crane;[1]
Aphrodité had her doves.   It was, with the Greeks, the
very acme of profanity to fright away the denizens of a
sacred enclosure.[2]   With the Germans and the Celts
divination from birds was as common as with the Greeks
and Romans.   Odhinn (or Wuotan) had his two hawks or
ravens whirling round his throne; and every morning
they flew ' earth's fields over '[3] to watch the ways of men.
We also know that among the Norsemen it was the
greatest gift of prophecy to understand the language of
birds—though a man might sometimes wish he had not
known it; for they told of the future, its evil as well as
its good.   In one of the Völsung lays of the elder Edda
there is a beautiful passage which tells how Sigurd, when
he had eaten Fafnir's heart, had his ears opened in this
wise, and heard the eagles above telling one another of
his own deeds, and what would be his end.[4]

The ' wise women ' of many different systems of mythology seem to possess in common the gift of being able to
change themselves into birds.   Perhaps the more immediate prototypes of the angels of mediæval Christianity
were the maidens of Odhinn,[5] at once amazons and
prophetesses, who were called Valkyriur (Walachuriun).
They were likewise called *swan maidens*, because they took
sometimes the form of swans.   In the Bible the Spirit of
God Himself, when it becomes visible to man, appears in
the shape of a dove.

The worship of birds is of all forms of animal worship
the most exalted and spiritual, because it has to do with

[1] Homer, *passim*, esp. *Il.* x. 274; xii. 200.
[2] Herod. i. 159.   [3] Grimnismál, 20.
[4] Fafnismál, 31 to end.
[5] I do not mean their prototypes in art, but in popular belief, at any
rate in northern Europe. Concerning these Valkyriur, see Chs. VII.
and X.

regions remotest from common earth. This is why the
holy birds linger long in late forms of belief, and survive
generally as the symbol of those gods and goddesses whose
proper dwelling-place is the heaven. A bird, for instance,
would come appropriately from Zeus, or Athenê, or Apollo,
the sky, the air, the sun, or from Odhinn, the storm wind,
but less appropriately from Dêmêtêr, the earth goddess,
or from Poseidôn, the god of the waves. And I suppose
that when we encounter the figures of winged beasts in
religious art, as we do so conspicuously in the religious
art of Assyria, we are to take it that the gods whom the
beasts symbolise have been raised from earth to heaven.
These mythic beings combine the majesty of the beast
chosen—the courage of the lion, say, or the strength of the
bull, or the swiftness of the horse—with the spirituality
and special sacredness of birds. Such winged creatures
are not unknown to Greek art.[1] They have made their
way into the religion of the Hebrews, and thence into
Christian belief; the cherubim, it seems, were the same
as the Assyrian and Phœnician griffin.[2]

Seeing that birds have attributed to them a gift of
prophecy, partly in virtue of the antiquity of their worship,
it is natural that all fetiches should be themselves oracular.
Prophecy belongs to the region of magic, and magic rites
are almost always a survival from some old form of belief,

[1] E.g. Pegasus. The griffin, too, is tolerably common in some Greek art.
Both come through Asiatic influences. Cf. Layard, *Nineveh*, ii. 461, for
Pegasus, and for the griffin next note.

[2] I mean etymologically the same, as well as the same in their original
representation. Kuenen supposes that the cherubim who stood upon the
ark of the tabernacle had the shape of griffins (*Rel. of Israel*, i. p. 280).
The cherubim are, he says, embodiments of the clouds; they are, therefore,
essentially the same as the Valkyriur of the North, who, I say, foreran the
Christian angels in the popular belief of northern Europe. It may be well
to add that the double eagle which in Christian art was designed to represent the double greatness of the Holy Roman Empire (spiritual and material
rule combined in one, or perhaps only the united Empires of East and
West) is likewise drawn from Eastern iconography. Texier, *Asie Mineure*;
also A. de Longpérier, *Revue Arch.* O. S. vol. ii. p. 76. The monument
bearing representations of this and other fabulous winged creatures was
appropriately discovered on the site of the ancient Pteria.

the meaning of which has been forgotten, and the use in consequence distorted. The earlier gods, which were near, and visible, and tangible, and a part of nature, became a natural means of communication between man and the later gods, who were supernatural and unseen. Wherefore the power of divining remained with the tree itself, and with the mountain and the river. The oracles of Zeus were conveyed by the whispering leaves of the oaks of Dodona; and the laurel of Apollo at Delphi is another instance of an oracular tree. We should not be far wrong in supposing that the fabulous ash, Yggdrasill, was magical in this way. We know, at any rate, that the wise women of the North, the Norns, lived hard by one of the roots of this tree of life. The *divining rod* has inherited its qualities from the divining tree.

The prophetic powers of mountains resided generally in their caves. The wise women, or witches, of heathen and mediæval legend had their homes always either in a wood or in a cave.[1] Among the Romans we know how a voice from a cave used to bring the prophecy of the sybil.[2] It was in a cave or cleft between two steep rocks that the Pythoness received her divine inspiration.

Finally, more than either tree or mountain, waters have been great in gifts after this kind. Rivers, fountains, and wells have, in all ages, been accounted sacred and prophetic. From our wishing-wells back to the fountain of Urd, from which the Nornir watered the roots of Yggdrasill, or to Mim's well (if this be not the same), whither Odhinn went to buy wisdom, is one continuous stream of illustration of this belief, which need not be here set forth in full. That the notion was as familiar to the Greeks, the fountain of Parnassus, by which Apollo's priestess stood, the poetic inspiration ($\mu\alpha\nu\tau\epsilon\iota\alpha$) of prophet and poet from Parnassus and Helicon, may serve to remind us.

It is no strained imagination, but almost a statement of sober fact, that belief so common among the nations,

---

[1] See Chaps. VII. and X.   [2] Æn. vi.

of these trees he plucked a little twig. Then from the wound thus made (as from green wood burning) came, with bubbling, steam and blood, and last of all a voice, which was the voice of Pietro delle Vigne, the minister of Frederick. Tasso and our Spenser have given us pictures founded on the same old-world belief.

What has been here sketched out concerning tree worship will apply, changing what should be changed, to the worship of mountains. The mountain is higher than the tree, more majestic and remote, and in a manner more abstract. It is of the two the less fitted to be the parent of a race or tribe; and we do not, in fact, find so often the belief in a descent from mountains as in a descent from either trees or rivers. Mountain worship is, in most respects, an advance on tree worship; for when, to the growing intelligence of mankind, the tree becomes relatively small, the high hill is still immeasurable and has its head buried in the clouds. And from this cause mountain worship is more often to be seen persisting into later phases of belief, and is less characteristic of the earlier ones. Zeus may, in times relatively far advanced, still be worshipped in the actual form of a mountain.[2]

Of the oracular character which belongs to the mountain fetich I have already spoken. Some of the most venerable and ancient temples among the Greeks

---

[1] *Met.* xx. 4, &c.   [2] See Ch. IV.

were situate in a deep gorge between high rocks, as, for example, the shrine of Apollo at Tempe and the temple of Dêmêtêr at Eleusis. The gods themselves, when they were not throned high on the mountain summits, as on Olympus, often found a dwelling-place in its deep clefts.[1]

The river fetich has some special qualities and associations which I shall speak of presently. It has others which it shares with the tree fetich. Among the latter is its position as a progenitor, and of this belief we have the most conspicuous examples in Greek mythology. In truth, worship of the river and mountain fetiches has found its chief partisans in Greece and in Italy, while the cult of trees was especially characteristic of the Teuton and the Celt.[2] The nations of Northern Europe lived in regions, as Tacitus describes them, 'either rugged with forest or dank with marsh,' but the Greeks in a bright land not much wooded. Wherefore a difference of creeds followed this difference of surroundings. In Greek mythology Oceanüs is found to have many of the attributes which in the Norse mythology belonged to the mythic world-tree Yggdrasill. It corresponds in many respects to the world ash, the symbol of life and of time, and to that other ash (if another it really were) from which the human race proceeded. For example, Oceanus was the beginning of all things, the parent alike of gods and of men. He was the first and the last, the Alpha and Omega of life. The etymology of the name Oceanus seems to show that the very foundation of his nature was as a primeval existence, a forefather.[4] Oceanus was the parent of all waters,

---

[1] Cf. *Il.* i. 495, v. 753; Hesiod. *Th.* 113 (στύχας ἀλύμποιο).

[2] There are frequent references to river worship in Homer (cf. *Il.* xi. 726, xx. —a council of the gods which rivers attend; xxi. 130; *Od.* v. 446), but, so far as I remember, none to the worship of trees. It is very probable that fountains were much worshipped by the Celts. We find in the Middle Ages numerous ordinances forbidding this form of paganism. See Capitularies, i. *tit.* 64, § 789, *c.* 63, and viii. *tit.* 326, *o.* 21. *Leges Luitprandi*, ii. *tit.* 38, § 1. *Vita Elig.* ii. 15.

[3] 'Aut sylvis horrida aut paludibus foeda.'—*Germ.* 5.

[4] See Ch. VI. Ogyges.

the encircler of the world.[1]   He included in his circle all
living nature, for beyond this river lay only the land of
darkness and of death.[2]   Oceanus, again, was complete in
himself, and so for ever returning upon his own course.[3]
Other rivers were the progenitors of special families—
Asopus, Inachus.   A descent from rivers is not at all
uncommon among Homeric heroes : witness Asteropæus,
whom Achilles slew beside Xanthus—' he was the son of
broad-flowing Axios '—and Menesthios, the son of Sper-
cheios, and others.[4]

   Fetichism discharged a great duty in that it first
formed the patriotic instincts, by giving to men a notion
of *fatherland* and an attachment to a particular soil.   The
fetich gods could not be moved, and in the worship of
them, in the sense of safety and sacredness which they
spread like an aroma round one spot, there was found just
the force needed to awaken a sense of nationality and of
fellowship among men.   The value of a safe, protected
spot must be great in proportion as all other places are
strange and fearful ; by the fetich worshipper the outer
world is not dreaded only on account of its visible
dangers—for the wild beasts who hover round, for the
savage men of a different tribe and an alien creed who
may be near—it is likewise ghost-haunted, and may be the
home of evil spirits and unseen unfriendly powers.   And
so, moved by this fear, all those who are akin draw near
together.   It has often been noticed how the sense of
kinship among nations springs more from a common
faith than from any other tie ; this outweighs the bonds
of blood, of language, and of country.   We see examples
enough of this even now, when the orthodox Slav is the
bitterest enemy of the Catholic Slav, when the Shiah
Persian or Afghan is more hateful than any common foe
to his Sunni brother.   It was well, therefore, that at first

---

[1] *Il.* xiv. 246, xxi. 196 ; Æsch. *Prom.* 636, &c.   [2] See Ch. VI.
[3] ἀψόρροος.   *Il.* xviii. 399 ; *Od.* xx. 65.
[4] *Il.* xxi. 141, &c. ; xvi. 173.

the ties of country and of kinship and of creed should have
been inseparably united.

Greek national life sprang up around some local shrine.
For the guard of the temple and the honour of the god,
towns or villages entered into Amphictyonies—associations of the neighbours to it—and these Amphictyonies
in time grew into States. 'Only one form existed in
ancient Greece for the combination of peoples—namely, a
common religious worship, which at fixed times assembled
a number round a generally acknowledged sanctuary, and
laid upon all the participators in it the obligation of
certain common principles. Such festivals—associations
or Amphictyonies—are coeval with Greek history, or may
even be said to constitute the first expression of a common
national history.'[1] The principle of the Amphictyony was
conceived in the genuine spirit of fetichism; for, to unenlightened minds, the temple itself is a kind of fetich. The
temples of paganism were, as an orator of the latter days
of paganism declared, 'the life and soul of the country;[2]
under their protection the peasant planted and sowed; to
their guardianship he committed his wife and child.' We
can guess, then, how dear in times far more ancient than
these must have been the river by which a tribe had settled,
the mountain in whose caves they lived, or the tree which
sheltered them.

So much for the characteristics of fetichism in its
prime. A hundred more examples might be given
of the worship of trees and rivers and hills, and of the
traces of such worship in later creeds. But the main
characteristics of the faith would return again and again,
and only grow wearisome by repetition. Nevertheless,
before we quite leave the subject we have to notice one
peculiar form of worship which seems to be connected with
fetichism and more peculiarly with the cult of rivers.

---

[1] Curtius, *Hist. of Greece*, i. 111.

[2] Ψυχὴ, ὁ βασιλεῦ, τοῖς ἀγροῖς τὰ ἱερά. Libanius in a speech to Theodo-
sius on behalf of the ancient temples.

I do not propose to enter into a discussion concerning the religious significance of animal worship, taken as a whole. The origin of it has never yet been satisfactorily explained,[1] and until it has been made more clear we are not justified in adopting arbitrary theories concerning it. Some peoples have furnished themselves with elaborate reasons for their worship of animals: they have made them symbolical of moral qualities, or even of some natural phenomena. Sekhet, the bright-eyed cat or lioness goddess of the Egyptians, was made to stand for the sun, or else for the moon, because the cat's or lioness' eyes shine at night; the eagle, in like manner, symbolised the sun. Explanations like these have always been given by people who had themselves advanced too far beyond the sphere of animal worship to understand its meaning. Such notions may have seemed satisfactory to Egyptian priests in the days of Herodotus; they cannot possibly seem so to a student of the history of belief to-day. Failing some better interpretation, we may assume that, beside that honour which was paid to superiority in size or strength, the reason for animal worship lay in some human feature or quality—the majesty of the lion, the walk of the bear, the human cry of the cat—suggesting thus the doctrine of the migration of souls. This would reserve for animals a great amount of reverence, such as that paid to dead ancestors, though this would still fall short of actual worship; and, perhaps, the cult of animals has always been rather an element in other creeds than a distinct creed itself.

From other kinds of animal worship, however, the worship of the serpent stands apart. It is of all forms probably the widest spread and most deeply rooted; and yet its origin is, of all perhaps, the hardest to understand. Fergusson suggests its great longevity as one reason, its deadly power—both mysterious and deadly—as another.

---

[1] For I think, as I have said, the totem theory quite insufficient to explain it; or perhaps I should rather say it is too sufficient a way.

The first, by itself, is certainly not reason enough ; besides, it would not be easy for man to ascertain this fact without paying close attention to this reptile, which would be in itself peculiar. And the objection to the other reason is that serpent worship—as Fergusson admits [1]—is not one which is strongly marked by fear.

For my own part, I believe in this one instance that the use of the animal is symbolical, and that in almost every case the serpent stands for the river. It would, of course, be impossible, or even if possible unsuitable, to produce in this place all the reasons which have led me to such an opinion. But there can be no harm if we turn aside for a moment to glance at the chief among them.

The river of rivers to the Greeks and Romans was that great Oceanus of which I spoke just now—the earth-encircling stream which flowed between the world of men and the kingdom of Hades.[2] The belief in that stream, as we shall see more clearly in a future chapter, was by no means confined to the classical ancients, but was shared in by all the members of the Indo-European family. It has been already said more than once, and shown, that the most primitive belief concerning the sea is that it is only a mighty river; wherefore it follows that if in any system of mythology a sea is found in the place which a river occupies in some other system, the myth concerning the sea is later than the myth concerning the stream. Now in the creed of the Teuton races we find generally that instead of the whole of man's earth being surrounded by a river like Oceanus, it is girt in ' by a wide and deep sea.' 'The gods,' says the younger Edda, ' made a vast sea, and in the midmost thereof fixed the earth.' [3] What, then, we are tempted to ask, has become of the river? Have the traces of that earlier myth quite disappeared ?

I believe that that river has been transformed into the mid-earth serpent ('miðgarðsôrmr'), called Jörmungandr,

[1] Fergusson, *Tree and Serpent Worship*, beginning.
[2] *Od.* xi., &c.   [3] Edda Snorra, D. 8.

who, in the later form of the mythology which we know, is described as lying at the bottom of the mid-gard sea curled up with his tail in his mouth.

Jörmungandr has been generally considered the personification of the mid-earth sea; I say he is rather the personification of the mid-earth river. Now the difference between a sea and a river is precisely this, that one is still and the other is continually flowing. But how is a river to lie all round the earth and yet be for ever flowing, unless it flows into itself? Here was the first difficulty which arose when men tried to reconcile the old and vague ideas of primitive belief with the exacter knowledge of later times. They generally met the difficulty by making the river flow in upon itself. The Greek Oceanus was imagined to flow in this returning way; it was, as we have seen, ἀψόρροος, returning everlastingly in its own bed. Jörmungandr lies, we are told, with his tail in his mouth, and that tail is continually growing *into his body.* This image certainly suggests the idea of a river flowing in upon itself like Oceanus.[1]

In this case, then, we seem to have discovered a river which is certainly transformed into a serpent. In the battles between Thorr, the hero god of the North, and this Jörmungandr we seem to see the prototypes of most of those dragon fights whose relation delighted the ears of Middle Age Europe, from the fight of Sigurd with Fafnir to that of our St. George. Here then are a large number of serpents and dragons whose connection with rivers is tolerably certain.

Now turn to Greece. The serpent fights· of Hellenic mythology—the combats of Apollo with the Python, or of Heracles with the Lernean hydra, or with the serpent Ladon, who guarded the apples of the Hesperides—show, even at the first glance, a close resemblance to those

---

[1] I have discussed this origin of Jörmungandr at greater length in a paper on the 'Mythology of the Eddas,' *Trans. of the Roy. Soc. of Literature*, vol. xii.

of Thorr with Jörmungandr. This alone would suggest
that the above-mentioned serpents might have had an
origin similar to the origin of the Norse sea-serpent. We
are not, however, limited to this argument by analogy.
In the case of the Python, at any rate, the close association between her and a river can be demonstrated. We
remember that the fight between Apollo and the Python,
as told in the Homeric hymn, springs directly out of the
enmity of the fountain goddess Telphusa to the sun god.
This Telphusa (or Delphusa) was, unquestionably, some
ancient fetich river, whose worship the Dorian cult of
Apollo displaced ; and so the myth describes her contriving
a stratagem to rid herself of her rival. She sent him to
the deep cleft of Parnassus, where the Python, her other
self, dwelt ; when Apollo had slain this monster, he
returned and polluted the fountains of Telphusa. M.
Maury, in his 'Religions de la Grèce,'[1] quotes from Herr
Forchhammer an ocular experience of the death of the
Python beneath the arrows of the sun god. In the great
amphitheatre of Delphi, whose very name was taken from
the concavity of the valley (δέλφυς, belly) which was the
site of the town, is poured, during the rainy season, a
rapid torrent which passes between the two rocks formerly
called Nauplia and Hyampeia. During spring the
waters dry up and evaporate, so that in summer the
torrent brings no water to Delphi. The fountains of
Castalia and Cassotis are supplied simply by the subterranean flow of the waters from Mount Parnassus. The
drying up of this torrent, through the heat of the sun
(Apollo), is the death of the great serpent. The writer
goes on to point out how the name of this serpent is first
Δελφύνη—that is, full of water (from δέλφυς and ύνος for
οἶνος; in this connection any liquid)—and afterwards
Δεφίνη, empty-belly (δέλφυς, ἰνάω). Ovid says that this
Python was born from the earth after the deluge of
Deucalion ; Claudius tells us that he devoured rivers, i.e.

---

[1] i. 134.

his tributaries. We must not, of course, consider the slaying of the Python as a local myth only; but it was localised at Delphi and there spoke of a particular stream.

The dragon fights of Heracles seem to group themselves in pairs; he strangles two serpents in his cradle, and in later life he kills the hydra and the serpent Ladon; but we must remember also that he fights with and conquers *two* rivers, Peneius and Alpheius.

The two great Vedic serpents are Ahi and Vritra. In the form which they wear in the hymns they seem to be symbolical of the clouds rather than of anything terrestrial. But, I think, it is quite possible that they were rivers before they became clouds, and afterwards were transferred from earth to heaven. Ahi and Vritra are still designated generally the 'concealers' or 'containers of the water.'

I will not go so far as to assert that serpents had originally no more than this symbolical meaning. I cannot pretend to account for their primitive worship. Only I take it for certain that, at a very early time, rivers became, through symbolism, confounded with serpents; that in all the mythologies which we have opportunities of studying, this identification has gone so far that the worship of the two is inextricably involved; and hence that the *cult* of serpents, in any wide extent, is dependent upon one among the three chief forms of fetichism. We have already disposed of the great original serpents—the *Urschlangen*, if I may so call them—of Greek and German mythology: the more we see of the countless tribe of their descendants, the more we shall be reminded of the progeny of Oceanus.

A characteristic of the river, noted in it more than in any other fetich, was that of being the 'oldest inhabitant' of the country where it flowed: the notion of the river having been there before man came, and possessing the land in its own right, was ever upheld. To this notion

the river owed, in part, its title of *king*.   Just so the
snake was pictured as autochthonous, first dweller in the
soil; whereby it became the guardian of ancient treasures,
whether these treasures were life-giving fruits, apples of
the Hesperides or of Eden, or, as in the vulgarer and
later German myths, only a great primeval hoard.[1]   The
snake is a child of earth, and symbolises the oldest dwellers
on the soil.   When Cyrus was marching upon Sardis,
a wonder was reported to Crœsus as he lay in that city.
The town was suddenly seen to be full of snakes, and the
horses on every side were trampling them to death.   And
this was taken for a sign that the new comers, the Persians, would overcome the men of Lydia.[2]   In Arcadia
rivers were addressed by the title of king (ἄναξ),[3] perhaps
as progenitors of the race or as first possessors of the
land.   The serpent, too, is often styled a king, and wears
a crown; this still more frequently in German and Celtic
than in Greek tradition.   The 'serpent king' is still one
of the most popular characters of modern folk-lore.[4]   In
Germany upon those days which are now become the festivals of the Church great honours are paid to him.   If he
comes and partakes of the cakes or sweetmeats prepared
for him and left upon the hearth, he brings luck to the
house.   He is thus a sort of guarantee of stability, like
the house tree itself.   Or we may fancy him some ancestor
of the house, who still watches over it.

The connection between tree and serpent worship is
very close, though not so intimate as some writers would
have us suppose.[5]   But, however intimate, it says nothing

---

[1] The term 'heathen hoard' (' hæðnum hord ') is used to describe the
buried treasure which Beowulf gained by slaying the fiery serpent (*Beowulf*,
4546).   The meaning, of course, is that the treasure was of immense
antiquity.

[2] Herod. i. 77–80.

[3] As by Odysseus, *Od.* v. 445.

[4] A. Wuttke, *Deutsche Volksaberglaube*, pp. 50–5.

[5] Mr. Fergusson has, I think, given a quite false impression by treating
of *Tree and Serpent Worship* as if the two were always associated in belief.
He is obliged himself to acknowledge that such is not the case.

against the symbolic character of the mythic serpent, and
its origin in the river; for the worship of trees and of rivers
is likely to go more often together than that of either of
these fetiches combined with mountains; for this reason,
among others, that the tree can scarcely grow save in a
land where streams abound. It is a fact that we cannot
let our thoughts rest upon any familiar religion without
at once recalling a dozen examples of tree and serpent
worship, which are as many instances of the survival of a
still more ancient fetichism. I am, however, ready to
admit that in the later form of creed the serpent often
plays a part which does not seem of right to belong to
the river. The fetich river is nearly always a life-giving
power: it is the predecessor of the *fontaine de jouvence*; it
is the Urdar fount from which were watered the roots of
the world tree Yggdrasill. The serpent is, on the contrary,
often a destructive and evil power, as was that 'subtle
beast' of Genesis, and Jörmungandr himself, with all the
dragons his descendants; as was the Python, or those an-
tagonists of Heracles the serpent Ladon and the Lernean
hydra. But even these destructive serpents are found
in close association with the tree of life. The serpent
of Genesis entwines it; Ladon guards the apples of the
Hesperides; Niðhögg, another Eddaic snake, is twined
round the roots of Yggdrasill.

Among instances of a more direct worship was that of
the brazen serpent set up in the wilderness which was
still worshipped by the Jews in the days of Hezekiah; or
(to confine ourselves to our proper province) the serpents
which were to be found in most of the temples of Greece;
one in the Erechtheum at Athens, which was kept close
beside the sacred olive tree, another in the temple of the
Great Goddesses. The reptile was, we know, before all
things sacred to Asclepios, and was kept in his house; as,
for example, in the great temple at Epidauros. It would
seem that the sun god has the special mission of overcoming and absorbing into himself this form of fetich;

this is why Apollo slays the Python and why the snake is
sacred to Asclepios.[1]

We now leave this anomalous form, serpent worship,
and return to the direct history of fetichism. It is evidently essential to the true fetich—I mean to the fetich
which is *worshipped* and not used only as a charm—that
it be a natural product and not the work of ·man. Men
could not begin by themselves creating their own gods : a
fact sufficiently obvious (though it has been lost sight of
by many writers) to anyone who considers what man's
creations really are. All making—that is to say, all *art*
—is no more than imitation and reproduction, and has, in
Sidney's phrase, 'the works of nature for his principal
object; to become, as it were, but the actor and player of
what nature will have set forth.' We cannot conceive the
process of mind by which man, who had never seen a god,
could make one, or how he could give bodily shape to
what had hitherto been but an abstraction of his mind.
Obviously, the made fetich must be an imitation of some
thing, and if that made fetich is held sacred it must be
because the thing which it resembled had been first
worshipped.

The later fetich, then—whether it be an *imitation* of
the earlier one or a *portion* of it, like the stick or stone
which an African savage sets up in his forest—exists only
in virtue of the earlier unmade one. It is impossible—at
least it has proved so as yet—to fathom the degree of
worship the African savage pays to this stock or stone,
or to say what ideas his mind associates with it. This
alone is certain, that his creed is a survival from earlier
phases of belief, and, like other survivals, is a thing
anomalous in itself. It may coexist with various different
shades of intelligence and of religious perception. The
stick or stone may still (in virtue of survival) be considered as in itself a thing divine, or it may be used as a

[1] Pausanias (ii. c. 23, § 1 ; see also x. 45, xxii. 11) says that Asclepios
was adored under the form of a serpent at Epidauros.

means of concentrating the mind on an unseen presence.
Those fetiches which have a distinctly magical character
—such, for example, as pyrites—not only allow of, but require the belief in unseen gods at the back of the visible
phenomena which give them birth; a thunder stone
could not be sacred till men had come to believe in a god
of thunder. Therefore this kind of fetiches, of which
writers have often spoken as if they were the products of
the earliest fetich-worshipping phase of belief, are not
really so.

The later fetiches are not without interest to our study
as survivals. I can imagine that the nations among whom
fetichism was once most rife have a special tendency to
reverence these concrete material objects. Fetiches of
this sort have always been very common in the Asiatic
religions; for which reason the highest Asiatic religion,
Hebraism (and Mohammedanism after that), set its face
against the imitation of anything which was 'in heaven
or earth, or in the water under the earth.' But not with
entire success. The conical-shaped stones (*maçcebas*) and
the stumps (*asheras*; the word also signifies a grove)
which were conspicuous in the religions of the Syrians
and Phœnicians were often adored by the chosen people.
An example of a Mohammedan fetich exists in the black
stone which is the central object of reverence in the
Kaaba at Mecca, and which all pilgrims salute.

The fetiches last spoken of may have bad some connection
with phallic worship. But when this was the case they
were used as symbols only; and it is impossible to believe
that the origin of their use lay in symbolism. Far more
reasonable is it to suppose that everything of this sort has
taken its place in worship because it was a survival and a
representative of the once divine mountain or divine tree.
Of course, in the instances just given, it is a case of survival—that is to say, of *superstitio* only. We know enough
of the creed of the Syrians and of the Phœnicians to be
in no danger of supposing that these asheras and maçce-

bas were their very gods; nor is there any fear lest the Mohammedan should confound with the veritable Allah the black stone of the Kaaba, though he kisses this at the crowning rite of his long pilgrimage.

Of the same kind with these Asiatic stones and stumps were the holy *objects* (*agalmata*—not yet images) of the Greeks. Take, for example, the two stumps joined by a third in the shape of the letter Π, which was worshipped as the image of the Dioskuri (Castor and Pollux).[1] A rough piece of wood, called the sceptre of Agamemnon, was worshipped at Argos; another 'which had come down from heaven' was worshipped at Thebes as the Cadmeian Dionysus. The thyrsus of this last god and the Palladium (*agalma* of Pallas) are other instances in point. Nor were the stone *agalmata* less numerous. There was the column which represented the Zeus Meilichios of Sicyon;[2] at Hyettus, in Bœotia, was a rough stone which men called the agalma of Heracles;[3] at Thespiæ, an antique agalma of Erôs (chief divinity of this Phryne city) of the same kind;[4] and at Pharæ (Achaia) were thirty stones of quadrangular shape, each bearing the name of some god. 'In truth,' Pausanias adds, when he has spoken of these last, 'among all the Hellenes rude stones once received adoration as things divine.'[5]

Objects such as these may, I have said, have been chiefly used to concentrate the mind on some inward idea, as children use sticks and stones to play with, and endow them with the names of real or imaginary persons. Savages will do the same in a most serious fashion; and the witch of the Middle Ages, following the example of children and savages in this, made a waxen image to represent an absent person. Yet in every case the image ends by being,

[1] Winckelmann, *Hist. de l'Art*, i. ch. i. [2] Pausanias imagines this to be the origin of the letter Π (viii.). [2] Max. Tyr. and Clemens Alex. ii.
[3] Paus. ix. 24, 3. [4] Id. ix. 27, 1.
[5] Paus. vii. 22, 3. Cf. Lenormant in the *Revue de l'Hist. des Rel.* 1881, Les Bétyles.'

to some extent, confused with the being represented, and
so becomes endowed with a sort of vitality and, if it is the
image of a god, with a sort of sacredness. The habit,
therefore, of regarding such mere blocks and shapeless
masses with religious reverence might continue into the
days of a refined creed. It did continue among the Greeks
into the days of high artistic conception, and by so doing
had an important influence upon the development of
Greek art.

After a while, as religion progressed toward a personal
and more human conception of God, the stones or the
blocks (or the trees as they stood) began to be carved into
rough likenesses of human beings. When the image of
the god was made out of a tree still growing, he was
called *endendros* (ἔνδενδρος). We have Zeus Endendros,
Apollo Endendros, Dionysus Endendros. The thyrsus of
Dionysus, made out of a vine prop, was sometimes shaped
at the end into the image of a rude bearded head. The
terminus of still later times was a relic of this curious
and noteworthy stage of belief.

This was in truth eminently a transition period of
thought; it was marked, as transition times always are,
by much confusion, by an attempted adaptation of the
older elements of belief to those new ones which had in
reality superseded them. When the thing—the stone or
stump—was no longer an actual god, it was still to men's
thought permeated by a divine essence as by a sap. So
that when a statue had to be made, a substance of such a
kind that it was in itself holy, that which had once been
a fetich, was found far more suitable for the purpose than
any chance fragment of wood or stone. Wherefore we
see many instances of oracular command to carve an
image out of some particular holy tree.[1] Clearly a higher
order of divinity would reside in an ill-made statue of this

[1] See Bœtticher, *Baumcultus*, p. 214. The original image of Athene
Polias was made from her sacred olive tree (Plutarch, *Themist.* 10).

sort than in the finest work of art which had no mystery
or holiness mingling with its substance.

The tree fetich was a thing prayed to of itself: its
existence independent of man, its nature not human
nature. The carved tree shared the sacredness of the
uncarved one, and the face upon it only implied this
much, that the fetich confessed a likeness to mankind. It
was never meant to assert an identity between the divine
and human characters. As these rude images (agalmata)
must have been the beginning of sculpture among the
Greeks,[1] it cannot but have followed that the remains of
the fetichistic spirit deeply affected the early development
of Greek art. We must not look upon the rude archaic
statue as in any way representing man's ideal of human
nature, or even his nearest approach to such an ideal.
The mouth with its fixed smile, the eyes with their dull
stare, were put there in the spirit in which they might be
suggested by writing the words *mouth* and *eyes* upon the
block; or as ' the plaster, or the loam, or the rough-cast'
stood for ' wall' with the performers of that ' tedious brief
play of Pyramus and Thisbe.'[2] The real life, I mean, of
the agalma, and its real influence upon the imagination,

[1] Greek national art was not, of course, a pure creation of the Greek
mind, but, in a certain degree, a legacy from Assyrian, Egyptian, and
Phœnician art ; for, no doubt, the mere delight in the representation of life,
as displayed in the earlier art of these lands without any special consideration for the thing represented, was the first thing which stirred in the
Greeks their æsthetic taste. But the art which was merely imitative was
not yet Hellenic. What was needed was that the Greeks should use the
power acquired by imitation for the expression of Greek ideas. As we
know, they did use it chiefly to express their belief about the gods and
heroes.

[2] It is well worth noticing about archaic art that it has a double way
of expressing itself, partly as a complete representation of the thing
designed and partly as a sort of catalogue of the parts which make up the
thing. Thus in a profile face the eye is always drawn as if seen full, not
because the artist ever saw it in that way, but because he knew there was
an eye at this place, and his full drawing of an eye was the only thing
which expressed 'eye' to his mind. In the same way the joints are
articulated in a very curious way. To borrow a term from heraldry, we
might call this 'canting art.' It forms, I think, an important stage in the
growth of hieroglyphics.

lay in the thing itself. That would quite alone be wondrous and mystic, whereas the expression given to it was but an accessory. With us it is the very opposite. The only meaning of the statue is in its expression; without that the marble is lifeless indeed.

If we succeed at all in realising a state of mind such as that of the worshipper of shapeless agalmata, we shall understand how an interest and a veneration might attach to the objects as *things* far greater than any which in later times attached to a statue as the realisation of an *idea*. This explains why we find so many instances in which an archaic image has been enshrined in the most holy place of a temple; while all around, used as accessories only, were the triumphs of a later art. None of these later statues—albeit they were statues of gods, and in some cases of the same god as he who dwelt within the shrine —could rival the ancient image in the popular affections. Twenty lesser instances of such a state of things will at once occur to the reader. The great typical instance is that of the Artemisium at Ephesus. Some remains of this wonder of the world have, in quite recent days, been recovered and brought to this country; and we may judge from them (if we were in doubt before) that in outward decorative art it was inferior to no production of its own age. In the holy of holies still stood the time-honoured image of the Ephesian Artemis, that hideous figure only part human, part bestial or worse, and part still a block. This had been the central object of all, from earliest to latest days. For the sake of this the three temples had risen one upon the site of the other.[1] A real Greek Artemis might adorn the sculptures of the walls, might be allowed presence as an ornament merely, but the popular worship was paid to the deformed figure within.

It seems not improbable that when an artist, such as Pheidias or Polycleitus, was commissioned to execute the

[1] J. T. Wood, *Discoveries at Ephesus*, p. 263.

great statue of any temple, as the Athenê of the Parthenon, the Zeus Olympios at Elis, the Hera at Argos, his
representation was more archaic and stiff than what the
artist would have produced if left to his own fancy merely.
I think the descriptions which we have of the greater
statues suggest such a custom in art.   There can be no
doubt that there was, relatively, far less room for the
sculptor's talent in the figure of the great Athenê
Parthenos—clad, as she was, in full armour with spear
and helmet—than in that other figure of the same goddess
which adorned the frieze of her temple.[1]   It is certain,
again, that we see this influence of tradition in early
Italian art.   The greater divinities—if I may use that
expression—are more stiff and conventional, more archaic,
than those who accompany them.   The Virgin and Child
remind us more of the primitive Byzantine type than do
the angels who fly around.   So late as down to the time
of Botticelli this difference of treatment can easily be
detected.

By far the most important and deeply interesting of
all the chapters in the history of design is that which
shows us the Greek sculpture passing away from these
traditions, leaving its archaic work behind it, and making
its thoughts really speak in the productions of its hand;
when the features no longer remain so many labels
expressing the *fact* of vitality, but are fashioned to show
the depth and meaning of life.   A supreme moment, for
example, I would call it in the life of the world when the
old archaic mouth, fixed and meaningless, has the lips
turned downwards, and begins to take that curve which

---

[1] It is of course obvious that a draped figure would be more seemly for
worship than an undraped one.   It is known that the people of Cos refused
Praxiteles' statue of the nude Aphrodite, and that it was in consequence
transferred to Cnidus.   On the other hand (at a much earlier date than the
time of Praxiteles), nude Aphrodites were portrayed on the friezes of
temple walls.   This witnesses, at any rate, to the distinction made in
popular thought between the great statue and those others which were
merely ornamental.

ever since has served to express depth of feeling and
greatness of soul. Sometimes we almost seem to detect
the moment of this transition.[1] When the step has once
been made, the change goes rapidly on, and soon the
human form keeps but slight and not entirely unpleasing
traces of its archaism. The stiff, expressionless face is
replaced by one which is only so far stiff that it shows
not the passing wave of emotion, but the fixed character
of the wearer. The limbs which formerly could neither
stand, nor sit, nor kneel with grace,[2] can do all these things
naturally, but they do not readily change from one atti-
tude to another, and there is not in the figures of this
time the portrayal of quick or dramatic movement any
more than of transient thought. This firmness of atti-
tude and expression, implying a certain self-reliance and
stability of character, is therefore in part an inheritance
from archaic tradition, but it not the less constitutes the
characteristic of the highest art.

And, without doubt, this age in representation, as
compared with any which follow it, is that in which the
thing portrayed is the most real and living to artist
and beholder; as what is ingrained and firm and seems
perpetual must always be more real, and so more venerable, than what is fleeting and passionate. The archaic
statue, in spite of its absence of expression, was always
looked upon as a thing quite real and living. And this
from two causes: first, because of the relic of fetichism
which made the mere thing—block of wood or stone—a
living existence; and secondly, because the carved image,
rude as it was, was still the first representation of a human
being yet put before the world. To us it is shapeless
enough, a thing of nought; to primitive man it was a
wonder. The stone, alive in itself and merely as a stone,

[1] I could point to two coins of Ænus, in Thrace, closely resembling each
other in style, which yet have this distinction, that the mouth of one is
essentially the archaic mouth, that of the other essentially the Greek mouth.
[2] See, for instance, the Æginetan marbles.

had in addition put on a likeness to human kind; it was
endowed with eyes, a mouth, a nose, could touch and
taste and smell. With some of the stiffness of the bygone
times the early fine sculpture inherited a sense of reality,
of wonder too and awe, attaching to the image itself, such
as could never belong to it when art grew more familiar.

All this was of a piece with early Greek belief, which
was at first unquestioning, taking the world as it found it,
and attracted with an intenser love for individual objects
in that world than other men had been. The grand style
of sculpture may be said to belong to the age of intense
and true belief in the divinity of nature.

We have thus seen two ways in which, outside its own
sphere, fetichism affected the development of thought.
One was in the direction of politics, by infusing into men
the germs of patriotism and a special attachment to the
soil on which they were born; the other was in the di-
·rection of art, by giving men a sense of the sacredness of
things as things, out of which reverence was in time to
grow the sense of the beauty and holiness of all parts of
nature.

The last effects of fetichism in the history of belief
were not done with even when the fetich had quite disappeared. If the worship of the river or, mountain left
deep traces in the hearts of the people, then the river
and mountain gods, or gods who suited best with such characters, would still hold sway with the people. Wherefore
beings who seem to have been born in this way from the
earth and the things of earth, often outlive all the other
members of a pantheon, and show themselves again when
they are least to be looked for. We shall see in another
chapter how such divinities seem sometimes longer lived
than all other portions of a creed.

When beings of the fetich kind make their reappearance under changed conditions of thought, it is like
the birth (which sometimes happens) from two white-

skinned parents of one who bears all the marks of the yellow-skinned races—an instance of what is called *atavism,* or reversion to the original type. To the lower orders of Egypt their great fetich god, the Nile, was probably more worship-worthy than the elemental deities who were honoured by the priests and upper classes. And it is no doubt on this account that we have to note the strange appearance as late as the end of the sixth century of our era, when Egypt and all Northern Africa had been long since Christianised, of the Nile god.[1] Ra and Amun, Thoth and Ptah, Osiris and Horus, had been long since slain by Christ and buried in oblivion; but this Nile god was imprinted deep in men's hearts, and was not yet forgotten. We find the Rhone worshipped in France down to the twelfth century, and the dead committed to its care —as the dead still are to the care of the Ganges. Fetichism survives in the honours paid to wells and fountains, common in Germany and in some parts of France, and in England known under the name of ' well-dressing,' a simple rustic festival, wherein procession is made to the well or fountain and flowers as offerings are cast therein. Some slight ritual, a rustic dance or something of the sort, accompanies the ceremony. Tree worship is preserved in the Christmas tree,[2] in which the boughs of the tree (like the oak of Dôdôna, green still though it is winter) are hung with flowers and ribbons. Tree worship survives in the dance round the maypole.

The fetich is essentially a local god; it is, therefore, a survival of the spirit of fetichism that habit among the Greeks (of which Plato complains [3]) of speaking of the statue as the god, and thus of speaking of particular shrines and particular places as being under the protection of the local god, who was really the local statue. Men

---

[1] Simocatta (vii. 16) relates the appearance in the Nile of a huge man, who was seen rising out of the river as far as his waist. He was believed to be the Nile god.—Maury, *Magie.*

[2] Though this is for *us* only a recent importation from Germany.

[3] *Republic.*

spoke of laying an offering on the knees of Athênê, because it was laid upon the knees of her statue. They spoke of their Apollo Lykæus, Apollo of Triopium, of their Ismenean Apollo, as if these were all separate divinities; as a Catholic might have spoken, or might speak, of Our Lady of Loretto, Our Lady of Lourdes, as if each were a special local Virgin. When, before the battle of Platæa, the Greeks and Persians stood face to face, an oracle promised victory to the Athenians if they would pay their vows to certain divinities, including Hera of Citheron, and to some local heroes, and if they fought in their own country, especially in the plain of Dêmêter Eleusina and Persephonê. The Athenians were perplexed with this answer. ' For,' said they, ' we are directed to fight upon our own soil, and yet to pay our vows to Hera of Citheron and to the local nymphs and heroes.' How could these help them, they thought, if they moved away from the territory over which their power extended, and yet this was Platæau and not Athenian soil. The difficulty was removed, we remember, by the gift of the district from the Platæans to the Athenians.[1] The existence of the difficulty shows the localisation of such a great goddess as Hera. This is one of the survivals from the days of fetich worship.

The last faint echoes of this belief are found in the uses of objects such as the *relics* of the Roman Catholics, the very *feitiços* from which the belief has received its name. The bone of the saint, the nail from the true Cross, are fetiches of this sort. In such instances as these the creed is so far dying out that it is degenerating into mere magic.

Every creed has its special kind of superstition, which is in fact *superstitio*, or the standing over of some ideas derived from the old belief into a new stage. The special superstition of fetichism is magic; wherefore we find magic common among savage races, many of whom, it is

[1] Plutarch, *Vita Arist.*

probable, are emerging from the earliest phase of belief. What I mean by magic is the belief in exceptional qualities residing in particular parts of matter, along with the recognition that these things are *matter* and have not a will of their own. As has been before pointed out, when any stone or any lion's tail *may be* magical it is impossible to suppose that the inherent power belongs by right to the thing. If a stone merely as a stone were endowed with power and will to do hurt or good, then by analogy every stone would be endowed with this power. There would then be no exceptional power in any, and magic would become swallowed up by the very commonness of it. Magic, of course, exists along with almost any form of belief, but also it may exist unaccompanied by anything which we can fairly call belief. It may be a *mere* survival. Travellers have often believed themselves to have discovered examples of magic rites without any religion. Tennent, we have seen, believed so.[1] We cannot, however, say whether the other element is really absent, whether these travellers have encountered a creed in a state of decay, or whether the deeper belief has been only hidden from them. ·On the other hand, we can point to some cases in which belief has been actually abandoned and the sense of magic has remained behind. In such a phase the belief in magic presents before us an exceedingly anomalous condition of mind; it is scepticism plus the superstition of fetichism. But, anomalous as it is, it is not infrequent. Magic generally becomes more or less prominent when belief is in a state of decay. We know how well this truth was illustrated by the practice of magic in Rome in the days of the Empire. In Italy in the days of the Renaissance we have not the same frequency of definite magical rites, but, on the other hand, we have the completest example on record of the prominence of the *magic sense* in belief.[2]

[1] Supra, p. 50.
[2] I do not think that magic and witchcraft should always be classed

Sismondi has given us a picture of the popular belief in Italy at this period. We see how there religion had become divorced not only from morality but almost from all recognition of a Personality at the back of the world of sense. What *was* recognised was the thing called priesthood, with certain mysterious rights which it possessed. The highest of priests, the Pope, was nothing as a man, and other potentates might make war upon him, cheat him, be cheated by him, and yet never touch the sacerdotal part. The disgraceful conduct of a prelate did not seem more disgraceful because of his ecclesiastical dignity; a Pope might use the basest treason, and men were not more scandalised because he was a Pope; and, on the other hand, his enemy might employ what force or artifice he chose to rob him of his earthly territories.[1] All this was only dealing with the priest or pope upon his civil side—that is to say, as a man. But touch the side of *doctrine*—that is to say, attempt to interfere with the stream of magical power which flowed into pope or priest—and you at once made yourself an outcast from all human sympathy. 'The very persons who, in secular affairs, put so slight a rein upon their ambition and upon their political passions, trembled only at the *name* of the Hussites. They did not ask if their doctrine was damnable, if it was opposed to the fundamental doctrines on which are based the structure of society and the relationship of man and God: all they cared to know was that the teaching was condemned; then their only desire was to destroy it by fire and sword.' It was not in these days, as in the Middle Ages it had been, a misconception of what the heretic believed that made men desire his destruction; it was really no question of belief at all. The Hussite was one who threatened to tap the sacred founts of power

together. The essential feature of the witch's craft is the compact with Satan; magic of the sceptical sort is a kind of bastard experimentalism—empiricism.

[1] See Sismondi, *Répub. Ital.* vol. ix. ch. lxx.

—not material power, but immaterial, magical—which hitherto had flowed in through the Church; and men were naturally willing to fight for their share of the gift, which they honestly believed themselves to possess, quite independently of their personal character. The relationship of this fount of magic to a Supernal Being was almost utterly lost sight of. Its source was no longer thought of. Rather was it deemed of a nature like the wind, of which men cannot tell whence it cometh. This alone they knew, that from old time it had belonged to the Church, to the priesthood, and had been transmitted from man to man by a regular rite, a kind of incantation. And now these Hussites would try and pollute or turn the sources. Should they not at all sacrifices be hindered from so doing?

I do not know that the whole history of human thought can offer us a better example than this of the belief in magic, unalloyed by any other kind of belief.

The clearly marked creed which follows next after fetichism is the worship of the great phenomena of the world, those phenomena, as I have before said, which are to a certain degree abstractions. The wind and the storm are not definite things, as trees and mountains are. In the class of phenomena we must place the heavenly bodies for they are not only celestial, but in a manner abstracted also. In this stage of belief it is not so much the disc of the sun which men worship as all the phenomena associated with sunlight—its brightness, warmth, vitality, and so forth. The sky god includes in his nature more appearances than are visible at any particular moment; the dawn too is, in part, an abstraction. All these existences belong to the second order of divinities. Most of the gods of this order are further distinguished by the fact that they reveal themselves only to one or two of the senses, while the fetich gods can be explored by all at once; the wind can be felt and heard only, the sun only felt and seen. It belongs to the mystery of our nature that of those things which we know least we can imagine most; and it is a part of the second stage in the growth of belief that the mind begins to supply from within what is no longer given by the senses without.

The earth and sea may seem doubtfully to belong to the higher class of divinities. But it is evident that neither earth nor sea, when thought of as a whole, is a finite object, but each an abstraction, or at least a generalisation. Nevertheless the sea may be narrowed in imagination to some particular bay; the earth may be confined to some particular mountain or valley. Wherefore these terrene divinities lie nearer to the race of fetiches than any celestial phenomena do; and we find they often slide back into the earlier class. When the creed has reached its higher developments the earth and sea gods and goddesses remain behind, to be cherished and specially worshipped by the lower strata of society.[1]

As all the following chapters of the volume will deal with divinities of this second and higher order, there is no need to say more about them here. There is, however, a small intermediate class of beings whom we, in the study of religious systems, are scarcely disposed to speak of as gods, who have yet in their time received no small share of worship, and who have filled in ancient creeds a wider space than we perhaps suppose. They belong, strictly speaking, to neither camp, and therefore they have been left behind in the march. We cannot call these gods anything better than the *generalisation* of the old fetiches. They thus form an exact middle term between these fetiches and those wider generalisations of nature worship. We spoke of them in the last chapter. They are the fetiches transformed just as the word tree is transformed by coming to mean not one particular tree but all the members of the grove. Supposing, for example, that the men who have once worshipped only trees come

[1] See Chapter V.

in time to worship the *wind* as the spirit of their forest,
then, as a middle term in this transition, they will have
worshipped the forest itself. If from having worshipped
the river they come (as we shall see they do) to worship
the cloud and then the air, as a middle term they will
have worshipped the generalisation of their rivers, or,
perhaps, for something more intangible than the rivers
themselves, the mists which rise up from them. The
divinities of this transition class are now lost to us—that
is to say, they survive only in a distorted form in the Undines, nymphs, and dryads of the creeds we know.

I imagine that the tree oracles of Greece portray this
stage of transition rather than real fetichism. The power
of divination which belonged to them was common to the
whole grove, and not to any particular tree in it; this, at
any rate, seems to have been the general rule. All the
trees of Dodona, for example, carried the message of
Zeus; nay, it was not so much the trees themselves
which did this as the wind which moved them. And yet
there was likewise here a remnant of individual tree
worship; for we read also of one particular oak, peculiarly
sacred to Zeus, bigger than all the other trees of the
wood, and remaining ever green all the year round.
Even a fragment of this tree could prophesy, for it was a
piece of this which Athênê placed in the prow of Jason's
ship 'Argo,' and that figure-head was as a pilot to the
Argonauts throughout their voyage.

The rivers change in their way as the trees in theirs.
They turn first into the mists which rise from the stream,
no longer tangible and fixed in form, but formless beings
—*apsaras*, as they were called in Indian mythology, who
anon float up into heaven and mingle with the clouds.
The apsaras (which means the *formless* ones) are, in later
mythologies, spoken of as if they were nymphs; but this
is after the anthropomorphic spirit has touched them; at
first, as their name well shows, they were nothing so cor-
poreal as the nymphs. In this stage of belief, man's

worship is passing on to a race of beings who are at best
but half embodied; who are not wholly ideal, and yet not
in the strict sense material. The mist rises up, becomes
the cloud, mingles with the air. While still on earth it
was the nymph or faun. The clouds in heaven are the
gandharvas (Vedic), the centaurs; in the North they are
the Valkyriur, Odhinn's swan maidens. Aphroditê, the
foam-born, and Athênê, at first Tritogeneia (water-born)
and afterwards the Queen of the Air, are of the same
confraternity.[1]

As it was the mist arising from the Delphic stream
which sent the priestess into her holy madness, we may
in the matter of oracular gift liken these exhalations of
the rivers to the winds which blow through groves such as
that of Dodona.

No need to tell how numerous were and are these
half-earthy divinities in India, in Greece, in heathen
Germany, among the Celts and Slavs. Their name is
legion—fauns, dryads, nereids, nymphs, Undines, gand-
barvas, and (more expressive than all other names)
apsaras, formless ones.[2] They are presented to us by
art as beings with human shape, sometimes mixed of
human and animal; others (the dryads, for example) are
of human and vegetable nature conjoined; in the heart of
the people they have scarcely a shape, but are a presence
only—the presence of their old friends the forest and the
stream. The doubtfulness of art concerning their shape
and nature portrays the uncertainty of popular thought

---

[1] See Chapter IV.

[2] It is, on the whole, exceptional to find these fountain beings of the
masculine gender. In Greece, however, the rivers were generally male,
the lakes female. This, I say, must be looked upon as rather peculiar. It
is noticeable that the gandharvas of Indian myth may be of both sexes,
but the centaurs are always represented as males. When the fountain
nymph is associated with that idealised fount which is known in myth as
the fountain of life, she becomes the Fate (Parca, Moera, or Norn). The
Scandinavian Norn is not distinguishable from the Valkyria; Fates, as
fées, fairies, returned again to their simpler universal character. The
Moiræ are connected with the Celtic Mairæ, from *mar*, *mṓir*, simply a 'maid.'

about them.   Atalanta is one of the most typical of these
stream maidens.   She was born on Mount Parthenon by
the banks of a *river*.   By a stroke of her lance she once
made water spring from the rock.[1]   Her name (ἀτάλλω)
expresses the *leaping* water.

Arcadia, where the old beliefs were the longest lived,
was the great home of nymph worship.   Of the same race
as the nymphs were the Muses.   They were called nymphs
sometimes.   They too were originally streams.[2]

Certainly one of the most beautiful among ancient
beliefs is that which has associated the discovery of music
with the sound of waters.   Next in importance after the
invention of writing comes, it seems to me, this art, the
production of harmonised sound.   In respect of its sponta-
neity it stands midway between drawing and writing.
The first is a purely imitative art, and, so far as we can
tell, spontaneous from human nature.   Writing is so little
spontaneous that it has been invented almost accidentally,
and once found has been passed on from nation to nation
and not rediscovered.   Music is more simple than writing,
and may have several different sources.   The melody in
the vibration of a single stretched string, as of a strung
bow, might easily be noticed.   Traditionally, music has
always been considered an imitative art, like drawing;
the vibrating string was supposed to mimic some melodious sound in nature; and among the many which we
hear—rustling of leaves, the cries of animals in hollow
distance, echoes from caves, and the wind amid pine trees,
or any of those softened murmurs which come to us from
the depth of the forest—none have been found so impressive as the music of waters.   The moaning of the waves
round the shore gave rise to the myth of the sirens; and,
whatever the truth may have been, the Greek undoubtedly
believed that some stream of Pieria or of Helicon had given

[1] Paus. iii. 24, § 2.
[2] The Lydians called the Muses νύμφαι (Steph. Byz. s. v. Τόρρηβος; Pho-
tius, s. v. Νύμφαι).

birth to Greek music. By these banks the Doric shepherd first learnt to string his lyre.

Or be it that music arose with Pan and the Arcadians, where too the worship of streams most prevailed. The flute of all instruments best suggests the bubbling sound of brooks. Perhaps the use of the lyre, the instrument of Apollo and Hermes, was only a higher order of music which came in with the worship of these gods and superseded the music of the pipe. If that be so then the contest with Marsyas is the rivalry between the old music and the new, expressing a deeper rivalry in creed and manners;[1] for the melodies of the flute or the pan-pipes are those of contemplative lives and dreamy ease, but Apollo was the introducer of war music and of the pæan.

The sober truth about Marsyas' skin was, I suspect, that it was a sheepskin placed in a certain river in Asia Minor in such a way that the water running through it gave it a tuneful sound; not less, however, is Marsyas the typical river god, who sets up his earthly music in despite of the airs of heaven.

The sound of this plaintive early music of nature, and the · thought of the simple Arcadian worship of the nymphs and satyrs, might well give men a fondness for the days gone by, and make them contrast favourably the old nature worship with the worship of gods after they had become transformed into personalities. I will not say that the gods, when they had grown personal and active, were at first, in any moral sense, the superiors of these peaceful deities of stream and mountain. At first the god who represented merely the power of will without its moral responsibility was a bad substitute for those early will-less *things*, the deified phenomena of nature; just as a child is a better thing to contemplate than a young man under the sway of his passions in their force. We can have small reverence for the new usurping Zeus of the

---

[1] See Prof. Percy Gardner, 'Greek River Worship,' *Trs. of Roy. Soc. Lit.* vol. xi.

'Prometheus Vinctus.' And this is why the poet in that play gives us so beautiful a picture of the nature god, Ocean, and the nymphs, which are the river mists, coming to sympathise with the Titan in his sufferings. And, as against Zeus the usurper, Prometheus appeals to all the divinities who are the pure expression of outward things—to the swift-winged breezes; the deep, uncounted, laughing waves; the all-seeing eye of the sun; and earth, the mother of all.

CHAPTER III.

THE ARYAS.

ONE of the singers of the Rig-Veda relates to us the birth of Agni, the fire, and its attendant circumstances. The fire itself is produced by the rubbing of two sticks; and so, naturally enough, we are told that these are the parents of the god. But, behold! the fire seizes upon these same sticks and consumes them; so Agni is scarce born when he devours those who brought him forth. This is a terrible truth to be obliged to tell.

> This deed now make I known, O earth, O heaven
> The son new-born devours his parents.[1]

The poet is shocked, as he well may be, at the thought of such a parricide, and would fain not tell the story but that he knows it true. And so he only adds, with humility of heart—

> But I, a mortal, cannot gauge a god;
> Agni knows and does the right.

Could anything better than such a passage as this express the condition of a belief which is dealing still with the phenomena of sense, and which has nevertheless got some way in the apprehension of moral truths; which is, in fact, well advanced in the second phase of belief, but not yet past it? First observe how completely we have here got beyond the earliest fetich worship and those beliefs akin to fetichism which we discussed in the last chapter. Agni is not simply a material thing. He is certainly

[1] Rig-Veda, x. 7, 9.

nothing which can be touched and handled; he cannot
even be fully apprehended by the senses; he is a *generalisation*, and therefore in part an idea only. Agni is not
one single flame, but then neither is he an abstract god
of fire. He is both one and many flames, and to his
character still clings the character of his element. It is a
fact that the flame consumes the wood which gave it life—
the father who created it and the mother who bore it.
Being so certain a fact, it must be told. Still Agni is a
divinity and knows what is right. The notion of righteous-
ness attaches to the god before he has clothed himself
in a human character or become subject to the laws of
man.

To the fetich worshipper the stick which produced the
fire would have been a god. Nay, there can be no doubt
that many among the contemporaries of this poet of the
Rig-Veda, and many in long subsequent times, *did* worship
as a god the fire drill, or swastika. This became in after
years personified in the person of Prometheus.[1] While to
that same fetich worshipper the fire itself would have
been too abstract and intangible a substance to be made
into a divinity. To the poet priest who chaunted· this
Vedic hymn it was quite otherwise. The wood itself was
mortal, for the wood itself was material; and just because
the fire was not material, but so subtle and mysterious,
just because it appealed so much to his imaginative
faculties, it was made into a god, and Agni was
worshipped. In the Vedic hymns Agni is often called
' an immortal born of mortals.'[2]

I do not pretend that the Vedic worshipper is always

[1] See Kuhn, *Herabkunft des Feuers*, where the myth of Prometheus
springing from the *pramantha*, or fire drill (also ' butter churn '), is very
beautifully worked out; also in the *Zeitschr. für vergl. Spr.* xx. 201. The
swastika symbol ⼂, so well known on Buddhist monuments, has been
interpreted as this fire drill; it has also, however, been interpreted as the
symbol of the sun. See E. Thomas and Percy Gardner, in the *Numismatic
Chronicle* for 1880. Schwartz (*Urspr. der Myth.*) connects Prometheus
with the whirlwind.

[2] R. V. iii. 29, 13; x. 79, 1.

a perfect example of man in the state of nature worship. Nor do I mean to say that Agni always adheres so strictly, as here he does, to his true character. The Vedic hymns are a miscellaneous collection of poems composed at various times—intervals of hundreds of years even between some of them—and handed down from age to age by oral tradition only. They therefore express many different phases of belief. Agni sometimes makes us forget that he is the fire. Sometimes he seems quite human as he comes down to drink the libations which are poured out for him and joins Indra in his battles against the enemy. Still we shall scarcely find in any historic creed such speaking examples of nature worship as are to be met with throughout the pages of the Vedic hymns. Nor, perhaps, does any Vedic god illustrate more fully in his character the various influences of *sensation* upon *belief* than does this god of fire.

In the instance just chosen we have seen the curb which external experience puts upon the satisfaction of the moral sense. Let us now look at the matter from the other side, and see what a point of spiritual and moral idealism may be reached without any departure from needful adherence to outward fact, without leaving the region of externals and 'those things which nature herself will have set forth.' In another hymn, earlier in date probably than the hymn previously quoted, there is again allusion made to Agni's birth from the wood. But in this connection we find that the god had likewise a parentage in the clouds, where he was born in the form of lightning. 'I will tell (or have told), Agni, thy old and new births.'[1] The new birth is from the wood; the old birth was from the clouds. The god, we see, lived first in heaven, and was there doubtless long before the race of man was seen here below. But somehow Agni descended from heaven

---

[1] R. V. i. 20. Notice in this hymn also for immediate and future use how Agni was born of the seven streams (vv. 3, 4), did not lie concealed there (9), and became a protector by his shining in the house (15, 18).

and became imprisoned in the wood, whence the act of man—first taught him by Manu [1]—can set Agni free. This re-birth from the wood is in very truth an incarnation of the fire god, for man too, we know, was descended from the tree; his flesh is made from the wood. Wherefore Agni clothes himself not only in a material but in a carnal form when he comes to earth.

Agni's birth in heaven was wondrous, miraculous even. ' Scarce born, he filled the two worlds '—that of the heaven, namely, and of the earth. This is an image, perhaps, of the lightning flashing suddenly, and seeming to fill all the space of air; or, perhaps, it is the red of morning, for that too is called Agni; or may be, again, it is the fire of the sun itself. In such an aspect of his being, the heavenly aspect, Agni is everything that is great: in moral strength as in physical force he stands next to Indra, far before any other divinity. And yet, for all that, Agni consents to become imprisoned in the wood; he has a life on earth and shares the toils and troubles of man. He is, on this account, among all the celestials, the god who cares most for human kind. ' Protect us,' the priest calls out to him in need, 'protect us by thy shining in the house.' We know how dearly cherished was that protection of the fire god. The most sacred function in the domestic life of the Aryas was the keeping alive the house fire; the duty of doing this was always assigned to the paterfamilias, and that which made men most desirous for heirs male, and made them, if they had none of their body, seek to gain one by adoption, was the wish that the same · fire should be kept alive when they were gone. Luck would desert the house, and the dead father would suffer in the other world, if the

---

[1] Manu (the thinker) is the typical first *man*, and the same with the Greek Minos (Benfey, *Hermés, Minôs u. Tartaros*). If we do not accept Kuhn's origin for Prometheus he too would be an equivalent of Manu. Prometheus and Manu perform the same office in respect to fire. Manu and Minos are of course lawgivers; so are Yama and Yima (Zend) also types of the first man.

fire went out; just in the same way that in earlier modes
of thought luck was fancied to desert the family or the
village if the house tree or the village tree died down, or
if the water of the fetich stream ran dry.

Another sacred duty was observed when the flame of
sacrifice was kindled, and again, in another shape, Agni
appeared on earth. On this flame libations were poured
of the intoxicating soma [1] juice, the sacramental drink of
Vedic Indians. Agni was invited to partake of this libation; and as the flame licked up the drink Agni was said,
in the language of the Vedas, to take his share of the
sacrifice, to drink of the soma. After this he sprang up
heavenward and vanished in air; he had gone back to his
celestial home. Thus man having first set Agni free
from his prison house the wood, was likewise the means
whereby the god reached once more the mansions of the
blessed.

There was one sacrifice more rare and more solemn
than the daily enkindling of straw or pouring of soma
upon the flame; this was when the dead man was burnt
upon the pyre and offered up, as it were, unto the god of
fire. Agni received the soul and bore it up to heaven. [2]

Thus in every way Agni is shown as a messenger
between heaven and earth: he comes down in the lightning and he returns in the flame of sacrifice. He is
constantly invited to call the gods down to the feast
which is preparing for them at the altar. He only among
the heavenly ones is seen to devour what is offered to him.

And, again, Agni may be sometimes the internal
flame, the source of all passion, of the passion of passions

---

[1] *Asclopias acida* is the botanical name of this plant. From its juice
can be concocted an alcoholic drink which was much cherished by the
Indians and Persians (by the latter called *homa*), and which played an
important part in their ritual. The soma drink was a sacramental draught,
and as such corresponded to the mystic millet water (kykeón) of the
Eleusinian celebrations.

[2] Of burning the dead, and the beliefs which attach to that custom,
more hereafter (Ch. VI.)

to primeval man, the most sacred of his emotions, love.
Soma is the god of wine, Agni of the other great motive
power in men's lives and beliefs.[1] This emotion being
accounted in primitive language especially holy, therefore
Agni is essentially the holy one. I would not wrest to
any fanciful resemblance the points of likeness between
this ancient divinity and the later *avatars* of Indian and
Christian creeds ; but it is evident the god stands ready
to take the part afterwards given to Vishnû. And whether
or no we choose to consider that the ideals which Vishnû,
and still more Christ, express are implanted in human
nature, it is evident that, without passing beyond his
legitimate functions as a nature god, Agni is able to
realise some of the qualities of such an ideal. He is incarnate, after a fashion, being born of the wood ; he is, in
a peculiar sense, the friend of man ; he is the messenger
and mediator between heaven and earth ; and lastly, he is
in a special manner the holy one, the fosterer of strong
emotion, of· those mystic thoughts which arise when in
any way the mind is violently swayed. Agni is all this
without laying aside the elemental nature in which he is
clothed. And this one example may prepare us for the
manysidedness of nature gods :—

.Agni is messenger of all the world

. . . . ? . .

Skyward ascends his flame, the Merciful,
With our libations watered well ;
And now the red smoke seeks the heavenly way,
And men enkindle Agni here.

. . . . . .

We make of thee our herald, Holy One ;
Bring down the gods unto our feast.
O son of might, and all who nourish man!
Pardon us when on you we call.

[1] See Ch. I.

Thou, Agni, art the ruler of the house;
Thou at the altar art our priest.
O purifier, wise and rich in good,
O sacrificer, bring us safety now.[1]

In one respect Agni is different from the other gods.
He alone, almost, is independent of climatic influences.
Not so the god of the wind, or of the sun, or of the sea.
People may live near the water, and see for ever before
them the broad, level, unploughed plain; or they may
live inland in close-shut valleys, watered only by one
small stream, on whom 'the swart star sparely looks;' or
they may live in the perpetual shade of woods, or on
broad arid plains where the sun's heat is well-nigh
intolerable; or in dark frosty lands, where the sun dies
during one part of his yearly round and is for this period
never seen by night or day. It is· impossible that the
gods of nature can remain the same with peoples exposed
to such varying influences. With fetiches it is different.
The differences between fetich and fetich are noticeable,
indeed, within a small locality, but in the sum, among a
large body of people, they may be expected to balance
one another. The differences of climatic nature gods are
wide and cannot be bridged over. We have but to study
and interpret the characters of some of the great sun-gods
of Eastern lands—Ra, say, or Moloch—to understand
the sort of sun these lands lay beneath; and we have only
to remember the differences in latitude and in the face of
nature between these Eastern countries and the countries
of Europe to see why the sun god is so different a being
in the creed of the Asiatic to what he is in the creed of
the European.

It is desirable, therefore, that, before we come to
examine any of the known creeds of the Indo-European
race, we should try to gain some idea of the earlier
climatic influences to which its ancestors were subjected,

[1] R. V. vii. 16.

while they were still one people, at the time in which the
germs of later creeds were but beginning to put forth
shoots.   Five distinct 'languages,' in the Biblical sense
of that word, have, it is well known, issued from the
Aryan nest—namely, the Aryas proper or later Aryas,
the Indo-Persic family, the Græco-Italic, the Celtic, the
Teutonic, the Lithuano-Slavonic.   Some of these have
kept no memory of that first home; some have believed themselves autochthonous, or children of the soil,
in the land where history discovers them.   Others (the
Norsemen, for example, out of the Teutonic family)
have had some vague tradition of an Eastern origin;
and one people, the Persians, have a tolerably clear and
consistent legend of the changes of home which preceded
their settlement in Iran.   But of course the story puts on
a mythic disguise.   It is related by their Zend Avesta [1]
that the good and great spirit, Ahura-Mazda, created in
succession sixteen paradises; but that the evil one, Angra-
Mainyus, came after him, like the sower of tares, and
polluted these paradises one after the other.   It is impossible to trace out a clear line of travel by the identification of these places.   Some cannot be identified; the
order of them has been misplaced.   But interpreting the
story by the rules which must guide us in reading mythic
language, we are, I think, justified in seeing the evidence
of a passage at some former time from the high land of
Bactriana toward the Persian Gulf, and this theory of an
original home in Bactriana would suit with what we know
of the movements of other Aryan races.

To the weight of this traditionary evidence we must
add the cumulative testimony of a number of small coinci-
dences, which, though each is slight in itself, afford not
inconsiderable evidence in the sum.   If we find that the

---

[1] First Fargard. Pictet (*Les Origines Indo-Européennes*, ch. i.) has devoted some space and much ingenuity to an endeavour to trace the course
of the migrations made by the Iranian people.   With what success I am no
judge.   Darmesteter repudiates the attempt (*Avesta*, Intr.)

species of metals, flowers, animals, trees, which the old
Aryans were acquainted with are those which are to be
found in Bactriana; if we find that the early life of these
Aryas was of the kind likely to be adopted in a country
such as that is, and under the influences of sun and sky
which that land is subject to, we are justified, I think, in
assuming the Persian tradition to be a true one. The
way in which we may rediscover the social and natural
surroundings of the proto-Aryas is that very method
whereby, in a former chapter, we arrived at certain conclusions touching the knowledge which our ancestors had
of horned cattle, of a sky god, Dyâus, and of the relationship of a daughter. For the method which was there
applied to but one or two things may, it is evident, be
extended to all the region of possible knowledge. The
late M. Pictet has used this method with eminent talent
and success; and amid many other conclusions concerning
the old Aryas he arrives at this, that their first traceable
home must have been in the Bactrian land.

This country is the one which lies westward from the
Beloor Tagh, northward from the Hindoo Koosh and all
the region of barren Afghanistan. It is a land once celebrated among the countries of the world for its fertility,
and though it has fallen now on evil days it is still one of
the best cultivated parts of Central Asia, in both a material and a moral sense.[1] The high ranges behind them
cut off the inhabitants from all communication with the
east and south. In the hills innumerable streams are
born, which, flowing westward, go to swell the waters of
the Oxus and the Jaxartes. The hills, the streams, and
the valleys which these last have hollowed out give a
peculiar character to the scenery, a character of perpetual
change. 'Bactriana,' says Quintus Curtius,[2] 'is in its
nature a very varied land. In some parts trees abound,
and the vines yield fruit remarkable for its size and sweet-

---

[1] Bokhara is at this day a centre of Mohammedan learning.   [2] vii. 4.

ness. Innumerable fountains water the fertile soil. Where the climate is favourable they sow corn; elsewhere the ground furnishes pasture for the flocks.' And a traveller of more recent date, Sir Alexander Burnes— one of the very few who in modern days have penetrated to this region—speaks in much the same terms of the variety in the aspect of nature, though he has less to say about the fertility of the soil.[1] From his account it is interesting to learn how many of the trees are familiar to European eyes; even the maythorn is to be met with there, though scarcely anywhere else in Asia.

Now it so happens that of the great monarchies of the ancient world, the earliest, those which seem to have passed on their traditions to all which followed, arose in lands the very opposite of the one here described. Egypt and Chaldæa have close resemblances in the main characteristics of their scenery and position. Each is by comparison a narrow strip of cultivable soil cut out of the desert, and each owes its fertility altogether to one cause, the great river or rivers which flow through its midst. In Egypt the irrigation from the Nile is natural; in the land of the Tigris and Euphrates irrigation is obtained by artificial means: this is all the difference between the two countries. Both, too, are singularly rich, and their riches seem the greater in comparison with the barrenness and poverty which lie at their doors. For Egypt and Chaldæa are, in reality, tracts reclaimed from one and the same desert—the great infertile belt which extends half round the world, stretching from the borders of China on the east to the western coast of Africa. Wherefore in such countries as Egypt and Chaldæa everything is present which is likely to attach the people to the soil on which they live, and to stay their imaginations from ever wandering to regions beyond those which they know

---

[1] For now irrigation has to be effected by artificial means, and where the canals have fallen into disrepair drought has ensued. See *Expedition of Lieut. A. Burnes.*

familiarly. Their fertile land is a land of life, but all around them lies the country of death. Such a state of things is likely to beget a certain dulness in the fancy and a settled routine in life; everything will determine men to a fixed society and government, and to a fixed religion. The great river is at hand to serve for the oldest and chief god of the land; the impossibility of travel rivets tighter that chain of association and of reverence and of fear which holds men close to the neighbourhood of their fetich. All these effects were produced in Egypt and Chaldæa. Feeling themselves so securely fixed in their home, and generally prosperous there, like men *quibus Jupiter ipse nocere non potest,*[1] the Egyptians and Chaldæans, and the successors of the Chaldæans, the Assyrians, gave themselves to a 'great bravery of building,' and the immense temples and tombs which arose all over their lands became a new race of fetiches, and also a kind of sentries and watch-towers to keep the people where they were. They were contented, but they were slaves. Their rulers were tyrants—the temporal rulers, their Rameses, their Tiglath Pilesers, and Sennacheribs—and the spiritual kings, their gods, fiercest and most cruel of all of whom was the great sun god, Moloch, 'the king' *par excellence.*[2]

The home of the Aryas, on the contrary—a land of innumerable streams and separate valleys, naturally divided into as many political districts—would be incompatible with the formation of a great monarchy such as those which sprang up in Egypt and Assyria. And we know that the beginnings of social life among the Aryas were not of the Asiatic kind; their political unit was the village, a cluster of homesteads, that is to say, a sort of miniature republic, associated under certain laws, and

---

[1] The Egyptian priests, Herodotus tells us, descanted to him of the *risk* of depending upon Zeus for fertility. They were, of course, right from a purely experiential point of view. Can we doubt that the respective characters of the religions of Egypt and Greece were affected by the different natures of their gods in this and other respects?

[2] Moloch is *melek*, a king.

each one governed, subject to these laws and customs, by its individual chief or head-man. This village community is the germ out of which the later institutions of European statecraft have had their rise. In the Indian village, in the Russian mir, and in the Swiss canton, we see it in a condition nearest to its original purity.

The effects of this beginning of social life among the Aryas has been visible in all their later history; one of the chief of these effects has been that they have never been apt to form themselves into very great or permanent monarchies. The kingdom of the Medes and Persians under Cyrus might, indeed, seem at first sight a striking exception to this rule; but it is not so much so as it appears. Although the monarchy of Cyrus certainly did resemble the autocracies of Egypt and Babylon, it could never have come into existence if these last had not preceded it. It was a distinct imitation of the great Semitic and African kingdoms, not a natural growth; and it was only achieved by un-Aryanising the people. The foundation of the permanent rule of Cyrus lay in the older and more settled monarchies which the kingdom of the Medes and Persians absorbed into itself. Chaldæa and Egypt were full of ancient cities, and it was the possession of such strongholds as were to be found there which gave its stability to the rule of the Achæmenidæ. The walled towns which had a short time before begun to spring up in the land of the Persians themselves were built in imitation of the older walled towns of Chaldæa. That this was the case is very well shown by the picture which Herodotus gives us [1] of the condition of the Medes at an earlier time, when they had first shaken themselves free from the Assyrian yoke, and his account of the foundation of their native line of kings. For a long time these Medes lived in separate villages, without any central authority, and lawlessness prevailed throughout the land.

[1] i. 96–98.

At length Deioces, the son of Phraortes, having attained
great influence by his justice and firmness, succeeded in
having himself raised to the throne. Desiring to secure
his power, he caused the city of Ecbatana to be built. It
was beneath the walls of this, its first city, that the foundations of the Median kingdom were laid. '

The conditions into which the Medes relapsed so soon
as they had shaken off the Assyrian yoke might be
matched in a hundred examples taken from the history of
people of Aryan stock at such a time as the pressure of
some firm hand had been removed.

Just in the same way, after the death of Charlemagne,
the Frankish nation split up from one into many kingdoms and duchies. So did almost all the Teuton peoples
who had joined in the invasions of the Roman Empire in
like manner split up when the fear of an opposing power
no longer kept them together. The Goths of Spain or of
Italy, the Lombards, and the English all tell the same
story which is told by the history of the Medes.

The Aryan religion must have been as republican and
as manysided, as was the social life of the people. Each
small assemblage of houses which stood beside a rivulet
or a lake, in the clearing of a forest, or under the shadow
of a hill, was a world unto itself. And no doubt each
village had its own fetich, its supernatural protector, in
the stream or tree which was in its midst. The village
tree has survived, if not as a divinity, at the very least as
a recognised institution almost to our own time. The
local worship of mountains and of streams in like wise
has left deep traces in the creeds of Europe. If the
remains of fetichism could be so vital, fetichism itself
must have had a lengthened sway. But the people could
never have become the Aryan *nation* had their notions of
unity been confined to the local fetich and the village
commune. They acquired an idea of a wider fellowship.
They spoke a common tongue, and in that language they
acknowledged themselves as one people—the *aryas*, or

noble ones—in contradistinction to the barbarians, ' the inarticulate,' or to the *turanians*, the ' wanderers,' who for them filled up the roll of outer humanity.

The beliefs of the Aryas expanded with their policy; or it were truer, perhaps, to say that their social life widened as their creed widened.[1] And with the change there came to the front the higher kind of gods who were pan-Aryan, and who at last put to silence the older but lesser village gods.

Something has been already said of the obvious advantage which, in respect of a permanent hold on men's minds, the elemental religion has over the fetichism which precedes it—the superiority which the worship of clouds, or skies, or suns, or storms has over the worship of trees and rivers and mountains. If a people change their home they cannot take the fetich with them; and therefore the nation will be without a god, unless either a new fetich is at once found (which is scarce likely) or men are willing to worship some part of nature which cannot be so easily abandoned. The nation is almost sure in such circumstances to turn and worship the great elemental gods.

But even if the people do not leave their homes, and only coalesce somewhat in national life, the elemental god has still an immense advantage over his fetich rival in respect of his *universality*. He alone can be the god of the whole people. Although in each village the people are still most inclined to fetichism, and the village stream or tree is in consequence more honoured than the sun or the wind, still that tree or stream has no claim to reverence from the men of another village. They have probably *their* individual village tree, who, rather than a friend, is a rival and an enemy to the other fetich. When neighbour communities cease being at war and become friendly, the union is likely to be signalised by the sacrifice to each

See p. 69.

others' prejudices of the rival gods: the thing they now need is a divinity whom all have worshipped alike. He must be something higher and more celestial than the fetich, a wider Nature god. This is, in fact, an instance exactly parallel to that seeming paradox of reputation whereby we are met with the difficulty that the greatest genius is never first in repute among his contemporaries. Why, it may fairly be asked, should future times be *always* so much more discriminating than present ones? To which the answer, of course, is that the great genius would never really have a majority of suffrages in any age, but that his suffrages, such as they are, go on accumulating from age to age, while his rival of one generation, the popular writer of that time, puts out of memory his rival of a previous generation. The popular writer, for the purposes of our illustration, represents the fetich god, for the elemental god stands the genius, and for the rivalry of different ages we substitute the rivalry of different localities.

Each separate village in old Bactriana had, we may suppose, its fetich god, while the gods of all the Aryan nations were the sky and the sun, the earth and the sea. The more the people gravitated together, the more did these universal deities come to the front, and the divinities of fragments of the people fall into the background. The decisive change was probably made when the migrations of the Ayras began, and all the fetiches had to be left behind.

For hundreds of years had the proto-Aryas inhabited their fertile Bactrian home, until they grew into a considerable nation; the older tribes backed against the eastern hills, the younger extending westward into the plain as far as the borders of the Caspian.[1] At length, either because they grew too large for the land they dwelt in or because they felt more and more the pressure of alien

[1] See Ch. VI.

peoples—those Tartar races who still form the population
of Central Asia—from what cause, indeed, we cannot determine now, they broke up into separate nations, which,
one by one, set off upon those long journeyings not destined to come to a termination until some at least among
the people had reached the very ends of the earth. The
fetich god could be no protection in the new unknown
world to which the travellers turned. But the sun went
with them; he even pointed the way they were to travel
as he passed on before them to the west.[1] The sky, clear
or cloudy, was still overhead; the ruddy morn and evening
showed their familiar faces; the pillar of cloud went
before them by day, and the pillar of fire by night; the
storms followed them on their path, and the moon with
all her attendant stars. These, therefore, were the gods
to whom henceforward they must turn to pray.

The younger tribes, whom we saw settled to the westward, were the first to migrate. They left behind them
the older inhabitants, the Aryas *par excellence*, from whom
afterwards descended the Indians and Iranians. But even
these had at last to abandon their country. Whatever
the reason for the others' departure, theirs, one would
suppose, must have been involuntary, under the force of
superior and hostile powers. For they did not go westward, but crossed the steep hills which were behind them.
The Iranians, as we saw, struggled to the high table-land
of Pamir, which tradition afterwards represented as the
land made evil by Ahrimanes. The Indians crossed the
Hindoo Koosh and debouched upon the plain of the Indus;
and it was during their residence in the territory of the
five streams, the Panjâb,[2] that these Aryas of India composed the body of their first sacred poetry—those Vedic
hymns which are a memorial not of their faith only, but
also, in an indirect way, of the still earlier Aryan religion
of Bactria.

[1] Ibid.
[2] The Ganges is unknown to the Vedic hymn-writers.

I

But let the reader be upon his guard—upon his guard once for all—against the notion that any distinct doctrine of mythology can be gleaned from the poems of the Veda. Something has already been said of the difference between mythology and religion, so far as to show how the presence of one must to a great extent preclude that of the other. Mythology, in a manner, precedes religion. Mythology is an interpretation of natural phenomena, through the enkindling of imagination indeed, and with some sense of worship going along with the interpretation, but by men not in that state of strong emotion which we may distinctly call religious. The tales of mythology are records of facts—of facts seen, no doubt, though an imaginative atmosphere, but yet regarded as passing events and not in a peculiar relation to the observer. The *ego* of the narrator of myths is not vividly present in his consciousness. With religion and with the literature of devotion it is very different. These imply an intense concentration of thought upon the spiritual (unsensuous) side of the external phenomena: they imply a condition of feeling in which the *ego* is of pre-eminent importance in relation to all outward things, in which the external world is regarded or neglected in exact proportion as it calls out an answering emotion from the human heart. The Vedic poems are of the religious kind; they are distinctly devotional in character, and are therefore rightly described as hymns. And thus being intended as vehicles of feeling, not as the records of events, they offer a marked contrast to those epic poems which are our earliest authorities for the belief of most other members of the Indo-European family—to the epos of Homer, for example, and the eddas and sagas of the German peoples. This gives the Vedas a certain poverty on the mythologic side; it also tends to make the beliefs which they record seem more advanced in development than they really are. Yet, for all that, the Vedas reveal some aspects of belief more primitive than are to be found either in Greece or in Scandinavia:

some facts without the light shed by which the religious history of the Aryan folk would have remained for ever obscure.

Professor Max Müller has already called attention to one remarkable phase of belief which the Vedas illustrate, and which, but for its survival in these hymns, would perhaps never have been noticed. He has called this phase henotheism,[1] by which is meant the worship of one god out of the pantheon as if he were the only divinity, and the passing on then to pay the same vows and honours to another deity. Henotheism expresses quite a different tone of mind from monotheism, and arises mainly, as in the last chapter was pointed out, from the shortness of memory which leads men to neglect and overlook that phenomenon which is not actually present, and so to forget for a time the god whose nature is bound up with this phenomenon. Wherefore it is evident that in the Vedas, where henotheism is so rife, we have got most near to the condition of belief in which the god was identified with that visible power of nature whence he took his name; to that state of things in which Indra was worshipped while active, but forgotten when he was not so. Indra is throughout the Vedas really the sky or the storm; and though he receives the general titles suited to a universal ruler, yet when we see him in action his deeds are those possible to a storm god only. Agni is in verity the fire, and his ways are the ways of that element alone.

It is through the combination of this genuine polytheism with the language of devotion that henotheism becomes conspicuous. Of course it was thought that the god would be flattered by being addressed in such a style of adulation as if he only were the lord and king. But men to whom all the gods seemed equally present, would

---

[1] What I have called *pure polytheism* is, as has been shown, a different stage of belief from that which is commonly called by the same name. This pure polytheism is in the most intimate relationship to *henotheism* (Ch. I.)

have felt the risk of offending quite as much the god who was really supreme. If there were anyone like Zeus, who was so mighty that if a chain were suspended from heaven, and he were at one end and all the other gods were pulling at the other, they could not displace him, then henotheism would not be safe; nor would it be possible. If there were no personal god sitting apart and directing all the rest, if every god were (more or less) limited within his own sphere, then the immoderate desire to obtain the special gift which this or that divinity held in hand, the carelessness of the savages about the future, and their natural forgetfulness that there were other powers and other gifts beside this one, would far outweigh the fear of losing some subsequent favour of a rival god. Henotheism, then, is only possible in a certain condition of belief; wherefore the discovery of it in a conspicuous form in the Vedas is a guarantee that we shall find much else that is really primitive in them.

We ought, before we speak of the actual Vedic creed, to try and get some notion of the pre-Vedic one which all our ancestors had in common, or at all events of that which the Aryas brought with them to their Indian home before the first Vedic hymn was raised. All the Indo-European people possessed in common, as we have seen, a sky god, Dyâus, whose name, connected with (if not sprung from) a root *div*, to shine, points him out especially as the bright heaven. The fact that those first cousins of Dyâus, Zeus and Jupiter, have little in their natures to suggest the bright heaven or clear sky, might lead us to suppose that the Indian Dyâus had been originally the heaven in all its aspects, the heaven by night as well as the heaven by day; but that his nature had been subsequently divided, and his character in consequence changed. If this was the case the rule over the night sky was given over to Varuna, 'the coverer.' Later on in Indian mythology Dyâus comes to signify the sun, but when it does so the word is feminine

—the sun is feminine in Sanskrit—and the masculine Dyâus is still a different being from the sun itself. Essentially, then, we must say that Dyâus was ever to the Indians the bright upper sky, the sun's home; but he was not the sun itself.

Dyâus was evidently one among the greatest, probably he was once *the* greatest god of the Indians in the pre-Vedic age. But in the hymns Dyâus is much neglected. Scarcely one is addressed exclusively to him, and the mention of him, when it occurs, is rather incidental than of the character of actual worship.

Dyâus has a proper companion and helpmeet in the earth goddess, and she, too, belongs rather to the pre-Vedic times than to the Vedic. It is so natural to imagine the heaven and the earth as the two first beings, the progenitors of all life in the world, that in every system almost they stand at the head of the pantheon. In a former chapter we saw how the New Zealand story represented the heaven and the earth—Rangi and Papa they are there called—as the begetters of all other living things, who yet required to be torn apart that their children might continue to live. This primary embrace of earth and heaven is what most primitive people would hit upon to account for the origin of all things. Wherefore we may believe that far back in the Vedic creed stood first of all the heaven father, and by his side the earth mother.

The Vedic earth goddess is Prithivi. Whenever Dyâus and Prithivi are made the subject of a hymn they are invoked together, almost as a conjoint being (Dyâvaprithivi). In such hymns the ordinary characteristics of Dyâus and Prithivi are held before our eyes: the two are represented to us strictly in their phenomenal existence. They have not the same power of choice and will, nothing of the strong personality, which belongs to Indra and Agni. Dyâus produces the rain, and sends down the fertilising streams; Prithivi bears on her bosom the immense weight

of the mountains, and from her womb sends forth tho lofty
trees.[1]

What is specially remarkable in the hymns to Prithivi
is that the singer, even while he is worshipping the earth
goddess, seems to have his thoughts still turned heavenwards, still to be thinking of the clouds and of the rain.
It is a peculiarity of the Vedic creed that it is eminently
celestial, and scarcely ever concerned with mundane
things ; and the tendency seems to express itself even in
the worship of the earth goddess. This fact has led
Professor Gubernatis[2] to declare that the original significance of Prithivi—etymologically 'the large, the extended'—was not the earth, but the heaven, and that
there were two Prithivis, the celestial and the terrestrial,
of which the celestial was the elder. This, I think, we
cannot say. In a former chapter we have seen how easily
divinities who were first known in the terrene days of
belief may get transferred from earth to heaven ; much as
the Assyrian bulls and lions, worshipped no doubt in days
of animal worship, had a pair of wings given them and
were straightway idealised and sent to heaven. I believe
that the great celestial serpents—the clouds—Ahi and
Vrita, the chief enemies of Indra, were once terrestrial
rivers ;[3] and I believe in the same way that Prithivi, from
being a mere earth goddess, got a place in the sky in order
that she might sit beside her spouse, the heaven god. We
shall see other instances of a transfer of this kind.[4]

As Prithivi thus remained a distinct being, and at the
same time lost her connection with the ground, appearing
henceforth rather as the consort of the heaven than as the
goddess of the earth, she became by name distinguishable
from the soil, which last was, in Vedic Sanskrit, known
under the name of Gau. Gau is an older word than
Prithivi, and was itself once *the* name of the earth goddess
(whence the Greek goddess Gaia). Prithivi was then only

[1] Cf. R. V. v. 84.   [3] *Letture sopra la M. Ved.* pp. 59-64.
[2] See Chapter II.   [4] See Chapter IV.

one of the epithets of Gau. But as religion changed Gau sank into insignificance and Prithivi came to the front. Just so in the Greek mythology Gaia (Gê) was the pure and simple earth; Dêmêtêr (Gê-mêtêr) was the earth with something more of personality added on. Gê, in Greek mythology, continued to be a goddess, but she was characterless; the force of personality remained with Dêmêtêr.

In the Vedic hymns we see Prithivi in her turn losing worship and losing individuality because the creed has become too celestial for her.

We cannot explain so easily the neglect into which Dyâus has fallen, which seems the more extraordinary when we remember how once widely worshipped and how ancient a divinity he was. Nevertheless the fact remains. Part of his nature Dyâus passed over to Varuna, who was also a personification of the heaven, but most often, I think, of the heaven at night. Varuna's name signifies the encompasser or coverer (root *var*, to cover or conceal); he is the same with the Greek οὐρανός. Varuna, however, did not succeed to the supremacy which Dyâus once claimed. That was transferred to Indra.

The raising of Indra to the place of highest god is the great advance which Vedic religion has made upon the older proto-Aryan belief. Dyâus is the father of Indra, just as Kronos is the father of Zeus and Ouranos of Kronos; and this alone would lead us to suppose that the heaven god was the older.[1] Now, however, Dyâus' chief claim to reverence is through his son.

[1] The sonship of Zeus to Kronos is a myth of comparatively recent birth in Greek mythology, and arises, as Welcker has shown (*Griechische Götterlehre*, i. 140), merely from a confusion of words. Kroniôn, which is the same as Chroniôn, was at first an epithet applied to Zeus, showing him as existing through all time—not so much 'born of time,' but rather the 'one of time,' the old one, a common way of speaking of gods (cf. the Unkulonkulu of the Zulus, the 'old, old' Waïnamoïnen of the Kalewala). When this meaning had been forgotten Zeus became merely the son of Kronos, and Kronos became a new being. The notion of personifying the abstract idea *time* would never have entered the minds of a primitive people. When Kronos came into being he was endowed with a certain

> Thy father Dyâus did the best of things
> When he became thy father, Indra,[1]

sings one of the Vedic poets. Evidently Indra is acknowledged as a later god, but also a greater than his forerunner.

If we succeed in understanding the condition of mind
necessary for that purely natural religion when the
divinity was by name identified with his visible counterpart—the sea or the sky, or whatever it might be—we
can realise how, to become so deified, a phenomenon must
be constantly present to the senses; or, if not always
present thus, it must at least recur so regularly and so
often that the notion of its existence is firmly impressed
upon men's thoughts. The sun is not always seen, but he
rises and sets with the most perfect regularity, and in
fine climates his face is rarely hidden by day. He, therefore, is fitted to be from the first among the greatest of
the nature gods. Yet even the sun is not, in most mythologies, the supreme god; very often he falls far short of
being so; and that he does this is owing, in chief measure,
to his disappearance at night. When men's memories

---

character, and this was really taken from the old heaven god—known as
Varuna, Ouranos—who, as we have seen, belonged to an age before that
in which Zeus came to be worshipped as a god of storms. In fact, Dyâus'
nature divided in twain; the heaven side went to Varuna, the storm side
went to Zeus; and therefore in the Greek creed Ouranos belonged to a
very early stage of worship, and corresponded almost exactly to the Latin
Saturnus. When Kronos appeared he assumed the character of Ouranos,
who was henceforward almost completely forgotten. The record of the
change, however, is distinctly preserved in the myths; for the birth of
Zeus from Kronos, the treatment of his children by the latter, &c., almost
exactly reproduce the relative positions of Kronos and Ouranos. Therefore, knowing as we do that Kronos is of later origin than either Zeus or
Ouranos, we are justified in removing this middle term, and we at once get
back to the birth of Zeus from Ouranos, the jealousy of Zeus entertained
by his father, and the way in which the newer god dispossessed the old.
If, therefore, I speak of the Greeks looking back to the Saturnian time of
their religion (Ch. IV.), I do not mean that there ever was a time when
Kronos was worshipped instead of Zeus, but that the Greeks looked back,
without knowing it, to the older worship of *their* Ouranos, which really
did precede the cult of *their* Zeus.

[1] R. V. iv. 17, 3.

are very short it will fare still worse with phenomena whose appearance is more uncertain or at longer intervals.

The state of belief which has been characterised as henotheism, and which consists in worshipping the phenomenon which is immediately ·present and neglecting those phenomena which are past, evidently arises immediately out of that still earlier phase of thought (still earlier and still more akin to fetichism) when the phenomenon to be recognised as ·divine must be always present to the senses. Henotheism is, in fact, a kind of reversion to this state of feeling : it forgets all phenomena which are absent, and makes a protest against the place of *memory* in a creed. For these reasons a storm god (or god storm) is not likely to have been placed high in the pantheon during the earliest days of nature worship. When, however, the divinity and the phenomenon were not so absolutely identified, when the notion of the former's possessing a separate existence has begun to creep in, the god could be thought of without the aid of visible presentation. He was still perhaps identified with the phenomenon in *character*, but he had now a different name from it, and so could be contemplated alone. He might be sitting apart. He might peradventure be sleeping or upon a journey. And the personality now became more impressive if the deeds of the god were somewhat irregular and arbitrary. This is the time for a god such as the storm god (Indra or Zeus) to rise to power.

We may suppose that in those climates where the Indian sung his song of praise—unlike ours—the heavens were most often seen in their garment of unblemished blue. Nothing is certainly more divine and impressive than such a sight—at first.[1] But there is withal some-

---

[1] I anticipate here some objection on the part of the acute reader. 'Such a phrase as *at first*,' he will say, ' imagines man awakening suddenly into the world, opening his eyes upon its wonders, and at once falling to the invention of a mythology grounded upon these *first impressions*. But

thing monotonous about it. This god has not his changing fits, his passion and his kindness. He is too serene
to be very ardently loved or feared, for that eternal calm
can have small sympathy with the short and troubled life
of man. With Indra it is very different. He is the god
of storms; he is the sky, but the sky of clouds and rain
and lightning. His coming is rare, but it is terrible.
Sometimes, doubtless, Indra seems to be worshipped only
when he is present and seen. But throughout the whole
Vedic series we see the awe which he inspires when
he does come; in them we seem to behold the very
flash of his arrows and to hear the reverberation of his
thunder.

I think that the evidences of a transfer of worship
from the older sky god to Indra are very clear in the
Vedic poems. There is a kind of rivalry between the two;
or when Indra's contest is not with Dyâus it is with Vâruna
($o\dot{v}\rho\alpha\nu\acute{o}s$). It is acknowledged by Vedic scholars [1] that
Varuna was worshipped before Indra, and Varuna is, in
one aspect, only another name for the older Dyâus. The
following hymn is a record of the rivalry between Indra
and Varuna. The poet makes them both uphold their

---

such an imagination is quite inconsistent with the slow development of
human faculties. There is nothing shorter lived in the human thought
than the sense of *wonder*.' This last statement is, in reality, only partially true. The sudden sense of wonder soon fades, but there is a slow
abiding sense which never leaves human nature, and which, if it did desert
mankind, would carry away with it all his power of poetry and all his
power of belief. Wherefore the *at first* of the worship of the sky must be
taken to mean that period during which man, having passed away from
fetichism, had not yet advanced beyond it far enough to be able to worship
any god who was not a constantly present phenomenon. The gradual
fading of the influence of the sky on belief is coeval with the slow development of the notion of a being, to some extent, apart from phenomena.
It seems to us possible in a short time to grow familiar with and weary of
any particular phenomenon, because we can now run rapidly back through
the stage of thought which human nature has taken ages to make complete. In this respect it was with Belief as it was with Reason: the
simplest and most obvious deductions which a child makes now in a few
hours took mankind centuries to make for the first time.

[1] By Roth and by Gubernatis (*Letture*, &c., 189).

claims to worship, and then he himself sums up between them, preferring the active and warlike god :—

VARUNA SPEAKS.[1]

I am the king, to me belongeth rule,
I the life-giver of the heavenly host ;
The gods obey the bidding of Varuna,
I am the refuge of the human kind.

. . . .

I am, O Indra, Varuna, and mine are
The deep wide pair of worlds, the earth and heaven ;
Like a wise artist, made I all things living ;
The heaven and the earth, I them sustain.

. . . .

INDRA SPEAKS.

On me do call all men, the rich in horses,
Who through the hurry of the battle go ;
I sow the dreadful slaughter there ; I, Indra,
In my great might stir up the dust of combat.

This have I done ; the might of all the immortals
Restraineth never me, nor shall restrain.

. . . .

THE POET SPEAKS.

That this thou dost, know all men among mortals ;
This to Varuna makest thou known, O ruler.
Indra, in thee we praise the demon slayer,
Through whom the pent-up streams are free to flow.

Such a change as that from Dyâus or Varuna to Indra is incidental to the transition from nature worship to the personal god. That it is so is shown by the fact that changes, identical in significance, have been made by other peoples of the Indo-European family. All have

---

[1] R. V. iv. 42. Varuna is the *coverer*, from root *var* (to cover, enclose, keep). Cf. Skr. varana, Zend varena, *covering*. This is very suitable for the night sky, and like that image of Lady Macbeth's—

'Nor Heaven peep through the blanket of the dark,
    To cry, " Hold, hold ! " '

abandoned Dyâus. The Teutons took in his place Wuotan
or Odhinn, who is first of all a god of storm. The Greeks
and Romans kept the name of the older sky god Zeus—
Dyâus—but they modified his nature in the same direction
in which Indians and Germans changed the natures of
their divinities. Dyâus meant originally the bright
heaven; Zeus was as essentially a god of thunder and of
rain—νεφεληγερέτα, the cloud-collector. He, and Jove
too, corresponded as to their natures almost exactly with
Indra.

Yet the unmoved, all-embracing heaven better realises
some ideals of a divinity than these fitful storm-gods do;
and if a people pass from the one to the other it will not
be without some loss. In its high moods the fancy will look
back to former days, when the gods were of a larger pattern
than those of to-day. Men will tell of some past Saturnian
reign when lives were longer and not so eager and bitter
as they have become, when their forefathers enjoyed the
fruits of earth without strife and labour. For, after all,
the sky of clouds is the lower sky. The Greeks, we know,
made a distinction between ἀήρ and αἰθήρ, the lower and
the upper air. Dyâus, when he grew to be Zeus, did in
reality sink from the latter to the former: he descended
to the cloud regions. According to one theory of etymology, Indra expresses the same change in his very
name.[1]

The world over which the cloudy Indra ruled was the
world of farm and valley and low fertile pastures; but the
mountaineer, whose way led him to higher ranges and on
to the great peak of the Himalayas, saw, as he climbed
upwards, that he had passed the heaven of rain and
thunder. The clouds, which used to seem so far overhead,
were now stretched beneath his feet like a carpet. The
storm flashed, but he was beyond its reach; yet still, far as

[1] This etymology is proposed by Gubernatis (*Letture*, &c., p. 188). I
am, I confess, inclined to look upon the derivation given with great suspicion, but I will not venture to pronounce positively against it.

ever above him, spread the highest vault of heaven, whence shone the sun, or on him looked the everlasting stars.

Wherefore the earlier associations never quite lost their hold, and the sky god asserted again and again his paramount influence upon men's imagination. As we are at present dealing only with Indian mythology, it is enough to notice how in time, in the Brahmin creed, Indra succeeded to the complete nature of Dyâus; while his active powers, along with his thunderbolts and lightning flash, were taken from him and given to a younger divinity—namely, to Vishnu. Vishnu is the Brahmin saviour, the incarnate god.

In truth, there is in this rivalry between Dyâus and Indra an element which is universal and ingrained in the religious instinct. At first, in such early times as these Vedic ones, the instinctive feeling is not consciously expressed, but expressed unconsciously by these changes of creed. We can now recognise the counter-workings of this instinct as independent of any particular phase of belief, as belonging not to this period specially, but to all time. The contest between the heaven and the storm gods is an expression of two diverse tendencies of the human mind when dealing with religious ideas. There is first an impulse upward, a desire to press the thoughts continually forward in an effort to idealise the Godhead; but by exalting or seeming to exalt Him to the highest regions of abstraction, this tendency is likely to rob the Deity of all fellowship with man, and man of all claims upon His sympathy and love. Then comes in the second impulse, which often at one stroke brings down the god as near as possible to the level of mankind, leaving him at the last no better than a demi-god or superior kind of man. One we may call the metaphysical or the religious, the other the mythological impulse; and we shall never rightly understand the history of religion until we have learned to recognise these two streams of tendency interpenetrating every system.

Indra, then, once rose to a supreme place because he was more active and changeful than Dyâus, and better satisfied those instincts which desire to see the deity like mankind. Soon he assumed the qualities and title which had belonged to his father, and clothed himself with the character befitting a Supreme God. In the Vedic creed, such as we see it, Dyâus has almost altogether faded away. Indra there represents the ideal godhead: he is the Father and the Supreme One, the god to whom all highest worship turns.

It results from this that in the Vedic hymns Indra has to a great extent put off his mythological nature, in order to clothe himself more completely with the majesty of divinity. The instinct of *worship* is devoted to him; the story-telling parts of the creed are reserved for lesser gods. Of Indra's deeds we shall have something to say hereafter; but there is not very much variety in them. On the other hand, we can have no difficulty in allowing that he, among all the gods of the Vedic Indian, exercised the deepest influence on belief. Next to Indra stood Agni. To say that among the most genuine and ancient hymns of the Rig Veda about 265 are addressed to Indra, 233 to Agni, while no other god can lay claim to more than a quarter of this latter number,[1] is enough to show in what direction, towards what parts of nature, the religious thought of these Aryas turned. We have a further witness to the supremacy of Indra and Agni in the fact that nine out of the ten books of the Rig Veda begin with a series of hymns addressed to them, as though their worship must precede all other. The worship of Indra is the central feature of Vedic mythology. As Dyâus has quite resigned his throne before the beginning of the Vedas, Indra must be looked upon in every way as the supreme

---

[1] Soma, indeed, can apparently do so; for the whole of one book (the ninth) is devoted to him. But, in fact, the hymns of this book are all of a ritualistic character: they are concerned with the ceremonies of worship in which Soma plays so important a part. But they are not written distinctly in praise of the Indian Bacchus.

god. He is still a representative of the storm; but as he is also the highest god, it is needful that he should be something more than this. He has already taken upon himself a great part of the nature of the older god of heaven. 'The might of all the immortals,' as we have seen, 'restrains him never.'

It was the power of the god which was most worshipped. He might be counted on for help as the special god of the Aryas,[1] just as Jehovah was the special god of the children of Israel. In a fine passage, which breathes the spirit of the Hebrew psalm, we are told how 'he shakes the heaven and the earth as the hem of his garment.'[2] Indra is often called upon, as Jehovah is, to show his strength and to confound those who have dared to doubt his supremacy; for here in India, as in Palestine, 'the wicked saith in his heart, There is no god.'

INDRA SPEAKS.

I come with might before thee, stepping first,
    And behind me move all the heavenly powers.

THE POET SPEAKS.

If thou, O Indra, wilt my lot bestow,
    A hero's part dost thou perform with me.

To thee the holy drink I offer first;
    Thy portion here is laid, thy soma brewed.
Be, while I righteous am, to me a friend;
    So shall we slay of foemen many a one.

Ye who desire blessings, bring your hymn
    To Indra; for the true is always true.
'There is no Indra,' many say; 'who ever
    Has seen him? Why should we his praise proclaim?'

INDRA SPEAKS.

I am here, singer; look on me; here stand I.
    In might all other beings I o'erpass.
Thy holy service still my strength renews,
    And thereby smiting, all things smite I down.

[1] R. V. vi. 18, 3.   [2] Ibid. i. 37, 6.

And as on heaven's height I sat alone,
To me thy offering and thy prayer rose up.
Then spake my soul this word within himself:
'My votaries and their children call upon me.'[1]

The enemies against whom Indra fights are not, however, generally speaking, earthly foes. I have heard critics speaking from the outside object to Vedic scholars the improbability that any people would have their thoughts constantly set to observe the heavenly phenomena and to sing of them. And I must confess that, at the time I read these criticisms, my prejudices—or prejudgments—went altogether with the critics. But such predispositions must give way to fact. We cannot determine beforehand what it is likely that a people will or will not think or believe.[2] And it is quite certain that almost all the Vedic hymns are concerned with the skyey influences, with the heaven, with day and night, with the sun, with morning and evening twilight, with the clouds and with the wind. The purely devotional parts of the hymns have a certain sameness; for the Vedic religion has already neared the conception of a single ideal god. So long as we are concerned with what Indra *is* we find that epithets are too few to express his greatness and the many sides of his character; but we find also that the same expression, or nearly the same, may be used of other gods, as of Agni or of Varuna or Mitra.

When we pass beyond the inward being and come to the record of the deeds which Indra *has* done (not those he is asked to do), we are face to face once more with the fresh world of nature. Treated in this way, no longer devotionally but historically, the nature of Indra is limited to the phenomena of storm. He kills the enemy,

[1] R. V. viii. 89. I have followed here, as in all other cases, the translation of Grassmann; Ludwig gives a somewhat different complexion to this dialogue.
[2] See what Schoolcraft says concerning the minute attention paid by the Algic tribes to the phenomena of the sky, *Algic Res.* p. 48.

it is true; he breaks down his strong citadel; he destroys his high hills. But who is this enemy? He is Vritra; he is Ahi, the serpent. 'Him the god struck with Indra-might, and set free the all-gleaming water for the use of men.'[1] What the serpent has done is to conceal the waters of fruitfulness which Indra sets free. The hills which Indra destroys are the mountains of Sambara— 'the shadowy cloud-hill of Sambara'[2]—very evidently the clouds themselves. The one great action of the god, which is referred to again and again and constantly prayed for, is the bringing the thunderstorm, and with it the desired rain.

In reading the description of these conflicts, we detect a slight confusion of mind on the part of the authors of the hymns. This confusion arises from Indra's being in a degree abstracted from those physical phenomena which are the substance of his nature; so that the same phenomena can be presented again to the imagination, and in a new light. Thus, though there can be no doubt that the great god is himself the storm, or still more strictly the stormy sky, and though this idea of course includes all the separate parts of the storm—the black clouds, for example, which hold in their bosoms the lightning or the rain—still it is quite possible to regard these parts as separate entities. The clouds may be the servants and the companions of Indra. When they appear in that aspect they are the Maruts, his band of warriors. Or the clouds may be enemies of the god. The darkness which

---

[1] i. 165, 8. The name Vritra is, I believe, from the same root, var (or vri), as Varuna. Possibly, therefore, it was originally only the darkness. This reappearance of one central idea (shown in root) in two forms should be compared with the identity of Thorr and Thrymr (Ch. VII.)

[2] ii. 24. Sambara (= samvara), from sam and vri, is a parallel example. It had not originally an evil significance, only meaning he who covers up or contains the source of abundance (sam and samba, happiness; but samb, to collect). This is an epithet for the cloud. But when Sambara grew into an opponent of Indra, the name was construed to mean the concealer, or secreter, or thief of wealth and happiness.

follows their spreading over the heavens seems to proclaim
them powers of evil.

In this way the clouds become those deadly serpents,
Ahi and Vritra; and now, behold! Indra has sent his flash
and they are dissolved in rain. This water, long desired,
expected long, they have concealed in their folds or coils;
and it is Indra who sets it free. Strong with his soma
drink, he hurls his bolt and strikes to atoms the stream-
concealing dragon.[1] In this aspect, therefore, the clouds
are very appropriately likened to Vritra, or to Ahi, or to
the mountains of Sambara.

Thus the storm and the constituents of the storm
are at once Indra and his companions, the Maruts,
and also the enemies of Indra. There is nothing more
common in mythology than such a double aspect of a
natural phenomenon, though at the same time there is
nothing more puzzling to the student, nor nothing which
seems to give a better weapon to the sarcasm of the
sceptic in comparative mythology, who accuses us of
making 'anything out of anything' when we interpret
myths in this way. Zeus is a storm god scarcely less than
Indra is; but beings of the storm also are the Cyclops and
(possibly) the Gorgon. Or if Medusa be, as I hold, the
moon, so too is the goddess Artemis. The eye of the Cyclops
is the sun; and yet the sun is not the less greatest and most
beneficent of gods. It is the same in the mythology of
the Teutons. Thorr, the god, is the wielder of the thunderbolt; but one of Thorr's great enemies, the giant Thrymr,
is the thunder likewise. The sun is Balder, the Beautiful,
brightest and best of the Æsir; or it is the eye of Odhinn,
which the god threw into Mim's well; or else it is the
head of the giant Mimr himself, which Odhinn cut off.

Indra being promoted to be the supreme one among
the gods, Agni takes the place next to him, and becomes
the messenger between heaven and earth. How well and
how consistently with his elemental nature he fills this posi-

[1] P. V. ii. 19.

tion we have already seen. Yet it is true that the being who in most mythologies—most Aryan mythologies, at any rate—is the human-like god and the friend of man is not the fire, but rather the sun. He is Apollo or Heracles, Thorr or Balder. The promotion of Agni to this place must therefore be reckoned a peculiarity of the Vedic religion, but it is one which it is more needful to point out than to attempt any elaborate explanation of the causes of it. Indeed, in all such cases the record of the fact itself is what we most want, not theories of how this fact came to be—theories which, as a kind of prophecies after the event, are very easy to fabricate. As the thing was so, we easily see that it would suggest a tone of thought in conformity with the articles of belief. It is easy to imagine the frame of mind which should choose an Indra for the supreme divinity rather than a Dyâus, or an Agni next to him rather than an Apollo or a Balder. But the important thing to notice is that the inclination was present among these particular people and at this particular time.

The human god is he about whom myths oftenest arise, and whose character is in consequence more varied than the character of the Highest. This rule is illustrated in the case of Agni, of whose manysided nature we have already noted the most important features. Twice born, once in the cloud and once again in the wood; descending from heaven in the lightning, and rising up again from the altar or the funeral pyre, Agni was, while on earth, always at the service of man, watching over him in the house. He was the eternal opposite of man's great enemy, the darkness; he was the chief protection against that and its multitudinous terrors. We cannot now realise the horror which men anciently felt of the dark, of its dangers from wild beasts, of the still greater spiritual dangers to which at night-time they felt themselves exposed. At night ranged abroad those evil ones, those unseen deadly foes who (in the words of one Vedic hymn) 'strike with hidden

but victorious powers.'   Therefore Agni is never allowed
utterly to leave the worshipper: *the house fire never goes
out.*[1]   This was the rule once among all the nations of the
Indo-European family; but before historic times it had
been more or less abandoned by most, and was preserved
in its strictness only by Indians and Persians.

In other Indo-European creeds—those at least of Greek
and Roman and Teuton [2]—we never find the worship of
the fire in its intensity, only the traces of what it has been.
In Hestia and Vesta it is not the whole character of Agni
that is presented to us, but only the house fire generalised
or epitomised as a great state fire.[3]   Hestia is called by
the Homeric hymnist the most revered of goddesses.[4]   At
Olympia, Pausanias tells us, the first sacrifices were made
to her.[5]   This surviving custom witnesses to the decay of
a higher kind of worship, as does the importance attached
to the maintenance of the fire of Vesta in Rome,[6] and to
the purity of the vestal virgins, and so forth.

In Germany traces of the same kind of fire ritual are
found, but diminished to a small compass.   At the present
day popular superstition forbids the letting out of the fire
on the hearth during certain sacred nights—Christmas
Eve, for example, New Year's Eve, or, according to some,
for all the nights of the 'Twelve Days.'   'If the fire goes
out on the hearth the money goes out of the coffer.'[7]   And,

---

[1] Concerning the laws and customs which have been founded upon the
need of this perpetual house fire, see, among many other writers, F. de
Coulange's *Cité Antique*.   It is doubtful whether the classic Vesta and
Hestia are from the root *ras*, to shine, or from *ras*, to dwell (see *Zeitsch.
f. v. Spr.* xvi. 160).   May it not be from both, and the identity of these
two roots witness to the importance of the house fire to the house?   No
man could dwell without a house fire.

[2] The fire god, Agni, retained his name only among the Slavonic
branch of the Aryan race.

[3] See above on root meaning of Vesta and Hestia.

[4] Hymn. in Aph. 18, 22.

[5] v. 14, § 5.   See also Plato, *Leges*, ix. 2.   Let us add that in Crete her
name was pronounced in the solemn oath before that of Zeus Cretagenes.

[6] These perpetual fires were not unknown in Greece.   There was one
kept up, for example, at Mantinea.

[7] Wuttke, *Deutscher Volksaberglaube*, pp. 63, 66, &c.

again, for a public recognition of the same duties we have
the custom of lighting bonfires on the hills on great days
of the heathen calendar— the Easter or Ostara fire, the fire
on Walpurgisnacht (May-day Eve), and the Johannisfeuer
(St. John's Day fire), which was more anciently the bale-
fire of Balder.[1]

The ritual of the fire is, in all these cases, but a faint
shadow of what among the Indo-European races generally
it had once been. Accordingly, the beings who are supposed to represent Agni represent but a small part of the
great personality of the fire god. Hestia or Vesta show
him as the house fire, the flame which has descended to
live on earth. Hephæstus and Vulcan show him in a still
meaner guise, as the forger's fire : this is the same character in which Agni is called in the Vedas Twashtar, the
fabricator. In such a guise as Hephæstus or Vulcan the
fire god has sunk almost below the level of humanity ; for
he is a lame, deformed being, the laughing-stock of the
Olympians.[2] Nevertheless this lameness and deformity
are not themselves of recent origin, but have their place
in the character of Agni, and are associated with some of
the most beautiful myths concerning him. Of these, however, I cannot speak now. What is peculiar to Hephæstus
and Vulcan is that they present this side only and forget
the higher ones.

It is evident that the novelty and wonder of fire had
been lost sight of by the Greeks and Romans and Teutons.
Fire had become an ordinary thing to them, and so they
were no longer in eager search for its presence throughout
the realm of nature. It is for some such reason as this

[1] See Chapters VIII., X.

[2] As for the northern Loki, he presents the fire in its worst aspect, a
being no longer divine, but one who never ceases to work evil against the
Æsir (Edda Snorra, D. 49). Nevertheless that Loki had not originally
this evil nature is witnessed by the Eddaic history itself. In a study on
the 'Mythology of the Eddas' (*Trs. Roy. Soc. of Literature*, vol. xii.), I
have discussed at some length the gradual deterioration of Loki, and
shown (I think the importance of the place he once held.

that, in the later creeds, the earthly fire is quite dissociated
from the heavenly one. With Agni it was very different :
from his heavenly birth he drew all the greatness of his
character. The god who was so near to man was yet seen
far away, not in the lightning only, but in the red of
morning. The Indian saw in the dawn a sort of picture
or allegory, if I may so call it, of the total universe, and
of the limitless extent of time and space. The Vedic
psalmist called the place of the sun's rising Aditi, 'the
boundless ;' for as he looked through the long layers of
level cloud he was swayed by the sense of endless space—
that sort of mental vertigo which seizes us sometimes when
we, too, gaze either upon the endless ranges of cloud on
the horizon or upward among the vista of the stars.
Through all the regions of morning and evening brightness the worshipper saw Agni shining, and so he called
him the son of Aditi, the boundless one.

Side by side, then, stood these two contradictory
notions—Agni, the endlessly extending vista of red clouds
at sun-rising or sun-setting, and Agni born from the
rubbing of two small sticks. Between the two, from one
to the other, extends the vast pantheistic nature of the
god. And yet to this external being we must add something more. Agni is also the unseen god, the internal
fire ; he is the kindler of all passionate longings, of inspiration, of the intoxication of thought and joy, of anger
and the burning desire of revenge.

Indra and Agni represent upon the whole, as has been
said, the strongly religious side of Indo-Aryan belief, as
opposed to the lighter mythological aspect of it. It
belongs to the scheme of these chapters to pass slightly
over this religious phase, which touches too closely upon
the later ethical development of belief. It is not our
object to discover what kind of emotion the gods called
forth from their votaries so much as what was the outward
aspect in which imagination saw the gods. Indra and
Agni, therefore, cannot occupy a place in our enquiries

proportionate to the place which they held in the creed of the Indian.

Agni, however, has many claims upon our attention on the heroic side. Being so human in some aspects of him, he was not always kept at the greatest heights of adoration, but descended often to the heroic level, and in doing so became the subject of divers myths and stories. His most striking appearance in this guise is that to which reference has been already made, his great act of parricide, which was acknowledged even by the singer to be scarcely becoming a god, but concerning the performance of which no doubt unfortunately could be raised. I will not assert that this notion contains in it the germ of the story related of so many heroes—Cyrus, Œdipus, Perseus, Orestes, Romulus, and others—namely, that, voluntarily or by accident, they have been guilty of this crime of parricide; but I think it possible that these personages may have had some connection with Agni, and that their story may be in part founded on the Agni myth. However, they are certainly not immediate children of the fire god.

Prometheus, on the other hand, is a direct descendant of the fire god. He was once not improbably the actual embodiment of the *fire drill*; but to a mythology not quite so literal he became an embodiment of fire, or the fire god. Fire has its evil and destructive as well as its beneficent aspect, and this bad side of the element is embodied in the Titan Prometheus. Though not a parricide, he is the foe of father-Zeus; and for his wickedness he is punished. This, at least, I take to be the earlier legend; for it is one in which Prometheus closely resembles the Scandinavian fire god, Loki, who is also the enemy of the gods, and who, for his wickedness, is chained upon a rock till the day of doom. Some returning thought of the goodness of fire and its benefits has again changed the Greek story, and restored the Titan by making him a martyr to his love of human kind and a victim of the

jealousy of the Olympians. In the story, therefore, of
Prometheus stealing fire from heaven, and giving it to
man, we have unquestionably the trace of an old Aryan
myth, which gave a similar part to Agni. This story
placed the fire god in opposition to some supreme being
in the Indian pantheon—may be to Indra or Dyâus. And
Agni was punished for his temerity. Perhaps he was
flung from heaven as Hephæstus was, and as, we know,
the fire itself is often flung. Perhaps he was chained to
a rock as Prometheus and Loki were chained.

From Agni and Indra we pass to gods less exalted in
the Vedic ritual, less near to realising the ideal of a godhead, but yet with individualities of their own. There is,
it cannot be denied, a certain indistinctness about the
celestial phenomena with which we are dealing in Vedic
mythology, as compared with those terrestrial fetich gods
which we discussed in the last chapter. But this seems
not unnatural when we consider that we have reached a
less material and a more imaginative region than we were
in before. Moreover, in the Vedas we are not even in the
region of pure phenomena worship, but in an intermediate
state between that and the *cult* of gods who have the
nature of man.

As the worshipped river grows shadowy and shapeless
in the mist-like *apsara*, 'the formless one,' so the nature
gods, in their turn, before they emerge again as human
beings, become first the pale semblances of what they once
were ; while they are, at the same time, the faint fore-
shadowings of what they will be, they are the phantoms of
human kind. They are no longer *things* ; they are not even
pure *phenomena* ; they are not beings with completely *human*
natures ; and so they hover in a middle state, and hang,
like the coffin of the Prophet, suspended between heaven
and earth. Take the sun god, for example. He was once,
it is certain, merely the bright disk which travels up
heaven's arch. But in the Vedas he is no longer this

only; the disk itself may be the wheel of his chariot. The sun god (Suryas) comes 'dragging his wheel.'[1] The sun god is here something unseen and imagined, but he is not yet humanised. Sometimes he is called a bull, sometimes a bird;[2] but it is not meant that he is really a bull or a bird. Still he is as much like these things as he is like a man. He is the great ruler of the day, the all-powerful, the creator—as it sometimes seems—of all the world. (For does not the world at his call become *visible*, and come out of darkness which is nothingness?) Yet for all his greatness the sun god has not such a free will as man has; he cannot rule and act in any way he chooses. He is compelled to follow his daily round; he 'travels upon changeless paths.' In one word, all his being is still united to the phenomenon which gives him his name, and which is to mankind his outward show.

It is essentially the same with the other divine parts of nature as it is with this particular one, the sun; the morning goddess is not the simple dawn, though she must be in all things like the dawn. The evening goddess must be like evening; the storm and fire gods must be like storm and fire. But all these things are seen through a medium of imagination, and not in the prosaic aspect of mere fact.

In no mythic poetry are we lifted up to a higher region of imagination than we are in the Vedas. It might seem as if such flights were too airy and unreal to have been made by genuine belief; and they would be so, perhaps, were it not that they start from the firm ground of a more primitive creed, to which the new beliefs are still partly tied. If a visible thing is no longer worshipped in them, still the divine being is so near the thing—the phenomenon—in all his ways, that the certainty which attaches to what the eye can actually see and the ear detect becomes his by inheritance. The worshipper was himself scarcely

---

[1] R. V. vii. 63.   [2] Cf. x. 177.

yet conscious of the distinction to be made between Indra and the storm, Ushas and the dawn, Suryas and the disk of the sun.

But it is harder still for us to understand such a state of belief than it was for men of that time to create it, seeing how much we have lost in these latter years all our sense of the mystery and wonder of nature. Fetichism appears to us but senseless magic when we cannot make the effort of imagination required to understand how the lifeless things which it chose for its gods were once not lifeless at all. The nature worship which followed fetichism will seem still more extravagant until we realise some part of the awe and splendour which were associated with natural phenomena, and which, by a necessary reaction, give to these vague appearances a character and being.

Turning now from the strictly religious side of Vedism, and from the beings who best represent that, we come first to two who stand next in majesty to Indra and Agni, and next to them receive the greatest meed of praise in the hymns. We want all the aid which imagination can lend us to understand fully the characters of Mitra and Varuna.

These gods are sometimes invoked separately, but far more often together, combined, in fact, into one being, Mitra-Varuna. When thus combined they become quite different beings from what they are when single, and it is in this combination that the peculiar refinement and difficulty in the conception of Mitra and Varuna has to be brought out.

Vârnna is properly the sky, meaning, as this word does, the coverer, the concealer, and becoming, as it becomes in Greek, οὐρανός. Varuna is not, however, the same as Dyâus, the bright heaven; it is rather the sky of night, and as such the god Varuna should be thought of when he stands alone. By himself, again, Mitra seems to be the sun; such a nature is implied in the root of the name— *mid*, 'to grow warm'—and also in an epithet which belongs peculiarly to him, 'the friend;' for the sun god in all Aryan creeds is, in an especial sense, the friend of man.[1] Mitra, moreover, has his counterpart in another Aryan system, namely, in the Iranian. Mithras of the Persians was, to all seeming, a solar deity. But then, as the sun is so often called the eye of Mitra and Varuna,[2] it is clear that when the two are joined Mitra cannot any longer be the sun. Now in the Norse mythology the sun is the eye of Odhinn, but in this case Odhinn is the heaven. We are justified, then, in saying that, joined together, Mitra and Varuna likewise express some aspect of the heaven. They cannot be absolutely the *same* thing; they are, then, *two* heavens, the bright and warm and the dark and concealing.

Let us note, again, that Mitra and Varuna are in a special sense the sons of Aditi, 'the boundless,' the limitless vista of clouds which we see at sunrise. There is a third Aditya associated with these two—Aryaman. He has no existence by himself, and seems to be brought in for the sake of making up an orthodox trilogy.[3]

In their fullest and most transcendental sense, then, Mitra and Varuna, the day and night sky, may be taken for personifications of day and night. When combined into one being, Mitra-Varuna, they are the image of the union of day and night—that is to say, of the morning. But the presentation of the ideas of morning and evening —the two are generally coupled together—to the mind are very various, and these take in mythology many different shapes.

[1] In the Vedic creed, however, we must say that the sun god is this *next after* Agni.

[2] R. V. i. 50, 6; 115, 1 and 5; vii. 63, 1; x. 37, 1. Sometimes of Mitra, Varuna, and Agni, i. 115, 1.

[3] We may compare these three with the curious trilogy who are introduced at the opening of the Younger Edda—namely, Har, 'the high;' Jafnhar, 'the equally high;' and Thriði, 'the third.' A being called Thriði could never have a separate existence apart from the other two. His very name shows why he was invented. In like manner Mitra and Varuna are evidently an equal pair, and Aryaman is Thridi, the third.

Mr. Herbert Spencer, noticing a dispute between two learned philologists—Max Müller and Adelbert Kuhn—concerning the nature of the Vedic Saramâ (which the one authority claims as the dawn, and the other as the wind), remarks upon the improbability of so unreal a phenomenon as the dawn being made into a god. He has his own explanation of the worship of the dawn, and although that is a thousandfold harder to maintain in face of the facts of mythology, we may admit the force of the objections to another's theory. The truth, as I fancy, is that the original god or goddess is not the dawn, but rather the wind of morning which ushers in the light, and which, blowing upon the face of the sleeper and awakening him so, may well seem the real messenger of day. In some places these morning breezes are very regular, and not less constant are those which accompany the sunset. Curtius, in the opening chapter of his 'History of Greece,' gives a beautiful picture of the regularity of the winds which govern the Ægean. Every morning a breeze arises from the coasts of Thrace and blows all day southward; at evening it goes down, and for awhile the sea is calm. Then almost imperceptibly a gentle wind arises from the south. We need not wonder if in early times the ideas of morn and even are merged in the notions of the wind at sunrise and sun-setting, and that they only after awhile became abstracted. Therefore Saramâ may be the wind and yet the dawn.

There may be more or less of idealism, less or more of simple sensation, intermingled in the conceptions of the dawn and of the sunset. The most material sense is that of the winds of morning and evening. These in the simplest form Mitra and Varuna are not. But that in a more general way Mitra and Varuna represent the horizons of morning and evening, or the morning and evening themselves, I do not doubt.

Here is one indication. Mitra and Vâruna are to be worshipped morning, noon, and evening; and Aryaman is

but the 'third,' the supplement of their being; so we may
say that Mitra, Varuna, and Aryaman are to be worshipped
morning, noon, and evening. Aryaman would thus correspond to the midday, Mitra and Varuna to the morning
and evening. Again—and this is a stronger indication of
the natures of Mitra and Varuna—Agni, says the Athar-
vaveda, in the morning is Mitra, in the evening (or at night)
is Váruna. Now Agni, as we have seen, is always present
in the clouds of sunrise and sunset: therefore to say that
in the morning he is Mitra, is to say that the red of dawn
is Mitra; that he is Varuna in the evening means that
the red of evening is Varuna. There being two reds, two
meeting-places of the day and the night skies accounts
for the combination of Mitra and Varuna into one Mitra-
Varuna.

I know that this attempt to fix for a moment the
shifting vane of popular belief cannot but create confusion
in the mind of the reader. The weathercock cannot be
held steady. But though it is always turning it never
shifts far from the normal point. I have but sought to
register each of these rapid changes. Let us now free
our thoughts from this analysis. We have to picture
Varuna and Mitra as a mighty Pair—not, as I have said,
human and yet not pure phenomenal—whose presence is
felt about the time when the division of the 'two worlds,'
the sky and earth, first becomes visible. This is all the
singer knows. He himself does not analyse and register
his thought. At the dim hour of twilight, before the sun
appears, he is aware of a mighty presence. In the
morning, so he tells us, when the sun's horses are being
unloosed, and while the thousand lights of the night
heaven are still to be seen, he catches sight of the princely
pair, the noblest of beings.[1] 'Heaven nor day, nor
streams nor spirits, have not attained your godhead, your
greatness.'[2]

[1] Read, for example, R. V. v. 62.
[2] Or, more literally, 'wealth' (R. V. i. 151, 9).

For Mitra and Varuna, then, the singer—the chorus of singers and of priests—stands watching before the day break. Ere the actual Dawn herself, the goddess Ushas, opens all her treasures, or the sun appears, these mystic Twain will approach, going together side by side through heaven;[1] 'possessors of three realms of air,' 'lords of the dew.'[2] They are coming; and now we hear the chorus rising in the still twilight.[3]

> If at thy rising, sun, thou shalt discover
> Us blameless to the twain Varuna, Mitra,
> Then, Aditi, we singers stand in favour
> With all the gods, and with thee, Aryaman.
>
> Now to the twofold world, Varuna, Mitra,
> Rises the sun god, gazing upon men,
> Guardian of those who stay and those who wander,
> Guardian of right and wrong among mankind.
>
> From his high seat seven steeds with rein he governs,
> Who bright anointed[4] him, the Light God bear.
> Unto your throne, both loving, he approaches,
> Summoning all things as his sheep the shepherd.
>
> Up now have climbed your mead-besprinkled horses:
> The sun god mounted up the flood of light.
> The three Adityas made smooth his journey,
> Varuna, Mitra, Aryaman, in concert.
>
> For these are the avengers of much evil,
> Varuna, Mitra, Aryaman, together.
> And in the house they cherish holy laws,
> The faithful sons of Aditi, and strong.

[1] R. V. i. 136, 3.   [2] R. V. v. 69; ii. 41, 6.

[3] R. V. vii. 60. The meaning of the first verse is somewhat obscured by the fact of its containing three vocatives, in the desire of the poet to include many divinities within one canticle. The first line is addressed to the sun—by anticipation, for he has not yet risen. The third speaks to Aditi or to the Adityas, Varuna and Mitra. Line four includes Aryaman in the address.

[4] Literally 'butter dripping.'

These are not to deceive, Varuna, Mitra.
The fool also shall they correct in wisdom;
Good heart and knowledge giving to the righteous
Upon his way, and from oppression freeing.

As lively watchers of the heaven and earth,
As wise ones bear they safe the erring mortal.
(In every river is there not some ford ?)
And they can hold us up in our affliction.

A sure, well-guarded shelter to the Sudas
Give Aditi and Mitra and Varuna,
Guarding their children, and their children's children.
Keep far from us thy wrath divine, O Strong One.

The sun is but the eye of Mitra and Varuna; and yet
they, like the sun, move for ever upon fixed paths; they
will have their way made straight through heaven.[1]
Wherefore, seeing that *right* is but *straight*, they who
move upon a straight road as Mitra and Varuna do, or as
Surya, the sun god, does, are likewise the lovers of justice
and of fixed law. 'The lords of right and brightness,'[2]
one poet calls Mitra and Varuna; and in the first
character, the lovers of right, they are perpetually addressed. They are pure from birth.[3] Moreover, they watch
over man, and they are, as the hymn just quoted says,
guardians of right and wrong (of the laws of right and
wrong) among mankind. They come as spies into the
house[4]—a beautiful image for the soft stealing morning
light—and of man's home they are, like Agni, the
guardians.[5]

The character of being messengers to man and his
friends belongs to the two Adityas in the next degree to
Agni; but of the two it belongs rather to Mitra than to
Varuna.

There are not, it has been said, many hymns addressed
to Mitra alone. But here is one in which his righteous-

[1] Cf. R. V. i. 136   [2] i. 23, 5.   [3] i. 23.
[4] ii. 67, 5.   [5] vii. 61, 8.

ness and yet friendliness are expressed with great sweet-
ness :— [1]

> To man comes Mitra down in friendly converse.
> Mitra it was who fixed the earth and heaven.
> Unslumbering mankind he watches over.
> To Mitra, then, your full libations pour.
>
> Oh, may the man for ever more be blessed
> Who thee, Aditya, serves by ancient law ;
> Sheltered by thee, no death him touch, no sadness,
> No power oppress him, neither near nor far.
>
> From sickness free, rejoicing in our strength
> And our stout limbs upon the round of earth ;
> The ordinance of Aditya duly following :   ·
> So stand we ever in the guard of Mitra.
>
> Most dear is our Mitra, high in heaven,
> Born for our gracious king, and widely ruling.
> Oh, stand we ever in his holy favour,
> Enjoying high and blessed happiness !
>
> Yea, great is Mitra, humbly to be worshipped,
> To man descending, to his singer gracious.
> Then let us pour to him, the high Aditya,
> Upon the flame a faithful offering.

Sometimes instead of Mitra, Varuna, and Aryaman we
have Agni associated with the first two and instead of the
last.   Suryas, the sun, for example, is called the eye of
Mitra, Varuna, and Agni.[2] And these three form an
appropriate trilogy in the second rank of worship after
Indra.   For, putting aside that great god who, sometimes
at any rate, appears an absolutely supreme ruler, as much
above all others as Zeus was superior to the rest of the
Olympians, putting aside Indra, Agni, Mitra, and Varuna
are the most godlike of all the beings of the Indian
pantheon.   They are, therefore, we may suppose, the most
nearly separate from the region of phenomena, the most
idealised of all the divine phenomena.

---

[1] iii. 59, 7.   [2] i. 115, 1.

For an example of the difference between Mitra and Varuna, as we see them in the hymns and that which they would have appeared had they been nothing more than the winds of morning in their *physical* sense, we may compare the two Adityas with the two Asvin. These last two were the Dioscuri of Indian mythology. By name they were simply the horsemen, or rather the charioteers—no actual riding on horse*back*, as in the later example of the Greek twin brethren, being imagined in their case.[1] As they were specially noted for the swiftness of their flight, they must, one would suppose, have been embodiments of winds. I have, in fact, no doubt that they were simply the morning and evening breezes, and essentially the same as the Sârameyas, the sons of Saramâ, the dawn. They were, too, *essentially* the same as Mitra and Varuna (as morning and evening), only that the latter were much more complex in nature and much more idealised.

A third representation of the dawn is the maiden Ushas, the sister of the Asvin, whom they carry away in their swift chariots when the sun pursues her. We see that the Vedic mythopœist is never weary of personifying this particular part of celestial nature. It accords with this peculiarity of his creed that the dawn is almost always the hour of his worship. The hymns sung at midday or at sunset are very few compared with those which usher in the day. Though it were perhaps 'to consider too curiously' should one attempt to give to each of these various personifications of the dawn a distinct phenomenal existence, yet for the sake of presenting them more clearly before the imagination, so that each may play his part

---

[1] They belong to a time when horsemanship, in the modern sense, was not yet known. We find that the word *atra*, a horse, comes, from its connection with the chariot of the sun (drawn by seven horses, the Harits-Charites), to signify the number seven. This is as much as to say that to the Vedic Indian the word 'horse' naturally suggested the sun god. Wherefore we cannot doubt that the Asvin had originally drawn the car of the sun god. Before Suryas had seven horses he probably possessed two only

in the Indian's mythic day, I will dispose them thus :—
The first white streak of light which showed the Indian
the separation between earth and sky opened before the
eye of fancy the illimitable space which seemed to stretch
beyond that break. This, which is what is called the
white dawn—*alba, aube*—was the entry of Mitra and
Varuna, the revelation of the 'boundless' Adityas. It
was through a twilight air, a windless twilight morning
air, that the song we heard but now broke upon our ears.
Anon springs up the breeze, or the twin winds (one, yet
double, because they are of night as well as of morning),
the Asvin, driving rapidly through the quickly lightening
space ; and after them comes their sister the Red Dawn,
Aurora, allied to Aura, the breeze, but not identical therewith. She is Ushas. Close behind her, in loving chase,
comes Suryas, the sun.

But let us leave this rapid catalogue of the morning
sights and follow at a slower pace the course of the
mythic day as its events are told us in the hymns. Let us
go back to our chorus of priests, still waiting till the sun
shall rise. Varuna and Mitra appear chiefly to the eye of
faith ; but other, lesser things are more real. These lesser
beings of the pantheon are, compared with the great
gods, like to heroes or demi-gods and goddesses. Even
the sun (Surya) we are compelled to place generally in
this category. First comes Ushas, the Dawn, opening the
dark gates of night. She brings forth her car and oxen
to run her course. With lovely dress she clothes herself,
like a dancer, and unbears her bosom to the sun god.
'Making light for all the world, Ushas has opened the
darkness as a cow her stall.' And once again uprises the
priestly chorus with its Muezzin call to prayer :— [1]

> Dawn, full of wisdom, rich in everything,
> Fairest, attend the singers' song of praise.
> Oh! thou rich goddess, old, yet ever young,
> Thou, all-dispenser, in due order comest!

[1] iii. 61.

Shine forth, O goddess, thine eternal morning,
With thy bright cars our song of praise awakening.
Thee draw through heaven the well-yoked team of horses,
The horses golden bright, that shine afar.

Enlightener of all being, breath of morning,
Thou holdest up aloft the light of gods.
Unto one goal ever thy course pursuing,
Oh, roll towards us now thy wheel again!

Opening at once her girdle, she appears,
The lovely Dawn, the ruler of the stalls.
She, light-producing, wonder-working, noble,
Up mounted from the coast of earth and heaven.

Up, up, and bring to meet the Dawn, the goddess,
Bright beaming now, your humble song of praise.
To heaven climbed up her ray, the sweet dew bearing;
Joying to shine, the airy space it filled.

With beams of heaven the Pure One was awakened;
The Rich One's ray mounted through both the worlds.
To Ushas goest thou, Agni, with a prayer
For goodly wealth, when she bright shining comes.

Unspeakably beautiful as poems are all these dawn
hymns, but not, like those addressed to the greater gods,
full of awe and worship. The singer has passed out of
that region, when he compares Ushas to a dancer, and tells
of her unbaring her bosom like the udder of the cow.
Nothing is there either, we observe, in the above hymn
of a strongly moral cast—no more mention of righteous-
ness and the guardians of the law. The blessings which
daylight brings are not of this sort. Daylight is the all-
dispenser, because, in making seen what was before hid,
she seems to give it to us once again. But she is not in
any other sense the creator or governor of the world.

Next after Ushas comes the sun god, Surya, himself.

Arise before us, Surya, again;
As sounds our song, come with thy coursers swift.[1]

[1] vii. 62, 2.

He comes for all men alike—the 'just and the unjust,' as
the Bible has it—dragging his wheel;[1] the eye of Mitra
and Varuna; he who rolls up the darkness like a garment:
he throws off his garment, his dark cloak.[2] 'Thou risest for
the race of gods; thou risest for the human race, risest for
all, thy light to show.'[3] The stars steal away like thieves
before the all-seeing god of day. He, like Agni and Mitra,
looks friendly down upon the world and the ways of men;
he sends the rays, his messengers, to earth. He is a
warrior, and comes waving his banner;[4] he is a charioteer,
and drives seven mares—the barits, or the charites of
Greek mythology. Sometimes his flight is winged by the
wind;[5] and sometimes he, with the Wind (Vayu) and with
Agni, forms another trilogy in the Vedic pantheon.

> From heaven shall Savitar protect us,
> And from the air the Wind,
> And Agni from the earth.
>
> O Savitar, thy fiery ray
> Is dearer than a hundred gifts.
> Protect us from the lightning crash.
>
> God Savitar, thy bright glance send;
> And oh, thou Wind, do thou too send;
> And, Forger,[6] bright beams forge for us.[7]

But that the sun god cannot, more than Agni, escape
the consequences of his actual nature, and therefore cannot conform to the law of mortals, we also see. Agni
devours his father and mother. Surya is the child of the
Dawn; and yet he pursues her as a lover, and at the last,
just before the day ends, he weds her. This marriage
can only take place at the last hour of the day; it is the
signal of the sun's own death. Here is the dark story of
crime which wrought the doom of Thebes: it is the

---

[1] vii. 63.
[2] iv. 13, 4, where the sun is addressed under the name of Savitar.
[3] i. 50, 5.   [4] iv. 13, 2.   [5] x. 170.
[6] Agni as Tvashtar, the forger.   [7] x. 158.

marriage of Œdipus and Iocaste. Here it is shadowed forth in the pure poetry of natural mythology; afterwards it was crystallised into a legend.

We might stay for ever at this sunrise, unravelling the myths which cling about this most human of the gods. But time will not stay; the day presses onwards, and each stage brings with it some new event. We saw, in the language of a Vedic poet,

> The watcher, him who never tires,
> Who wanders up and down upon his path,
> Veiling himself in things alike and unlike,
> Who goeth here and there about the world.

And now we must let him pass on his way and note what follows.

The breezes, which were gentle in the morning, and for that reason were feigned to be the sons of Prishni, the dew,[1] strengthen as the day grows older; they overcloud the sky, and the storm approaches. This is the coming of Indra in his might. The calm of morning is forgotten; the battle of midday begins. Midday is the time of labour and duty, and to the fiercer Aryas the word duty meant war. It is for this great contest that Indra has long been arming himself. The hundred citadels of Sambaras, where the giant has hid the rains which were meant to water the earth, are now seen towering in the sky, peak above peak, battlement over battlement. Against these Indra sallies forth to fight, but he does not go alone. The sons of Prishni, who are the winds or the storms, have been preparing themselves likewise. At first they were things of nought; now they are mighty heroes armed with the flash and the thunder. 'They spring up of their own strength; they are dight in golden armour; their spears send forth sparks of fire.'[2] These

---

[1] Prokris.   [2] ii. 34; vi. 66, &c.

are the 'unapproachable host' of Maruts,[1] who wander through the paths of air in their swift cars; sometimes they come so near the earth that men hear the crack of their driving whips.[2]

Where is the fair	assemblage of heroes,
The sons of Rudra,[3]	with their bright horses ?
For of their birth	knoweth no man other,
Only themselves	their wondrous [4] descent.

The light they flash	upon one another;
The eagles fought,	the winds were raging;
But this secret	knoweth the wise man,
Once that Prishni	her udder gave them. [5]

Our race of heroes,	through the Maruts be it
Ever victorious	in reaping of men.
On their way they hasten,	in brightness the brightest,
Equal in beauty,	unequalled in might.[6]

One hymn of the Rig Veda seems to be adapted to this storm hour of the day, and to describe the very moment when Indra comes forth to battle, and there is joined by his comrades. This hymn has been translated by Prof. Max Müller, and of his translation I avail myself.[7]

First speaks the sacrificing priest :—

With what splendour are the Maruts all equally endowed, they who are of the same age and dwell in the same house! With what thoughts! From whence are they come?

[1] The Maruts are probably connected etymologically with Mars (cf. Z. f. v. Sp. v. 387, &c.; xvi. 162).   [2] v. 63, 5.
[3] Rudra is also a storm god. His name means the *flash*; that of the Maruts the *storm*.   [4] Unique.
[5] Prishni being here and in many other places imaged as a cow.
[6] vii. 56. This poem has quite an Eddaic ring; it is curious, therefore, to find that the truest counterparts of the Vedic Maruts are to be sought in the Valkyriur of the North (see Ch. VII.) The hymns addressed to the Maruts, which occur in the first book of the Rig Veda, have been completely and admirably translated by Professor Max Müller. I forbear, then, from giving more than one example of these, beautiful as they are, and content myself with referring the reader to Professor Müller's translation.
[7] The hymn is from R. V. i. 165.

THE MARUTS SPEAK.

From whence, O Indra, dost thou come alone, thou who art mighty? O lord of men, what has thus happened unto thee? Thou greetest (us) when thou comest together with (us) the bright (Maruts). Tell us, then, thou with thy bay horses, what thou hast against us.

INDRA SPEAKS.

The sacred songs are mine, (mine are) the prayers; sweet are the libations! My strength rises; my thunderbolt is hurled forth. They call for me; the prayers yearn for me. Here are my horses; they carry me towards them.

THE MARUTS.

Therefore in company with our strong friends, having adorned our bodies, we now harness our fallow deer with all our might; for, Indra, according to thy custom, thou hast been with us.

INDRA.

Where, O Maruts, was that custom of yours, that you should join me, who am alone in the killing of Ahi? I, indeed, am terrible, strong, powerful. I escaped from the blows of every enemy.

THE MARUTS.

Thou hast achieved much with us as companions. With the same valour, O hero, let us achieve, then, many things! O thou most powerful! O Indra! whatever we, O Maruts, wish with our heart.

INDRA.

I slew Vritra, O Maruts, with (Indra's) might, having grown strong through mine own vigour; I, who hold the thunderbolt in my arms, I have made these all-brilliant waters to flow freely for man.

THE MARUTS.

Nothing, O powerful lord, is strong before thee; no one is known among the gods like unto thee. No one who is now born will come near, no one who has been born. Do what has to be done, thou who hast grown so strong.

Indra.

Almighty power be mine alone, whatever I may do, daring
in my heart; for I indeed, O Maruts, am known as terrible; of
all that I threw down I, Indra, am the lord.

O Maruts, now your praise has pleased me, the glorious
hymn which ye have made for me, ye men! for me, for Indra,
for the powerful hero, as friends for a friend, for your own sake
and by your own efforts.

Truly, there they are, shining towards me, assuming blameless glory, assuming vigour.   O Maruts, wherever I have looked
for you, you have appeared to me in bright splendour. Appear to
me also now.

The Sacrificer speaks, and so ends.

Who has magnified you here, O Maruts? Come hither,
O friends! towards your friends.   Ye brilliant Maruts, cherish
these prayers, and be mindful of these my rites. . . . .

We see from this that the Maruts have no very distinct existence or purpose alone; and, indeed, their
appearing always in the plural number would be enough
to show us that they are regarded rather as heroes than
as gods. It is very possible they were often confounded
with the dead ancestors.[1] Wherefore their coming to the
fight must be taken as prototypical of the coming of the
Greek heroes to the great fields of battle—to Marathon,
for example, and to Platæa. It is interesting to see in
the Greek legends that the Dioscuri are often associated
with the heroes and dead ancestors; for the Dioscuri are
the same with the Asvin, and therefore, as the winds of
morning and evening, are the proper companions for the
storm gods. The Maruts are all equal: none is before or
after another; none is greater or less than another; 'of
the same age, dwelling in the same house, endowed with
equal splendour.'[2] Their proper sphere is the midday;
sometimes, though, they come awakening the night. They
slay the elephant, the buffalo, the lion; they are unerring
marksmen; they draw milk from heaven's udder; they

---

[1] Gubernatis, *Letture*, &c., p. 150.   [2] i. 165.

milk the thunder cloud.[1] 'To whom go ye, ye shakers, and by what art, along these airy paths? Strong must your weapons be, and mighty ye yourselves, not like the might of wretched mortals.'[2]

And so they play their part. The last scene shifts to day's ending, when the sun god is again prayed to ere he leaves the earth, for he is going to that other world, his nightly home, where he will meet the dead fathers (pitris) of the tribe. Savitar is especially the evening sun. He unyokes the steeds who have borne him along his tedious path; he calls the wanderer to rest from his journey, the housewife from her web, and all men from their labour; he watches all things ever dim, and dimmer and a glory done. And now, in a more subdued note, the singer pays his final vows to this god, and commits himself and all that he holds dear into his care.

> Savitar, the god, arose, in power arose,
> His quick deeds and his journey to renew.
> He 'tis who to all gods dispenses treasure,
> And blesses those who call him to the feast.
>
> The god stands up, and stretches forth his arm,
> Raises his hand, and all obedient wait;
> For all the waters to his service bend,
> And the winds even on his path are stilled.
>
> Now he unyokes the horses who have borne him;
> The wanderer from his travel now he frees;
> The Serpent-slayer's[3] fury now is stayed;
> At Savitar's command come night and peace.
>
> And now rolls up the spinning wife her web;
> The labourer in the field his labour leaves;
>
> . . . .
>
> And to the household folk beneath the roof
> The household fire imparts their share of light.
>
> . . . .

[1] i. 64, 8. [2] R. V. i. 39.
[3] Indra's? I have, to avoid monotony, taken some slight liberties with the voices of the verbs in this poem.

He who to work went forth is now returned;
The longing of all wanderers turns toward home;
Leaving his toil, goes each man to his house:
The universal mover orders so.

In the water settedst thou the water's heir,[1]
On the firm earth badst the wild beast to roam,
And in the wood the fowl. Nothing, O god,
Great Savitar, thy will dares violate.

And, as he can, each fish in the womb of water
(Who restless flits about) seeks now his rest;
The bird[2] makes for his nest, cattle for their stall:
To their own home all beasts the sun god sends.

'Tis he whose ordinance none dare slight; not Indra,
Rudra, Varuṇa, Mitra, Aryaman,
Nor evil spirits even.   Savitar,
On him, on him, with humble heart I call.

[1] The fish.   [2] *Lit.* 'the egg's son.'

CHAPTER IV

ZEUS, APOLLO, ATHÊNÊ.

Αἲ γὰρ, Ζεῦ τε πάτερ καὶ ᾽Αθηναίη καὶ ῎Απολλον.

WOULD that it were more easy to draw out of the bright and varied fabric of Greek religious thought those threads which form the main substance of the tissue; those deep and essential beliefs over which the rest of the religion and mythology of Hellas is but a woven pattern. But for many reasons this is very hard to do. First, because Gieece or Hellas can scarcely be looked upon as the country of a single people, while it holds such a variety of national sentiment, and shows as many instances of national discord as of unity. And secondly, because the shifting and subtle fancy of the people afforded a very unstable foundation for the building up of any creed; so that what was believed among them one day might very likely be laughed at the next. Just by reason of this same subtlety and swiftness of thought, Greek religion, at the time of our first contact with it, has already passed through its earlier stages, and polytheism is seen no longer in a condition of growth, but of decay. Homer and the writers of the Homeric cycle alone show in the formation of their mythology anything approaching to a direct contact with nature. They crystallise belief, and the later poets draw from them; yet even with Homer the age of creation has ceased, the age of criticism and scepticism has begun. At any rate the gods have strayed far away from the region to which by nature they belong. They have become anthropomorphised: imagination is occupied in following their lives and deeds as it would the

lives of mortals. Fancy and the dramatic and creative
faculties have as much to do with them as has genuine belief; there is no longer a warranty that the character and
actions of these gods will follow the simple lines of fact.

Once, when a god was truly a nature god, and when
the phenomena of nature were all truly divine, the lightning and the hail, the frost and the dew, the wind and all
the waves of the sea, were alike strange and mystic; and
the alternations of these things were chronicled with
reverent awe. It was inconceivable then that man should
set himself to *invent* stories of their doings, because all
invention must fall infinitely short of the wonder of truth.
In Homer we discover that much of this feeling has
already died away. The thunderer is still the thunderer,
but he is also a quarrelsome husband, a tyrannous and
capricious king. Hêra, his feminine counterpart, is queen
of heaven; but she is also the very type of a shrewish
wife. It follows that in spite—nay, in part because—of the
wondrous richness and variety of Greek religious myths,
it is not in these that the character of nature worship can
be most effectually studied; wherefore, perhaps, the constant battle which rages round the interpretation of Greek
mythology. The Teutonic myths are simpler and far more
meagre; but they show us, more clearly than the Greek
do, the history of their growth. The Vedic hymns, though
they tell us no tales, are more deeply imbued than the
Iliad and the Odyssey are with a conviction of the reality
of all they describe, and the gods themselves are nearer to
nature. Let it be, then, with an eye often directed to
these neighbour systems—to the Teutonic and Celtic
beliefs upon the one side, and upon the other to those dis-
cernible in the Vedas—that the student set himself to
the task of unravelling the intricacies of Greek mythology.

The comparative method we require is something
much deeper than the comparison of mere words and
phrases. The more we look into the history of Aryan
creeds, the more are we struck by the recurrence in them

of certain fixed sentiments or forms of belief, which express themselves through different personalities in the different systems. And we soon come to see that thought has in these cases been governed by laws scarcely less rigid than those which have determined it in the formation of language. It is probable too that, as in the case of language so in the case of mythology, a great number of the laws of development are confined to the special race with which we are dealing, and have been different among Semitic people, different again among Mongols or Negroes.

Unless we can fathom the deeper sources of religious thought in Hellas, we can never understand her mythology, which is but a stream flowing from those deep fountains; we must first find out where lay the real belief—that is to say, the germ of genuine emotion—then we shall be able to understand of what nature was the *Aberglaube* which imagination and poetry fostered from that seed. Now, so far as the later and historic Greece is concerned, I have no doubt that the invocation quoted a moment ago—

Would Father Zeus, and Athenê, and Apollo—

occurring so frequently in Homer,[1] really gives an answer to our first enquiry, and that the trilogy or trinity, thus specially united, represents the highest attainment of Hellas in the idealism of belief. And if we imagine a Greek, in the solitude of his chamber, or in the more moving solitude of woods and meadows, stirred with some sudden strong religious impulse, we may guess that the image of one of these three greater divinities, the image of Zeus, of Apollo, or of Athenê, would be likely to rise before his mental sight. These three deities, therefore, are they who have in the end given the tone to Greek thought on religious matters, and to their natures those of the other divinities have insensibly been obliged

[1] *Il.* ii. 371; iv. 288; vii. 132; xvi. 97. *Od.* iv. 341; vii. 311; xviii. 235; xxiv. 376.

to conform themselves. And though we have special
divinities locally honoured, and in particular places held
to be supreme, as Hêra at Argos, Aphroditê in Cyprus,
Hermês in Arcadia, Dionysus in Thrace; such local worship must not be taken as evidence against the universal,
the pan-Hellenic character of the other. Because in the
Middle Ages at Tours St. Martin was more often invoked
than Christ or the Father, and at Cologne the Three Kings,
St. Remigius at Rheims, St. Ambrose at Milan—at each
place, that is to say, its special patron saint—it does not
argue that any of those who practised these special forms
of worship supposed that in the governance of the world
at large the saints were more powerful than the Trinity.
No more must we suppose that, though the rivalry of the
Greek cities led to the upholding of each city's patron in
opposition to some other god, the Greeks had not likewise their points of religious unity, or that there were no
personalities specially selected for contemplation in that
universal sense, who must of necessity have been the chief
gods of Hellas.

  In the Greek images of the gods there is often so little
individuality that, if we took away some external attributes
or symbols which accompany the figures, and which are
no more than a kind of labels to them, we might be in
danger of confounding one divinity with another; of mis-
taking Athênê for Hêra, Hermês for Apollo, Poseidôn or
Hadês for Zeus. In the case of the Panathenaic Frieze,
for instance, that sculptured procession which once
adorned the second wall of the Parthenon, we do really
find ourselves in such a dilemma. In the centre of the
composition is a group of persons, whom, by their size,
above the mortal stature, we know to be intended for gods,
but for what particular ones among the Olympians it is
still a matter of dispute. In the case of one or two we
are able to fall back upon the helping symbol—as the
shoes and petasos of Hermês; the ægis of Athênê; the
wings of Erôs—but we shall never get beyond a probable

conjecture for the greater number. The difficulty does not arise solely nor even chiefly from the disfigurement of the faces in this case. Some of them, at all events, are well preserved; yet we cannot say that these are distinguishable by the countenance alone. Poseidôn, for all the character which he displays, might as well be Zeus.[1]

I do not say that in general the antiquarian is left quite at a loss. His skill is to interpret small signs which would be unnoticed by common observers; to read, as it were, the mind of the artist, and not look from the position of those for whose sake the artist wrought. But the existence of such means of discrimination does not affect the general truth of the proposition, that to the ordinary glance, to anyone not initiated into the secrets of the worker, there would be such a class likeness among certain orders of the divine beings that no single individuality would seem to step out from among them. And if we take this art to reflect—as art always seems to reflect the best—the popular religion of the day, we must confess that no very strong individuality would have been felt to attach to any one among the gods.

But art itself comes at a late epoch in the history of Greece, and no condition of thought which existed then is proof of like thoughts in the heroic age, centuries before, when as yet Greek sculpture was scarcely born. The religion which finds such an expression as in the sculpture of the days of Pheidias is very different from the creed of primitive times. Polytheism has come near to its latter days when the gods have grown so much alike, and when all seem to express the same ideal. So far as the Greek gods are now not men, so far as they contain some divine nature in them, this nature is the same for all. And the god-like *idea*, or, to put it more in the

---

[1] See *Guide to the Elgin Room, British Museum*, by C. T. Newton, Michaelis' *Parthenon*, and Flasch's *Zum Parthenon*. Some of the points in dispute are very curious; that, for example, between the maiden Artemis and the sad matron Dêmêtêr as the bearer of the torch.

language of philosophy, the abstract conception of a god, will soon attach specially to some particular member of the pantheon, who, like the later Zeus of the Greeks, will thus become *the* god *par excellence*, ὁ θεός ; then the monotheistic goal will have been reached. For when in character the gods have become much the same, the difference between one and another of them must depend altogether on external surroundings. Some may have a greater majesty in the eyes of their worshippers, and receive more reverence; but it is because their rule is wider, not because they are in themselves different from their brothers. But for the limit of their various domains all the gods would be alike ; they are many kings, whose empires are not of the same extent, yet still all kings. And the most powerful anon becomes in heaven; as he would become on earth, an over-king to all the others, the *bretwalda*, as it were, of the Olympian realm, until at last he brings the rest under him, and reigns alone. He is the single *god* ; the other divine powers sink to positions like those which occupy the saints of the mediæval calendar.

Amid this general uniformity in the representation of the Greek divinities there is nevertheless one point of separation. The goddesses are all alike and all young ; the matron cannot be distinguished from the maid : but among the gods there is the difference between the bearded and the beardless one, the mature god and the youthful god—in a word, between Zeus and Apollo. And it is the Zeus and Apollo images that convert to a likeness to themselves those of the other gods. That fair young face which we see in its dawn in archaic sculpture, and follow downwards, as it grows continually in beauty and dignity, is most often the face of an Apollo. Zeus is just as much the ideal of the grave, mature ruler, the divine counsellor and just judge, the γέρων of the heavenly assembly.[1] ·

[1] Not. of course, precisely the Spartan γέρων, member of the γερουσία, who must be sixty years of age. Zeus we might imagine from thirty-five to forty. He would then be five to ten years above the lowest limit for the Athenian βουλή.

made up of two sections—those who went round by the
Hellespont and those who came down to the coast of Asia
Minor. It was these last who were known to the Semitic
nationalities, certainly to the Phœnicians, perhaps to the
Canaanites and Israelites; it was these who were designated
by the name Javan. The word Javan we may translate into
Ionian. Wherefore, in calling these Asiatic Greeks (as a
body) Ionians, I would not be thought to make a nicer
distinction than their neighbours the Phœnicians made.
It is true that the word was not understood in so wide
a significance by the Greeks themselves, at least not by
those of historic times. In these historic days we find
the Asiatic coast divided among three Greek nationalities,
only one of whom retained the ancient name of Ionians.
The others called themselves Dorians and Æolians, and
all three, even the Ionians, imagined themselves to have
been planted there not by migrations from anterior Asia,
but by colonisation from the opposite coast of European
Greece. The Dorians had been planted in this way.
Many even of the Ionians may have been brought, by a
backward wave of migration, from the West to the East.
But the name of the Ionians was far anterior to these
recorded migrations: so, too, was the first settlement of
Greeks on the coast of Asia Minor.

The Yavanas, or Ionians of Asia Minor, mingled with
the Oriental nations whom they found there, some of
whom had attained no small degree of civilisation. And
the Ionians doubtless acquired many of their arts. Especially from the Phœnicians, the seafarers of those days,
do they seem to have learnt the art of navigation, which
was known only in an elementary form to the older
Aryans. There are, common to the Indo-European family
of languages, words for *oar* and *rudder*, but none for *sail*;
and we may conclude from this that sea voyages were
unattempted by the Aryas of the prime, or by the
Yavanas when they formed one nation. Those of the
Græco-Italicans who crossed the Hellespont could well

have accomplished that feat with only such boats as had plied upon broad rivers. But the Greeks of the Asiatic coast soon learned a higher art of navigation. Presently a great part of the people passed on, and settled upon the countless islands of the Ægæan and upon the eastern coast of European Greece. One of the Greek words for *sea* is quite peculiar to that language—not shared, I mean, by other Indo-European ones—and is likewise peculiarly significant. It is πόντος, which means literally a path.[1] Can we doubt that the habit of looking upon the sea as a 'path,' a way, was first opened to the minds of the Greeks when they from their Phœnician neighbours had learned to make the water their road to new lands?

In the formation of the Greek nation, then, there were two elements. The earlier and ruder people, who travelled by the Hellespont, were the first to set foot on the mainland of Europe; the other body came by immigration from the coast of Asia Minor, and brought some civilisation with them, and all the elements of a higher life.

Of course this was not accomplished in a day: the passage into Greece of the men from the Asiatic coast must have been especially slow, for they had nothing to tempt them to leave the rich land in which they were. The settlers on the other side of the Ægæan could have been no more than the overflow of their population. Each successive wave which came overlapping the previous one was more deeply imbued with the nascent

---

[1] Connected with the Skr. *pantha, patha* and our *path.* It may be that there is a Teutonic name for *sea* from the same root, viz. the A.S. *faïthi* (Pictet, *o. c.* i. 113). No nautical terms were originally common to the Greek and Italian languages, save those that are also common to the Indo-European family. This shows that the Greeks discovered the art of sea navigation after they had been separated from the Italian stock.

In reference to the effect of movement upon the development of belief, the decay of fetichism, &c., it is worth noticing that the very active nature of the whole Greek race is exemplified by the number of *verbal roots* in the Greek language.

The Latin *pontus* is, I believe, borrowed direct from πόντος. *Pons* is related to *pantha.*

civilisation of the Asiatic Greeks, more nearly Hellenic in character as compared with the character of those who had wandered far round by the Hellespont. These last formed the Pelasgic element[1] in Greek society.

The migrators from the Asiatic coast found people of more or less Semitic extraction settled in many of the islands, and in those parts of the eastern shore of European Greece which they first occupied. It is hardly to be supposed that the other travellers (whom we have called Pelasgians), after they had gone round by the Hellespont, found the lands into which they debouched quite bare of inhabitants. But of these earlier people we know little or nothing. They were probably a peaceful pastoral race. Their very existence had been forgotten by the men who ousted them from their homes; for, in historic days, the Greeks of Europe generally looked upon themselves as autochthones—that is to say, sprung from the earth on which they dwelt.

The later travellers from Asia, who had grown to a more complete self-consciousness and to a stronger sense of nationality than their Pelasgic brethren could feel, came later than the others had done to the European coast. When they did come, they found in European Greece a race somewhat like to themselves in language and character, but much ruder in manners, with no memory of the time when they all together left their Aryan home, but, on the contrary, deeming themselves children of the soil and firmly settled there. These people had developed a certain civilisation, marked by solid stone architecture—unless this were, as I rather suppose, the work of a still earlier race, and only adopted by the Greeks—and they had some cities. The name, Pelasgians, which they received from the new comers

---

[1] Pelasgic, according to a recent derivation, which seems to me sound, is from the root of the Skr. parasja (paras *far* ja *go*), and means not, as was by the Greeks supposed, 'the old,' but 'the far wanderers.' See paper by R. Pischl, *Zeitschrift für vergleichende Sprachforschung*, vol. xx.

from Asia, whatever its original meaning, came in time
to distinguish the older and ruder civilisation, which had
first appeared in Greece, from the newer or truly Hellenic
civilisation, which came from Asia. The Hellenic culture
superseded the Pelasgic culture ; and, but to a less extent,
Hellenic belief superseded Pelasgic belief.

It is needful to take into account these details of the
prehistoric existence of the Greek people, so far as they
can be reasonably conjectured ; because the character of
their existence, and the scenes among which that life has
been passed, must go far to determine the people's future
creed. When the proto-Greeks entered upon their life of
change and migration they were still in the main a nation
of shepherds. They had lived in a land of hill and valley
and rushing mountain stream, and after their wanderings
had begun their lot still lay amid scenes not dissimilar.
They travelled first to the hilly Caucasus, and thence to
the central table-land of Asia Minor, a region compounded
of barren heights and more fruitful lower lands ; and
thence they passed (many of them) into Thrace and
Macedon and Epirus. Here, even in the cultured and
historic ages of Greece, the inhabitants remained amid
wild scenes a rude bucolic race. Those who settled on
the western coasts of Greece proper, though now in
sunnier regions, were, in days near to historic times, confined to the most barren and stormiest parts of them ; for
the mild eastern coasts had fallen into the hands of the
Ionian peoples.[1]

The western people it was who first gained from their
Italian neighbours the name of Græci (Γραικοί),[2] which

---

[1] The character of Macedon and Thrace—the region beyond Mount
Olympus—is admirably described in the beginning of the seventh book of
Curtius' *Griechische Geschichte*. The distinction which I have drawn
between the two orders of civilisation, the Pelasgic and the Ionian (or
Hellenic), is geographically between the kingdom of the Ægean, which
included the islands and both coasts of that sea, and the regions to the
north and west.

[2] Connected with the Gaelic word *creach*, a hill. This name forms a

of Ithaca might serve for all this part of Greece. It was 'rough, not fit for use of horses, yet not too barren.' Now, as the older Greeks were by degrees pushed backwards and backwards from the south and east by the more enterprising Ionians, and as the Ionians must in historic, or nearly historic, times have departed much more than the old Greek people had done from their primitive faith, it is in the north and west of Greece that we must look for the traces of the earliest creed of the Greek race.

During their days of wandering the gods of the Greeks were doubtless chiefly those heavenly bodies who travelled with them as they travelled, and some elemental substances —one of the chief among these fire—which they had learned to worship while they were in Bactriana ; their fetich-worshipping instincts remaining, from necessity of travel,[1] in a sort of abeyance, until in a new settlement fresh objects of reverence should be found to take the place of the others. The protecting Heaven, and next to the Heaven the Sun, who shed his brightness on their path, and when he rose in the morning ran before them on the road they were to take, were their ever-present gods. The first of these we *know* they worshipped, him whom, under the name of Dyâus, they had known in their cradle home. This Dyâus-Zeus remained the chief god of all.

One may fancy that the Germans and the Slavs, during their migratory period, underwent an actual degeneracy

natural contrast to Ἕλληνες, the inhabitants of low-lying and *marshy* lands ; just as the old Greeks of Greece proper form a contrast to the Ionians, who imparted their civilisation to the Hellenes of later date. For when the marsh is drained it becomes fruitful, like the rich *Argos*.

Compare the description of Ithaca, given above, or of 'black Epirus' (*Od.* xiv. 97), with the description of hollow Lacedæmon, 'where, in the wide plain, is wealth of lotus and cypress and rye, and broad fields of wheat' (*Od.* iv. 601-608 ; cf. also *Od.* xiii. 414, ' Lacedæmon of broad lands').

[1] See Chapters II. and III.

in culture. Their condition, when they first emerge into
the light of history, seems more barbarous, nearer to the
condition of a nomadic and hunting people, than the
state of their Aryan forefathers in their settled home.
Whether, in their time of want and difficulty and struggle,
the Greeks likewise passed through a period of degeneracy
we cannot be sure. They could not, at any rate, have
advanced much during their wanderings, for they were
still a savage people when they obtained a lasting settlement in Greece. Their gods, too, were doubtless of a
rude and savage kind. Dyâus underwent the same change
of character which, in the last chapter, we followed
out in the growth of Indra worship, when we saw the
heaven god giving place to a more human and active god
of storms. We see that this happened by noting what
character belongs to Zeus and Jupiter, when they appear
in the creeds of Greece and Rome. The nature in which
Zeus and Jupiter most agree must have been the character
of the Dyâus-Zeus of the proto-Greeks and proto-Romans.
These gods are essentially the pictures of the stormy sky.
They are both alike the wielders of the thunderbolt, and
guardians of the wind and rain. Even in Homer the Ionian
Zeus, though he has grown to be much more than merely
this, is essentially a storm god. We have seen how the
very imagery which described his nod was drawn from the
natural imagery of the cloudy sky ; and it is needless to
recall all the passages wherein Zeus shows in this character. The Greeks, for all the beauty of their sky and
air, had many opportunities for watching the phenomena
of storms ; for their land is varied in its character, subject
to sudden atmospheric changes, nursed upon the bosoms
of the two seas upon which it looks. Nor, I think, is
anything more noticeable in Homer than the number and
the beauty of the similes which he has gathered from such
watching.

Over all such doings in the air Zeus has as close and
special a control as Poseidôn over the waves. Zeus is not

the land was far more wild and storm-bound, and there the
special god of that race, the Pelasgic Zeus, assumed a still
gloomier aspect. Here it was that the wind, driving in
from the Mediterranean, rolled up great masses of cloud
which broke upon the high inland ridges, such as Ithome
and Lykæon,[4] so that these mountains, visible cloud-
collectors as they were, became the very embodiments of
the god. It is in these regions that we find the deepest
traces of the worship of the Pelasgic Zeus, the god of
rugged mountains and of gloomy forests. On coins of

---

[1] νεφεληγερέτα : consider the force of such an address as κύδιστε
μέγιστε, κελαινεφὲς, αἰθέρι ναίων.

[2] *Il.* vii. 4 ; xii. 252 ; xi. 27 ; xii. 279, where Zeus sends the snow.

[3] *Il.* v. 520_5.

[4] The epithet of Zeus, Ζεὺς λυκαῖος (Paus. i. 38, 5 ; viii. 2 ; 1 Callim. *H.
in Jov.* 4), is probably a reminiscence of the ancient meaning of his name,
dyâus, the shining. The title is also applied to Apollo. Nevertheless
there is evidence that Zeus was specially worshipped on Mount Lykæon.
May not, then, the name of this mountain have been taken from the name
of dyâus, of which lykæús is a simple translation ? If this be so, it suggests
an example of a relapse into fetichism. The mountain was first masculine,
ὁ Λυκαῖος : later neuter, τὸ Λυκαῖον. Other epithets of Zeus show him to
have been specially worshipped on mountain-tops, e.g. ἄκριος, κορυφαῖος.   ·

Ithome and of Megalopolis—this last place was under the
shadow of Mount Lykæon, the highest peak in the Peloponnese—we see the Pelasgic Zeus seated upon a rock;
whereby we learn where his dwelling was.   There is
a similar representation of the Olympian Zeus upon the
coins of Elis; and this indicates that here even the Olympian Zeus kept the character of his Pelasgian forerunner.
The Zeus of Dôdôna was worshipped in much the same
fashion on Mount Dicte, in Crete.   Zeus, like Odhinn, the
wind god of the Teutons, loved to haunt the darkest and
most inaccessible groves.   One of these was at Elis;
another, more awful still, at Dôdôna.   The oak, which
was Odhinn's tree, was also Zeus's.[1]   The wind which
whispered through the oaks of Dôdôna brought the oracle
of the god.   He is commonly portrayed with a crown of
oak leaves.

In all this we see the mingling of an older fetichism
with a new creed.   The mountain—Lykæon or Ithome—
preserved its former godhead when it was worshipped as
the very Zeus.   It was not only the grove of Dôdôna that
was holy, but a certain evergreen oak in it was peculiarly
so.   This oak no doubt was confounded in popular imagination with the deity.

It is not to be supposed that either the European
Greeks or the Asiatic Greeks, either the Pelasgians or the
Ionians, were uninfluenced by the creeds with which they
came in contact.   If the Pelasgians met with men in
quite a primitive state of fetich worship, this would tend
to stir in them reactionary leanings towards the primitive
religion which they had left behind them in Bactria, and
once more local gods would spring up, local mountains and
streams would be worshipped; indeed, we have already

---

[1] Especially the edible oak (φηγός).   From this Zeus received the
epithet φηγωναῖος, which he sometimes bore.   See Zenodotus *apud* Steph.
Byzant., *Frag. de Dodona.*   Jupiter had the name Jupiter *fagutalis* (Varro,
De Lingua Lat. iv. 32, 1), which may have belonged to him before the
fagus changed from an oak into a beech.

seen such things long continued to be worshipped in
Greece. Gradually, no doubt, there came to be a separation between the creeds of the more active and intelligent,
those who were truer to their own nationality and to their
gods, and those who sank down in the social scale and
mixed with the earlier natives of the land. The peasantry,
who had in their veins the blood of this older stock, came
to have a separate code of belief, connected with the cult
of Pan and of the Arcadian Hermês, and of many a local
satyr and nymph, and this creed, if it was not hostile to
the worship of Zeus and Apollo and the other Olympians,
at any rate passed it by without much attention.

Often we find the two religions existing side by side,
and at peace; but this peace could hardly have been
gained save through previous war. In such a case, when
the gods of the new comers put to flight the established fetich gods of the land to which they came, it
might seem to the eye of history like some great combat
between the visible things of nature, the Titanic mountains and trees, and the subtler, unhandled, but greater
celestial powers. That memorable *gigantomachia*, or war
between the gods and Titans, does in truth lie at the
threshold of all advances in culture; only by breaking up
the peaceful, settled life of the prime do men begin to
advance in civilisation. We cannot wonder if between
such mighty forces the battle was grievous; so that, as
Hesiod tells us, the tramp of the contending armies shook
the earth, and echoed far below to the depths of shadowy
Tartarus.[1]

Seen by peasant eyes, the same combat and the in-
coming of Zeus and his army were the inroad of a fierce
new power into the woods and valleys of the land. In
such eyes, the age before Zeus was a golden time; those
days were days of peace and plenty, and the memory of
them was cherished at rustic firesides. The husbandmen

---

[1] *Theog.* 664.

believed in them, and called them the Saturnian age, the age of gold, to which had succeeded an age of bronze, i.e. of war;[1] after which had followed a still worse age, the age of iron, and of slavery, with its iron chains. It is Hesiod, who sympathised at heart with the peasant state, and had no love at all for war or adventure, who has given us this tradition, a peasant's legend of the three ages of the world.

From whatever side we view the contest, the result was the same—Kronos, who represented the earlier time,[2] and with him all the Titan brood, had to flee far away to the extreme borders of earth, where stands Atlas, the Titan's son, and keeps the gates of the outer world, and where Day and Night, treading upon each other's heels, alternate pass the brazen threshold; and beyond Sleep and his brother Death, the sons of murky Night, have their home; there must the giant race abide.[3] There sits Iapetus, the father of Atlas and of Prometheus, and with him Kronos, joying neither in the splendour of Helios Hyperion nor in the breath of winds, for deep Tartarus is all around.[4] Zeus it was who dispossessed these of their rule, and who took a dreadful vengeance upon one Titan, only because he had been too much the friend of the human race. Apollo contended with the shepherd Marsyas—type of the Arcadian life—and inflicted upon him a cruel punishment. These new comers are the gods of will, no longer the simpler divine things of nature.[5]

But as, when an invading nation has subdued another, the war of extermination is arrested by marriage, and the

---

[1] Weapons having been made of bronze in the epic age.

[2] Kronos was essentially a Pelasgic god, as the form of his name, Kronos for Chronos, shows. Pelasgic words take κ for χ, e.g. κρησνός for χρηστός. See Maury, *Relig. de la Grèce*, i. 263. Maury likens κρόνος to γέρων. It is possible the name may have been a name for Dyâus (or Ouranos), and not have arisen in the way Welcker supposes (see p. 119, note). In either case we may take the actual form of this divinity to have sprung up in Pelasgic days.

[3] Hesiod.   [4] *Iliad.*   [5] See p. 96.

wives of the conquerors, taken from out of the inferior race, preserve its blood ; so I suppose that there was some compromise effected between the new deities and the old, and that the compact was solemnised by the marriage of the god of heaven to the goddess of earth. The earth goddess, though her worship is allied to fetichism, is of a nature far more abstract than any mere fetich: In every creed she stands as the natural counterpart and partner of the heaven, representing the principle of production, as he does that of generation. Thus in the New Zealand tale of Tanemahuta, which was referred to in the second chapter, the great productive principles were called Rangi and Papa, the Earth and Heaven. The closeness of their embrace threatened to destroy all the children whom Papa had brought forth. In the Vedas by the side of Dyâus sits Prithivi, the Earth.

Each of the wives of Zeus, therefore, I imagine to have been at one time or another the goddess of the earth. These wives are many.

Ζεὺς δὲ θεῶν βασιλεὺς πρώτην ἄλοχον θέτο Μῆτιν.
δεύτερον ἠγάγετο λιπαρὴν Θέμιν. . . . .
τρεῖς δὲ οἱ Εὐρυνόμη χάριτας τέκε καλλιπαρῴους.
Αὐτὰρ ὁ Δήμετρος πολυφόρβης ἐς λέχος ἠλθεν.
Μημοσύνης δ' ἐξαῦτις ἐράσσατο καλλικόμοιο.
Λητὼ δ' Ἀπολλῶνα καὶ Ἄρτεμιν ἰοχέαιραν
γείνατ' ἄρ' αἰγιόχοιο Διὸς φιλότητι μιγεῖσα.
Λοισθοτάτην δ' Ἥρην θαλερὴν ποιήσατ' ἄκοιτιν.[1]

To Hesiod many of the persons here enumerated were embodiments of qualities—that is to say, of abstractions merely. Mêtis was Thought, Themis was Law. Almost all of them, however, were originally personifications of some part of nature, and the greatest number were earth goddesses. Themis was so, for she was a Bœotian earth goddess.[2] Eurynome is a counterpart of the 'wide' Prithivi. Dêmêtêr (γη-μήτηρ) is another representative of Prithivi-matar, mother Prithivi, mother earth. She,

---

[1] Hesiod. *Theog.* 886 sqq.   [2] Maury, *l. c.* i. 81.

perhaps, inherited most of the character of the old Aryan
goddess.   Hêra, too, was once the earth.

Not only the wives but the mother of Zeus also was an
embodiment of the earth.   She was Rhea, the wife of
Kronos.   As Kronos was, we have seen, probably only an
older form of Zeus, a middle term between the Zeus whom
we know and the Dyâus who was worshipped by the
Aryas, so Rhea may be an older form of Hêra.   Rhea was
originally goddess of the Phrygians,[1] and the Phrygians
represent the earliest form of that nationality which gave
birth in time to the Hellenic race.   As the Phrygians
gave birth to the Greeks, so did Rhea to Hêra.   The
former of these two names is unquestionably connected
with the Sanskrit root *ira*, earth, which in Irish becomes
ire, whence *Erin*, Ireland.[2]

Concerning the worship of the earth goddess it is not
my cue to speak in this place; for of this we shall have
something to say in the following chapter.   All that we
need do here is to take account of this form of worship,
as constituting an integral part of the religion of the
early Greeks.

But Hêra, whatever her origin, was in many ways
different in character from the other wives of Zeus.   And
that she was different shows that in her person the worship of the earth goddess had undergone a change.   It is
one of the signs of the change and the advance of a creed
when the celestial divinities come to displace the terrestrial
ones, or else to effect a change in the natures of the latter.
In this instance the heaven god has absorbed the individuality of his consort, and has given her instead of her old
character a nature modelled upon his own.   It is simply
as the Queen of Heaven that Hêra appears in the Iliad.

[1] Such at least is the opinion of Maury.   From Phrygia Rhea was
brought to Crete, where in the historical days she is first met with.

[2] One etymology proposed for Hêra is 'lady,' connected with the
Latin *herus*, the German *Herr*.   See Maury, *l. c.*   Welcker (*Gr. Götterleh.*
i. 362) adopts that from ἔρα, earth, the Sanskr. *ira*.   Herodotus tells us
that Hêra was a Pelasgic goddess (ii. 50).

In Norse mythology we have just another such example of the development of an earth goddess into the simple feminine of the supreme god. Frigg, the partner of Odhinn, and Freyja, the goddess of the earth, were originally one person;[1] but their individualities became separated in order that they might fulfil the requirements of a double nature. One, as the wife of Odhinn, was the counterpart of the heaven god; the other was not divorced from the functions which belonged to her own being. Hêra, then, changed her character from what it was in Pelasgic days; but still we must reckon Hêra as one of the divinities belonging to that early time. There is a Pelasgic Hêra as well as a Pelasgic Zeus.

Another god whose worship is also as antique, according to my theory, as that of Zeus, or Dêmêtêr, or Hêra, is Poseidôn.[2] Poseidôn I suppose to have been the first sea god of the Greek nationality. The people could not have arrived at the borders of Asia, they could not have crossed the Hellespont, nor have settled in their new homes in European Greece, without learning to worship the dark waste of water which hemmed them in on every side. Poseidôn was the first embodiment of this phenomenon; he it was whom the first mariners made their patron god. But afterwards Athênê—in a way which we shall presently trace out—became the goddess of sailors, and the newer generation of navigators worshipped her and neglected Poseidôn. Hence the rivalry between the two. Odysseus is the type of the newer generation, and Odysseus is persecuted by Poseidôn and saved by Athênê.[3]

There is in most creeds a god of earth as well as a goddess, with a certain difference between them. The god

[1] The name *Frigg* is not improbably connected etymologically with *Prithivi* (Grimm, *D. M.* i. 303).

[2] Kuhn believes Poseidôn to have been originally a god of heaven, and to have undergone the same change which passed over the Vedic Varuna (see *Zeitsch. für verg. Sp.* i. 455, &c.) This question does not concern the character of Poseidôn as the god of the Greeks.

[3] See below.

N

of earth represents the active powers of generation, the goddess the passive. The former is the god of the seed or of the power of the seed in the ground rather than the mere receptive power of earth. The receptive power of earth such deities as Prithivi or Dêmêtêr represented. The earth god of the Greeks was the god of the hidden treasures of generation and of growth (Ploutôn). Ploutôn came to be confounded with Hadês; but I doubt whether Hadês or Aidoneus are the proper names of this Pelasgic god. Rather I should suppose him to be represented by Zeus Chthonius, earth Zeus; a title equivalent to earth god.[1] Hadês was originally only the personification of the tomb; afterwards, however, he entered into the inheritance of the forgotten earth god and became Hadês Plûtôn. Another part of the belongings of this earth god were given over to one of a younger generation, to Dionysus.

It would seem, then—and this is quite natural—that the Pelasgic gods for the most part belong to the elder generation of the Olympians. They are Zeus, and Dêmêtêr, and Hêra, and Poseidôn, and Hadês. In addition to these it is impossible to believe but that the older Greeks had their sun god. The sun is too important a being to be left out of any system in which the celestial gods are worshipped at all. In no system does the sun appear as a parent god, but always in a relation of sonship to the sky, out of which he seems to spring. Therefore the sun god of the earlier time must have been one among the younger generation of the Olympians. He was not Apollo, who represents the later culture of the Hellenic race. Nor was he Helios. We must look out for some one among the second generation of the gods who could have been the sun god of this age. He must be one who afterwards fell somewhat into the background, because he had at last to give place to Apollo. Two gods, I think, represent this divinity

[1] Zeus being in this case a *general*, not a *proper* name (θεός). See Ch. I.

—Arês and Heraclês. The sun of western Greece was not that bright being who shone over the Ægæan and its islands. His character was adapted to that of the Pelasgic Zeus; he was the day star, shining red in the storm or battling with the clouds, rather than the same sun shining in pellucid air. The traces of this first sun worship—which was displaced by the *cultus* of Apollo—are to be sought first in the person of Arês the fighter, χάλκεος Ἄρης, brazen Arês, who ruled in warlike Macedon and Thrace; next in Heraclês the labourer, who was the god of the Peloponnese and of its peasants. There can be no question that in prehistoric times the worship of the first of these two was far more widely extended than we should suppose from reading Homer or the poets after Homer. Traces of Arês worship are to be found in the Zeus Areios, who was honoured at Elis, and in the name of the Areiopagus of Athens.[1] But of course the god's real home was farther north. He was the national deity of the Thracians;[2] his sons led to Troy the men of Aspledon and Orchomenus in Bœotia, and his daughter Harmonia was the wife of Cadmus.[3]

The Arês who appears in Homer has no longer a foundation in the phenomenal world. He has become little more than an abstraction, the spirit of the battle, to be placed by the side of such beings as Eris, strife, Phobos, fear, Deimos, terror, and the rest.

The adventures of Heraclês are precisely those most commonly ascribed to a sun god. Read side by side with those of the Teutonic Thorr[4] (Donar), they show how

[1] For the chief traces of the worship of Arês in historic days see Pausanias.

[2] Cf. especially Herod. v. 7, where we are told that Thrace was the principal seat of his worship.

[3] See Welcker, *Gr. Götterlehre*, i. 413–424, on Arês as a sun god. For some curious evidences of his worship in Macedon and Thrace, furnished by the coins of these districts, see *Num. Chron. for* 1880, p. 49, by Prof. P. Gardner.

[4] I think it is because they have not studied the Greek mythology side by side with the Norse, that most writers have spoken of Heraclês as almost

primitive must have been the worship of Heraclês and the myths which gathered round that worship. He perhaps differs little from some god known to the ancient Aryas. But when Apollo came and showed a higher ideal of the god of the sun, Heraclês' divinity suffered much abatement until he sank at last to be a demi-god, holding only by sufferance a place on Olympus.

These Pelasgians were half-savage men. The gods of tempest whom they honoured—the Zeus of the stormy heights and wind-grieved forests; the black Demetêr, fit images of the unsown earth; Rhea, worshipped in hollow caves; the red and angry sun; dark-haired Poseidôn, the god of tempestuous seas—these were well fitted to their needs of worship; they could never have satisfied the religious wants of Hellas. In the person of the Greeks, it has been well said, humanity becomes for the first time completely human; before, it was half bestial, like the satyrs of Arcadia or the centaurs of Thrace; its creed was unformed and unsightly like its gods, who were still represented by blocks of wood and stone.

But, as Greece grew to perfect manhood, the gods became softened in nature. The Pelasgic Zeus changed into a god of Olympus, the true image of a king in heaven. Elis and its groves opened to the new sovereign, who took his seat there unopposed. None were more instrumental in this change than they who introduced the new sun god, Apollo, in the stead of Arês or Heraclês, and a new heaven-born Athênê, who outshone the earth goddesses, Rhea, or Demetêr, or even Hêra herself. The revolution, however, was a quiet one, like those slow changes we learn to think of as creating new worlds or new systems of planets. In the nebulous mass of the old Pelasgic society, as yet without coherence or national

identical with the Tyrian Melcarth. See Curtius, *Griech. Gesch.*, for a recent example. So far as concerns the representation of Heraclês in art, I can well believe there was an indebtedness to Phœnician influence; and this extended, perhaps, to some special myths, but not to the whole conception in the popular mind.

existence, a vortex of more eager life was set up; and this, ever widening, drew into itself the best part of the race, until a new Hellas arose to take the place of Greece.

As for the processes whereby the Apollo worship and the Athênê worship were introduced, at these we can do little more than guess; and yet concerning the first of these tradition does seem to afford us some clue; and that which tradition appears to sketch out we may—making due premise that the story is not to be taken for certain fact—present in something of the form of a continuous narrative.

The authors of Apollo worship as a Hellenic belief were, it would seem, the Dorians—at first a small tribe, not worthy to be called a nation, who lived in the extreme north of Greece, where Mount Olympus separates Macedon from Thessaly. They were Zeus-worshippers; by their conquests and settlements they carried the cult of the Olympian Zeus over the whole land of Greece; and because they worshipped Zeus, the old chief god of the Pelasgians was never deposed from his throne. But the Dorians were before all things the votaries of the sun god, Apollo; and with them the religion of Apollo travelled wherever they went. The outbreak of these men of the north from the bosom of the Pelasgic world, was in some respects like the outbreak upon the Roman Empire of certain Teutonic peoples from the vast unexplored forests of Germany, and from the shores of silent northern seas. Like the Scandinavians, from being mountaineers, these men took to the sea, and became pirates. They haunted the islands of the Archipelago, and passing onward, sometimes resting where they came, sometimes defeated and forced to retire, they got at last to Crete, and founded the first Dorian kingdom there.

The tradition of Minôs points not obscurely to the time when Crete was the ruling state in the Greek world. The kingdom of Minôs extended, no doubt, over most of the islands of the Ægæan, and over part of its Asiatic and

European shores. And Minôs was a Dorian, Crete a
Dorian land.[1] At this time, therefore, it was that the
great extension of Apollo worship probably took place,
whereof the deepest traces were in after years discovered
in Caria, in Lycia, and in the Troad. It is likely enough
that Apollo worship was not moulded into its final shape
until such time as the Dorians of Thessaly had been long
in contact with the Ionians of Asia, and that it passed
through many lower forms before it reached the condition
which we admire. There is evidence of the existence of a
sun worship of a not exalted character in the same land of
Crete. The bull-headed Minotaur can hardly have been
anything else than a sun god, one of the Asiatic stamp:
the Cnossian labyrinth has a totally Oriental appearance,
and reminds us of that celebrated garden of Mylitta in
Babylon which Herodotus describes.[2]

There is no doubt that it was through much commerce with other peoples, through much friction and inter-
change of ideas, that the Greek religion in its entirety,
the *cult* of Apollo and of Athênê alike, grew to be what
they were. But let us not say that Athênê and Apollo
were on this account less truly Hellenic. It was with the
history of belief as it was with the history of art; the first
forms were borrowed from the East, from Phœnicians,
Assyrians, or Egyptians. But that which infused life into
these forms, which placed a spirit in their bodies, and a
breath in their members, that was wholly Greek.

Even before the time of Minôs—that is, before the
Doric kingdom in Crete had put to silence the older

---

[1] I do not mean to say that the original Minôs was a Dorian. Minôs
was really to the Greeks no one else than what Adam is to us, what
Yama was to the Indians, and Yima to the Persians. But as Yima grew
into the hero, Yamshîd (Jamshîd), so Minôs became the typical earliest
king. The first *kingdom* of the Greek race was the kingdom of Minôs,
in Crete. This was, perhaps (as suggested, p. 166), originally an Ionian (or
Yavan) kingdom, but at the time to which Greek tradition points back it
had become by conquest a Dorian one.

[2] Herod. i. 199.

Doric rule in Olympus—the shrine of Apollo had been founded on Delos. Delos was afterwards deemed to be the navel of the earth; because, being in special favour with Apollo, it might be thought to stand under the eye of the midday sun. It was also deemed the birth-place of the god, because it lay in mid-Ægæan and the sun is born from the sea; and also probably because it was one of the earliest shrines of the deity. This island, standing as it does half-way between Europe and Asia, and half-way between Olympus and Crete, is a type of the *cult* of Apollo, which was the meeting-point between the Oriental and the Occidental Greeks.

Last of all, the Dorian migrations which took place about the tenth century before our era, starting from the Doric tetrapolis, the cities of Erineus, Bœum, Pindus, and Cytinium—for to this neighbourhood the Dorians of Olympus and Tempe had gradually moved—carried the Delphic worship of the god over the whole Peloponnese. Thus by example, or more direct enforcement, the new creed spread on every side, until the god was honoured wherever the Greek tongue was spoken—

Through the calf-breeding mainland and through the isles.[1]

The old poems—those two hymns, for example, which have been joined into one and called the Homeric hymn to Apollo—have not very much which is reliable to give us out of their tradition. The mythic journeys of the god have but few grains of history interspersed in them, and these grains are not easily discoverable. On the other hand, the Homeric hymn tells not obscurely other facts which are in their way historical; it relates the nature and the deeds of the sun god as he presented himself to the eyes of those who composed the hymn. We know how nearly the sun god has always touched the sympathies of man-kind, and how he has generally assumed an office more

[1] Hymn. in Apol. 21.

human than that of any other nature god. The sun itself has many aspects. There is therefore enough in the nature of the sun god to furnish more than one individuality. There are high sun gods and low sun gods and suns who are but demi-gods or heroes. The manhood of Apollo never sinks him low. He is human in his sympathics, and in many incidents of his life, but he is also completely god-like in dignity.

Son of the 'Concealed' (Leto), or, in other words, of the Darkness, Apollo was born in suffering upon the island of Delos. The hymn tells how his mother first wandered from land to land, and how one coast after another refused to receive her, dreading to give birth to the Far-Darter because of the anger of Hera. But at last she came to rugged Delos, and to her prayer that island listened : there for nine days[1] she laboured in pain and could not be delivered, because Hera hindered the birth. But at length the hour was accomplished, and then the bright one leaped into light, and all the attendant goddesses gave a shout (we have here an echo of an old belief —petrified in the myth of Memnon—that at the hour of sunrise the horizon sends forth a sound[2]) and Delos grew all golden. Then the goddesses washed him in fair water, purely and holily, and (beautiful picture of the sun wrapped in the golden-threaded clouds of dawn) they wrapped him in a white robe, and around it did a golden band. Thus arose the Far-Darter, the god of the silver bow, whose arrows are the rays, whose golden sword is the heat of the sun.

The hymn has much to tell us concerning the tradition-

---

[1] The mystical number nine is especially connected with Apollo (cf. the nine muses) and with the sun ; its curious repetition in the Odysseus myth (see note to p. 303) is the best justification for those who would interpret the wanderings of that hero as a sun myth. I think, however, I have shown in Ch. VI. that the sun myth may have had its influence upon the story of Odysseus without being in any sense its real foundation.

[2] I imagine that the origin of this myth is the realisation of the *birth* of the sun, and the cry of pain which mother Nature (or mother Earth) gives at that hour.

ary spread of Apollo worship, mingling these details
with others which belong purely to the nature myth.
But we have not a complete biography of Apollo, as we
have of Heracles, and for the reason that a *life* implies a
death, and Apollo does not die.   He is immortal, unchangeable among the Olympians, next in majesty to his
father.   All the gods fear him as he goes through the
house of Zeus, and all rise from their seats when he
passes, stretching his wondrous bow.   He is in this hymn
a terrible and proud god, who lords it over mortals and
immortals.   If Apollo's name do really mean 'the destroyer,' we cannot doubt that once he was as fierce and
dangerous as Arês himself.   The sun hero is ever a warrior.   The dark coils of cloud against which Indra
launched his thunderbolt wait to devour Apollo, unless he
can destroy them first.   The cloud serpent Ahi is in this
case the Python; and the serpent destroyer is not now
the god of storm, but the sun.   No sooner has the god
been born than he begins his life of adventure and of
war.

His first journey was that which brought him to
Delphi.   The bright open country pleased the god, and he
wished to found a temple there.   But he was turned from
his purpose by the river goddess, Telphusa, who fraudfully
persuaded him that the place, with its flocks and herds of
wild horses and its races and charioteers, was an unfit
place for the solitude of his shrine, and would have him
pass on to the gorge of Parnassus.   This she did because
she desired to keep her renown in the land, and she
hoped that Apollo would be killed by the serpent who
inhabited the ravine.   The god then passed on, and
founded a shrine at Crissa (whence it was afterwards
moved a little inland to the historic Delphi).   Here he
discovered the great serpent.   Hera had brought this
monster forth, like neither to gods nor mortals, a bane to
men.   And her the Far-Darter slew with his arrows, and
she writhed among the woods, and gave up her life, spout-

ing forth blood.   And the sun rotted her carcass, whence
she was called Pytho after death.

This last myth has a general and a local significance.
The general significance is the war which, according to
many different mythologies, the sun god carries on against
the river god.   The great river which is the sum of all the
lesser fetiches of this kind is the earth river, which flows all
round the world and which the Greeks knew by the name
Oceanos.   Perhaps in its widest significance the contest
between the sun god and the river is a combat with this
earth river.   For this is the destroyer of the sun.   Into
Oceanos the sun sinks every night and dies.   The river
smothers him in its coils and puts an end to his life; and
before that could happen there must have been a battle
between the two.   This, I suppose, is the general significance of the fights between the sun god and the river;
combats which come forward so conspicuously in the case
of the Norse god Thorr and the earth-girding serpent
Jörmungandr.   And yet this typical battle is enacted
again every time the sun dries up some local stream; so
that in the story of the Python-slaying, beside the deeper
significance which made it the same as the contests of
Thorr with Jörmungandr, of Heraclês with the Lernean
hydra, and the combats between Indra and Ahi, there is
the relic of a lesser local myth which recorded only the
drying up of the stream of Mount Parnassus.

Much might be said in this place of the myths related of Apollo; for the myths which belong to the sun
are in most systems more numerous than those which
attach to any other phenomenon.   But the subject of sun
myths has perhaps received an undue amount of attention
in comparison with the myths of any other part of nature;
and therefore there is no need to stay long upon them
here.   Among the sun myths which characterise best the
nature of Apollo we will glance at one or two.

In the whole repertory of folk tales there is none more
touching nor none which is a greater favourite in popular

lore than that which tells of the hero hiding his greatness for a while in a servile state, or beneath a beggar's
gabardine, receiving the sneers and slights of his comrades in patience, because he knows that his time will
come and he can afford to wait. The story naturally attaches to the sun, as his life is the type of the heroic
one; and, as we see from the above history, it does not
pass over Apollo. For the god was born upon the smallest
and ruggedest of all the Ægæan islands; all other lands
rejected him because he was under the ban of Hera. And
like the prince when he throws off his disguise and gilds
all things with his greatness, and arms himself for heroic
deeds, so does Apollo seem when he makes Delos most
honoured of all places and rich with many gifts. According to another tale, Apollo was, after the slaughter of the
Python, for purification from blood, condemned to become
a servant and to feed the horses of Admetus; at another
time he served Laomedon and built a wall for him round
Ilium. All these stories have the same intent.

Again, the sun is the wandering god. No sooner was
Apollo born than he started upon his travels. He went
to rocky Pytho, playing upon his harp. From Olympus
he descended to ' sandy Lecton to the Magnesians, and
went amid the Perrhæbians.' Or, according to another
part of the hymn, taking the shape of a dolphin, he guided
men from Crete to Crissa, that they might spread abroad
his fame in that region. This plunging of the god into
the water, and his taking the shape of a fish, is the setting of the sun; and the birth of Apollo in the mid-Ægæan
is his rising. Both are alike parts of the sun's daily
journey.

Another example of the connection between Apollo's
history and popular lore is to be found in the story told us
by Apollodorus, how soon after his birth he was carried
away on the back of swans to the country of the Hyper-
boreans, where he remained until a year had run out.
This is in no way different from that common Teutonic

legend of the *swan knight* who as a child is borne away by birds of the same species to some distant land, some earthly paradise, and returns at last in the like fashion. In the case of Lohengrin the knight comes in a barge which a swan is dragging along as he swims; and so, in this example, Apollo's dolphin voyage and his swan flight through the air are, in a manner, combined into one picture.

The wandering Apollo led the Dorians to Crissa. But I do not think this was the only occasion on which he became their guide. The sun, in all migrations and in all wanderings, is ever the leader; and I have no doubt that Apollo had been at the head of all the adventures of the Doric race. But when these last had adopted Heraclês from the men of the land to which they came, they transferred this character of leader from the god to the demi-god. As K. O. Müller says, 'everything which is related of.the exploits of Heracles in the north of Greece refers exclusively to the history of the Dorians, and conversely all the actions of the Doric race in their earliest settlements are fabulously represented in the person of Heraclês.'[1] To account for the migrations of the Dorians, a so-called 'return of the Heraclidæ' was invented and placed under the special guidance of Heracles.

The transfer to this last god or demi-god of some of the deeds of Apollo had two causes, and has two aspects. In one aspect it was a reassertion of the importance of the older demi-god, of him, that is to say, whom the Pelasgic Greeks had worshipped before they knew Apollo. But it has another significance beside this. Heraclês remained essentially the lower divinity, the peasants' god; Apollo was the god of the higher race. Wherefore it was natural to ascribe to the former those deeds which were most essentially human in character. Apollo was raised to a loftier and remoter sphere so soon as he had been

---

[1] *Dorians*, Eng. translation, p. 56.

purged of the more human parts of his nature, and these had been passed over to Heraclês.

We note the effects of this change in one matter of supreme importance belonging to the mythic history of the sun. We have already seen how necessarily it belongs to the sun's nature that he should be born weak, and suffer hardships in his childhood; how it belongs to him that he should be a wanderer and a fighter. But not less than all this it appertains to his character that he should *die*. It is this last act which makes the nature of the sun god approach the nearest to human nature. Wherefore it is an action sure to be brought into prominence in the case of a sun god who has sunk some way toward the human level, and is sure to be as much as possible suppressed in the case of a god who has come to be raised very high above the level of mankind. This truth is illustrated in the persons of Heraclês and Apollo.

The death of Heraclês is the most impressive incident in all his varied history. No one who reads the account of it can, I think, fail to be struck by the likeness of the picture to an image of the setting sun. The hero returning home, has reached the shore of the Ægæan, when Lichas comes to meet him, bearing the fatal shirt poisoned with the blood of Nessus. At starting upon his voyage Heracles puts it on, and straightway the burning folds cling to his body, just as the sunset clouds cling round the setting sun.[1] Feeling that his end is near, Heraclês orders Lichas to make him a mound upon Mount Œta— on the *western* shore of the Ægæan, as we note—and there is he burned. The flame of his pyre shines out far over

[1] All this has been better said in Sir G. Cox's *Mythology of the Aryan Nations*, and in the same writer's *Tales of Ancient Greece*. I am, I confess, among those who think that the learned writer has used too much ingenuity in hunting out possible 'sun myths.' But that this story and many others are sun myths I feel no manner of doubt. The universality of *folk tales* argues nothing against the existence of nature myths of this kind. Even if many of the tales had been invented before nature worship began, they would inevitably get transferred to those gods whose characters they fitted.

the sea as the sun's last rays shine out in the light of the fiery sky. So, too, in a Northern myth, Hringhorni, the funeral ship of Balder—that is to say, the barque of the sun—is described as drifting out burning into the west. The Northmen never upheld the idea that their gods were immortal, and therefore it was no difficulty to them to tell of the death of the sun. Neither was it difficult for the Greeks to tell of the death of Heraclês, because Heraclês was not one of the true Olympian gods. He had only by sufferance his place on Olympus, and had left behind him in Hades (as a sort of pledge) his shade, which still stalked about those darksome fields.[1] It was far harder to realise that Apollo could ever have suffered death, and accordingly we find that the memory of that part of his career was almost forgotten in the latter days.

Yet there are relics of myths which were myths of Apollo's dying. One is this. When Apollo had slain the Python, he had, as we have seen, to purify himself; and part of his purification consisted in serving in the stables of Admetos, and in tending his horses on the sides of Pierus.[2] Now Admetus, as Otfried Müller has shown, is really one of the by-names of Hades; so that Apollo's service in this case is a descent to the under world. No doubt but this is some relic of an earlier myth, which gave to the great battle between Apollo and the Serpent a different ending from that now known to us, making the god worsted and not victorious in his fight with the powers of darkness. Another indication of a descent to hell is found in the share which Apollo takes in the recall of Alcestis from the realm of Death and her restoration to her husband. It is here that the likeness between the Greek god and the Christian Saviour which has been insisted on by

---

[1] *Od.* xi. 601. Heracles also makes a temporary descent to Hades, and brings back Cerberus. This combat, and that of Heraclês with Thanatos, in the story of Alcestis, are instances of victory over death on the part of the hero.

[2] *Il.* ii. 766.

many writers reaches its culminating point. Of course
every sun god must descend to the world of shades, but
all do not rise again: none rise more victoriously than
Apollo does, harrowing Hell, as it were, and bringing
back the spoils in the person of Alcestis. Just so, according to Middle Age tradition, did Christ, after going down
into Hell, spoil from its clutches the patriarchs of the Old
Testament, Adam and Abel, Noah, Moses, Abraham, and
the greatest among the seed of Abraham.

> Io era nuovo in questo loco,
> Quando ci vidi venire un Possente,
> Con segno di vittoria incorronato.
> Trassaci l' ombra del Primo Parente,
> D' Abel suo figlio, e quella di Noè,
> Di Moisè legista, e ubbidiente
> Abraam Patrarca, e David Rè,
> Israel con suo padre, co' sui nati,
> E con Racbele per cui tanto fe'
> Ed altri molti; e feoegli beati.

The history of the development of Apollo's character,
then, is the gradual exaltation of his nature to suit the
growing needs of men. All that was lowest in it, and all
that seemed inconsistent with the highest degree of power,
all that was fierce and rude, all that was too human in
weakness, could be transferred to one of the older sun gods—
to Heraclês, say, or to Arês—until at last the god of Hellas
became the prototype of the highest development of Greek
culture. In Homer he is not only the greatest of all the
sun gods; he is superior in character to almost every
other deity. In the Iliad, though Zeus is the most mighty
of the two, Apollo's is certainly the more majestic figure.
There is. something very suggestive in the remoteness of
Apollo from the passion of partisanship which sways the
other Olympians; first the terror of his coming to revenge
a slight done to himself, and then his withdrawal for a
long time from all part in the combat after that injury
has been thoroughly atoned for.

One cannot help seeing a certain analogy in the characters and positions of the chief actors in the drama of the Iliad, Agamemnon and Achilles, and those two heavenly spectators Zeus and Apollo.[1] Zeus is the king of gods, as Agamemnon of men, and, despite the fact that Zeus sides with the Trojans, there is a bond of union between the god and the mortal. Agamemnon always addresses himself first to Zeus, even to the Zeus who rules on Ida, and when the Achæans are sacrificing some to one god, some to another, his prayer is to the King of Heaven.[2] The likeness between Apollo and Achilles scarcely needs to be pointed out. Achilles is a sun *hero* and Apollo is a sun *god*; that is really all the difference between them. Each is the ideal youth, the representative, one might fairly say, of ' young Greece,' that which was to become in after years Hellas. Achilles is from the very primal Hellas, whence the whole country eventually took its name. Apollo and Achilles have the same sense of strength in reserve and an abstinence from participation in the battle going on around : each is provoked to do so only by some very near personal injury.

M. Didron, in his interesting work on Christian iconography, gives us a sketch of the relative positions in art occupied during the Middle Ages by the two first persons of the Trinity, whence we can gather their positions in popular belief, of which art is the mouthpiece. We find that at first God the Father never appears ; His presence is indicated by a hand or by some other symbol, He has no visible place in the picture ; and when at last He takes a bodily shape, His form is borrowed from that of His Son. It is Christ who, in the monuments of the fourth to the tenth centuries, is generally portrayed performing

---

[1] On the whole it must be noticed that Zeus and Apollo, unlike Athéné and Héra, do not engage personally in the fight—Apollo does so once or twice—but use their powers as nature gods. Zeus especially acts in this way : Apollo does so in the case of the demolition of the Achæans' wall (bk. xii.) See also the great fight of the gods in the xxth book.

[2] Cf. *Il.* ii. 403, 412 ; iii. 276.

those works which in the Old Testament are ascribed to Jehovah; Christ makes the world, the sun and moon, and raises Eve out of the side of Adam. Before the tenth century the usual type of Christ is a very young man. After that century He is some thirty years of age; and then the Father begins to be seen. He is fashioned in nearly the same manner, and is no older and no younger than His Son. This implies that, during the early ages of Christianity, Christ had quite excluded the Father from the thoughts of most men; and I think we have only to read the literature of this time—the profane literature especially, the histories or memoirs—to see that such was the case. The reason of this was that Christ was the active Divinity; the history of His life and death, His labours and sufferings, was constantly before the popular mind. He absorbed all characters of the Trinity into His individual person.

A similar thing, we have seen, happened in the case of Indra and Dyâus, and of Zeus and his predecessor; the change might have been enacted once more in the case of Zeus and Apollo. And perhaps this would have happened if the Dorians had worked out their religious history for themselves. For the Doric Zeus was an abstract and inactive god; he alone never would have received, never did receive, great religious honours. 'The supreme deity, when connected with Apollo, was neither born nor visible on earth, and was perhaps never considered as having any immediate influence on men.' [1]

As this Doric religion met with the Pelasgic creed, and the active and the passive Zeus had to be rolled into one, and the Apollo to conquer a place for himself in the belief of all Hellas, there was at first, I doubt not, some conflict between the rival systems; much like that conflict between the earthly Agamemnon and Achilles. Sometimes Apollo appears higher and sometimes lower than Zeus.

[1] Müller, *Dorians.*

In Homer's picture the father is far more susceptible of human passion, far less self-contained and self-reliant, than his son : but then on the other hand Hesiod, writing in the mainland of Greece a century or two later, neglects Apollo almost completely. So that the view which Homer presents of Zeus and his son may have been exclusively an Ionic one. And, concerning Zeus, I think we can see that very late—as far down, for instance, as the time of Æschylus—two very different pictures might be presented to the popular mind, the one that of the usurping god of the Prometheus, the other the Zeus to whom the Suppliants pray.

The mountains have given way to Zeus in a Titan struggle against the new gods ; the trees have been carved into images of unseen powers; the fountains, dissolving themselves into mists, have floated heavenwards, and thus a new race of ethereal beings has supplanted those who were born on earth.

An intermediate stage it was while the mist still lingered above the river and the cloud upon the sea. At such a time took place the birth of some among the great goddesses of Greece. Aphroditê, for example, is one among this sisterhood of the mist-born ones, rising as she does from the foam and coming as she comes over the waves of the far-sounding sea, borne on the soft spray; and another sister is Artemis, who is in reality a river nymph. But chief of all that company is Athênê Tritogeneia, the daughter of Triton.[1] Triton means not water in the abstract, but some definite form of it, as a particular inlet or river or strait, and the Athênê of each place had no doubt her parentage in the particular piece of water known to that place. It were not too much to say that the Athênê of Athens was the child of Ilissus —no mean god even in late times, for he had his place

---

[1] She is called also ποττία, θαλασσία, εὐπλοια—sea-born, in a word, like Aphroditê.

on the pediment of the Parthenon—and that out of the worship of that very river first sprang the conception of the Athenian goddess. For of course each place had its local fountain and local nymph. It was a matter of chance which of the fountain goddesses attained pre-eminence and extended her name over the rest. This alone is certain : whatever the history of Athene's origin, whichever among the worshipped mists it may have been who was her prototype, the subsequent career of the goddess was such as to make her peculiarly adaptive to Greek ideas; so that she became at last the most truly Hellenic of all the watery divinities.

The same fate did not attend all. Aphroditê was born in some region where she was subject to Oriental influences ; from which she received into her nature most of the peculiar characteristics of the neighbouring Eastern goddesses, such as the Astartê of the Phœnicians, the Mylitta of the Babylonians. These were properly earth goddesses, and had all the sensuous character which belongs to this order of beings. And so Aphroditê became earthy and sensuous. Yet she is to be seen in other guises. She was sometimes represented armed like Athênê, and in such guise she was scarcely distinguishable from Pallas.

If, then, it was an accident of birth which transformed Aphroditê into Kupris, an accident of birth and of education, it was an accident also which rescued Athênê from such blighting influences. There are two genealogies for the race of goddesses. One is of the earth, and then the deity is Prithivi or Demeter, who marries the heaven god, and becomes either the ideal mother goddess or else, like the Mylitta of Babylon, the Cybelê of Phrygia, the Astartê of Tyre, a goddess of sensuous delights. The other birth is from the stream or the sea, and then, if she follow her natural instincts, the goddess rises heavenward, and becomes first the cloud, and after merges into the wind or the air. It belongs to the essential cha-

racter of such an one that she is not sensuous. Her
special characteristic is her maidenhood. Athenê is ever
called in Homer Maid Athenê (Pallas-Athenê). Parthenos,
another word for virgin, was her peculiar title. Indeed,
it was so recognisedly a sufficient designation of her at
Athens, that her temple was called the Parthenon simply,
instead of the more natural Athenaion (Athenæum). In
the Homeric hymn addressed to her she is called Corê
(κούρη). In another Homeric hymn, addressed to Aphroditê, it is said that there are but three whom the Queen
of Love has never subdued, and these are Hestia, Athenê,
and Artemis.

And here let me turn aside a moment to point out to
the reader how the essential identity in the characters of
Athenê and Artemis is indicated by their virgin natures.
We know how universally the latter goddess was celebrated for her chastity and modesty, so that even to see
her naked, as Actæon did, was a mortal offence, which did
not fail to meet with mortal punishment; while, on the
other hand, it was a sin no less deadly for Artemis'
maidens to offend against the moral sense of the goddess
by breaking their vows of maidenhood—as in the case of
Callisto. Now we find Athenê sufficiently designated as
Parthenos, the maiden *par excellence.* And yet those who
had known both Athenê and Artemis could never have used
the names Pallas and Parthenos as synonyms for Athenê.
Seeing, then, that chastity is the leading characteristic of
Artemis (as the most important myths about her show),
and that the chastity, i.e. the maidenhood, of Athenê was
so necessary and distinctive a part of her nature that she
was known as *the* maiden, we are justified in saying that
Artemis and Athenê were of identical nature.

Artemis was originally a stream; she was of the same
nature as her attendant nymph the 'leaping' Atalanta,[1]
one of the great mythic huntresses of antiquity and un-

---

[1] ἀτάλλω, to leap.

doubtedly a fountain. Athênê, too, was originally born of
the stream. Both were, on account of this birth, pure
maidens; and being such, both became afterwards confounded with the moon.[1] Apollo and Athênê are necessarily closely connected, as the idealisations of the young
male divinity and the young female divinity; still closer,
however, is the relationship between Apollo and Artemis.

Artemis, then, was at first the same as Athênê. The
two had the same origin in the outer world of phenomena,
and for awhile their characters must have unfolded side
by side. But the circumstances of their after lives were
very different. Artemis was a goddess chiefly of the less
cultured populations of Greece—that is to say, of those
who dwelt in the interior of the Peloponnese. Athênê,
on the contrary, became the tutelary divinity of the most
highly civilised city in all Hellas. She daily waxed
greater, and the other waned. Athênê's history was preserved by the best literature of Greece; Artemis was left
in the shade among her Arcadian shepherds, and fell
down to the second rank of goddesses. This difference in
their respective histories was partly accidental: it was, at
all events, independent of their essential natures, and
arose only out of the varied fortunes of their votaries.
Therefore what we have to say of the birth of the tutelary
goddess of Athens, of her first issue from the phenomena
out of which she was formed, and the earliest pages of her
history, may apply in great measure to Artemis as well.

I have said that at first there may be as many Tritogeneias as there are separate pieces of water to give them
birth. Pallas-Athênê, $\dot{\eta}$ $\pi\alpha\rho\theta\acute{\epsilon}\nu$os, was once the special
maiden goddess of Athens, sprung from the water which
watered Athens: no more than this. Or, if more than
this, she was at all events the goddess of only one section

---

[1] Athênê's relationship to the moon appears in many ways. As a
mariner's goddess she was confounded with Astartê. She was also identified
with the Gorgon (cf. the expression $\gamma o\rho\gamma\hat{\omega}\pi\iota s$), and, whatever Medusa was
at first, she came to be thought of as the full moon.

of the Greek race. Aphroditê was the water deity of
another section—of the Cypriotes, for example, and those
Greeks who came most under the influence of Asiatic
thought. Artemis filled the same place with a third
division—the shepherd races of the inland. Athênê stood,
in a fashion, between the two; she was more Asiatic than
Artemis, more Greek than Aphroditê. So she was destined to lord it over all her compeers. One of the Tritogeneias must inevitably have risen to pre-eminence, and
have thrust the·others into the shade. When this event
did happen, Aphroditê became the goddess of an abstraction—Love. Artemis became the moon.

Gods and goddesses who once ruled over much greater
phenomena often seem to find a last refuge in one or other
of the heavenly bodies. Even Jupiter lived to be confounded with a star. Astartê, who was originally (I suspect) an earth goddess, came to be, like Artemis, identified
with the moon. The great Mitra and Varuna, of whom
we spoke in the last chapter, descended first to become
the Asvin of Vedic mythology, and then descended further,
to be in the persons of the Dioscuri confounded with the
morning and evening stars. But to return to Athênê and
her history.

This goddess succeeded in absorbing in herself the
highest parts of the characters of Artemis and Aphroditê.
She also in a certain measure subdued Hêra to follow her
nature. It has been said that Hêra was more a goddess
of heaven than of earth. But she was this, not in virtue
of her own nature, but of her being the wife of Zeus.
And in leaving her rightful element, she left behind her
some of her individual character. Hêra had not the same
rights in the heavenly regions which Athênê possessed.
When we see Hêra and Athênê acting in concert, as we
do throughout the Iliad, we must regard Athênê as being
actually, if not in name, the leader. Hêra's being is
merged in Athênê's: she forgets that she is a wife; she
acts of her own will and not in proper obedience to her

husband. Hêra is a cloud when she and Pallas come flying down to the Grecian ranks side by side like two doves sailing through the air. She is a heaven goddess when she steals the thunders of Zeus. But Athênê does not need to steal from Zeus; she wears the ægis by right; and the ægis is the thunder cloud.

Zeus, from being the heaven, became the stormy sky and even the cloud; Athênê, in a contrary way, being first the cloud, was refined as time went on into the air and into the sky. She came eventually to be the Queen of the Air: but we must not so think of her at first. She was originally a stormy goddess; and when not the cloud itself, then the wind or the thunder storm, which are born of the cloud. To her and to Zeus alone did the ægis belong by right: each, it would seem, had their own ægis, that terrible corselet fringed with Horror and girt about with Fear, whose true nature is not difficult to divine.[1] The origin of the cloud in the water is soon forgotten, and so was the first birth of Athênê. To Homer —the epic Homer—she was only Tritogeneia, daughter of Triton. But to the author of the Homeric hymn and to all later mythologists Athênê had another and a higher parentage: she was born again to be the daughter of Zeus. The story of this Athênê's second birth (it is really a second birth and like that of Agni from the wood, only she ascends from earth to heaven and he comes down from heaven to earth) is that which became so favourite a subject for vase paintings and sculpture, and which is in the hymn thus told:—

' I begin my song to Pallas-Athênê, the glorious grey-eyed goddess, wise in counsel, having an untender heart, the revered virgin, our city ward and mighty; Tritogeneia;

---

[1] 'And about her shoulders she threw the ægis fringed with Horror, which Fear rings round ; thereon was Strife, and Might and chilling Rout' (*Il.* v. 738 sq.) And again, in *Il.* xv. 329, αἰγίδα θυσσανόεσσαν. The fringe is the lightning which issues from the cloud.

whom counselled Zeus alone brought forth from his reverend head, clothed in her warlike golden panoply, shining
on every side.   And awe possessed all the immortals who
saw this thing.   But she quickly leapt from the immortal
front of ægis-bearing Zeus, shaking her bitter spear, and
great Olympus quaked in fear before the wrath of the
grey-eyed one.   And round the earth a horrid sound re-
sounded, and the sea was stirred and tossed its purple
water.   Then suddenly the salt wave stood still, and Hyperion's glorious son (the sun) stayed long the going of
his swift-foot steeds until the maid (κούρη) took from her
immortal shoulders that godlike armour; and counselled
Zeus rejoiced ! '

'Having an untender heart;' and why?   What is
this *wrath* of the grey-eyed goddess which all fear?   It is
the rage of the storm.   The very word used here. (βρίμη)
is expressive of the grinding thunder.   It means literally
not so much the mere emotion of anger as the outward
expression of it, such as snorting.   Athenê is cruel
because the lightning is cruel, grey-eyed because the
cloud is grey.   She has been the river and the river mist;
but that is forgotten.   What she seems now is the storm
cloud begot in the heavens—in the head of Zeus.   Her
golden panoply is the storm all armed and ready with the
flash.   For see how the old nature meaning of the myth
peeps out under its thin disguise.   Dread possessed all the
immortals when she 'leapt forth in a moment'—as the
lightning leaps from heaven—brandishing a *sharp spear*;
and great Olympus shook before her snorting.   The storm,
we see, had begun.   'And all about the earth a horrid
din went round. . . .'
  Presently we pass to another image closely allied to
these images, but somewhat different from them.   Just
now Athenê was the storm itself, almost the lightning
itself, when she leapt forth from heaven.   But change the
image a little; let her be simply the cloud; then her arms

are the thunder and the lightning. The Vedic Maruts
have the same panoply. 'They put on golden armour;
their spears send down sparks. They lift the mountains;
the forest trees shake before them.' When the lightning
has gone forth and the thunder rolled, then Athênê, the
cloud, has laid aside her weapons. Who does not know the
stillness with which nature awaits that moment of flash
and crash? Here it is recorded how the salt wave stood still
and the glorious sun stayed the going of his steeds, until
the maid put from her shoulders that immortal panoply:
and counselled Zeus rejoiced—the sky itself grew clear.

It is in her aspect as a grim storm goddess that Athênê
first appears to us in Greek poetry. It is in virtue of this
fighting power that she is πολιάς, city guardian. We see
that well enough by the epithets which follow one another
in the hymn. Athênê is 'untender-hearted' (ἀμείλιχον
ἦτορ ἔχουσα), and therefore 'revered' (αἰδοίη); and because
she was so dread and so revered she was the best of
guardians for the city. Wherefore it was that the oldest
temple to Athênê at Athens was the temple of Athênê
Polias, and therefore was it that she was worshipped in so
many towns under that name.

There is so much likeness between the natures of Zeus
and Athênê, both being at one time personifications of the
sky and at another time personifications of the storm,
that it need not surprise us to find that the epithet
πολιεύς belonged especially to Zeus. But we do not appreciate the full force of such a phrase as applied either to
father or daughter, if we only think of the *polis* of
historic days. Let us turn for a moment to think of prehistoric times—that is to say, of days when Zeus and
Athênê partook much more of the elemental nature from
which they had sprung, than they ever seem to do in
literature. In such days the πόλις was not the ordered
city, the centre of a busy life, suggestive only of the 'sweet
security of streets,' and remote from fear of the unseen
power of the storm. It was, on the contrary, a little

palisaded *village*, situate in a wild country, surrounded by lonely tracts of forest and of marsh. Each village was a tribe and a nation to itself; and there was war slumbering or awake between each community and its neighbour. Over the wild region which surrounded this little oasis of human life presided the God of Storms. If he was friendly to the village, if he was a true city-ward to it, then he howled with destructive vengeance round the tribe which was coming to its attack. This was the ancient character of the Ζεὺς πολιεύς. When we come to study the beliefs of the German races, we shall find in their social condition a better example of the community which I have been imagining, descended from the *village community* of old Aryan days. We shall see how among the Germans each collection of houses cut itself off from neighbouring villages by a *mark* or forest track, and how this mark was ever placed under the guardianship of the God of Storms.

It seems strange that Athênê and Zeus should have remained such distinct individualities, and yet that there should have been really so little distinctive in their two natures. If we compare either their possessions and attributes, or their most characteristic deeds, we shall see that very many of these are partaken of by both. There often is no clear distinction between Zeus and Athênê. She is then little else than the feminine counterpart of her father. As we have seen, each was essentially a city guardian; and Athênê alone beside her father possessed the ægis and wielded the thunder.[1] There is something very appropriate in the way that in Homer the goddess and the god are made to take opposite sides in the Great Siege. The storm may well have seemed to range itself now with one camp, now with another. The thunder might come from Ida, and then it was sent by Zeus;[2] or

---

[1] In *Il.* ii. 447 Athênê is shown as possessing an ægis of her own; in v. 733, &c., she borrows that of her father; in xi. 45 Athênê and Hêra together thunder.   [2] Cf. viii. 170; xvii. 593.

it might come from the west, whitening the waves of the
sea, and then it was Athênê and Hera flying together from
Olympus. But in the double natures of both Zeus and
Athênê there is full scope for a difference in their outward
appearance. Zeus is not only the stormy sky; he is likewise, and more rightfully, the clear heaven. He may be
a passionate and changeful being, or he may be the all-
knowing, the wise counsellor, the just judge.

Such changes as these belong partly to the change of
Athênê's natural character, partly to the development of
her ethical nature. They can be observed passing over
the goddess of Homer, and they become more noticeable
when we pass on to poets later than Homer. In the
Iliad the goddess appears essentially as the fighter, 'Aθήνη
πρόμαχος,[1] a character which is, as we have seen, intimately connected with her old name of Athênê Polias.
In the Odyssey another side of her nature becomes conspicuous. She is there the wise counsellor (πολύβουλος,
πολύμητις), and a divinity appropriately adored by the
cunning seafarers and merchants for whom the Odyssey
was written.

I will not say, however, that this side of Athênê's
character, 'the wise one,' was not of very ancient origin,
and has not as much as her fierce, stormy character its
origin in the phenomenon from which she grew. Nay, in
some respects it even seems to have the oldest birth. We
have seen how Athênê was first of all water-born, whereby
she was called τριτογένεια, πόντια, θαλάσσια, εὔπλοια. She
was also a daughter of Metis, who was in later times
'Counsel' (an abstraction), but in her earlier days a water
nymph, a daughter of ocean.[2] This birth from Metis had
a certain connection with the epithet πολύμητις; and it is

---

[1] Athênê is not called *Promachos* in the *Iliad*, but that word more than
any other expresses her character there. Compare especially *Iliad*, iv. 439,
where Athênê is coupled with Arês and with Deimos, Phobos, and Eris;
v. 29, where she is again in special opposition to Arês; v. 333, where her
name is coupled with that of Enyô.

[2] Preller, *Griech. Myth.* i. 150.

not difficult to show what that connection was. Metis was
an Oceanid. The Oceanids were not the waves, but the
rivers. And rivers have always been associated with prophecy. Every mythology has its wise women, who are
the guardians of a fountain or stream. In the Eddas
such beings are to be seen in the 'weird sisters three'
who keep the well of Urd, which stands under Yggdrasill.
Originally these three maidens were themselves personifications of wells or streams. The Pythoness was the water
of Delphi, and was one with the nymph Telphusa; later
on she was the wise maiden of the sacred stream. The
wells of knowledge or of magic, or the fountains of youth
which we meet with in myth and legend, are no more
than the narrowing to particular instances of the magic
and sacredness and healing gifts which were once universally attributed to streams. And it so happens that of
the many kinds of supernatural power which these as
fetiches once possessed, their knowledge and cunning remained with them the longest. Wherefore the serpent,
which is in every mythology symbolical of the river, is
everywhere held to be 'more subtle than any beast of the
field.' It is not difficult, then, to see whence Athênê
draws her cunning and wisdom.

By the process of the survival of the fittest, this was
the part of the goddess' nature which lived the longest;
because, as men advance in civilisation, they set more
value upon intellectual gifts and less value upon mere
animal courage and capacity for fighting. Hence the
very noticeable change which, as we shall presently see,
has passed over the character of Athênê when we turn
from the Iliad to the Odyssey.

An important deed of Pallas beside those which she is
made to perform in Homer, was the help which she gave
to Perseus in his expedition against the Gorgons. Besides
the ægis, Athênê possessed the shield into which Medusa's
head had been fixed, and which was hence called the *gorgoneion*. The adventure of Perseus is most evidently a pure

nature myth, and the gorgoneion must therefore belong to Athênê in her nature character. Concerning Perseus there is no doubt. He is the sun, the hero who, like Surya, 'wanders up and down upon his path,'[1] veiling himself in things alike and unlike (i.e. hiding his form in the petasos of Hermês). We have first to note him on his western journey, how by the fitful winds he was borne through endless space, and from the lofty sky looked down on the far-removed earth, and sped over all the world; how he saw Arcturus cold and the claws of Cancer, and was carried now to the east, now to the west. And then, following him on his journey, we may see him at day's decline staying on the borders of Atlas' kingdom, upon the edge of earth, where the sea is ever ready to receive the panting horses of the Sun and his wearied car.[2] Here Perseus is not the sun seen as the *god* who travels upon right and changeless paths, but as the *sun hero* who is essentially a wanderer. The Medusa head, as we see it in early art, presents a hideous face, with the tongue lolling out and sharp teeth agrin. It is, in fact, the strange misshapen *waning* moon, which before dawn we may see hanging over the western horizon. Soon the rising sun will strike it dead. Medusa herself is a kind of goddess of death, the queen of that western world of shades. As art advanced, she grew milder, until she became like Hypnos, a soft embodiment of rest. But she was Death for all that.

Some have supposed, however, that the Gorgon was not originally the moon, but the storm, and to this notion her connection with Athênê gives some colour. For the truth is, Athênê and Medusa are one and the same being seen under different aspects. Athênê herself is called gorgon-faced (γοργῶπις),[3] and I have little doubt that she

---

[1] Rig Veda, τ. 177, 3. [2] Cf. Met. iv. 622 sqq.

[3] Γοργῶπις or γοργωπός is of course a general synonym for fierce-looking, and as such is applied to Hector—῾Εκτωρ . . . Γοργοῦς ὅμματ' ἔχων (Il. viii. 348, 9). But as a special epithet of Athênê it has a deeper meaning than 'fierce' only.

was once represented by a face not unlike that archaic gorgon one. Such an instance of absorption by a divinity of his or her earlier being is very common in the history of mythology. The Gorgon must, then, have been at first the storm, and afterwards the waning moon. The battle of the sun god and the cloud is universal; and this may have been the first meaning of Perseus' slaying Medusa. Afterwards a more fanciful mythology would convert it into the death of the moon.

Athenê's being the daughter of the cloud and also of the water—to inland men of the river, but to those by the coast of the sea—gave her a peculiar connection with navigation, and made her the special patroness of those among the Greek nationality who first practised such an art. There was an additional reason for her becoming the goddess of sailors, and that was a certain amount of confusion between her and the Phœnician Astartê. To inland men she—or I would rather say the maiden goddess, the Parthenos, the Pallax—came to be represented by Artemis; to those who were most orientalised she was merged in Astartê or Aphroditê; while to the intermediate class she kept her proper individuality.

Now this intermediate class was formed of precisely the men who made Hellas what it was. They were the Javan, the Ionians, the dwellers by the sea of either coast, the adventurers, the merchants, the lovers of art. Wherefore Athenê became patron of all these pursuits. She was the sea goddess of the newer men, in opposition to Poseidôn, who was the sea god of the Pelasgians. Whence the contest between them.

These I take to be the chief constituents which go to make up the character of the water-born goddess. Some essential features of this character are to be traced all through the history of Athenê worship, until (shall we say) she reappears in neo-Platonist and Christian mythology as the Divine Sophia or as the Virgin herself. But of course Athenê's ethic being tends continually to dim her natural being. We shall do well to adhere generally to the rule laid down that we ought to seek in Homer alone for anything like a nature god or goddess; wherefore, in concluding this sketch of Athênê, we will turn back again to recapitulate in a few words the leading features of her character as that is portrayed in the Iliad and in the Odyssey.

We have first to remember that Athênê is always Tritogeneia here, and we must therefore think of her always as the cloud in some form. In the Iliad she is the storm cloud especially. Zeus thunders from Ida[1]—that is, from the Troy side—and his seat is there;[2] while that of the rest of the gods is on the European side—namely, upon Olympus.[3] Thus Zeus becomes an image of the storm which from landward bears against the Greeks. Apollo (the sun), too, came from the east, and so he seemed to be ranged upon the side of the Dardanians. Apollo came from Pergamos to oppose Athênê coming from Olympus; but when the sun had sloped toward the west, Apollo's power to help his allies failed him. 'So long, then, as the sun was climbing to mid-heaven the weapons reached both sides with equal power, and the people fell; but when the sun had passed on towards eventide, then were the Greeks the mightier in despite of fate.'[4]

And now for the Greek befriending deities.[5] Athênê is meant to be the chief and leader of these. Hêra seems sometimes the leader, for this is suitable to her place as Queen of Heaven; but her genius is really overpowered—

---

[1] viii. 170; xvii. 593.   [2] viii. 397, &c.   [3] viii. 438, &c.

[4] Il. xvi. 777, &c. The morning is more taken account of than the evening. This is perhaps why both Apollo and Arês seem on the side of the Easterns. The sun was really so till midday. The other deities who side with the Trojans are Artemis and Leto (who go with brother and son); Xanthus, a local river god; and Aphroditê, of Eastern origin.

[5] The divinities who side with the Greeks, the Westerns and the invaders, are Hêra (only because her nature is overpowered by Athênê's), the two rulers of the sea, Athênê and Poseidon (one as the storm, the wind, or cloud, the other as the sea itself), Hermes (god of the West and of Death; see Ob. VI.), and Hephæstus. See book xx.

'rebuked, as it is said Marc Antony's was by Cæsar '—by the genius of Athênê. We see this the more plainly when we have followed the history of the goddesses into the second epic; for there we find that Hêra has sunk to insignificance, while Athênê retains all her ancient power with something added. Even in the Iliad Athênê sometimes orders and Hêra obeys;[1] and this seems a very remarkable thing when we remember the difference of their nominal positions and the actual difference of a generation between them. Generally Hêra and Athênê go side by side, flying together,[2] or driving side by side in the chariot.[3] Wherefore we may take them for two embodiments of the storm or the storm cloud coming 'in speed like doves' to meet Zeus, who comes up from the other side, whitening the Ægæan as they pass over it. It has been already noted how both Athênê and Hêra can wield the thunder.

Before we leave Athênê's character in the Iliad we must notice the epithets which attach to her. Tritogeneia has been spoken of; Polybûlos ($\pi o\lambda \dot{v}\beta o\upsilon\lambda o s$) is the same as Polymêtis ($\pi o\lambda \dot{v}\mu\eta\tau\iota s$), and belongs of right to this river-born goddess. Agelia ($\dot{a}\gamma\epsilon\lambda\epsilon i\eta$) she is frequently named, a word of doubtful significance which may be rendered 'forager' or 'shepherdess' ($\dot{a}\gamma\epsilon\lambda\eta$), both epithets connecting Athênê with Artemis; but the second probably the original one. In this case the clouds may be the sheep, and Athênê may be likened to the wind. Gorgôpis

---

[1] viii. 381.

[2] v. 778. Athênê often takes the form of a bird (especially of a swallow). Moreover, the winged sandals ($\pi\epsilon\delta\iota\lambda a$), which characterise Hermês in sculpture, are Athênê's property as well. Now, Hermês is the wind (see Ch. VI.) As Athênê has the $\pi\epsilon\delta\iota\lambda a$, so has Freyja, the chief among the Valkyriur (see Ch. VII.), a feather robe (fiaðrhamr). The Valkyriur correspond to Athênê in nature.

Next to the wind the sun may be presented in the form of a bird. He is addressed as one in the Rig Veda. On *Il.* vii. 57 Heyne comments, 'Ridiculum hoc, si Minerva et Apollo in vultures mutantur aut vulturum speciem assumunt. Comparatio spectat ad hoc solum, quod in arbore considunt et pugnam inde prospectant' (vol. v. p. 318). Heyne, however, did not suspect the nature origin of these divinities. See *Zeitsch. f. verg. Sp.* xv. (1866), 88 sqq..   [3] viii. *l. c.*

($\gamma o \rho \gamma \tilde{\omega} \pi \iota s$), fierce-eyed, may also be rendered Gorgon-faced, and affords in either signification good reason for supposing that Athênê and the Gorgôn were once the same.

Now we pass on to the Odyssey, where Athênê reigns almost supreme. Odysseus is, in the language of the German legends, Athênê's *Liebling*; his failures and successes typify the fortunes of Athênê's special votaries. And who are these? They are the merchant pirates, the sea rovers, the discoverers, the Greek Hawkinses and Drakes, whose time of power succeeded to the older aristocratic days commemorated in the Iliad. The poet of the Iliad sang to the rich and powerful princes of the Ægæan shores; the poet of the Odyssey, too, sang in coast towns of the Ægæan,[1] but no longer to petty kings, rather to the merchantmen and the loungers in the market. Of these cunning 'many-deviced' traders Athênê is the patron saint. The worship of her is so fervent that it admits no rivalry in her own domain, and therefore she has driven to the background the older god of the sea. Athênê and Poseidon had been friendly in the Iliad; in the Odyssey they are constantly opposed. And because Odysseus puts out the eye of the Cyclops, who is Poseidôn's son, and yet eventually escapes the vengeance of the Sea God, Athênê must be held to triumph in the end.

'Once,' says the author of the 'Imitation,' 'the children of Israel said to Moses, *Speak thou to us, and we will hear thee. But let not the Lord speak unto us, lest we die.* This, O Lord, is not my prayer, but with humility and with fervour I say to Thee, as Samuel the Prophet says, *Speak, Lord, for Thy servant heareth.*' The awfulness which enwrapped the God of the Jews disappeared in the milder nature of Christ. The greatness of a prophetic mission is no longer needed to gain a hearing of the Deity; and

---

[1] He is quite ignorant of the geography of Ithaca, and indeed of all coasts beyond Cape Matapan. See Bunbury's *Geography of the Ancients*.

the voice of the Lord is now still and small and uttered in
the human breast, not amid the thunders of Sinai.   This
characterises the change from the older to the newer
creed; something of the same kind was the revolution
which the worship of Apollo and of Athenê brought about
in the religion of Greece.   It was in this case, as in
the other, a meeting-point between God and humanity;
and though there is little moral resemblance between
Christianity and the religion of Hellas, yet there was
in this particular matter a likeness in the development of
each.

The belief of Christianity is a belief in the beauty of
holiness; the creed of Hellas was a belief in the beauty of
the world and of mankind.   Nature was no longer terrible
to those who had grown to understand her better.   They
were not only in a new nature, but they looked upon nature
with new eyes.   Once Zeus had embodied all that seemed
most impressive in the world around—the dark rugged
land, the storm heard in the forests, and the sea raging
against the shore.   And he was in himself the soul of such
scenes.   To him might have been addressed the words of
Patroclus to Achilles—

Grey ocean bore thee, and the lofty rocks; for cruel are thy
    thoughts.

But when Apollo and Athenê had taken their place
beside Zeus, men saw the sun rise in a milder majesty, and
the airs grew calmer, and the hills were clothed with
purple brightness.   From the bare mountains of Thrace,
from windy heights and perilous seas, the Greeks had passed
to the Ægæan, to its safe harbours and its thousand laughing islands; they had exchanged the lonely life of shepherds
for the security of streets, for commerce, and for luxury.
Apollo was a lover of nature, but not in her most terrible
aspects; ' the high watches pleased him and the far-reaching mountain-tops, and the rivers that run into the deep,
and the shores stretching down to the sea, and the sea's

harbours.'[1] Wherever on the Asiatic coast some promontory extended commanding a wide horizon there was sure to have stood from old times a temple to the sun god. From such places, from those high watches, men saw him as he rose, and prayed to him when he sank into the waters. He went, they deemed, to an unseen divine land whither the dead heroes had gone before. And before he quite descended he seemed to stand as a messenger between men and that future world. It was not so much the far-off heaven of the gods to which he was going, as to the happy land of the blessed set apart for mortals; and the two worlds between which he stood were both human habitations, though one was the world of the living and the other of the dead. Therefore Apollo was always the friend of man and accessible to human prayer.

Hear me, O King, who art somewhere in the rich realm of Lycia or of Troy; for everywhere canst thou hear a man in sorrow, such as my sorrow is.[2]

The rare capacity for art, which was the inheritance of the Greek race, must soon have lightened its first fear of nature, both in making the latter more familiar and in raising man in his own eyes by showing him himself able in a way to fashion nature, and therefore possessed of some part of the creative faculty which belongeth to God. Athênê and Apollo were not associated only with the beauties which sunlight and calm air can give, but with those fashioned beauties which are the aim of all artistic striving. Athenê was the patroness of the goldsmith's art, of cunning workmanship and of embroidery down to the housewife's skill. All the arts were Apollo's care; but most of all *music*—that is to say, rhythmic movement of limbs or of words with the harmony of sound accompanying such movement; for such the Greek understood by his word music, which meant for him the sum of all culture. The Pelasgic Zeus had chosen for his home the

---

[1] Hymn in Apol.　　　　[2] Prayer of Glaucus, *Il.* xvi. 514 sqq.

groves or the bare mountain-tops.   But Apollo's dwelling
was a house made with hands; to him were dedicated
some of the earliest temples.   Apollo gave the Greeks the
first need of surpassing the shapeless images which had
been sufficient representatives of the other deities.   Among
early sculptures the statues of Apollo are by far the most
frequent; and we must consider the later images of other
youthful gods—of Hermês, for example, or the beardless
Dionysus—as no more than variations upon the original
Apollo type.

The wonderful ideal type of Greek manly beauty may
thus in a manner be ascribed to the worship of this sun
god; the ideal of womanhood, to the worship of Athênê.
For it were unreasonable to suppose that the perfections
of Greek sculpture represented the realities of life.   The
humanity of the god or goddess was always an exalted,
idealised manhood.

We have, then, traced the history of these Hellenic
deities through a series of changes corresponding to certain
definite phases of religious growth, and in these phases we
have seen how a change of outward circumstances implied
a parallel change in ethic and in inward development.
The first appearance of Zeus upon the scene—the Greek
Zeus, I mean, as distinguished from the Indian Dyâus—is
indicative of the dawn of the anthropomorphic spirit,
when the phenomenon which moves and acts has obli-
terated that which was constant.   As yet there was no question of an ideal man, no desire for ethic or for any moral
law; all that was needed was that the god should have
that one human quality of will and power; and this the
Pelasgic god essentially possessed.   Then came the rise of
morality; the gods not only became men, but they became
ideal men; and in this change Apollo was the conspicuous
figure.   The statues of Apollo express the very perfecting
of an anthropomorphic creed.   But after a while this in
its turn failed to satisfy the needs of men, for they
required their divinity to be something more than human,

more even than the ideal human nature; he must be an abstract being, an idea which could find no embodiment in visible form. And with this wish arose again the old supreme god of the whole Greek race to give a name to the abstraction. The Zeus whom Æschylus' suppliants invoke is neither the Zeus of the East nor of the West, of grove nor temple; he is not the god of Olympus any more than of Dôdôna; he is merely *the* God, the King of kings, like the Hebrews' Jehovah.

'King of kings, happiest of the happy, and of the perfect, perfect in might, blest Zeus.'

And we know how the very priest of Dôdôna called upon him in the same strain:

Ζεὺς ἦν, Ζεὺς ἔστι, Ζεὺς ἔσσεται, ὦ μεγάλε Ζεῦ, 'O mighty Zeus, which was and is and is to be.'[1]

---

[1] See Pausanias, x. 12, § 5.

CHAPTER V.

MYSTERIES.

THE greater gods of Greece—those at least who, in the heyday of worship, had the deepest influence upon national belief—were the intrusive gods, the divinities of new comers into the land, the patrons of warriors and sea-faring men. Such gods were the Olympian Zeus and the Apollo of the hardy mountaineers of Tempe, and Athênê, who had brought the Ionians from Asia to Greece, who had shown Greek colonists the way to new countries, and who taught men skill in arts and cunning in trade. But behind these gods stand, half hidden in shadow, other deities of older birth, they who had been worshipped in ancient days by the simple and settled folk of the same lands, by the mere peasant, the shepherd or the planter. Such were Pan or Hermes of Arcadia, Dionysus of Thrace and Macedonia ; such were Dêmêtêr and Dionê and Themis. The names of the beings are for the most part distinctly Aryan ; but in character the gods are pre-Aryan, for they belong of equal right to all nations whose lives are of a quiet kind. Like gods, if with different names, must from age to age have been worshipped on the soil of Greece. If Athênê and Apollo called out a greater measure of enthusiasm and took a larger share in the fostering of Hellenic culture, Pan and Dêmêtêr had, in humbler fashion, a scarce less assured sway over the hearts of their votaries.

This is why in every land a mystery hangs about the worship of the gods of the soil: it is because of their great antiquity. At a time when other creeds are novel theirs is still antique, and many strange, dim associations cling about that creed which the worshippers themselves can scarcely understand. It lies nearer than do other parts of the religion to the primal fount of all religion.

It was said in a former chapter that almost before we arrive at any definite belief among men, and certainly before we reach their developed *mythology*, we find them giving expression to their wild emotions by dances and gestures not less wild. Almost before there is a worship of things there is a sort of worship of emotion; and this gathers especially about two phases of strong excitement, the one created by love, the other by wine. Passion, mental or bodily, is the soul of all religious excitement; that is to say, it is the soul of all belief. The Veddic charmer does after a fashion shadow forth the religion of all mankind; the darweesh and the fakeer display in their strange dances something which is older and more of the essence of human nature than the dogma of Islam; the Christian Flagellant, he who joined in a Procession of Penitents or in a Dance of Death, was the brother in faith of these two, and had got back to a point where no difference of creed could divide. And just in the same way, before the creation of any formulated myth touching the gods of Greece, earlier that the constitution of any Olympus, must have come some ritual observance of this unrestrained, passionate sort. When the pantheon was made, this emotional worship associated itself with those divinities in it who were of oldest birth—that is to say, with the chthonic [1] or earth gods. In after times, when the primal

---

[1] We use this word chthonic with some freedom when we apply it to the first earth gods of the Greek pantheon. The chthonic divinity was essentially a god of the regions under the earth; at first of the dark home of the seed, later on of the still darker home of the dead. But at first an earth divinity was not worshipped under this aspect. It was—and this is especially true of the earth goddess—not the underground region, but the surface of the earth that was worshipped. Therefore, when we speak of Prithivi, or Gaia, or Dêmêter, or Tellus, or Ops, in their earliest forms we cannot call them chthonic divinities. Later on they become more nearly so.

condition had been passed, the same rites, unexplained and
mysterious, were reverently preserved.

The earth itself is a woman: Prithivi, Dêmêtêr.
Perhaps, however, it is neither as Prithivi nor Dêmêtêr
that we ought to think of the goddess to whom the first
chthonic rites of Greece were paid.   For the rituals which
grew into the mysteries may have existed in the land
before the coming thither of Zeus and his pantheon.   But
the older names are gone; we must needs use those which
have been handed down to us.   In time Dêmêtêr came to
hold a place as near to the hearts of the lower orders of
the population, the descendants of the conquered nationalities, as she ever held to the hearts of their conquerors,
and a far nearer place than she held with these latter in
their conquering days.   For it is only by a peaceful and
settled race that the earth goddess is ever held in high
esteem.   This is why it was that the Dorians, the most
warlike among all the nations of new Greece, were ever the
most hostile to the *cult* of Dêmêtêr.   After their invasion
of the Peloponnese, the worship of that goddess had to
hide itself in the rustic retirement of Arcadia, and for long
years—so Herodotus declares [1]—Arcadia was the only portion of the Peloponnese where it was preserved.

There is in most creeds an earth god as well as an
earth goddess, though the former is the less important
personality.   He represents rather the germinal power of
the ground than the simple earth, and he is therefore less
essential to primitive belief than the goddess is.   This is
why he always holds an inferior place.   He is sometimes
the son, sometimes the husband, of the earth.   In Roman
mythology he appears as Liber, who is the son of Ceres
and the brother of Libera, who is a kind of second Ceres.
In some of the Asiatic creeds, to which we shall refer
anon, he is the husband of the earth goddess, but he is also
almost on a level with human nature; he is the Adonis

---

[1] Herod. ii. 171.

to the Cyprian Aphroditê, the Anchises to the Aphroditê of the coast of Asia Minor. Of Greece proper the earth god is for some places Dionysus, for others Ploutôn, for others Pan. Dionysus was not, I suppose, a god of native birth, but became Greek by adoption, and was worshipped especially in the north. Ploutôn, or Hadês-Ploutôn, must not be confounded with that later Hades the embodiment of the tomb. Ploutôn is often spoken of as the son of Dêmêtêr.[1] In the Eleusinian myth the same divinity, Hades-Ploutôn, was her son-in-law. Dionysus held the same relationship.

Zeus himself had to take upon him part of the nature which had belonged traditionally to this god of the soil. Just as there was, as well as a Zeus Olympios, a Pelasgian Zeus to embody the worship of the older race, so there was, as the representative of a creed still earlier, a Zeus Chthonios, or Zeus of the Earth. Such a title implies a complete reversal of Zeus' character as the ruler of heaven. Zeus is indeed husband of the earth goddess, but by right only because the heaven is married to the earth. Nevertheless, we notice that in the Greek pantheon there is no god to whom the surface of the earth is assigned for his special kingdom. In the division of the universe by lot among the three sons of Kronos, to Poseidôn was given the hoary sea, to Hades the pitchy darkness, to Zeus the wide heaven in the clouds and air. The earth was common to all three.[2] The reason of this probably is that these three sons of Kronos are all later comers than the original earth god.

The divine beings who in the historic ages of Greece were the heads and representatives of chthonian worship were Dêmêtêr and Persephonê, the Great Goddesses, as at Eleusis they were called. It was no doubt because of the high antiquity of their *cult* that to them belonged in a

---

[1] Dêmêtêr was said to have brought forth Ploutôn in a thrice-ploughed fallow in the island of Crete.

[2] *Il.* xv. 187 sqq.

special degree the title σεμναί, *reverend, holy*; there was
something awful and mysterious about them which the
other gods had not.   The god who was most associated
with these in worship was Dionysus, who was in historic
days but the pale shadow of what he (or his predecessor) had been when invested with their full character
as earth gods.   Nevertheless the shape which he took
in Greece seems to be one which the earth god has
generally assumed in the later forms of the Aryan religious systems.   The association of three beings of the
same kind as these three—that is to say, a mother, a
daughter, and a male divinity who is husband or brother
of the last—seems generally to belong to the scheme of
Aryan earth worship.   The same trilogy appears in the
Ceres, Libera, and Liber of Rome, and in the Frigg,
Freyja, and Freyr (Freke, Frowa, and Frô) of the Teutons.

   More primitive, perhaps, than the formulated worship
of Dêmêtêr, Persephonê, and Dionysus in Greece was that
form of earth worship whereof we catch faint glimpses in
the legend of Pan and his rustic compeers.   These were
honoured by country dances and unelaborate rites—wild.
dances and processions, no doubt, suiting the tastes and
tempers of those who used them, but not yet turned into
any distinct ritual.   In the Greece of historic times these
early rites had been already supplemented by very defined
ceremonies, called by the name of mysteries.

   The celebrations which have handed on their title for
a general name in future ages, the Greek μυστήρια, are,
when we first catch sight of them, great religious revivals,
for even then they preserve in tradition a something which
has been half forgotten.   They have already departed far
from their original use, and this we see when we compare
them with like ceremonies observed among less cultured
races.   We cannot translate μύστης, nor any of its deriva-
tive words, quite into the primitive sense of them; and our
modern translations, *mystic* and the rest, are separated
from this primitive meaning by a gap which centuries of

religious growth have made. A writer upon the myth of Demeter and Persephonê[1]—the story which formed the foundation of the mysteries which were enacted at Eleusis —computes that we can trace its history for a thousand years. No portion of a creed, no ceremonies connected with that belief, could remain unchanged so long. For example, the element which we naturally associate first of all with the idea of mystery is its secresy, and yet this element the early mysteries contained only in a secondary degree. In the Eleusinia, it is true, the pledge to silence concerning the holy rites was strictly exacted, and is said to have been strictly observed; yet Plato, we know, complained of the easy accessibility of the rites themselves, and Plato lived in days when the motive cause for secresy and exclusiveness had been long in operation.

When Greek thought had been aroused to speculation upon the origin of the world, upon primal existences, upon the difference between good and evil, upon the cause of either, upon a hundred subjects, in fine, whereof it had formerly no conceit, men fancied that during the ecstasies of emotion to which the mystic rites gave rise they caught sight of a solution to the difficulties which oppressed them. And perhaps not wholly without reason; for at such times imagination anticipated the slow steps of logic, and seized hold on new truths almost without knowing how. But these men chose to believe further that the same truths had been revealed to their ancestors and had been by them obscurely handed down in an ancient ritual. The forefathers themselves had no thought of such depths of philosophy; these were added in later times, when the old significance of the rites had been obscured or quite forgotten. Those which *they* instituted were the natural expressions of human emotion; scarcely more complicated and abstruse than the dance of our Veddic devil charmer, or than a war dance of Africans or Maoris.

---

[1] Foerster, *Raub u. Rückkehr der Persephonê.*

It is because of the original simplicity and naturalness of such rites as these that, on whatever side we look, within the bounds of Hellas or abroad, rituals of the same ·kind meet our eye. The Eleusinia of Attica had their rivals in the Thracian and the Samothracian mysteries in honour of Dionysus and of the Cabiri: nay, we know that almost every town of Greece had its own circle of ceremonies, and its formal worship of one or other or of all of the earth divinities. Outside the bounds of Greece are first to be noted the Phrygian rites of Cybelê, most near among Oriental rituals to those of Hellas.

There was in Asia Minor the worship of Cybelê and Sandôn, and in Cyprus that of Aphroditê and Adonis; there was the wounded Thammuz mourned by Tyrian maids, and in Egypt the dead Osiris wept and sought for by Isis. .'The rites of Ceres at Eleusis differ little from these'—the rites of Osiris and Isis (it is Lactantius who is speaking). 'As there Osiris is sought amid the plaints of his mother,[1] so here the quést is for the lost Persephonê; and as Ceres is said to have made her search with torches, so (in the Osiris mystery) the rites are marked by the throwing of brands.'[2] The closer we examine into these various rituals and their attendant myths, the more shall we be struck by their general similarity and the more clearly shall we see that in origin and first intention they were all the same.

What is the meaning of this likeness? The Greeks supposed that many of their beliefs and forms of worship had been received from the Egyptians. But we know now that an adoption of this kind from another race is very rare in any mythology, and may be left out of account in this case: so that, when resemblances such as those we

---

[1] The writer is mistaken here, for Isis was the wife, not the mother, of Osiris.

[2] Lactantius, i. 21–24. Though this writer is not an authority for the early ceremonial of the Isis rites, still, from what we know of the conservative nature of the Egyptians, we may fairly conclude that these had not changed much even so late as in the days of Lactantius.

have noticed are to be found in the religions of many different peoples, they spring out of the fundamental likeness of all religions, as being products of human thought. This was the case with the mysteries: they had their root in instinctive expressions of emotion, not in any particular story nor in any traditional worship. When we find the Eleusinia adopted and initiated in later times and in distant places, we are not to assume that these phenomena are the result of direct missionary efforts on the part of its votaries, but rather that all men had a natural inclination to this form of worship.

No more ought we to suppose that these rites themselves were transplanted into Greece or into Attica from any earlier home. It was in part true, no doubt, that the rites of Dionysus were introduced into the Eleusinian mysteries from Thrace; but it was only a partial truth. For though Dionysus himself may not have been originally known at Eleusis, some other earth god, for sure, was known. Dionysiac worship was said, we know, to have been founded by Orpheus. And then men went further, and attempted to find a derivation, also from Thrace, for the Eleusinian worship of Dêmêtêr and Persephonê. Eumolpos, the fabled introducer of those rites, is called by late writers the son of Boreas (the north wind), or else of Poseidôn and Chionê—that is to say, of the sea and of the snow. By this was meant that Eumolpos had come from northern Greece. The ancients always made things happen in the way of importation and personal influence: the worship of a god in their traditions is generally said to have been introduced into a land by some particular hero. But such is not the usual history of religious ideas. Either they spring up naturally or they never flourish at all.

The truth is that mysteries of this kind are almost universal, and it is a matter of chance which among many birth-places of them attains celebrity, and comes to be thought the mother of all the rest. Eleusis, which means the place of ' coming '—that is to say, the coming of

the New Year—cannot originally have been a designation
of one or two particular spots only; for each locality must
have had its special place at which the spring and spring's
greenery were thought to come back and appear once
more to the world.   In a Norse mythic poem which really
tells the story of the marriage of Persephoné and Dionysus
in a different guise, it is related how a maiden, Gerð (the
Earth),[1] agrees to meet the sun god, Freyr,[2] 'in the warm
wood of Barri,' where Barri signifies simply 'the green.'
Thus any green wood might be the meeting-place of Freyr
and Gerð: but no doubt each locality fixed upon its special
Barri wood.   Just so each place had once its Eleusis, or
the place of spring's coming; but one place eventually
outlasted and outshone all the rest.   Yet even in late
days there were more places with this name than one:
there was an Eleusis in Bœotia as well as in Attica.

We can account in this way for the fact which has
sometimes been commented on as strange, that the
Eleusinia are not spoken of by Homer (the epic Homer)
nor by Hesiod.   The reason is to be found, not—as some
have alleged—in the lateness in time of the Eleusinian
form of worship, but in the commonness of such festivals
and the number of places in which they had their seat.
The importance of the special Attic celebration was of late
growth, for it was due in chief measure to the supremacy
of Athens.   So far as the *institution* of the rites went,
that was too old to be followed back in the history of
belief.

Three or four hundred years ago men had a use for the
word *mystery* which we have since laid aside.   It was
applied to those primitive representations which were the
first divergence from the old miracle plays in the direction
of the secular drama.   Guilds used to be formed out of
the laity for the enactment of these 'mysteries,' which,
becoming a little more secularised still, were afterwards

---

[1] Gerði = earth.

[2] At first an earth god, and afterwards a god of summer and of the sun.

called 'moralities.' It has been questioned whether the
word, when thus used, had any etymological connexion
with the Greek μυστήριον.[1] But that is a matter which
concerns us nothing. This much is certain: that the
mystery of the Middle Ages represented in many ways the
character of the early Eleusinia and other celebrations of
the same order. All these were essentially dramas. They
were, if you will, miracle plays; for the miracle which they
played was that old, long-standing wonder of nature, the
return of the New Year and of all that it brings with it,
the reclothing of Earth-in the greenery which Winter has
stripped off and hidden away. Goethe, counting the stages
by which melancholy gains a sway over man's mind, notes
how at last it begets in him such a distaste of life, such an
intense *ennui*, that the very return of spring strikes his
fancy only as a thing foregone and wearisome through
constant repetition. To man in primal days (but it need
not be so to him alone) the same event appeared ever new,
and so wonderful and joyful that no colour could paint, no
language could dignify it enough. Man sought to present
the glad coming of summer in such a way that it should
appeal to all the senses at once; he sang it in endless
rhymes, he made myths about it, and then he enacted the
story in a drama; and thus he laid the foundation not of
the mysteries only, but of all dramatic representation.

We do not, it is true, know much of those other rites,
Egyptian, Asiatic, or half Hellenic, which I spoke of just
now; but what we do know is enough to convince us that,
like the Eleusinia or the Dionysiac festivals, they took
their rise in the same desire for the symbolic portrayal of
two great events: first, the sorrow of Nature when the
warmth of the sun is withdrawn and the fruitful growth
of plants and grasses is stayed, and then her joy when
these are all restored. The advent of spring was the

---

[1] The terms *moralities, mysteries,* sprang up only at the end of the
Middle Ages. *Mystery* is supposed by some to be derived from *ministerium,*
i.e. a guild, and to have had the spelling changed by false analogy.

'good spell' of the heathen peoples; the death of summer was their book of doom.

As the Eleusinia constituted the chief Greek festival in this kind, and the one concerning which we have most information, though even here our information is meagre enough, I will take this alone as a sample of the Greek mystery, and allow a slight sketch of that to stand for the rest. We all know the story upon which the drama was founded. The tale has come down to us in a hymn, which was, we may suppose, chaunted at such time as the rites of Dêmêtêr and Persephonê were celebrated. Plays then, as in later days, required their prologue, which set forth the history of the piece about to be enacted. So this Homeric hymn tells the tale of the rape and return of Persephonê almost in the form in which her history formed the subject of a mythic drama at Eleusis.

It tells us how the girl Persephonê was wandering with her companion maidens in the Nysian plain, gathering crocus, and rose, and hyacinth, and fair violets, and, more beautiful than all, the narcissus.[1] The deceitful earth sent up this flower to allure the goddess away from her fellows; it was a wonder to be seen, for on it grew a hundred blossoms, which sent forth their fragrance over the laughing earth and the salt waves of the sea. But, as the maiden stooped to seize the prize, the wide earth gaped apart, and the awful son of Kronos leaped forth and bore her away shrieking in his golden chariot. But none of mortals or immortals heard her call, save only Hekatê (the moon) in her cave, and Hêlios (the sun), who sat apart from the other gods in his own temple receiving the fair offerings of men. . . .

But an echo of the cry reached Dêmêtêr, and grief seized her mind. She rent her veil and put from her her dark blue cloak, and like a bird hurried over land and sea seeking her daughter. For nine days she wandered

---

[1] The name of this flower is supposed to bear a special allusion to the sleep of death, or of the winter earth (*ἄρκη, numbness* or *deadness*).

thus, a torch in her hand; until at last Hekaté came to
meet her, likewise bearing a light.   And these two, carrying their torches, sped forth together until they came to
Hêlios; and the goddess spake to him. 'Do thou, O
Sun, who from the divine air lookest down upon all earth
and sea, tell me if thou hast seen any one of gods or
men who against my daughter's will has forcibly carried
her away.'   And he answered, 'Queen Dêmêtêr, I grieve
much for thee and for thy slender-footed daughter.   But
know that Zeus, the cloud-gatherer, has done this thing,
giving thy daughter to his brother Hadês for his fair wife.
Cease then, goddess, from immoderate grief.   Aidôneus,
who is king of many, is no unseemly kinsman among the
immortals. . . .'
    When Dêmêtêr had heard this she was filled with
sharper grief and with anger against the cloudy son of
Kronos, and quitting Olympus, she wandered among the
cities and rich fields of men, obscuring her godhead.   At
length she came to the house of King Keleos, the ruler of •
Eleusis.   There she sat down by a well in the guise of
an old woman.   And the daughters of Keleos saw her as
they came out to draw water, and they knew her not, but
spake to her. . . .   And Dêmêtêr became nurse to Demo-
phoôn, the son of Keleos and of his wife Metaneira.   She
fed him on ambrosia and breathed sweetly upon him as
he lay in her breast.   At night she concealed him in the
strong fire, like a brand, secretly, without his parents'
knowledge.   And she would have rendered him immortal;
but Metaneira, foolishly watching at night, saw it, and
smote her side and shrieked out. . . .   And fair-haired
Dêmêtêr put from her in anger the child, and laying him
upon the ground, she spake to Metaneira. 'Oh, foolish
thou! how hast thou erred!   For by the gods' oath I
swear, by the unappeasable water of Styx, I would have
made thy son immortal and given him unending fame.
But now he cannot avoid death and his fate.   But un-

dying glory shall be his, because he has sat upon my knee
and has slept in my arms. Know that I am Dêmêtêr. . . .'
Then, as she spake, the goddess changed her guise, and
cast off from her her eld. Beauty breathed round her,
and from her fragrant garment spread a sweet odour; far
shone the light from that immortal flesh, and on her
shoulders gleamed her yellow hair, till the house was filled
with the sheen of it as with the lightning. And she left
the palace. . . . And when morning came Keleos summoned his people and told them what had happened, and
bade them build a costly temple to fair-haired Dêmêtêr.
And here the goddess sat down, far apart from the councils
of the gods. Nor while she was there did the earth yield
any seed; in vain men ploughed, and white barley fell
into the furrows in vain; until Zeus sent his messenger,
Iris, to entreat her to return. And, one after another,
came all the immortals with gifts and honours, but she
obstinately turned from all their words.

Then at last Zeus sent down unto Erebus his golden-
wanded messenger to lead away Persephonê from the
murky land, that her mother might be comforted. . . .
And Hadês did not disobey the command of Zeus the
king. Persephonê rejoiced and leaped up in joy. But
he (Hadês) had craftily given her a seed of pomegranate,
that she might not remain for ever above with holy
Dêmêtêr. Now Hadês yoked his steeds to the golden
chariot, and Hermês seized the reins and the whip and
drove straight from the abodes of death, and, cutting
through the deep darkness, they came to where Dêmêtêr
stood. . . .

But because Persephonê had eaten the fruit of the
pomegranate she must still pass one-third of the year
below with her husband; two-thirds she spends on earth
with her mother.

The history which we have just narrated, and which
occupies the first ·portion of the Homeric hymn to
Dêmêtêr, commemorates a nature myth of unfathom-

able antiquity. Towards the end of the hymn the poet strays into legends which have more to do with the supposed origin of the Eleusinia and with the teaching to mankind of the use of agriculture—elements neither of them, as I shall presently point out, belonging to the earliest myth of the earth goddess. Wherefore, over this latter portion of the Homeric hymn—telling how the goddess Dêmêtêr came again to earth, to the Rarian plain, and how the corn sprang up as she passed, how she made the whole earth blithe and fruitful, how she at last appointed the 'law-dispensing kings,' Triptolemos, and Diocles, and Eumolpos, and Keleos, to preserve her rites—over all this we will pass.

Dêmêtêr is γῆ-μήτηρ, mother earth. Persephonê was called at Eleusis Corê, the maiden, or, more literally still, the 'germ.' Eleusis is 'the coming,' not originally, I suspect, of Dêmêtêr to earth, but of the returning spring. And we may see how truly in this poem, even though it has an epic form, all the dramatic instincts are satisfied. The Norsemen had their celebrations (a kind of mystery, too) of the death of the earth in winter, or perhaps one should rather say of that visitation which is peculiar to Northern climates—the total extinction of the sun himself during the coldest months. The festival (or fast) was called the bale or death of Balder. It was kept by the lighting of great fires, called the bale fires.[1] But, strange to say, the season chosen for this celebration was not winter, when the sun was really hidden, but summer—nay, the very height of summer, Midsummer's Eve. It was thus, by taking the sun at the moment of his greatest power, that a dramatic force was given to the miracle play which enacted the sun's own overthrow. Just the same spirit is visible here. Persephonê, the maiden, the

---

[1] In the Middle Ages the bale fires changed their names, and became St. John's fires (*Johannisfeuer*, *feux de St. Jean*), and under these names are still kept up in Germany and some parts of France, and in the west or extreme north of Scotland. St. John's Day of course occurs at Midsummer.

image of spring, is found playing in the meadows and gathering the flowers of the early year at the moment when Aidôneus comes to carry her below. Rightly this rape should have been made to happen in the autumn; but then the force of contrast between life and death would have been lost. So it happens in the spring; and probably the chief Eleusinian feasts were originally at this season.[1]

On the other hand, though the changes of the year are gradual, those between day and night are rapid and impressive. Granted that the time of year is fixed as it is, both here and in the Northern myth, the drama will be the most effective if the time of day in which its action falls is made to be the evening. Balder's bale fires were lighted at sundown, and kept burning all through the night. And here also, reading a little between the lines of the hymn—that is to say, making allowance for some extension of time in a story which is told epically, not dramatically[2]—we can gather, I think, that the rape of Persephonê was originally thought to happen just at sunset, and then the search for her to extend throughout one night. Behind the expanded season myth lies the more primitive myth of light and dark. For see how the positions of the sun and moon are incidentally told us:—

> And her companions all vainly sought her.
> Of gods or mortal men none heard her cry,
> Saving two only, the great Perseus' daughter,
> The goddess of the cave, mild Hekatê,
> And bright Hyperion's son, King Helios,
> He too gave ear unto that call; for he,
> Taking from men their offerings beauteous,
> In his own home sat from the gods away.

[1] *Originally*. As is afterwards suggested, it is probable that their transference to autumn denoted a change from a feast which merely celebrated the return of the year to one which was more distinctly a farmer's festival.

[2] Such allowances in interpreting any particular *form* of a myth we must always be prepared to make.

The sun is away from Olympus because he is near his setting; he is sitting in his western tent by the homes of men. Hekatê, the moon, hears from her cave; for she is still below the earth. And now Dêmêtêr, who has caught a faint echo of that cry of anguish, hurries over the earth with a torch in her hand, seeking Persephonê: it is night. Anon she encounters Hekatê, who comes to meet her, likewise carrying a light: for now the moon has risen.

There is no reason why the Eleusinia, or some festivals of a like kind, may not have existed before the familiar use of agriculture. Dêmêtêr is much more than the patroness of the husbandman's art; she is the earth mother herself, the parent of all growth. The coming of spring would be not less welcome in days when men lived upon the proceeds of hunting, upon flocks and herds, or upon wild fruits. All life is in the hands of the fruit-bearing goddess.

Γαῖα καρπὺς ἀνίει, διὸ κλήζετε μητέρα γαῖαν

chaunted the Dôdônian priests.[1] And they might have sung the same to Gaia or to Dêmêtêr (Mother Gaia) ages before corn had been first sown.

But agriculture was introduced; and the special importance of earth's fruitfulness as the cause of the growth of the grain came in time to throw into the background the earth's other miscellaneous gifts. Nevertheless this change was long in taking place. The myth which is connected with this aspect of the Eleusinia—that is to say, their aspect as celebrations of the new birth, not so much of the year as of the ear, and as the special glorification of the husbandman's art—is the myth of Triptolemus. He, said the legend, was charged by Dêmêtêr to spread abroad her worship, and to teach men the mystery of sowing corn. His name explains his position in the myth: he is τρίπολος, the thrice-ploughed furrow. In

[1] Pausanias, x. 12, 5.

later days Triptolemus grew to be a very important character in the Dêmêtêr legend. But in the Homeric hymn, which is probably almost contemporary with Hêsiod—that is to say, not later than the eighth century before Christ [1]—Triptolemus plays no very leading part. He is one (the first, it is true) among many kings who are said to have received the command of Dêmêtêr to institute her rites. 'She went,' says the hymn, ' to the law-giving kings, to Triptolemus and horse-driving Diocles, and the might of Eumolpos, and to Keleos, leader of the people, and to them she told how to perform her holy service.' Moreover, all this history of the institution of the mysteries forms a separate part of the hymn, and is in no way connected with the main legend which was related just now.

The worship, therefore, of Dêmêtêr in her character of goddess of husbandry has a second place in the intention of the mysteries. In later times, say from the beginning of the fifth century, when the history of the great goddesses begins to be common in art, Triptolemus is rarely absent from such representations. He commonly forms one of a group which contains Dêmêtêr and Persephonê, Hadês, Hekatê, and Hermês. In one part of the picture may be the god of the under world ; in the other is Triptolemus in snaky chariot, scattering abroad the grain. When this change had taken place, and the character of Triptolemus had become an essential in the Persephonê legend, the mysteries had come to be much less rejoicings at the return of the spring than a sort of harvest homes, rejoicings for the ingathered wealth which earth had yielded.

When agriculture is in its infancy men do not sow in the autumn. They plant some quick-growing corn, which takes a few months only to ripen; and what is sown in the early spring is reaped before the summer. The French name for buckwheat, *blé sarrasin*, is derived from the use by the Tartars of this grain, which can be sown

---

[1] Lenormant, however, puts it later. See Daremberg and Saglio's *Dictionnaire des Antiquités*, art. ' Cérès.'

during the short sojourn which the nomadic people make in one spot. Therefore in early days the festival of Dêmêtêr and Corê would naturally fall in the spring. Later in time there came to be two festivals—the one dedicated to the coming up (anodos, ἄνοδος) of Corê or the germ, the other to her descent (kathodos, κάθοδος) into the infernal realms. The second was Persephonê's marriage with Pluto—that is to say, it was concerned with the most germane matter of the Eleusinian myth—it was, beside, the festival of the sower, and was for these reasons the greatest. Yet we observe that in being held in the autumn it runs counter to the picture which is presented to us in the Homeric hymn. The anodos was associated with the worship of Dionysos; it was celebrated in his month, the flower month, and was supposed (it was an addition to the old legend) to celebrate the marriage of Persephonê with that god.

Whether the mysteries were, as at first, feasts to the spring, or, as later on they became, feasts to the goddess of agriculture, harvest homes, they were, before all things, peasant festivals. They belonged, I have said, to the autochthones, the simple early inhabitants of the soil. To that belonging they owed their vast antiquity. Conquering nations passed over the land and left these rustic rites unchanged, adhering to one place, handed on by an everlasting tradition from generation to generation.[1] At

---

[1] Enough has, I imagine, been said in this and in the previous chapter to show that Dêmêtêr was one among the oldest divinities worshipped in Greece. Herodotus tells us so much (ii. 171). Pausanias says that she was known as Dêmêtêr Pelasgis (ii. 22, 10). She was called by the same title in Arcadia, the very home of all that was most ancient in Greek culture (Herod. l. c.) We have seen how obstinately her worship was maintained there.

Persephonê is not really to be distinguished from Dêmêtêr. For Dêmêtêr herself often appears as a maiden as Δημήτηρ Χλόη (Paus. i. 22), and this is identical in meaning with the name κόρη given to Persephonê. Dêmêtêr is spoken of as daughter of Γῆ κουροτρόφος (the nursing earth). Moreover in artistic representations it is very hard to make a distinction between mother and daughter. (See on this subject Gerhard, Gr. Myth. § 240, 4; and in Akad. Abt. ii. 357; and Overbeck, Gr. Kunstmyth. ii. 442,

last this creed, which had rested quiet 'under the drums and tramplings' of many conquests, began to rise again. The down-trodden race vindicated its old power; and the stone which had been overlooked in the first building of the Greek and Roman religions became the headstone of the corner.

All the charm of the unknown belongs to celebrations such as these, whose beginnings lie covered up by so many centuries of neglect. In Rome the festival of the Lupercalia kept alive the memory of a society of shepherds and hunts-men who lived before cities had been built or even agricul-ture established. The same feast lived to witness the fall of the Republic, to see a 'kingly crown' thrice presented to the Republic's destroyer;[1] and, lasting far beyond that, it saw the fall of the religion of Rome after the fall of its old government; it survived the introduction of Christianity, and was celebrated as late as in the reign of Anthemius. One may almost say that it is commemorated still at the Carnival. The Eleusinia had as long a life. They were finally crushed out by the monks who entered Greece in A.D. 395 in the train of Alaric's invading army; and that these proselytists should have exerted themselves in the

---

448. See the Harpy Tomb of Xanthos for an example of the likeness be-tween the two goddesses.)

From this I am led to believe that some parts of the myth of the two Great Goddesses may be repetitions, as the same adventures would have to be attributed to each. Thus I imagine that the wanderings of Dêmêtér belong of necessity to her as a goddess of earth, and quite alone express the notion of the change from summer to winter—the change in *appear-ance* of the earth being mythically represented as a change from place to place, a change in *space*. This will become more clear when we compare with the Dêmêtér mysteries those of which we have some traces among the Teutonic folk (see Ch. VII.) It follows that the rape of Persephoné and the wanderings of Dêmêtér are mythic repetitions of the same notion.

This leads us back to a still earlier form of the mysteries when Dêmêtér and Persephoné were not united, but separate.

See Daremberg and Saglio's *Dict. des Ant.*, art. 'Cérès,' by F. Lenormant, for the traces of Dêmêtér worship in Greece.

[1]   'You all did see that on the Lupercal
       I thrice presented him a kingly crown,
       Which he did thrice refuse.'—*Julius Cæsar*

matter shows that the faith had still a hold upon the affections of the people.

It has been said that there is in these rites another element beside the mere joy of living and of seeing the earth live again, or one may at least say a more eager and passionate expression of that joy. The substratum of phallic worship, which lies at the root of many elaborate rituals such as these, accompanies them in their after development. Therefore is it that in close relationship to the mustêrion stands the orgê. Both words have been handed down for perpetual use in later ages. In historic times the orgy belonged more especially to the later Dionysus, the wine god. The mystery still belonged to Dêmêtêr.

In such conceptions as this Bacchus, or the Vedic Soma, or Agni, are worshipped beings half physical, half abstract. On the one side is the thing, the honeydew, the wine, which excites passion, or the fire which symbolises it; on the other side, the emotion itself. But men do not analyse their complex feelings into their different elements; they do not recognise that fire is a symbol of the passion, or that the wine is only a cause of the tumultuous emotions which they feel. The wine or the fire they believe enters into them and itself *constitutes* the mental condition which they know. Therefore in worshipping the vine men did in fact worship the strength of their feelings, and these produced in them that emotional state which is necessary to belief, and which lies at the foundation of all religions. To produce such a condition of mind was the object of the orgy; which, in giving a more distinctly emotional, gave in the end a more distinctly religious character to the mystic festivals.

In another way also, pleasanter to contemplate, religious excitement was maintained—namely, by the supreme influence of music. Tradition shows us how early was the use of this stimulus in the Eleusinia. There was at Eleusis a family which claimed the hereditary office of chief priest (hierophant) in the celebrations. They were the Eumolpidæ; and they pretended an eponymous ancestor, Eumolpos, who was supposed to have been the first priest of Dêmêtêr and Dionysus at Eleusis, and to have introduced their mysteries there. In reality Eumolpos is nothing more than the 'sweet-voiced one,' the leader of the choir. The name Eumolpidæ is that of an office, not of a family: it must have been in later times that the office became hereditary and gave its designation to a single house. But that these sweet singers (*eumolpoi*) should have claimed the credit of originating the Demetric worship argues a vast antiquity for the choral performance therein, when the leading singer was likewise the officiating-priest.

The excitement which is wrought of old observances, imperfectly understood, the halo at once of mystery and of antiquity, grew up rapidly around the ritual of the Eleusinia. Strong emotion not much restrained, fostered by music and a kind of holy drama, and surrounded by much that is ancient and unexplained—these are ingredients which in all ages will produce the same effects. Let us note that all the 'mystics' in the modern purely religious sense —all those, I mean, who have enshrined their thoughts of God in a halo of rapt emotion—have turned to such dramatic pictures as the Greeks rejoiced in at Eleusis; and the converse holds good, that wherever we find these dramatic celebrations we may be sure that the doctrines which they contain will take sooner or later a genuinely mystic complexion. St. Francis of Assisi is the typical 'mystic' of the Middle Age. His biographer [1] has recorded the care with which he prepared, and the pleasure he took in the enaction of, a drama representing the birth of Christ, as nearly like the drama we have been describing as the difference between their two subjects. and the lapse of intervening centuries would allow.

[1] Thomas of Cellano in *Acta SS. Octobris*, tom. 2.

'The day of joy approached, the time of rejoicing was near. The brothers (of the Order of Franciscans) are assembled from many places; the men and women of the country round, according to their capacities, prepare *candles* and *torches* for illuminating the night, that night whose shining star lit up all future days and years. At length came the Saint, and finding everything prepared, saw and was glad. Even a manger is got ready and hay procured, and an ox and an ass are brought in. Honour and praise are given to simplicity, to poverty and humility, and Campogreco is made as it were a new Bethlehem. . . . The night is illumined like the day, and is most grateful to men and animals. The peasantry approach and with new joys celebrate the renewal of the *mysteries*. He (St. Francis) imitates the voice of woods, and the rocks rejoicing answer. The brothers sing, paying their meed of praise to the Lord. The Saint stands before the procession, heaving sighs, bowed with emotion and suffused with a wondrous joy. They celebrate the solemn service of the *Mass*.'

Is it not by a true instinct that the Church which claims to be built by a mystic power, and to transmit its spiritual influence through channels unsounded by reason, shrouds its acts of worship even now in a veil of half-explained drama, and wraps its dogmas round with a garment of melodious sounds?

There can be no question that the mystæ in the Eleusinia, with precisely the same intention as St. Francis, re-enacted in a certain defined series of dramas the chief details of the myth above narrated—that is to say, the loss of the maiden (Corê), the journeys of her mother, the sorrows of the goddess by the well, the honour done her in the house of Keleos, the preparation of the mystic drink by which Dêmêtêr was delighted and which became the sacrament of her votaries,[1] and finally the restoration

---

[1] This mystic drink, kykeôn (κυκεών), is described as having been made of meal and water flavoured with mint.

to her of her daughter Persephonê. And then perhaps came, as a pendant to this, the institution of her rites and the command to Triptolemus to spread abroad the worship of the Great Goddesses.

In this history of Dêmêtêr there are some features which constantly recur in the myths of earth goddesses wherever they are found; others are peculiar to the Greek legend. It has been already said that the mission of Triptolemus belongs to the later, and therefore less essential, parts of the legend. There are, again, some parts of the Dêmêtêr myth—as describrd in the Homeric hymn— which have been somewhat distorted from their original and universal shape, and made to take a peculiar character. This has been the case with the history of the wanderings of Dêmêtêr. In the Greek legend they are represented as if undertaken solely in search of Persephonê. In reality the earth goddess is by virtue of her very nature a wan- derer, and is always represented as passing from place to place. Dêmêtêr's journeyings are of the very essence of her character, and could not have been omitted from any myth concerning her. But at the same time they could not have depended entirely upon the doings of Perse- phonê, for this conclusive reason, that Persephonê and Dêmêtêr are only different forms of the same individuality.

We see that the earth goddess is a wandering goddess when we come to examine the myths which concern her and the ritual observances which have sprung up in her honour in many different lands. We have compared Dêmêtêr with some of the chthonic divinities of the East, of Egypt or of Asia. Among these it is well known that Isis is supposed to have wandered from land to land, and in the ritual observances dedicated to this goddess no small part consisted in dragging her image from place to place. The Ephesian Artemis, another earth goddess, was also borne about. When we take occasion, as in a future chapter we shall do, to confront with the myth and ritual of Dêmêtêr the myth and ritual of the earth goddess of the Teutonic races, we shall see that the latter divinity was also noted for her wandering nature. The essential meaning of the myth in every case is this: the earth goddess becomes identified in thought with the green earth, and in spring she is deemed to come back again to those who are waiting and longing for her. And the idea is made more real by a dramatic representation, which in spring time carries the goddess from village to village, from farm to farm, as though her coming there did inaugurate the new year.[1]

But in course of time the earth goddess becomes separated in mythology from the divinity of spring, and then a Persephonê, or an Osiris, or an Adonis, or a Freyr, or an Odhur,[2] a daughter, a lover, or a husband, has to play a second part in the ritual beside the earth mother. Owing to this kind of change, the wanderings of Dêmêtêr have taken a new character in the Greek myth. They are there represented as being undertaken in the search for a lost daughter—that is to say, as following after the departing spring, rather than as announcing its coming to the earth. Agreeably with the change in the story, the received myth about Eleusis itself was that it was only the place to which Dêmêtêr had come in the course of her wanderings in search of Persephonê. That which allows us to correct this account is, first, the comparison of this myth with the myths of other earth goddesses; and, secondly, the appreciation of the fuller meaning which the early form of the story would give to the name Eleusis.[3]

The Homeric hymn speaks of Dêmêtêr going over land and sea, but in language somewhat vague; in the drama the details of these wanderings were doubtless represented. All we know from the hymn is that the goddess went like a bird over the land and water; that for nine days she traversed all the earth. From a comparison of this myth with those preserved in the Roman form of Isis

---

[1] This idea is beautifully put forward by Lucretius, ii. 597-64
[2] See Chapter VII.   [3] See supra.

worship or the Teutonic earth worship, we gather that
in all these cases the sea voyage was a very important
element. ·A boat was dragged about during the Isis
festival in Rome, and a boat was the symbol of the
Teutonic earth goddess. This part of Dêmêtêr's journey
was, I imagine, alluded to in the phrase ἅλαδε μύσται,
'To the sea mystics l' which was called out on the second
day of the Eleusinian celebrations. As none did betake
themselves to any sort of sea voyage, the phrase has,
naturally enough, been found puzzling to commentators.
Some have said that it meant that men were to wash
themselves in the sea; but that explanation is surely inadequate. The day itself of the festival was called by the
name ἅλαδε μύσται; the mere act of ablution could hardly
have filled up the chief part of that day's ritual. I rather
imagine this name to have been a relic from a time when
the supposed sea voyage of the goddess was literally imitated by her votaries, though this custom was afterwards
omitted and the journey was made by land.

Next after this followed certain sacrifices made in the
city of Athens, and then was formed the procession to go
from Athens to that holy spot Eleusis. This journey might
be matched by those other ritual observances alluded to just
now, the bearing about of Isis, or of the Ephesian Artemis,
or of the Teutonic goddess. It was in itself a sort of drama :
it represented in its way the wanderings of Dêmêtêr, and so
in a degree anticipated the drama which was afterwards
to take place at Eleusis. In this initial procession, however, it was not an image of Dêmêtêr which the mystæ
carried with them as they went, but an image of the boy
Iacchos, who was identified with Dionysus and here stood
for the young year. It is this initiatory procession which,
as I suppose, contains in it the most primitive elements of
the ritual of the chthonic divinities. The wild dances
and processions in which all these rituals take their rise
precede the building of temples or the possibility of any
more formal dramas.

As the accounts which have come down to us of this great Greek festival are from the latter days of heathenism —nay, the best account is from the pen of a Christian father [1]—they necessarily exhibit the confusion of those elements which time had brought together to form a latter-day mystery. And we have before us the task of distinguishing what is new from what is ancient in them. There are descriptions of some processions such as might have been made a thousand years before, and there are symbolic phrases and rituals which betoken an age not long before Christ. But it so happens that the order of introduction into the ritual of each element in it roughly corresponds with the place of that portion in order of performance; so that the first days of the mysteries contain the most antique constituents, and we gradually, as we approach the end of the festival, come to newer and newer additions.

The half-forgotten drama of the procession was more ancient than the conscious formulated drama which took place at Eleusis; yet even these later additions did little else than repeat, with elaborations, the story which the first parts were designed to set forth. On the whole the wonder rather is that the simpler myths and earlier rites should remain so clearly distinguishable than that they should be here and there overlaid and hidden.

The greater mysteries, the Eleusinia properly so called, began in the autumn, in the middle of the month Boedromion.[2] The first day was called the day of the collection (ἀγερμός) or assembling. It was in truth a carnival which preceded the nine lenten days of the regular celebration: the noise and tumult on this day contrasted strangely with the silence and seriousness which were enjoined upon the mystæ when the festival had begun. The second day was called ἅλαδε μύσται, the meaning of which has been explained. The sea voyage was commuted

---

[1] Clement of Alexandria.
[2] The month which commemorated the defeat of the Amazons.

to a mere bathing and purification in the sea.   The third
day was that of sacrifice to Dêmêter in the temple at
Athens; the fourth, also of sacrifices—of firstfruits—to
Dionysus in his temple there; the fifth, of sacrifices to
Asclepios—a god who in those latter days had come
to be confounded with Iacchos, and so with Dionysus.
Then on the sixth day was formed the processional *cortége*
to Eleusis, carrying along with it the image of Iacchos,
represented as a boy bearing a torch like the Egyptian
Horus.[1]

These initial days of the festival reproduce its character
in the earliest times when peasants and shepherds did
service to the universal mother.   The dress of the mystæ
up to this time seems to show a consciousness of the
antiquity of the ceremonies which they renewed.   This
dress was a simple fawn or sheep skin (νεβρίς).[2]   On the
sixth day this costume was exchanged for a more civilised
dress to be worn at the inner mysteries.   During these
inner mysteries the door is closed to us.   Only the
initiated might partake in them, and they were forbidden
to speak of what they had seen and done.   The eighth and
ninth days, which ended the feast, were devoted to the
initiation (μύησις and ἐποπτεία) and to the grand dramatic
performances in the great temple at Eleusis.

But though we have been left outside the sacred
enclosure, shall we be far wrong if, in picturing what is
doing within (while making allowance for the difference
of age and the difference of subject), we allow our minds
to wander to St. Francis and his brethren assembled from

---

[1] Horus is the image of the rising sun, in contrast with Osiris, who is
the setting sun, or the sun after setting.   In a wider sense—that is to say,
in the great myth of the death of Osiris—Horus seems to be taken for an
image of the new year.   Iacchos also undergoes changes of meaning.
Sometimes, perhaps, his torch-bearing image was deemed only the morning
star, for this thought is expressed in the apostrophe in the 'Frogs'—

νυκτέρου τελετῆς φωσφόρος ἀστήρ.

[2] Νεβρίς is of course properly a fawn skin.   It was the general dress of
the Bacchantes.   It is probable that a sheep-skin often did service for it.

all Italy, with their torches alight, the manger prepared, with the ox and the ass in their stall, the hymn rising in the still night, the solemn excitement of the Saint as he administers the holy mystery of the mass? The Greeks, too, had their. torchlight procession, their veiled figures moving from side to side in mimic quest of the lost Persephonê; they had a sort of eucharist in the mystic drink kykeon; and for a processional chaunt let us listen to an ancient chorus which has come down to us, perhaps, from these very Eleusinia:— [1]

STROPHE.

Over the wide mountain ways
The Holy Mother hurrying went,
Through woody tracts her steps she bent,
By the swift river-floods' descent,
Or where upon the hollow coast
The deep sea-waves their voice upraise,
Loud in her lament
For her nameless daughter lost.
And the Bacchic cymbals high
Sent abroad a piercing cry.
So ever in her car, along
By yokèd wild beasts borne,
She seeks the virgin who was torn
From her virgin choir among.
In the quest, by her side,
Fleet as storms two others go—
Artemis of the bow,
And armed Athênê, gorgon-eyed.

.   .   .   .   .

ANTISTROPHE.

Now with many wanderings worn,
Her daughter's foot-prints, hope-forlorn,
·The goddess stayed from following.
The snowy Idæan heights she passed,
Pitifully sorrowing,
And in the snows herself down cast.

[1] Though misplaced in the *Helen* of Euripides.

And all the while from earth's broad plain
Men reap no more the golden grain,
Nor for the flocks green pastures grow,
No leafy tendril sprouts again.
She will the human race o'erthrow,
The city streets to desert turn.
No victim dies; no longer burn
The altar cakes; the fountains now,
By dews unfed, no longer pour;
She hath forbid their crystal flow—
For the maiden sorrowing so
Now and ever more.

It is evident that Persephonê was naturally little connected with thoughts of death, of the next world and of
future judgment. The allusions to her myth which we
have gathered together—and these are the most important
to be found in the range of Greek literature—the remains
of the Eleusinian festival which have come down to us,
make it clear that it is essentially as a goddess of spring
that Persephonê was worshipped, and that the mysteries
speak far more of the sorrows of Dêmêtêr above the earth
than of Persephonê beneath it.   We are not brought face
to face with the kingdom of Hadês, as (for example) we are
in the myth of the death of Balder, a story which in other
ways nearly resembles the myths of Persephonê.   What
likeness is there between this queen of the shades and the
Norse goddess Hel, whose table is Hunger, Starvation her
knife, Care her bed, and Bitter Pain the tapestry of her
room? Of course Persephonê was acknowledged as a ruler
of the dead.   She and her story are often painted upon
cinerary urns and upon tombs.   Still we must confess that
in her nature there is far more of Corê, the maiden, than
of Persephonê; and that this latter name, which means
light-destroyer, is as little appropriate to her whole character
as Apollo, the destroyer, is appropriate to the sun god.[1]

[1] Preller has discussed at some length and with much learning the
probability of their being two Persephonês, whose diverse natures became
united into one (*Demeter u. Persephone*, Introd.)

Moreover, where the Homeric story comes to an end the arrangement was that Persephonê (albeit she is called Persephonê there) should spend two-thirds of the year above the earth, one-third only below it. To the author of this hymn she was evidently not first of all a goddess of death; the god of torment has not yet taught her how to frown and how to chide. I think, therefore, that we may determine without much hesitation that the myth, and the mysteries which preserved that myth, had at first only a very slight connection with theories about death and a future.

Of course the image of the seed, perishing that it may rise again, speaks with a natural and simple appropriateness of the hope which may accompany the consignment of a dead man to the all-nourishing earth. But it speaks only through the voice of an allegory; and if there is one thing which the history of belief teaches us more clearly than others, it is that allegories of such a kind as this, the *parables* of nature, are not among the first lessons which man learns from her. Man's earliest myths are direct histories; they are *meant* at least to tell only of what happens before his eyes or what he credulously believes to be among the doings of the physical world. They are not mystical interpretations from these actions, or images transferred from the world of sense to the region of feeling and thought.

It is not the less true, however, that we can trace alongside of the simpler and earlier story of Dêmêtêr and Persephonê the growth of a deeper mystery which touched upon thoughts of the other world. And when the goddess of the very fulness of youth and of spring had come to be confounded with the ruler over the shades, men had before them, no doubt, a lesson of the deepest significance. 'In the midst of life we are in death.' This was now the text which came at the end of the fasting and feasting, the torchlight processions and triumphant hymns, and the nameless orgies after them. Has a more solemn

trumpet sound of warning ever rung in the ears of
humanity than this? Were these things, then, only a prologue to a dance of death? How changed must have
become the mysteries when such a belief had found
entrance!

> The world seemed not the place it was before.

We wrongly credit the Hellenes with a complete carelessness of their destiny in a future state. Such may have
been their prevailing tone; such must have been the
prevailing tone of a life so vigorous and joyful as their life
was. Greek art has little to tell us of thoughts about
another world.[1] But there must always have been a
minority who were not indifferent to these things; and a
little before the historical period their views (upon the
speculative side at least) gained a measure of strength.
Greece had been long connected by some tie with Egypt,
whose inhabitants, among all the nations of antiquity,
were most deeply imbued with thoughts about death and
the other world. Pythagoras, however, was the first Greek
writer who professed to have drawn much from the wisdom
of the Egyptians. Another source to which Pythagoras
and some of his followers have evidently been indebted is
Persia. We still feel, and in great measure through the
medium of the Platonic philosophy, the effects of Persian
teaching upon that great primal crux of religion the
origin of evil; a teaching which has spread its influence
over every Western land. Before the second age of Hellenic literature, the age of the drama and of lyrical poetry,
of Æschylus and Pindar, Greece had greatly altered from
its first simplicity. Colonists had gone out far and near,
had settled in Italy, in Gaul, and on the far shores of the
Pontus or at the mouth of the Nile. Even before the days
of contest with Persia, Greek soldiers were held in such

---

[1] It would have had more to tell had the paintings of Polygnotus come
down to our time. He covered two walls of the Cnidian pilgrims' house
(lesché) at Delphi with paintings representing the world of shades and the
punishment of the wicked (Paus. x. 25-31).

esteem that they went as mercenaries to the capitals of the greatest Asiatic monarchies, to Nineveh and Babylon as well as to Thebes. Greek merchants too traded with these countries, and Greek noblemen and philosophers frequented their courts.

Many questions which to the Eastern mind and in these time-worn States were quite familiar, were almost new to such a young people as the Hellenes; and the result of this intermixture of ideas was that Greece entered upon its philosophical stage; its mind became questioning and sceptical, which had once been simple and credulous. As the new ideas passed from State to State they saw the old Homeric religion crumble beneath their tread. And as the fixed faith of former times decayed, it left an unsatisfied craving for religious emotion of all kinds.

The mysteries had by this time gained every requisite for answering to feelings so excited. They were very old; but, as the origin and true meaning of them had been forgotten, they could not be exploded as easily as could the plainer teaching of the Homeric religion. All the stimulants to emotion which we have dwelt upon before, the secrecy of the mystery, the tumultuous excitement of the orgy, were to be found within them; and, in addition to these motives, they now added a new one, a hint concerning the great mystery of mysteries, the mingling of death with life. The worship of ancestors and the sacrifices to the departed went hand in hand with festivals of flowers and the honours of Dionysus.[1] All this must have given to the ceremony a new character. It must

---

[1] The Anthesteria, the festival of flowers, was especially set apart for honours to be paid to the dead (see Pauly, *Real-Encyclopädie* s. v. *Mysteria* and *Bacchus*). A black cock is the victim most often associated with the deities of the under world, and Persephonê is very frequently represented (especially so upon urns) with this bird in her hand. Now as the cock is the herald of morning, it belongs rather to the goddess Corê than to the infernal deities. It is, in fact, also sacred to Apollo. It is probably, therefore, only an after-thought which makes the cock a black one, a change corresponding to the change in Persephonê's nature. In the Northern mythology three cocks are to proclaim the dawn of the Last

have thrown over the festival a quite new air. of sadness, which was very different from the emotion with which men had looked upon the play which told only of the death of earth's greenery. The seeds which were now planted were the bodies of beloved relatives; they would not spring up again with the returning year. The mysteries entered upon a fresh phase. It was after this transition from the old to the new mysteries that art began to busy itself much with the story of the Great Goddesses. The artistic representations of the myth occur frequently on cinerary urns. Dêmêtêr herself became more a picture of maternal sorrow than she should naturally have been. In some of the statues of Dêmêtêr—as, for example, in that beautiful one from Cnidus in the British Museum—we have an image of the true *mater dolorosa* of the Greek creed. It is evident that the mother mourns for her daughter as for one dead. Nevertheless the ultimate consolation of the goddess was suited to teach men that they need not sorrow as those that have no hope.

The teaching concerning the expectation of a future life may have been the real substance of the latter-day mysteries; it may, I mean, have been the special subject on which silence was so important—the boon of knowledge to which initiation opened a door. It was perhaps then, when this doctrine crept into the Eleusinia, that the strict oath of secrecy was instituted. On the first day of the ceremonies the sacred herald, by public proclamation, enjoined silence and reverence on the initiated.[1] Afterwards those who were about to witness the holy drama were required one by one to swear secrecy. Wherefore Demosthenes says that those who have not been initiated can know nothing of the mysteries by report.

Day, that great Armageddon of Teutonic religion called Ragna-rök, the Doom of the Gods. Over Asgard—Gods' Home—a golden cock crows, over Man's Home a red cock, and over Hell a cock of *sooty red*.

[1] Εὐφημεῖν χρὴ καθίστασθαι τοῖς ἡμετέροισι χοροῖσι, 'Speak reverently, and stand aside from before our holy choir,' as Aristophanes parodies the ceremony.

One would fain know why the mystæ deemed secresy so important. Did they think that they could, as it were, keep the privilege of immortality to themselves by not divulging too freely how it was won; that the envious upper powers might withdraw it from mankind if all rushed in to share the gift?[1] Such a gift might well seem a strange one at the hands of the jealous gods, as it was indeed most precious. Would it be wise to distribute its benefits broadcast? When, owing to many circumstances, but chiefly owing to this, that they were the mysteries of the most thoughtful and spiritual nationality of Hellas, the Eleusinia became *the* mysteries of Greece, and all sought admission to their privileges, this admission was at the outset charily granted. At first only Athenian citizens might 'partake;' anyone born out of Attica needed to get himself adopted by an Athenian family. Afterwards initiation was allowed to all Hellenes. 'If these things contain some secret doctrine they ought not to be shown to all at no more cost than the sacrifice of a common pig:' so Plato complains of their easy accessibility. Subsequently the same rites were granted to the Romans. Barbarians were always excluded.

Again, one would like to know what ideas the initiated had touching that future for which they were in some unknown way preparing themselves. I should not think it strange if, in the height of their mystic rites, in the midst of blazing torches, of the sounds of music, of wild cries to Dionysus,

> Ἴακχ', ὦ Ἴακχε,
> νυκτέρου τελετῆς φωσφόρος ἀστήρ,

in the gloom of night, among sacrifices and the memories of friends not long since departed, the enthusiast became transported to think that he was no longer in the upper

---

[1] In the same spirit a woman of the Orkneys, when asked to repeat a charm which she had for driving away evil spirits at night, expressed a fear that the auditor would publish what she told him. 'And then,' said she, 'all the gude o' it to me wad be gane.'

workaday world, but had really been carried across the
dreaded Styx to the asphodel meadows and the banks of
the forgetful stream.   In the Middle Ages, during the
fever of those darker mystic rites, which used at times to
sweep over the people like an epidemic, and which cul-
minated during the fourteenth century in the horrible
Dance of Death, it was common enough to find the performers fully persuaded that they had passed the limits of
mortality.   Sometimes they deemed they were in heaven,
more often that they were damned in the world below;
some fancied they had got into an intermediate state
which was neither purgatory nor heaven nor hell.

Aristophanes, in his wild way, shows us a picture of
this kind of belief.   The portrait is distorted certainly, but
not perhaps very unlike the original.   The picture occurs
in the ' Frogs ' when Bacchus is preparing to descend to
the lower world, in order to fetch thence his favourite
Euripides.   And before making the journey he goes to ask
the way of Heraclês; for Heraclês, as we well know, had
been more than once into the land of shades.   The hero then
forewarns Dionysus how, when he has descended beneath
the earth and crossed the Styx, he will find himself in a
new world in no way distinguishable from that where he
now is—sunny meadows like those he is leaving, and
the bands of the initiate singing their songs to Dêmêtêr
and Dionysus, just as they sing them at the mysteries.
In truth, it is the damnation of Peter Bell :—

> It was a party in a parlour,
> Crammed just as they on earth were crammed;
> Some sipping punch, some sipping tea;
> And by their faces you might see
> All silent and all damned.

There is a fine Aristophanes-like touch of genius in
putting this force upon our fancy.   In the original play
the scene would be imagined[1] to shift for a moment

[1] The change of scene during the Greek plays was never more than
indicated to the imagination, not forced upon it, as with us.

to the banks of Styx, and to show Charon and his boat;
and then the meadows which men could actually see from
their seats, and the sun-light which fell upon them where
they sat, would be transformed (by imagination) to a
scene in Hadês.

When Dionysus has been standing a little while in
these meadows 'a mystical odour of torches breathes
round him,' and behold the chorus of the mystæ come in
calling upon Iacchos—without knowing that he is present
—and imitating in all respects the action of the mystæ
upon the upper earth, though the chorus which they sing
is (agreeably to the character of the comedy) a burlesque
of the chaunts which might have been heard during the
Eleusinian celebrations.[1]

It was not, however, concerning the future state alone
that the priests of the mysteries professed to impart a
revelation. There were a hundred questions undreamt of
of yore which in the latter days began to press for solution
upon the sharpened intellect of the Hellene. His age of
faith had gone; his age of philosophy had begun. As the

Keep silence, keep silence; let all the profane
From our holy solemnity duly refrain;
Whose souls unenlightened by taste are obscure;
Whose poetical notions are dark and impure;
    Whose theatrical conscience
    Is sullied by nonsense;
Who never were trained by the mighty Cratinus
In mystical orgies poetic and vinous;
Who delight in buffooning and jests out of season,
Who promote the designs of oppression and treason;
Who foster sedition, and strife, and debate—
Are traitors, in short, to the stage and the State.
Who surrender a fort, or in private export
To places and harbours of hostile resort
Clandestine assignments of cables and pitch;
In the way that Thorycion grew to be rich
From a scoundrelly, dirty collector of tribute.
All such we reject and severely prohibit.

Frogs, Frere's translation. This admirable translator only errs occasionally by throwing too strong an air of burlesque over Aristophanes' lines. This has been the case here.

firm belief of former days decayed it left behind an unsatisfied craving for emotion of all kinds—such longings
are the residuum of dying creeds—and these the mysteries
were by their nature peculiarly fitted to satisfy. They
alone could raise men out of themselves until in the ecstasy
of their holy rites all the difficulties of life and of thought
seemed to fade away. Without the aid of much definite
dogma they formed a natural counterpoise to the growing
scepticism of the age.

And then this age of growing scepticism was in a sense
likewise an age of growing morality. The notion of a
moral law, at least, was more constantly present than it
had been of old time. I do not say the practice was
an improvement upon that of bygone days; but the
development of man had reached that stage when right is
no longer a thing of instinct or habit; when righteous-
ness is seen not to be an affair of this or that occasion,
but to stand apart from all occasion, abstract and eternal.
The ' categorical imperative' of this sense of right and
wrong had risen, as it had never risen before, to be a force
in the world. And beside this power that of the old
supernatural beings seemed shadowy and unreal. Even
the scoffer Aristophanes witnesses to this important
part of what we may call the new mysticism. This consisted not of religious excitement, still less of physical
excitement or orgies only, but rested in some measure
upon purity of morals. It may seem strange that a form
of worship which still included many obscene rites—and
tLe Eleusinia, in common with all other mysteries, seem to
have done this—could have set itself up as a preacher of
morality: it must seem strange to us, who have so long
associated purity of morals in this particular with purity
of morals in every relationship, till the phrases 'an
immoral life,' 'a moral man,' have gained a technical
significance. The ancients acknowledged no such necessary interdependence between different kinds of goodness.
Excesses, licensed excesses, as they were, during the cele-

bration of the holy rites, did not afford a reason why the priest should refrain from warning away from the celebration all those who were stained with usury or avarice, or other vices of bad citizenship.

But, in truth, had the inconsistency been greater than it was, it would not be a thing to wonder at in the new mysteries. All the simplicity of the early festival had passed away, and in its place had come a strange compound of definite doctrine and of fancied revelation; of unexplained and unexplainable excitement; of some hope of the future combined with much fear of the mysterious upper powers who were but symbolised under the names of Dêmêtêr and Hadês, of Dionysus and Persephonê. Of such kind were the mysteries of historic times.

The final stage of Greek religion—we may call it the third stage, that of Homer being the first, the age of Æschylus and Pindar and of the rise of philosophy being the second—was that during which Platonism faded into Neoplatonism. It was in this last condition that the worship of Dêmêtêr came to mingle with the time-honoured mysteries of Isis. The likeness between the two goddesses had been acknowledged from of old, but this similarity was not the result of a transmission of religious ideas from Egypt to Greece. It was only a likeness which sprang from the identity of the impulse which produced both mysteries. It was not until the days of the Alexandrian kingdom that the Oriental creeds first began to exercise a strong attractive power upon Greek thought.

Whatever effect the learning and the religion of the Egyptians may have had upon individual historians, such as Herodotus, and upon individual philosophers like Pythagoras, it is certain that it had no deep influence upon the Greek belief during the latter's heyday of development. It was after the decline of belief in Greece and in Rome that men were found seeking new forms of mystic excitement in the dark places of Oriental creeds. Before the time of Alexander the Great, Greece had no doubt absorbed

something of the philosophy of Persia and of Egypt;
but these first lessons were as nothing compared to those
which came to her after her conquests in Asia and Africa
had been completed. In this old world the energy and
culture of the Greeks transformed the dull life which they
found there, and now Greek scepticism, which had perhaps
first been awakened by contact with the East, paid back
with interest all it had received, and began to unmoor the
Asiatic peoples from the anchor of their former creeds.
But then, again, the Hellenes in their turn received in
exchange some of the mystic spirit which by this process
they had set free to wander through the air. It was easier
to take from the Asiatic his positive belief than to quench
his religious nature itself, and his love of emotion and
mysticism. It was through the marriage of Greek philosophy with Oriental mysticism that there sprang up in
Alexandria that strange system of teaching to which has
been given the name of Neoplatonism.

It is no part of my purpose to attempt here to follow
this new philosophy—so unlike the calmly reasoned
systems of Plato and of Aristotle—along the dark labyrinth through which it chose to wander. Inferior as Neoplatonism is to Greek philosophy, properly so called, in
intellectual breadth and logical capacity, obscured as it is
throughout by a turbid atmosphere of mysticism and fan-
tastic creation, it has this element of superiority over the
older philosophy, that a keener moral sense displays itself
everywhere in it. It possesses a certain spiritual insight
which to the other would have been impossible. For this
keener moral perception belonged to the age in which
Neoplatonism sprang up, and to the conditions to which
the development of human thought had attained. Yet, as
has been said, this spiritual insight was not incompatible
with any actual backsliding in the sphere of positive duty.
There needed Some One who, by example as well as by
precept, should vivify and bring to practical fruit the
doctrine of right for its own sake; and He was yet unborn.

It is easy to understand why, amid all this confusion of thought and the kind of anarchy which spread throughout the sphere of moral life, now that the emotions were left as the only guide to men, the mysteries should have held their place with a redoubled tenacity, and exercised a deeper influence than they had ever gained before. Now, not the Eleusinia alone, but the mystic rites of almost every nation were incorporated into the ritual of the Greeks. What was the separate fascination which each of these rituals held we cannot tell; but we can well understand that the times were favourable to those orgies of feeling, that intoxication of the faculties, which all the mysteries alike fostered, and in which all had their root.

It is from the time of the New Platonism that we must date the growth of the mysteries of Isis and Osiris into that form of which Plutarch has left us a picture in his treatise upon those two divinities. Nevertheless the mysteries of Isis and Osiris could never have had an importance calculated to rival the Eleusinia so long as the Greek supremacy remained. But from Greece—that is to say, from the New Greece, whose capital was Alexandria —these mysteries spread to Rome. And it is chiefly as a phase in the history of Roman belief that the later Isis worship is interesting to us.

Under the Roman supremacy it would follow, as a matter of course, that the Eleusinia should fall considerably from their former consequence. Before the Roman supremacy, though much of Greek intellect and enterprise had deserted the original Hellas, though Athens had been eclipsed by Alexandria, yet it was to Greece proper that men's thoughts still turned with supreme reverence as to the mother of all wider Greece. They honoured its ancient festivals, its Olympia, its Eleusinia, as the institutions under which their country had grown so great, and which were most truly representative of Hellenic nationality. But all this was changed when Rome became the ruling

power of the world, and when even the Greeks put off
their ancient pride of race to be enrolled in the number
of her citizens. The Romans had no mysteries, properly
so called, of their own. They had had, indeed, in old days,
like all other nations, their festivals of the spring, such
as the Lupercalia. But these had never been developed, as
the Greeks had developed the Eleusinia, into a mystery of
what we have called the new kind. For the wants of
their new state of religious excitement their native
religious system was therefore unprepared. One would
have supposed the Roman natures themselves were un-
suited to this phase of belief; but the event shows the
contrary. Almost every kind of Oriental mystery found
in the latter days of the Empire its enthusiastic votaries
in Rome; but none more so than the rites of Osiris and
Isis, or of Serapis and Isis; for under the latter names
these Egyptian divinities were there most frequently
honoured.[1]

From the time of Alexander, when Greece entered
into such close relations with Egypt, and Alexandria
began to assume the supremacy which anciently belonged
to Athens, Isis worship began to spread in Greece,
and to rival in some degree the native Eleusinian rites.
Traces of Isis worship are found in Epirus, in Thespiæ
in Bœotia, in many of the Greek islands—as, for example, in Delos, Chios, and Cyprus [2]—even in Athens
itself. To Rome this worship spread through the
Greeks, but was here at first discountenanced by law.
Apuleius says—unless he has been misunderstood—that
Isis worship was known in Rome in the time of Sulla
the Dictator.[3] And for a long period no Isis temple
might be built within the walls. Even in the time of

---

[1] Serapis was originally a divinity quite distinct from Osiris; but the
two came to be united into one being.

[2] See Pauly, *Real-Encyc.* s. v. *Isis* (L. Georgii).

[3] Some read Sybilla for Sulla, which would make the statement useless
as a datum.

Augustus this prohibition held good, though there was in his day a celebrated temple of Isis without the walls.[1] Agrippa was strongly opposed to the new cult. He forbade the worship of Serapis or of Isis within a mile of the city. The cult was not received into general favour until the .time of the Flavian emperors. Domitian was its special votary ; his life had once been saved by his assuming the disguise of a priest of Isis. Marcus Aurelius built a great temple to Serapis. Commodus was priest of this cult ; so were Pescennius Niger and Caracalla. Thus these mysteries went on growing in importance till Christian times. It is strange to see these sober Romans throwing themselves as wildly as the rest of the world into this wild game ; to find an Apuleius—not a pious nature, one would suppose—pawning his last coat to buy initiation into the rites of the goddess. There was not much belief at this time, perhaps, in the efficacy of the rites to bestow immortality ; no more than there was any longer a firm belief in the existence of the gods commemorated. Still the ceremonial remained, though the myths on which it was founded had been rationalised and the belief from which it once drew all its support had faded away.

We can only guess at the form which the original myth of Isis and Osiris wore, or at the rites which commemorated the myth ; though we have every reason to believe that both myth and ritual followed the usual course of the worship of the earth goddess. Nevertheless there are in Egypt some peculiar characteristics in the changes which in certain seasons pass over the face of earth. For there the whole country is submerged during the Nile's overflow, and all life there is for a time destroyed. These peculiar effects of Nature seem to be reflected in the Osiris myth. Death takes in it a larger share than he does in the corresponding story of Persephonê ; and whatever note of triumph may accompany the conclusion of the history, it is pitched in a more subdued key than in the Greek legend.

Plutarch, writing in the first century of our era, just about the time when the Isis worship at Rome was in its greatest ascendant, gives an account of the Isis myth and then a theological explanation of it. Both are characteristic of the last stage in the religion of antiquity. The earlier forms of the story which related the death of Osiris, the mourning of his wife, her search for his body, and the revenge for his death, are lost to us. In the hands of the Greek the Egyptian tale stands evidently deeply indebted to the Dêmêtêr myth. The main differences, however, remain. The lost being is a man and not a woman (it is so, as we shall see hereafter, in the Norse version of the Dêmêtêr story), and this man is the husband of the earth goddess.

Typhon (Seth), the Genius of Evil—thus the story runs in Plutarch—made a conspiracy against the life of Osiris. And this is how he accomplished his purpose. He challenged the god to see if he could get himself into a certain chest which he had previously prepared, much as the fisherman in the Arab tale induced the jinnee to show his power by returning into the bottle from which he had just escaped. And, like that Arab fisherman, no sooner had Typhon got Osiris well into the box than he clapped down the lid and fastened it, and pouring melted lead over it to make it secure, he carried it away. Then begin Isis' wanderings in search of her husband. At length she heard that the chest, which was now Osiris' coffin, had been taken to Byblos, on the most eastern mouth of the Nile, and hidden there in a tamarisk tree; and further, that the tree had grown all round the chest, so as to hide it. Isis found, when she got to Byblos, that the tamarisk had been cut down, and was now a pillar in the king's palace. There she went as Dêmêtêr to the house of Keleos, and became nurse to the king's son. She

let him suck at her finger instead of her breast, and by
night she placed him in the fire, that his mortal parts
might be consumed away. But the mother seeing the
child all aflame, screamed out, and by so doing robbed him
of the immortality which would have been his. Then the
goddess discovered herself, and asked that the pillar which
upheld the roof should be given to her. She cut open the
tree and took out the chest, wherewith she set sail to
Egypt. 'It was now morning, and the river Phædrus
sent forth a bitter wind. . . .'

Isis went next to find her son Horus, leaving the
chest in an obscure and desert place. But Typhon, as he
was hunting by night (see how the day myth still lingers :
Osiris is brought back in the morning and lost again at
night), came perchance upon it, and knowing what it
contained, he took out the body of the god, tore it into
fourteen fragments, and scattered them hither and thither
over the land. Then Isis set out once more in search of
her husband, travelling in a boat made of papyrus reeds.
. . . When she met with any one of the scattered remains
of Osiris she buried it.

After these things Osiris came from the dead and
appeared unto Horus, exhorting him to avenge his father.
And Horus fought with Typhon and slew him.

The Eleusinia were devoted in about equal parts to
painting the sad journeys of Dêmêtêr, and her joy at again
beholding her daughter. Persephonê spends a third of
the year only below, two-thirds upon earth. Joy and
sorrow are about equally tempered; this is the lesson of
the Dêmêtêr myth. But in the Egyptian mysteries sorrow
has the foremost place. Osiris is only found when dead,
and found only to be lost again. And though Typhon
too is slain, and Horus victorious, this is like a second
part added on to the original story; it cannot bring com-
pensation to the wife who has lost her husband. And so
Plutarch speaks of the 'sober air of grief and sadness'

which appears in these ceremonies. This was a cult which had grown old in length of years. The gladness of heart which inspired all the mysteries at their beginning had passed away, and a sober sadness taken its place. In this instance, moreover, we have clearly brought before us the conflict between good and evil which in the earlier mysteries—not yet divorced from their close connection with nature—nowhere appears. Rites such as these rites of Isis, pictured things more solemn than the changes of the year. 'Her mysteries,' says our author, 'were instituted by Isis to be the image, or indication rather, of what was then done and suffered, as a right consolation to those other men and women who might at any future time be in a like distress.' A divine being suffering that her sufferings should be a consolation to humanity! Do we not here seem to be drawing near to the mysteries of Christianity?

Of the same late character is Plutarch's *explanation* of the story. He discusses and dismisses other former interpretations—which do indeed preserve some features of the original and natural origin of the tale—in favour of his own, which passes beyond and includes all these. Some have said, he tells us, that Isis was Egypt, and Osiris the Nile, and that Typhon was the scorching heat of summer, which dried up the stream; or that Osiris was the heaven, and Isis the earth; that he was the sun and Isis the moon; or lastly, that the god was the principle of productiveness in nature, Isis the recipient of the seed. They are all or none of these things. Osiris is the principle of good in nature, or in the soul of nature and of men.[1] Typhon is the opposite, the evil principle. The great Persian theory of the dual government of the world is here invoked, and referred directly to the teaching of Zoroaster and the Magians. 'There are two beings equally concerned in the ordering of terrene affairs, a good and a bad divinity, a

---

[1] Ψυχὴ τοῦ Παντός. *Isis and Osiris*, 49.

god and a dæmôn. Out of the war of these two principles
—for they are eternally united and yet for ever striving
one to subdue the other—is produced the harmony of the
world.' As Euripides says, 'good and evil cannot be
parted, though they are so tempered that beauty and
order are the issue.' . . . And this opinion has been
handed down from theologians and legislators to the poets
and philosophers, an opinion which, though its first
author be unknown, has everywhere gained so firm and
unshaken a credence as not only to be spoken of both by
Greeks and barbarians, but even to be taught by them in
their 'mysteries' and sacrifices—that the world is neither
wholly left to its own motions without·some mind, some
superior reason, to guide and govern it, nor that it is one
such mind only that, as with helm or bridle, directs the
whole; but that all the irregularities which in this lower
region we behold are due to the two great and opposing
powers, one for ever trying (as it were) to lead us to the
right and along a straight path, the other striving as
constantly to bring us in the contrary direction and to
error.

Certainly this great conflict between good and evil is a
riddle deep enough in the world's history. And men were
at this time beginning to learn how great and terrible a
mystery it was. The thought of it haunted all the philosophy of the days in which Plutarch wrote, and only
partially cleared away with the triumph of Christianity.
This, it seems, was now the lesson which was taught by the
mystic rites of Greeks and Romans. Man had no more
to do with the fresh returning spring, with peasants'
festivals, or with harvest homes. What meaning would
such old rites have had for the city life and the elaborate
civilisation of those latter days? And so their mysteries
were turned into epitomes of the teaching of philosophers,
or the speculations of moralists on the origin of good and
evil. To this the rustic festival of early days had grown,
to this its final stage.

Then came Christianity and silenced—silenced apparently—both the newer mystic cult and the older nature worship. The Mystics themselves became Christians, as Clemens Alexandrinus did, and burnt what they had adored. In the year A.D. 391 the great temple of Serapis at Alexandria was set on fire by order of the government. And about the same time the monks who came into Greece in the wake of Alaric's invading army put a perpetual finis to the worship of the great goddesses at Eleusis. Yet how strange is the tribute to the vitality of the ancient earth worship in this fact, that the last blows which Christianity levelled at its rival, paganism, should have struck at that form of creed. Zeus and Apollo and Athênê were far less dangerous to Christianity than the gods who had in reality preceded Zeus and Apollo and Athênê, the gods of farm, and village, and the cottage fireside, than Pan or Demeter, than Persephonê or Dionysus. This is perhaps the meaning of that legend which said that before the birth of Christ a mysterious voice ran along the shores of the Ægean, proclaiming as a herald of the triumph of the coming creed, not the death of Zeus or of Apollo or Athênê, but that the far older god of earth and earth's fruitfulness, that Great Pan himself was dead.

CHAPTER VI.

THE OTHER WORLD.

§ 1. *The Under World, the River of Death, and the Bridge of Souls.*

THERE are some phases of past thought—not far removed from us in time—into which it is all but impossible to gain real insight; difficulties, and questions which were new once, but have now been settled for ever, experiments not long ago untried which have now become a matter of daily experience, and conditions of life and society which have not long passed, and yet seem to us infinitely remote. But there are some questions, though they have been asked continually through all the past history of man, and though men will never cease from asking them as long as the human race endures, which seem still as far from solution as they ever were: there are some future experiences upon which mankind is always speculating, and which yet can never become present experiences so long as we are what we are—those questions, I mean, which concern the destiny of man after death, the character of his journey to the undiscovered country, and the sort of life he will lead when there.

Some would dissuade us from the continuance of these, so they deem them, unfruitful speculations; but it is very certain that man must change his nature before they will lose their fascination for him; and till he does so change he can never read without sympathy the guesses which past generations of his kind have made toward the solution of the same problems. To them, indeed, these solutions

have lost their interest, as ours will soon do for us. Whatever lot that new condition may hold in store, eternal
pleasure or eternal pain, they have tried it now; whatever
scene is concealed by the dark curtain, they have passed
behind it. This is certain; as that we soon must. So
long, however, as we remain here upon this upper earth,
we must be something above or below humanity if we
refuse ever to let our thoughts wander towards the changes
and chances of another life.

   Not, indeed, that questions of this sort have ever had
for the majority of men in one age, or for the collective
mass of humankind, an all-absorbing interest. If we
choose to look closely into the matter, and to judge of
men's opinion as it is displayed in their actions (the only
real opinion), we shall at first, perhaps, be struck by the
slenderness of the belief which they possess in a future
state. For it is slight compared with their 'notional as-
sent,' that which they think they believe concerning it.
With the majority of us faith upon this matter is at best
but shadowy; of an otiose character, suitable for soothing
the lots of others, and sometimes, alas! called into requisition to alleviate the stings of conscience for the pain
which our own misconduct or neglect has introduced
therein.

   It will be said that there was once a time when one
aspect, at any rate, of the future, its terror, was realised
with an intensity, and exercised an influence over life and
conduct, such as are unknown in our days. Perhaps this
was so; certainly these times were not ordinary ones.
But in our estimate of the Middle Ages we are, I think,
apt to lay too much stress upon the force which faith had
over the men of those days. We forget the other side
of the picture. There was on the one hand the orthodox teaching; and whenever the Church moulded completely the popular belief, this world was seen as if covered
beneath a pall, and the next shrouded in still darker
gloom. As the orthodox or monastic view of life was like-

wise the literary one, the picture of the world as it was
drawn by the Church has come down to us almost unre-
lieved by brighter colours. There was, however, another
spirit at work, the spirit of the laity; and for laymen at
least, whatever priests might say to the contrary, life had
still its pleasures, and, in the indulgence of these, thoughts
about the next world were then, as now, laid to rest.
Beside the deeper course of the main stream of belief this
under current may be distinctly traced, a rivulet of ancient
paganism; whether this were the génuine heathenism of
new-converted lands, or the sort of paganism or atheism
of countries which in comparison with their times were
almost over-civilised—such countries, for example, as
Italy or Provence. Provence began a kind of renaissance
of its own before the time for a renaissance had come; it
gave a new direction to the impulses of chivalry, it fostered *la gaie science,* and sent out its companies of troubadours, plying their art to call men away from thoughts of
the Day of Doom, and to drown with their songs the
perpetual chaunting of masses and the toll of bells. We
cannot overlook these elements in mediæval life. The
Gothic cathedral is a lasting memorial of the genius of
Catholicism; but if we examine it closely, and look in
neglected corners or at the carvings beneath the seats, we
shall see strange sights, not provocative to holy meditation.
Dante strikes, no doubt, the truest note of his age; but in
the pauses of his stately music you may hear the laughter
of Boccaccio.

In truth, that term ' dark ages' overrides our fancy;
' we can never hear mention of them without an accompanying feeling, as though a palpable obscure had dimmed
the face of things, and that our ancestors wandered to
and fro groping.' [1] On the other hand, neither have the
most light-hearted and sceptical of people been able to
shut their eyes utterly to the warnings of death. We are

[1] Elia.

wont to think of the Greeks as a people of just such a
light-hearted and in a fashion sceptical temperament,
and to contrast the spirit of Hellas with the spirit of
mediæval Europe. Truly little thought of death or of
judgment after death seems to disturb the serenity of
Greek art—such as that art has come down to us.
Thanatos (Death) is scarcely to be found;[1] even the
tombs are adorned with representations of war and the
chase, and with figures of the dancing Hours. And yet
we know that Greek art was not without its darker side.
It had, like mediæval poetry, its Dante—Polygnotus,
namely—who adorned the pilgrims' house at Delphi with
frescoes representing the judgment and the tortures of
the damned—a Greek Campo Santo.[2] These, had they
been preserved, would have given us a different idea of
the Hellenic mind in the presence of the fact of mortality, and shown us how easily we are led to exaggerate
the divergence in thought between different nations and
different times.

Where no knowledge could be gained from experience,
man has been driven, in solving such a question as that
of the character of our future life, to interpret the allegory of nature; and his interpretations have not varied
very much from age to age. Wherefore it is that, as far
back as we can test the belief of men, we find certain
theories touching the fate of the soul after death, which
represent in the germ at least the prevalent opinions of
our own day, and out of some of which our opinions have
arisen.

[1] It has been suggested that among a group of figures sculptured upon
the drum of a column brought from the Ephesian Artemisium, we have a
representation of Thanatos. The figure is that of a boy, young and comely
as Love, but of a somewhat pensive expression; upon his thigh a sword is
girt, such as Erôs never wears; his right hand is raised, as though he
were beckoning. With him stand Dêmêtér and Hermês, both divinities
connected with the rites of the dead.

[2] Pausanias, x. 28.

Belief sprang up at once from the mere effort of language to give expression to the unseen. Casting about for a name for the essential part of man, the soul of him, and using for the abstract conception such a physical notion as seemed least remote from the former, language at first identified this soul with the breath. All the Aryan tongues give us examples of this identification. The Greek ψυχή, *spiritus*, is allied to ψύχω, to breathe; in Sanskrit we have *átman*, soul, in Latin *animus*, *anima*—all three derived from original roots *an*, *anti*, breath, and allied to the Greek ἄω, ἄημι, as well as to ἀσθμα, a heavy breathing. *Spiritus* has the same meaning: it is allied to the Slavonic *pachu*, odour; *pachati*, to blow. The German *Geist* and our *ghost* are probably in part onomatopoetic, and suggest the idea of breath by their very sound. Like the vital spark itself, the breath is seen to depart when the man dies. But whither has it gone? This is the first question concerning the habitat of the soul; and the purely negative, purely scientific answer is but to confess ignorance, and to say that the breath has disappeared. The answer actually given advances a little way beyond this toward the beginning of a myth. The breath has gone to the 'unseen' or the 'concealed place;' as the Greeks said to Hadês (ἀ.ειδής),[1] as our Norse ancestors said to Hel.[2] Thus out of mere migration we have the beginning of a myth; the *spirit* becomes something definite, and the *place* it has gone to is partly realised.

This Home of the Dead, this 'unseen' or 'concealed' place, must needs be dark; and it is, of course, natural that there should be much confusion between the home of the living soul and that of the dead body, so that the

[1] It is true that another derivation has been given for Hades. It has been associated with the Sanskrit Aditi, the boundless, which may·be a name for earth (cf. Prithivi), though I rather believe it (as Max Müller says it is) a name for the heaven or the expanse of the dawn. See Maury *Religions de la Grèce*, ii. 278.

[2] Hel from Icl. *et helja*, to hide.

former becomes more or less identified with the grave.
In a more expanded sense the Home of the Dead may be
thought of as a vast underground kingdom to which the
grave is but the entry. It was always imagined that if
the dead man did return to the upper world he came
through this passage and out by the grave's mouth; and,
apparently, it was generally thought that he could return
no other way. It was also deemed that for awhile—for
a lesser or a greater while—the dead man lingered about
the funeral mound: thus soon after death the man's
ghost might be seen, but not (generally) long after death.
Along with the earliest traces of human burial we find
tokens of the custom of placing food and drink with the
dead body. The object of this may have been to furnish
the ghost with the means for beginning his journey to the
underground kingdom, and so of hastening his departure
from the neighbourhood of living men; for it is certain
that there was nothing of which primitive man stood more
in dread than of the appearance of a ghost. In the remains of the second Stone Age we find proofs that the
departed were pacified by such like gifts of food and
drink; they were in these days further honoured by the
erection of immense monumental tombs, which even now
present the appearance of small hills. The pyramids of
Egypt are a relic of the same custom of mound-raising
among primitive men. At the mouth of the Stone Age
grave mounds was held the death wake or funeral feast,
traces of which are still discoverable. Within the grave
was placed the body of the hero, or chieftain, surrounded
by implements of war and of the chase, by food and drink,
and also by dead captives and wives.

It is impossible for us to pronounce with certainty
what was the original intention of rites such as these,
which continue quite late in the development of civilisation. Was it supposed that the body itself came to life
and required the food which was left for it in the grave
before it arrived at its last home? Had it a journey to

make to get to the underground land? Was the food
intended only·for that intermediate condition of travel?
Before we have any means of testing men's belief upon
these points, the rites which might have expressed it have
become in a great degree symbolical, and their simpler
meaning has been lost.[1]

The prehistoric grave mounds witness in a curious
way to the prevalent notion that the grave mouth was the
gate by which ghosts returned to 'walk' the earth. To
prevent these apparitions the men of prehistoric days had
recourse to a strange practical method of exorcism.
They strewed the ground at the grave's mouth with sharp
stones and broken pieces of pottery, as if they thought a
ghost might have his feet cut, and by fear of that be pre-
vented from returning to his old haunts. For unnum-
bered ages after the days of the mound builders the
same custom lived on, whereof we see here the rise.
Turned now to an unmeaning rite, it was put in force for
the graves of those, such as murderers or suicides, who
might be expected to sleep uneasily in their narrow
house. This is the custom which is referred to in the
speech of the priest to Laertes in 'Hamlet.' Ophelia had
died under such suspicion of suicide that it was a stretch
of their rule, says the priest, to grant her Christian
burial.

> And but the great command o'ersways our order,
> She should in ground unsanctified have lodged
> To the last trumpet: for charitable prayers
> Shards, flints, and pebbles should be thrown on her.

The grave becoming in this belief *ipso facto* the entrance to Hadês, burial was necessary for admittance into
the other world. The soul who had not undergone this

---

[1] The funeral feast held in honour of the dead (of which the twenty-
third book of the *Iliad* gives a good example for prehistoric days) is of
course only a relic of the feast in which the dead partook. Of a still
earlier form of the ceremony we have fine examples in the tomb paintings
of Egypt. At these the dead is present,

rite flitted about aimlessly around the spot where his shell, the body, lay. This is the superstition concerning a murdered man. By the 'polluted covert' the ghost stands, to show where the horrid deed was wrought. By virtue of an easy transfer of ideas any other form of interment—burning of the dead when that was customary—became also the needful passport to the land of shades. Among the Homeric heroes we see every effort made to secure the body for this purpose; and when the corpse of Hector cannot be recovered, some faint image of the funeral rite is performed by burning his clothes.

This belief, too, explains why Elpenor, the comrade of Odysseus, is found by the latter, when he goes to visit the home of Hades, still wandering on the hither side of Styx; and why Patroclus' ghost comes to the bedside of Achilles, and reproaches him that his funeral rites have not yet been performed. In truth, the belief in the importance of funeral rites is too widespread and too well known to need further illustration in this place.[1]

Among those nationalities with whom the belief in an underground kingdom was most in force, the home and the condition of the dead must alike seem dark and cheerless. Enough of the old belief concerning the vanishing breath remained to make the future itself shadowy; and so perhaps it was a place of emptiness and hollowness, a no-life rather than one of positive pain, that made the early hell. 'The senseless dead, the simulacra of mortals,' Homer calls the shades; and the same thought is expressed by Isaiah when he says—

> Sheol shall not praise Thee, Jehovah,
> The dead shall not celebrate Thee;
> They that go down into the pit shall not hope for Thy truth:
> The living, the living shall praise Thee, as I do this day.[2]

---

[1] So Virgil:

> 'Hæc omnis quam cernis inops, inhumataque turba est;
> Portitor ille Charon; hi quos vehit unda sepulti.'—Æn. vi. 325.

[2] Isaiah xxxviii. 18, 19; cf. also Genesis xxxvii. 35, 1 Samuel xxviii. 19.

But when this under world takes a form of greater distinctness, and men begin to try and localise it beneath particular spots of the earth, they imagine more definite roads leading to it; and names, such as Styx and Avernus, which were purely mythical, assume a geographical character.   Approaches of this kind to the realm of darkness are the *Höllenthäler*, hell's glens, and the like, of which we meet so many in Europe.   All-very deep caves and abysses are believed to lead thither.   In a more imaginative way, and in the language of a finer poetry, the downward road is spoken of as the 'Valley of the Shadow of Death.'

But no living man ventures to the bottom of this dark valley; or if he do go he shall scarcely return.   The secrets of that place are well kept.   And great was of old the fear of the infernal deities, lest men should pry into their prison house.   Wherefore Hades cried aloud when Poseidôn was shaking the earth, lest that god should rend it asunder and disclose his mansions to the day—'mansions dolorous fearful which the gods themselves loathe.'

The inanimate *place*, the very cavernous hollow, becomes anon gifted with life; and the mere *privation* of an earlier faith grows into 'a more awful and confounding *positive*.'   Hell becomes a being.   Most likely this being was at first endowed with the figure of some ravenous animal, some bird or beast of prey, a wolf, a lion, a dog, a hawk, as the experience of each individual people might direct.   Greek mythology had its Cerberus, Norse mythology its Fenris wolf.   In a mythology a shade more elaborate the same thing is represented by imaginary creatures —dragons, griffins, or what not.   The dragons which we meet with in mediæval legend were once, most of them, in some way or other, embodiments of Death.   At the door of Strassburg Cathedral, and in one of the stained windows within, the reader may see a representation of the mouth

Sheol is misrendered 'grave' in our version.   It means 'the place of the dead,' not the place of dead bodies only.

of Hell, in the form of a great dragon's head spouting flame.

Anyone who is acquainted with mediæval sculptures and paintings knows how common it is to find this kind of imagery, which exists in virtue of the reversion of popular mythology to primitive forms of thought.

Of a like origin with this hell dragon are most of the fabulous monsters, half human and half animal, whom we meet in Greek mythology—the harpies, for example, the sirens, or the gorgons. If the underground kingdom is seen in the form of a man, he is a monstrous man, such as the ogre of our nursery tales. This ogre is a descendant of the Orcus of classical times, and, I doubt, he better shows us the primitive conception of that being than do any representations in art of the god of hell.

No people have painted the destructive aspect of death, the *negative* theory of a future, with a sharper outline than did the Greeks and Hebrews. What a contrast to the teaching of modern religions is the line—

They that go down into the pit shall not hope for Thy truth.

Yet Greeks and Hebrews have not abstained from endowing the 'unseen place' with some personality. In Greek literature we may almost trace the processes by which Hadês, from being impersonal, becomes personal, and then returns once more to be merely a place. Of a man dying it is not seldom said in Homer that 'hateful darkness seized him:'[1] here was a half-personality which was calculated soon to lead to a complete one. Hadês is accordingly generally a person in Homer. The Icelandic goddess, Hel, went through the same transformation that we can trace in the case of Hadês. From being the concealed place she grew to be the queen of the dead, and then again degenerated to be only the home of the dead. Of the thousand other images of horror to be met with in

---

[1] E.g. *Il.* v. 45.

different creeds—devouring dragons, fire-breathing serpents, or dogs who, like Cerberus, threaten those who are journeying to the underground kingdom—the most part can, from their names, be shown to have arisen out of the merely negative images of death, the 'unseen,' the 'coverer,' the 'concealer,' the 'cave of night.'

In contrast with all these myths stand those which after death send the soul upon a journey to some happy home of the departed, to a paradise which is generally believed to be in the west. If the first are myths of hell, the second series may be fairly described as myths of heaven. Nor can it be clearly proved that the more cheerful view of the other world is of a later growth in time than the one which we have been describing, seeing the evidence which the Stone Age interments seem to offer upon this point. For if the dead man had need of his weapons of war, of his captives and his wives, his life to come could not have differed for the worse from his life here. And if, among historic peoples, the earlier Hebrews were the exponents of the gloomy Sheol, the most hopeful picture of the soul's future finds expression in the ritual service of the Egyptians. To come nearer home, among all those peoples with whom we are allied in blood, the Indo-European family of nations, we shall find the traces of a double belief, the belief, on the one hand, in death as a dim underground place, or as a devouring monster, and the contrasting belief in death as a journey made towards a new country where everything is better and happier than on earth.

There is nothing distinctively Aryan in the notion of a journey of the soul after death. Every nation has possessed it, and almost every people, moreover, has associated it with the travel of the sun to his setting. But there is something in this phase of belief which makes it, wherever it appears, more national and characteristic than the other creed touching the under world; and that is the necessity

which its mythology is under of changing according to
the geographical position of those who hold it. The paradise whither the soul was imagined travelling was certainly
in one sense 'another world,' but it was not so in the sense
in which *we* use that term. The ancient paradise was in
no way distinctly separated in thought from the earth on
which men lived; and the way to it was always supposed
to lie somewhere in this visible world. Therefore the idea
of heaven varied according to men's outlook over this
earth. The Egyptian, for example, saw the sun set behind
a trackless desert which he had never crossed and never
desired to cross while alive. This desert was in his belief
a twilight land ruled over by the serpent king Apap.[1] It
lay upon the left bank of his sacred Nile, while the cities
of the living were upon the right bank; and so the
Egyptian 'Book of the Dead' gives us a picture of the
dead man's journey, in which all the geographical features
of Egypt reappear. The ritual shows the departed twice
ferried across a sacred River of Death (the Nile), travelling through the dark land of Apap or of Amenti, ever
advancing *towards the sun*, light breaking upon him the
while, till he comes to the Palace of the Two Truths, the
judgment hall of Osiris: Osiris being the sun which has
set. Last of all we see him walking into the sun itself,
or absorbed into the essence of the deity.

Our Aryans used the same imagery, with variations of
local colouring. In both myths there is the same childlike
confusion of thought between the subjective and the objec-
tive; between the position of the myth-maker and that of
the phenomenon out of which he weaves his story. Because
towards sunset the sun grows dim and the world too, it is
imagined that the sun has now reached a dim twilight
place, such as the Egyptians pictured in their region of

---

[1] Apap; the immense, a personification of the desert, and hence of
death. He may be compared with the great mid-earth serpent (midgard
worm) of the Norse mythology, which is a personification of the sea and
death in one. See infra.

Apap, or the Greeks in their Cimmerian land upon the borders of earth. But when the sun has quite disappeared, then inconsistently it is said that he has gone to a land which is his proper home, whence his light, whether by day or night, is never withdrawn. The twilight region is the land of death; the bright land beyond is the home of the blessed. Such are the general notions which among a primitive people correspond to our Hell and our Heaven.

In a former chapter we were able to present some picture of the Aryas in their early home by the sources of the Oxus and of the Jaxartes. We must once again recall this picture if we wish to gain an insight into the origin of their beliefs concerning the journey of the soul and the other world. We saw how one division of the race, the older portion, those from whom were to spring the Indians and the Iranians, had their settlements close against the eastern hills; while in a circle outside these lay the tribes who were to form the nations of Europe, and who before they broke up and started on their wanderings bore a common name, Yavanas, the younger or else the fighting members of the community. At the present day a broad belt of desert lies between the fertile valleys of Bactria and the Caspian Sea. While Bactria is inhabited by a settled and agricultural people, the great Khuwaresm desert produces only vegetation enough to support a few Cossacks and wandering Turkic tribes. But there is sufficient reason to believe that this was not always the case; but that a great part of what is now dry land was once the bed of the Caspian, which was joined on to the Sea of Aral, and extended in every direction farther than it now extends. The Caspian is known to have fallen greatly in its banks, and not at a remote period, but within historical times;[1] the process of shrinking would in a double way tend to the creation of desert, both by exposing the dry

---

[1] Wood, *Shores of Lake Aral.*

T

bed of the sea and by rendering the other land sterile
when so much neighbouring water was withdrawn.

The root-word which appears in the European class of
languages with the meaning of ' sea,' stands in the Indian
and Iranian tongues for ' desert.' Can we explain this
fact better than by supposing that after the European
nations had left their home, their brethren who remained
behind, and only long after migrated to India and to
Persia, came to know as a desert the district which their
fathers had known as the sea ?

Oysters, it is known, will not live save at the mouths
of rivers, and philology furnishes us with proofs that these
shell-fish were known to the European races while they
were still one people.   There can be no question that the
Greek ὄστρεον, the Latin ostrea, the Irish oisridh or oisire,
the Welsh oestren, the Russian ustoru, the German Auster,
our oyster are all from the same root.[1]   Therefore the
Yavanas while they lived together must have lived by the
sea.   Some have thought that the growth of the desert
coinciding with a parallel growth of the Aryan people first
set our ancestors upon their wanderings.

How much more roomy a place the sea occupies in
men's thoughts than is warranted by their real familiarity
with it ! Into the mass of sedentary lives—themselves the
great majority—it enters but seldom as an experience,
provided a man live only a few miles inland.   And yet of
all countries which possess a sea-board how full is the
literature of references to this one phenomenon of nature !
The sun and moon with all the heavenly bodies, the num-
berless sights and sounds of land, are the property of all;
and yet allusions to these are not more common in literature than allusions to the sea; one might fancy that man
was amphibious, with a power of actually living in and
not only by the water.   Charles Lamb acutely penetrates
the cause of a certain disappointment we all feel at the

[1] Pictet, Origines, &c., i. 514.

sight of the sea for the first time. We go with the
expectation of seeing all the sea at once, the commensurate
antagonist of the earth. All that we have gathered from
narratives of wandering seamen; what we have gained from
the voyages, and what we cherish as credulously from
romances and poetry, 'come crowding their images and
exacting strange tributes from expectation.' Thus we are
already steeped in thoughts about the sea before we have
had any sight of it ourselves, and only from the sea's great
influence acting through the total experience of mankind.
'We think of the great deep and those who go down into it;
of its thousand isles and of the vast continents it washes;
of its receiving the mighty Plata or Orellana into its
bosom without disturbance or sense of augmentation; of
Biscay swells and the mariner

> For many a day and many a dreadful night
> Incessant labouring round the stormy Cape;

of fatal rocks and the "still vexed Bermoothes;" of
great whirlpools and the waterspout; of sunken ships and
sumless treasures swallowed up in the unrestoring depths.'
This tribute which our expectation pays to the importance
of the sea in men's thought shows us that we must not
narrow the sea's influence in mythology by the limit of
man's mere experience of it. Few among the Aryans
lived by the Caspian shore. But still the tradition of the
Caspian appears in one form or another in the beliefs of
all the race. The tradition of the sea, of its real wonders
and its greater fancied terrors, must have passed from one
to another, from the few who lived within sight and sound
of the waters to many quite beyond the horizon to whom
it was not visible even as a faint silvery line.

Only the Yavanas lived by the Caspian shore. The
memory of the Caspian, however, is to be found more or
less distinctly in all Aryan mythology. For to the Aryan
race generally this sea stood in the same position which

the desert occupied to the Egyptian. Their backs were towards the mountains, their faces towards the Caspian. All their prospect, all their future, seemed to lie that way: when their migrations began, they were undertaken in this direction, towards the west. And, most important of all, their sun god was seen by many quenching his beams in the waves: the home of the sun is the home of *souls.* What more natural, nay, what so necessary, as that the Aryan Paradise should lie westward beyond that water?

It has been said that the Indian word for desert corresponds etymologically with the European word for sea: that word must have been in the old Aryan something like *mara,* from which we get the Persian *měru,* desert,[1] the Latin *mare,* the Teutonic (German and English) *meer.* But from identically the same root we also get the Sanskrit and Zend *mara,* death, the Latin *mors,* the old Norse *murdh,* the German *Mord,* our *murder,* all signifying originally the same thing.[2] What, then, does this imply? The word which the old Aryas used for sea they used likewise for death; and how would this have been possible unless this Caspian, their first sea, were likewise the Sea of Death, an inevitable stage upon the road to Paradise?

Though I speak of a sea it must not be forgotten that to primitive man, who has not yet explored its tracts, the sea is but the greatest among rivers. The Greek Oceanus was a river and yet the parent of all waters: the true parent of Oceanus was the Caspian. It would be natural for the Aryas to suppose that this measureless stream surrounded all the habitable earth, and that beyond it lay the dim region of twilight, the Cimmerian land which Odysseus visited.

The sunset and the ways were o'erdarkened, for now we had come
To the deep-flowing Ocean's far limit, the shadowy home

---

[1] To the Vedic Indians the word Meru came to stand for Paradise.
[2] Fick, *Vrg. Wörterb. der I.-G. Sp.* i. s. v. *mar.*

Where the mournful Cimmerians dwell; there the sun never throws
His bright beam when to scale the high star vault in morning he goes,
Or earthward returns from the midday to rest; for the gloom
Of night never ending reigns there—a perpetual doom.[1]

The cosmology of the Eddas has been, perhaps, partly shaped by the peculiar circumstances in which the Eddas arose, and the special character of the land (Iceland) in which they had their birth; but still we have traces in the Eddas of a belief which was common alike to Greek and Icelander. In the Norse poems the world is pictured as supported in the centre by the great tree Yggdrasill, and in the midmost of all is the city of the gods, Asgard, the Æsirs'-(gods'-)ward. Around lies the green and fruitful earth, man's-home; and this in its turn is surrounded by the mid-gard sea. Beyond that sea is a land of perpetual fog and ice; a weird and phantom land, possessed by beings of another race, hateful to men. This Northern Hades is called *Jötunheimar*, giants' home. The mid-gard sea, which is a sea of death, and at a still earlier time must have been a river of death, is personified in the mid-gard worm, the serpent Jörmungandr, who lies curled at the bottom with his tail in his mouth, encircling the world. He ever waxes in length, and his tail grows into his inwards; and this, as we noted before, is in exact analogy with the Greek Oceanus, which returns to flow into itself. If rivers are ever typified by serpents, then the greatest river of all, the earth stream, is typified by the mightiest of serpents, by this Jörmungandr.

We spoke in a former chapter of the fight between the sun god and the great river serpents of mythology, of Apollo with the Python, of Thorr with Jörmungandr. That combat has a deeper significance when we take into account that the serpents are images of death and personify

[1] *Od.* xi. 12 sqq.

the River of Death. Thorr is slain by his adversary, and
Apollo (according to one myth) after his fight with the
other has to visit the realm of Hadês. This is no more
than saying that the sun, like mortal man himself, has to
quench his beams and die in the mighty earth stream.

Gradually the notions of the River of Death and of
the Sea of Death from being one became two, and other
changes likewise sprang up through the natural confusion
of mythology between all the various types of mortality,
between the under world, Hadês, which was reached from
the grave mouth, and the river passage or the long sea
voyage which were required to get to the land of souls.
Hadês itself shifted between a place beneath the earth
and another far away in the west. Odysseus, to get there,
had to sail for many a day and many a weary night to the
extreme boundary of Ocean. But when he had got there
he met his companion Elpenor, whom he had left a little
while ago dead on Circê's island. Him the hero asked how
he could have come under the dark west more quickly
than Odysseus had done, sailing in a ship.[1] From such an
instance as this we see how far the original meaning of
the myths had been forgotten, and how a confusion had
sprung up between the Hadês under men's feet and the
Hadês at the end of the death journey, lying far away
in the west. It was in virtue of a similar amalgamation
of ideas that the mortal river soon found its way to the
under world. In the Greek mythology the one subterranean stream expanded into four—abhorred Styx, sad
Acherôn, Côcytus, Phlegethôn. These have all grown
mythopoetically out of ocean; as much as they were
feigned actually to flow from it. The Norse under world
had its subterranean river, named Gjöll, the sounding,
from *gjalla*, to yell, as Côcytus, from κωκύω, to cry. Of
Gjöll, as we shall meet with it again in another chapter,
I need say no more here.

---

[1] *Od.* xi. 51 sqq.

A desert, such as the Egyptian desert, or a sea like the Caspian, forms a natural barrier between the living and the dead. Without such a bar, if men supposed that some happy land lay to the west of them, it would be hardly possible that they should refrain from an attempt to get there, living. In the Middle Ages the myth of the soul's journey was translated into this literal shape, and became the myth of the Earthly Paradise, with an outcome of frequent expeditions—more by many than we know of now—to find it. At last these expeditions ended happily in the discovery, if not of a deathless land, at any rate of a new world.

They were not religious, heavenward-looking men who, in Mr. Morris's poem, set out in quest of the Earthly Paradise; and no doubt the bard has been guided by a true instinct, and that of all those mediæval mariners who were lost in their search after St. Brandon's Isles none knew that they had found what they were seeking—Death.

Must we not, then, place among such journeys that of the king Svegder Fiolnersson—whom we read of in the Ynglinga Saga[1]—who made a solemn vow to seek Odhinn and the home of the gods? Asgard had lost its grand supersensuous meaning in his days; it was simply a city of the earth, and a place to be got to. Snorri tells us how Svegder wandered many years upon his quest, and of the strange way he found what, unknowingly, he had been seeking. One day he came to an immense stone, as large as a house. Beneath it sat a dwarf, who called out to him that he should come in there if he wished to talk with Odhinn; and being very drunk, Svegder and his man

delusions of the same kind; and long before they had summoned up courage sufficient to navigate the Mediterranean they had invented the myths of their western islands of the blest, to which yellow-haired Rhadamanthus was taken when expelled from Crete by his brother Minôs, or of those gardens kept by the daughters of the West,[1] where decay and death could not enter.

The two myths of the Sea of Death and of the River of Death, which had sprung from the same source, became, as time went on, divided in their characters. The wanderings of the Aryas would necessarily bring about this effect: first, by showing to some peoples the difference between the sea and a river; and secondly, by transferring to other seas the myths which had originally gathered round the Caspian.

The terrors of the Sea of Death, wherever it was, would gradually diminish; and though the early belief would not be abandoned, there would grow up beside it the parallel conception of a distinctly Earthly Paradise. The earliest Paradise is, I have said, in a sense an earthly one, seeing that its site is not absolutely removed by thought from the earth. While somehow it cannot be reached save through the portal of death, mythology never acknowledges that the dead do actually leave the world of man. This inconsistency of thought—if it is one—could be preserved without difficulty among a sedentary people. The Egyptian, perhaps, never enquired why living men might not cross the desert to the house of Osiris. But when a nation begins to move, the thought springs into its mind, ' Why is death the only road to the home whither our fathers have gone? May we not arrive at the immortal land by an easier, or at any rate by a less painful route?' Come what may, they resolve to try. All the Western Aryas reached the sea at last; wherefore it is in the mythology of the European races that we must look for the best

---

[1] Hesperides.

examples of the Sea of Death and of the Earthly Paradise which lay beyond. The elder Aryas, the Indians and Iranians, remained much longer inland; wherefore their River of Death never was confounded with the sea; it remained in clear colours and sharp outline in their creed.

We cannot doubt that from the belief in the River of Death arose the custom of committing the dead to the sacred Ganges; [1] for just as the Hindu kindles a funeral fire on the boat which bears the dead down this visible stream of death, so used the Norseman to place a hero's body in his ship, and then having set fire to that ship, send it out seawards on the tide. And again, as by the Indian the Ganges is the being entrusted with the care of the dead, so to the Gaul the Rhone was the river of death. Nismes became the great necropolis of southern Gaul; for at that place it was customary to cast the dead into the river. The custom survived even into Christian times. [2]

In a more distinctly mythical guise the mortal stream appears in the Indian mythology under the names Vijarânadî and Vaiterani. What the Vedas have to tell us touching this river has been considerably amplified in the Brahmanas. In one tradition we meet with both the sea and the river of death. It is said that all who leave this world come first to the moon, 'heaven's immortal door.' This gate few only pass; the rest, agreeably to the doctrine of the transmigration of souls, return thence to earth, some as rain, some as worms, insects, lions, tigers, fish, dogs, men. But he who has known Brahma goes along the god's way, and comes first to the world of Fire, then to that of the Wind, then to that of the Sun, to that of the Moon, that of the Lightning, that of Indra, that of Prajâpati, at the end to that of Brahma; and this last

---

[1] The Indian *Gangâ* (Ganges) is turned into a mythic river, and is made, like Oceanus, the parent of all waters. This shows the Ganges to be identified with the River of Death.

[2] Michelet, *Histoire de France*, L. iii. 'Tableau de France.'

world is surrounded by a *deep sea*, deep as a hundred other seas, and with black waves made by the tears of human kind. From this sea flows a river, the 'eternal stream' (vijarâ nadi), which makes men young again. It is, in fact, the forerunner of our mediæval and more modern *Fontaines de Jouvence*. The true origin of the *Fontaine de Jouvence* is the same as the origin of this vijarâ nadi: that is to say, both are rivers of death, and men are made young by passing them, only when they thus pass into a new life. Near this 'eternal stream' is the tree Ilpa, which bears all the fruits of the world: the Tree of Life in all European (and Eastern) tradition stands beside the Fountain of Youth. When the good man shall come to the world of Brahma, Brahma will say to his attendants, 'Receive this man with honour; for he has passed the stream Vijarâ nadi, and will never more be old.' Then five hundred Apsaras will come to meet him, bearing flowers, and fruits, and clear water.[1]

This is the River of Death seen in its sunniest aspect. The reverse side of the picture is suggested by the other name of it, Vaitaranî, 'the hard to cross.' Into this seething flood the wicked fall. On the other side is Paradise—that is to say, the home of the Pitris, or ancestors. That the dead man may gain a passage over this dreadful stream, a cow (called anustaranî) was offered up.[2] Vaitaranî, another poem says, lies 'across the dreadful path to the house of Yama,' the king of hell.

So much for this river as it stands alone. A most important change must have been wrought in belief when the custom of burning the dead was introduced. It would seem that our Aryan ancestors themselves were the introducers of this rite. We can easily understand

---

[1] Cf. Pindar, Olymp. Odes, ii. v. 75 sqq. ed. Boeckh. See Weber, *Indische Studien*, i. 359 sq.; Weber, *Chamb.* 1020.

[2] Another cow is offered up *twelve days* after the man's death. This last fact is important in connection with the myths of Hackelberg, told in this chapter and in the tenth chapter. See Kuhn in Haupt's *Zeitsch. für deut. Alterthum*, v. 379 and vi. 117, also in his own *Z. f. verg. Sp.* ii. 311.

how the custom may have arisen. When the god of fire
is such an important being as the Vedas show him to
have once been, the thought of committing the dead to
his care seems simple and natural. Agni, as we have
seen, was the messenger between gods and men: he
called down the gods to feast at the altar, and he took
from the altar the smoke and odour of the sacrifice to
heaven. When the funeral fire had been lighted the
same divinity took with him the soul of man to his last
abode. Now, fire worship such as that of Agni was not
originally peculiar to the Indo-Aryas: it was in them but
a survival of a state of belief common to the whole Aryan
race, whereof we have seen in a former chapter numerous
proofs.

Or was it that the sun, who, as a wanderer, traced
out beforehand the journey of the soul, who himself sank
into the new world behind the waves of the River of
Death, did also in another way suggest the burning of
the corpse? The sun gods, Apollo and Heraclês, Thorr
and Balder, do in sundry ways and in divers actions
present the ideal life of human kind. These are the
heroes of heroes; whatever kind their death was it must
have been the one most worthy of imitation. The two
great fire funerals mentioned respectively in Greek and
Norse mythologies are the funerals of sun gods.

The one is that of Heraclês. The hero, when he felt
the clinging torment of the shirt of Nessus, and knew
that his end was near, ordered his funeral fire to be
lighted on Mount Œta, on the western shore of the
Ægean.[1] This myth must have been invented by Asiatic
Greeks, who saw the fiery sunset upon that sea. Again,
the body of Balder, who had been slain by his brother
Höder, was placed upon the dead god's ship Hringhorni,
a funeral fire was lighted on the ship, and it was then

---

[1] The funeral fire of many a hero is lighted near the sea-shore, as in
this case of Heracles. Cf. Achilles, *Il.* xxiii. 134 ; Beowulf, 6297. In other
cases of Norse funeral fires they are lighted on a *ship*. See Ch. VIII.

sent drifting into the sea. This is the barque of the sun
sinking in the waves. Most of the great epic heroes—
many of them sun heroes—followed the same custom of
fire burial. Of the Homeric funerals we need not speak.
Sigurd and Brynhild mounted their pyre, and on it placed
their horses, dogs, and falcons, all they had prized most
on earth.

Burning the dead, however, never seems to have been
a universal practice; rather a special honour paid to
warriors and kings. But then we must remember that
immortality itself was not, in ancient belief, granted to all
men alike, only to the greatest.

We see at once that, with the use of fire burial, many
of the old beliefs had to be given up—all those, for instance, which depended upon the preservation of the bodily
remains. Of old time men had buried treasures with the
corpse in the expectation that they would be some kind of
use to it; the body itself was then imagined to descend to
the under world, or to travel the western journey to the
sun. But now the body was visibly consumed upon the
pyre, on which too were placed, by a curious survival of
old custom, the precious things which would formerly have
been buried with the dead man in his grave. The body
and these treasures were consumed, had gone; but
whither? Had they perished utterly, and was there
nothing more now left than that earliest belief of an
'Α-είδης—a nowhere? Were none true of all those myths
which told of the soul passing to a home of bliss? Instead of giving up this faith, the Aryas only transformed
it; they spiritualised it and stripped it of the too material
clothing which in earlier times it wore. The thought
which had once identified the life with the breath came
again into force. Or if some visible representation of the
essence of the man was still desired, men had the smoke
of the funeral pyre, which rose heavenwards like an ascending soul.

In the Iliad, after Patroclus' spirit (ψυχή) has visited

Achilles in his dream, it is described as going away crying shrilly and entering the ground like smoke:

ψυχὴ δὲ κατὰ χθονὸς ἠΰτε καπνὸς ᾤχετο.[1]

We meet with the same imagery in long after years and in a far distant land, when, in the description of the funeral fire of Beowulf the Goth, it is said that the soul of the hero 'curled to the clouds,' imaging the smoke which was curling up from his pyre. There is even a curious analogy betwen two words for smoke and soul in the Aryan tongues. From a primitive word ˙dhu, which means to shake or blow, we get both the Sanskrit word dhuma, smoke, and the Greek θυμός, the immaterial part of a man, his thought or soul. Θυμός was not a mere abstraction like our word mind, but that which had a certain amount of separate individuality, and might even continue to live when the body had been destroyed.[2]

In these ways, by a change in the opinion of men mingling with a survival of old custom, the funeral rites were reformed, and the inanimate things—the food, the weapons, the clothes—which would once have been buried with the dead, were now burnt with him. Of such reformed rites we have a complete picture in the funeral of Patroclus, and the picture is one which in all essential details might serve for any of the Aryan folk. Oxen and sheep were slain before the pyre of the hero, and with the fat of their bodies and with honey the corpse was liberally anointed. Then twelve captives were sacrificed to the manes of the dead Patroclus; they and his favourite dogs were burned upon the pile. In this instance it is the complete burning, as formerly it had been the complete

---

[1] Il. xxiii. 100.

[2] The exact character of the θυμός, how far it was an entity separate from the body, I have discussed in another place, 'The Homeric Words for Soul,' in Mind, October 1881. There is one example in Homer of the θυμός continuing to exist after the body (Il. vii. 131); but I believe this is the only one.

sepulture, which constitutes the needful passport to Hades.
And so when the fire will not burn, Achilles prays to the
North and the West Winds to come and consummate the
funeral rite.   All night as the flame springs up·Achilles
stands beside it, calling upon the name of his friend and
watering the ground with libations from a golden cup.
Toward morning the fire dies down, and then the two
Winds, according to the beautiful imagery of the myth,
their work done, 'return homewards across the Thracian
sea.' [1]

Hector's clothes, as we have seen, were burnt as a sort
of substitute for his body; Patroclus' treasures were consumed with him.   The same customs were observed at the
funerals of the Teutonic heroes and heroines, Sigurd,
Beowulf, Brynhild, and the rest.[2]   Cæsar tells us how the
Gauls burnt with the dead all that they had loved.[3]   Evidently, therefore, the inanimate things, the weapons or
garments, as well as the captives and dogs, were believed
to survive in a land of essences for the use of the libe-
rated soul.

To the question, 'Whither does man's essence go when
it rises from the funeral fire?' the answer, if a wish alone
urged the thought, would be, 'To the gods.'   We find
that in the beliefs which were most associated with the
habit of burying in the ground the notion of a future
union with the gods was not strongly insisted upon.   The
western land, for instance, whither the sun was thought
to go at night, must not be confounded with the real
home of the gods, with Olympus or with Asgard.   The
Greek islands of the blest were not the seat of the gods;
nor was the house of Yama, which the Indians spoke of
as their land of the dead; nor, in fact, has any other
earthly paradise been so.   But, among the myths which
sprang up in the age of burning the dead, the hope of

---

[1] *Il.* xxiii. 193–230.   [2] Beowulf, 6020; Helreiö Brynhildar, &c.
[3] D. G. vi. 19.   See Pictet, *Les Origines*, &c. ii. 519, for examples of the
same custom among more modern nations.

union with the heavenly powers gained a measure of strength. The gods of the Aryan were before everything gods of the air. As the soul, made visible in the smoke of the funeral pyre, was seen by men to mount upwards, to 'curl to the clouds,' the notion of the soul's having gone to join the gods—chief god Dyâus, the sky—was impressed more vividly upon men's minds.[1] But as the notion of the western journey was not abandoned, a natural compromise was made, and the soul was now sent upwards to travel along the path of the sun: its journey now lay in heaven, and it was led towards its final home by the Sun or by the Wind. Still the path of the deceased lay westward; the home of the dead ancestors was still beyond the same western horizon; there was still an Oceanus to be crossed and a dark Cimmerian land to be passed through.

The path thus taken by the soul becomes to the eye of faith a *bridge* spanning the celestial arch, and carrying men over the River of Death. And men would soon begin asking themselves where lay this heavenly road. Night is necessarily associated with thoughts of death— 'Death and his brother Sleep'—and of the other world. The heavens wear a more awful aspect than by day. The sun has forsaken us and is himself buried beneath the earth; while at once a million dwellers in the upper regions, who were before unseen, appear to sight, those stars which in so many mythologies are associated with souls.[2] Among the stars we see a bright yet misty bow bent overhead. Can this be other than the appointed Bridge of Souls? The ancient Indians called this road

---

[1] 'If, after having left the body, thou comest to the free air, thou wilt be an immortal god, not subject to decay and death' (Phocylides, *Sylb.* p. 97). In the case of the ordinary sacrifice, if the flame mounted upward the sacrifice was accepted (cf. *Il.* i. 462; *Od.* iii. 459; see also Maury, *R. de la 'G.* ch. xiii.) The same idea would naturally accompany the burning of the dead.

[2] For example, in Hebrew belief (cf. Kuenen, *Rel. of Israel*) and in Russian folk-lore (cf. Ralston's *Songs of the Russian People*).

God's Path (panthânô devayâh), because, besides its
being the way of souls to God, it was likewise the way of
God to men.   They also called it cow path (meaning
possibly cloud path), and this designation appears again
in the Low German name for the same heavenly bridge,
Kaupat (Kuhpfad).   From the ancient appellation, cow
path, it is probable that we get the more widely spread
name of the 'Milky Way.'

In the Vedic hymns the Indians oftenest speak of the
Milky Way as the path of Yama, the way to the house of
Yama the ruler of the dead.

A narrow path, an ancient one, stretches there, a path untrodden
 by men, a path I know of.   .
On it the wise who have known Brahma ascend to the world
 Swarga,[1] when they have received their dismissal,

sings one.   Another prays the Maruts, the Winds, not to
let him wander on the path of Yama, or when he does so,
when his time shall come, to keep him, that he fall not
into the hands of Nirrtis, the Queen of Naraka (Tartarus).[2]

The Maruts in this instance are appointed the guardians
of the soul; and there is something very appropriate in
the performance of the office by these wind gods.

Agni, the fire god, is of course the one who first of all
takes charge of the soul when it leaves the funeral fire.
But next after Agni it seems appropriate that the soul
should be given in charge to the Wind.   The duty is not,
however, undertaken by the Maruts only; in other passages we find as guardians of the bridge two dogs, and
the dead man is committed to their care.   But these dogs
are also personifications of the Wind.

Give him, O King Yama, to the two dogs, the watchers, the
four-eyed guardians of the path, guardians of men.   Grant him
safety and freedom from pain.

 [1] Swarga, the *bright* land of the blessed.   The word is from the root *swar*,
to shine.
 [2] R. V. i. 38, 5.

And it would seem from many other instances that these two dogs of Yama have the special mission of taking charge of the dead who travel to the bright paradise beyond the bridge.

Thus stands out in beauty and completeness the myth of the Bridge of Souls. A narrow path spanning the arch of heaven, passing over the River of Death, or over the dwelling of Nirṛtis, Queen of Tartarus, it reaches at last to the country of the wise Pitris, the fathers of the nation. These Pitris have gone to heaven before, and since their death have not ceased to watch over the men of their race. The path is guarded by two dogs, the hounds of Yama, wardens of the way, and likewise psychopomps, or conductors of the soul along this strait road.

While the European races worked up into wondrous variety, as we shall see anon, the story of the soul's journey over seas, the myths of the River of Death and of the Bridge of Souls were cherished most by the Indians and Iranians.

The two hounds of Yama recall in the first place the primitive image of the underground world as a devouring creature : thus in this respect they both of them resemble the classic Cerberus. Their common name is Sârameyas, which connects them with the wind of dawn, Saramâ ;[1] and this, as we have seen, was also the wind of evening. The Sârameyas are said to be 'born of the evening wind'— that is to say, they are beings of the night. In this respect they recall both in character and name the Greek Hermês ; for the word Ἑρμῆς, Ἑρμείας, is nothing more than a transliteration of the Sanskrit Sârameyas. Taken together, then—that is to say, under their common name, Sârameyas—the two dogs are like two Hermês ; they are two wind gods. Hermês combined in his being the natures of both the wind of morning and the wind of evening ; he was the god who sent men to sleep or awoke them from sleep,[2] the leader of shades to the under world,

---

[1] See Chap. III.   [2] *Od.* v. 47 ; xxiv. 4 ; &c.

und also — we shall see this more fully hereafter — the bringer back of men from the world of death. All these characters belong to the dogs of Yama in virtue of their common name. They are under this name not unlike the Asvin, who, as we saw, were the two winds, that of morning and that of evening.[1]

Individually, again, the dogs are called Cerbura, the 'spotted,' and Syama, the 'black.'[2] The etymological connection between the first of these two names and Cerberus scarcely requires to be pointed out. It is evident, therefore, that the dogs of Yama contain in their nature the germs of two distinct but allied creations of mythology—first the wind god, who is also a god of evening, of sleep and of death; and secondly the hell-hound, who is the personification of the yawning tomb. They may sometimes be simply images of night. The names 'spotted' and 'black' may seem to indicate the starry and the dark night sky.

From being personifications of night it is an easy step to becoming gods of sleep. Sleep and Death are ever twins; and the dead man is, in other creeds beside this Indian one, given into the hands not of one brother only, but of both.

Πέμπε δέ μιν πομποῖσιν ἅμα κραιπνοῖσι φέρεσθαι,
Ὕπνῳ καὶ Θανάτῳ διδυμάοσι.[3]

One of the hounds may have represented the temporal, the other the eternal, sleep. Wherefore we need not be surprised to find a single Sârameyas prayed to as a divinity of slumber and the protector of the sleeping household, as here in a beautiful hymn of the Rig Veda :—[4]

Destroyer of sickness, guard of the house, O thou who takest all shapes, be to us a peace-bringing friend.

Bay at the robber, Sârameyas ; bay at the thief. Why bayest thou at the singer of Indra ? why art thou angry with me ? Sleep, Sârameyas.

---

[1] Chap. III.   [2] Wilford in *As. Res.* iii. 409.
[3] *Il.* xvi. 681; cf. also *Theog.* 758.   [4] R. V. vii. 5

The mother sleeps, the father sleeps, the hound sleeps, the clan father sleeps, the whole tribe sleeps; sleep thou, Sârameyas.

Those who sleep by the cattle; those who sleep by the wain; the women who lie upon couches, the sweet-scented ones—all these we bring to slumber.

Do not these verses breathe of the fragrant air of early pastoral life?

Sleep and Death are twin brothers, and therefore it is that, like Sarpedon in the Iliad, the dead man is given to them to be borne along his way. 'Give him, O King Yama, to the two dogs. . . .' As dogs the Sârameyas represent the horrors of death and of the under world; as the winds they are the kind guardians of the souls. No doubt their terrors were for the wicked only, and so they are apt images of death itself.

The Persians knew the Bridge of Souls under the name of Kinvad (pul Kinvad), and with this bridge are connected one or more dogs. Wherefore it is evident that all the essential parts of the Indian myth were inherited by the Persians also. In one Fargard, or chapter, of the Vendidâd [1] it is narrated how the soul of the wicked man will fly to the under world 'with louder howling and fiercer pursuing than flees the sheep when the wolf rushes upon it in the lofty forest. No soul will come and meet his departed soul and help it through the howls and pursuit in the other world; nor will the dogs who keep the Kinvad bridge help his departing soul through the howls and pursuit in the other world.' And again in another place [2] it is told how 'the soul enters the way made by Time, open both to the wicked and to the righteous. At the head of the Kinvad, the holy bridge made by Ahura-Mazda, they demand for their spirits and souls the reward for the worldly goods which they gave away here below. Then comes the strong, well-formed maid,[3] with the dogs at her sides. She makes the

[1] Fargard xiii. The translation is from Darmesteter's translation of the *Zend-Avesta*.　　　　　　　　　　　　　　　　[2] Fargard xix.
[3] We meet with this maiden keeper of the bridge in Norse mythology (see Chap. VIII.)

soul of the righteous go úp above Hara-berezaiti;[1] above
the Kinvad bridge she places it, in the presence of the
heavenly gods themselves.'

From the Persians the bridge became known to the
Hebrews, and from the one or the other source it passed
on to the creed of Islâm.   Sirât is the name of the bridge
so vividly described by Mohammedan writers.[2]   It is finer
than a hair and sharper than the edge of a sword, and is
besides guarded with thorns and briars along all its length.
Nevertheless when at the last day the good Muslim comes
to cross it a light will shine upon him from heaven and
he will be snatched across like lightning or like the wind;
but when the wicked man or the unbeliever approaches
the light will be hidden, and from the extreme narrowness
of the bridge, and likewise becoming entangled in the
thorns, he will fall headlong into the abyss of fire that is
beneath.

The Bridge of Souls cannot be always the Milky Way
even in the mythology of India; for in one hymn,[3]
though not a Vedic one, we read—

Upon it, they say, there are colours white and blue and brown
and gold and red.

And this path Brahma knows; and he who has known
Brahma shall take it, he who is pure and glorious.

Here the singer is evidently describing the rainbow.
In the Norse cosmology the rainbow has the same name
as the Indian path of the gods.   The Eddas call it As-brû,
the bridge of the Æsir, or gods.   Its other name is Bifröst,
'the trembling mile,' and this name may have been originally bestowed upon the Milky Way, for this when we look
at it seems always on a tremble.   Supposing the myths
which once belonged to the Milky Way to have been
passed on to the rainbow, the name of the former might
also have been inherited by the latter.

[1] The heavenly mountain.   [2] Sale's *Koran*, Introd. p. 91.
[3] Vrhadâraṇyaka, *Ed. Pol.* iii. 4, 7-9.   See Kuhn, *Zeit. f. v. Sp.* ii. 311, &c.

Asbrû, or Bifröst, was the bridge whereby the Northern gods descended to the world. One end of it reached to the famous Urdar fount, where sat the weird sisters three—the Nornir, or fates. 'Near the fountain which is under the ash stands a very fair house, out of which come three maidens named Urðr, Verðandi, and Skuld (Past, Present, Future). These maidens assign the lifetime of men, and are called Norns. To their stream the gods ride every day along Bifröst to take council.'[1] It was right that these awful embodiments of time and fate—Past, Present, Future—should have their dwelling at the end of the Bridge of Death.

Odhinn is the natural conductor of the dead to the other world, for he is the god of the wind, and therefore corresponds, in a certain degree, to the two Indian dogs, the Sârameyas. 'Odhinn and Freyja' (Air and Earth) 'divide the slain,' says one legend—meaning that the bodies go to earth, the breaths or souls to heaven. In the Middle Ages, when Odhinn worship had been overthrown, and the gods of Asgard descended to Hel-home—that is to say, when from being divinities they became fiends—Odhinn still pursued his office as conductor or leader of souls. But now he hounded them to the under world. Odhinn the god was changed into the demon Odhinn, and one of the commonest appearances of this fiend was as the Wild Huntsman. To this day the Wild Huntsman Hackelberg[2] is well known in Germany. The peasants hear his awful chase going on above their heads. He is accompanied by two dogs, and he hunts, 'tis said, along the *Milky Way*.[3]

A gentler legend concerning the Milky Way is that which we find preserved in a charming poem of the Swede Torpelius, called the 'Winter Street'—another of the

---

[1] Edda Snorra. D. 15.

[2] This name, Hackelberg, shows the Huntsman to be really Odhinn. The name is transformed from Hackel-bärend, which means 'cloak-bearing.' Now the cloak of Odhinn is one of his peculiar possessions.

[3] Of this Wild Huntsman I shall speak more fully in future chapters (Chaps. VII. X.)

names for this heavenly road.   And with this in the form
in which it has been rendered into English [1] we may close
our list of legends connected with the River of Death and
Bridge of Souls.   The story is of two lovers :—

Her name Salami was, his Zulamyth ;
And both so loved, each other loved.   Thus runs the tender myth :

That once on earth they lived, and, loving there,
Were wrenched apart by night, and sorrow, and despair ;
And when death came at last, with white wings given,
Condemned to live apart, each reached a separate heaven.

.   .   .   .

Yet loving still upon the azure height,
Across unmeasured ways of splendour, gleaming bright
With worlds on worlds that spread and glowed and burned,
Each unto each, with love that knew no limit, longing turned.

Zulamyth half consumed, until he willed
Out of his strength, one night, a bridge of light to build
Across the waste—and lo ! from her far sun,
A bridge of light from orb to orb Salami had begun.

A thousand years they built, still on, with faith,
Immeasurable, quenchless—thus the legend saith—
Until the winter street of light—a bridge
Above heaven's highest vault swung clear, remotest ridge from
ridge.

Fear seized the Cherubim ; to God they spake—
' See what amongst Thy works, Almighty, these can make ! '
God smiled, and smiling, lit the spheres with joy—
' What in My world love builds,' He said, ' shall I—shall Love—
destroy ? '

The bridge stood finished, and the lovers flew .
Into each other's arms : when lo ! shot up and grew,
Brightest in heavens serene, a star that shone
As the heart shines serene after a thousand troubles gone.

[1] By E. Keary, *Evening Hours*, vol. iii.   The name of the bridge, the
Winter Street, has a genuine Teutonic character.   The story, however, cannot be purely Teutonic ; not at least in the form in which Torpelius tells
it.   The names of the lovers are Hebrew.

§ 2. The Sea of Death.

Of all the European races the Greeks were the first who took in a friendly fashion to the sea; a fact pretty evident from what we can trace of the routes taken by their brother nations, and indeed indicated by the peculiarity of the Greek names for the sea, names not, like *mare* and *Meer*, connected with death, but θάλασσα, salt water, or πόντος, a path.[1] The advantages of situation which Greece enjoyed are to be credited with this circumstance. As Curtius points out so well, where Europe and Asia meet in the Ægæan, Nature has made no separation between the two worlds. 'Sea and air unite the coasts of the Archipelago into a connected whole; the same periodical winds blow from the Hellespont as far as Crete, and regulate navigation by the same conditions, and the climate by the same changes. Scarcely one point is to be found between Asia and Europe where in clear weather the mariner would feel himself left in solitude between sky and water; the eye reaches from island to island, and easy voyages of a day lead from bay to bay.' It was in this nearness of shore to shore, from the invitation of the islands spread out like stepping-stones across the calm Ægæan, that the Greek people, when their wanderings brought them to the limits of Asia Minor, did not hesitate long before they crossed over to European Greece and joined the two shores under the dominion of one race.

Very early in prehistoric days, long before the age of Homer, they had become familiar with their own Greek sea, with all its islands and all its harbours; but it was long after this that their mariners had rounded Cape Matapan; longer still before the first Greek had sailed as far as Sicily. Some tidings of the distant lands of the Mediterranean were brought by Phœnician navigators, and afterwards by their own more adventurous sailors;

[1] Connected with the Skr. *panthas, paths* and our *path.*

subjects with which they deal, the diversity of interests which they represent. The Iliad is a tale of land battle, and the theatre of its action is limited to the known world of the Greek, the two shores of the Ægœan; the Odyssey

---

[1] The expedition of the Argonauts was always held in Greek tradition to have preceded the expedition of Odysseus. It belongs to the 'antiquity' of Homer. No circumstantial account of it, however, is to be found until a much later date than that of the Odyssey; therefore it is right to consider the latter poem as the first great epic of the Sea of Death. That the voyage of the Argonauts was originally of the same kind as the voyage of Odysseus, and undertaken in *the same direction*, seems highly probable. In after years the former was transmuted into an expedition to Cholchis and to the river Phasis. But there is no trace of that form of the legend in Homer. All that is there said is that Jason's voyage was made to the house of Æetes (*Od*. xii. 70). Nowhere is it said that the land lay to the eastward; nothing in the earliest tradition points to that voyage in the Euxine and up the Phasis, which we meet first in Pindar and afterwards in a more elaborate shape in Apollonius Rhodius. The *golden fleece* might seem (to a lover of dawn myths) to suggest the dawn; but it does not so any more than do the apples of the Hesperides. The myth of these latter is a myth of sunset. Æetes is the brother of Circê, and son of Helios and Persê. He is, like Circê, connected with the setting sun, and so with death. He is a kind of god of death, and for that reason is called 'death-designing' (ὀλοόφρων).—*Od*. x. 137.

[2] Cf. especially *Od*. vii. 165, 316; ix. 270; xiv. 57, 283–4; xvi. 422.

is a song in praise not of war, but of seafaring adventure,
and the hero of it is not a type of the warrior, but of the
navigator.   For Greece, in prehistoric days, . had her
gallant band of Columbuses and De Gamas, of Drakes
and Hudsons, and it was these discoverers who paved the
way for Greek supremacy over seas.   Such men had
different views of life and a different worship from
those of the settled nobility of Greece, the Ionian princes, for instance, for whom the Iliad was composed;
and this divergency in views of life and worship appears very strikingly on a comparison of the two great
poems.

The original sea god of the Greek race had been
Poseidôn; but in the Odyssey Poseidôn is superseded by
Athênê,[1] who, when we put aside Zeus, stands by far the
first among the remaining divinities.   The Odyssey seems
to be written expressly to glorify Athênê, and to display
her power; for she is the active divinity throughout.   She
wields all those forces of nature which in the Iliad are
made the peculiar possession of Zeus himself, controlling
the storm and sending the lightning.   No other deity
appears actively upon the scene, saving the rival of
Athênê, the older sea god, Poseidôn, and he is defeated
in his endeavours to bring destruction on Odysseus.   With
Athênê the Odyssey glorifies the sailor and a sailor's life.
It celebrates all the luxuries which the voyager brings
home from foreign lands; and chiefly among them those
treasures of art which, first introduced by the Phœnicians,
were beginning at the time in which the Odyssey was
composed to stir the spirit of young Greece.   Of the sailor,
as goddess of the sea (Tritogeneia), of the merchantman,
to whom she gives prudence and the power to deceive, of

---

[1] In the *Odyssey* we see a transfer to Athênê of some of the powers
over the sea, which in the *Iliad* belong exclusively to Poseidôn.   In the
Odyssey, moreover, we find that Zeus has to a great extent delegated to
lesser gods the control over the phenomena of nature which were once
specially his, and that the powers of wind and storm are swayed alter-
nately by Poseidôn and Athênê.   See particularly bk. v

the artist, whom she endows with cunning of hand, Athênê
is alike the patroness.

But there are further points of difference between the
Iliad and the Oydssey. The nivigator had other dangers
to encounter than the warrior had, and different adventures to relate. The Western Sea, to which men's
thoughts were beginning to turn, and where Odysseus'
adventures lie, was not to their fancy fraught with earthly
terrors only, nor with dangers that were measurable and
known; it was full of untried wonders, bordering as
it did close upon the other world; nay, in a manner it
was the other world, for it was the Sea of Death. The
Odyssey is full of images of death, though they are not
self-conscious ones, only mythical expressions first used for
the passage of the soul from life, and then made literal by
their transference to the actual Western Sea. All this
produces a marked distinction in character between the
Iliad and the Odyssey. Long before the first outward-
bound navigator had rounded Cape Malea, all the coasts of
the Ægæan had become part of the familiar world of the
Greek; outside this only was the world of the unknown.
The Iliad tells us what the Greeks thought about the
known region. Myths no doubt mingled with the legend
of the fall of Troy; but that story is, in Homer, essentially
realistic; it is rationalistic even. The very powers of the
immortals and their deeds seem petty and limited.

And it may be that in this circumstance lies an element
of superior greatness in the older poem; for a poet can
only attain the highest altitudes he is capable of when
the material of his art is composed, I will not say of fact,
but of belief which has become so constant and familiar
as to take almost the shape of fact. That sense of reality
which drags down prosaic minds is for him the proper
medium of his flight: no sham beliefs or half-beliefs are
at his best moments possible to him. We should, perhaps,
never have had the 'Divine Comedy' unless the vulgar
literalness of priestly minds, confounding metaphors with

fact, had in its pseudo-philosophy mapped out the circles of Heaven and Hell, as an astronomer maps out the craters of the moon. The poet of the Iliad has over him of the Odyssey an advantage, so far as the former is dealing with the known regions of Greek life and as the other is cast abroad upon a sea of speculation and fancy.

Not of course that even the later poem had not to its hearers the air of a narrative of fact, or was without some foundation in experience. Some writers have attempted to explain the Odyssey as nothing more than a myth of the sun's course through heaven. But there is too much solidity about the story, too thorough an atmosphere of belief around it, to suit with a tale relating such airy unrealities as these. The Greeks who first sang these ballads must have been thinking of a real journey made upon this solid earth. But it is easy to see how many images and notions which had first been applied only to the sun god on his Western journey would creep into a history like that of Odysseus. Undoubtedly the sun myth had first pointed out the home of the dead as lying in the West; and nothing is more natural than that a people whose hopes and wishes carried them in the track of the wandering sun should, when they came to construct an epic of travel, make the imaginary journey lie the same way.

They would interweave in their story such truths—or such sailors' yarns—as Phœnician mariners or adventurous Greeks brought home from the distant waters, with many images which had once been made for the sun's heavenly voyage, and others which had been first applied to death. Their geography would be mythical; for they could have no accurate notion of the lands which they spoke of;[1] but

---

[1] Mr. Bunbury, among more recent writers, has admirably shown how completely mythical is the character of the geography of the *Odyssey* (*Geography of the Ancients*). See also Völcker, *Homerische Geographie*; and Welcker, in *Rhein. Mus.* vol. i. N.S. p. 219, 'Die Homerische Phäaken,' on the pretended identification of Scheria and Corcyra.

told them might lie in the Western seas. Now in reality there was only one thing which at the bottom of their hearts they believed actually did lie there—namely, Death; and beyond that death the home of the departed souls. Therefore their stories of the Mediterranean do almost all, upon a minute inspection, resolve themselves into a variety of mythical ways of describing death, and upon this as upon a dark background the varied colours of the tale are painted. It need take away no jot of our pleasure in the brilliant picture presented before us to acknowledge this. Behind the graceful air of the poem, sung as a poem only, we hear a deeper note telling of the passionate, obstinate questionings of futurity which belonged not more to Greece three thousand years ago than they now belong to us.

The tale of the great traveller could not at the first have been so full as we find it in its present shape. Evidently fresh adventures have continually been interpolated in the history, to give it richness and variety.[1] Myths at the outset are not rich nor varied; they are almost always confined to a single theme, and the action in them obeys the rule of ' unity ' more strictly than do those of the most classical dramas. It is probable, therefore, that many single stories have been rolled into one to make this great epic. We notice, moreover, that one series of events occurs in a narrative related during the course of another

[1] *Cohort. ad Græcos*, xxix.   [2] Cf. Butcher and Lang, *Od.* 2nd ed. p. xxiv.

series. All the events which Odysseus recounts while sitting in the hall of Alcinoüs, though they are supposed to tell the earlier history of his voyage, are no doubt additions to the original tale, which follows directly the course of the poem till the wanderer is brought to the island of the Phæacians, and then takes up its interrupted thread when his story is finished and Alcinoüs prepares his return voyage to Greece. An experience of the growth of myths and epics teaches us to look upon the two series as two distinct legends which have in this awkward way been forced into one story; one being more expanded than the other, and therefore perhaps of a later date.

Looking into the two series of adventures more closely, and comparing them together, we discover that many circumstances of one appear to be retold in a different shape in the other. Take, for instance, the life of Odysseus with Calypso and with Circê, and the manner of his deliverance from each. Both Calypso and Circê are nymphs and enchantresses; with each Odysseus passes a term of months or years, living with her as her husband, but longing all the while to return to his own wife and his own home; from each Hermês at last sets him free. What if the Calypso and Circê episodes both repeat in reality the same myth? And what if Odysseus' other great adventure, the voyage to the Phæacians, have likewise its counterpart in the expanded story? The question of the real identity or difference between the two series of adventures can only be decided when we have had time thoroughly to test the significance which there is in the points of their apparent likeness.

Meanwhile who is Calypso? Her name bespeaks her nature not ambiguously. It is from καλύπτειν, to cover or conceal. She is the shrouder or the shrouded place; the literal counterpart of the Norse Hel, which word is, as has been said, from the Icelandic *helja*, 'to hide.' How, then, can Calypso be anything else than death, as she dwells there in her cave by the shores of the sea? How

so nakedly as Calypso's name shows hers, yet we easily recognise by it *death* in one of its many guises—a ravenous animal or bird, a hawk or a wolf.[1]

For my part, I think that the tale divides at the point where we see Odysseus in the house of one or other of the two enchantresses; and that, starting from the island of Ogygia on the one hand, and from that of Æœa on the other, we have before us two successive pictures of the fate of a man's soul *after* it has passed the house of death. And I think, again, that the wanderings of Odysseus before he comes to the island of Circê may be taken for an image of the Western Sea on *this side* of the dark portal, the Western Sea which, though full of suggestions of mortality, has not yet quite become the Sea of Death. One order of pictures we may call cosmic, or belonging to this world; the other is hypercosmic, and appears only when we have passed the boundary which separates this world from the next. But of course this distinction expresses only the general character of the two parts of the epic. That general difference does not hinder the

---

[1] Κίρκος (whence κίρκη) is given as both *hawk* and *wolf* in L. and S. It is most likely from a root *krik*, meaning to make a grating sound, and therefore probably originally applied to the bird (cf. our night-jar). We may, then, compare Circê with Charôn, 'an eagle.'

two orders of ideas, the *worldly* and the *other-worldly*, from mingling at many points. They are, indeed, so closely allied as to be not easily distinguishable. The whole journey, including both images of death and images which apply to the region beyond death, is foreshadowed in the earlier parts of the voyage, in those parts which precede the arrival at the house of the Queen of Shades. It is, in fact,. as if we had first to pass through the Valley of the Shadow of Death, and while there to anticipate in a faint show the clearer vision which will come after dissolution itself.[1]

[1] There being, according to my view, only one essential idea at the bottom of the myth of the Odyssean voyages—namely, the idea of death and the next world—it follows that the chief adventures of the hero must constantly repeat themselves in new shapes.

The essential myth of the Sea of Death divides itself into three parts —viz. Death, the Earthly Paradise, and the Return Voyage to the Land of the Living. Of these the first two are the most important and the most constantly repeated. They should always recur in the same order. It may help the reader to a due understanding of the myths if I tabulate them in the order in which they were supposed to occur under the heads above mentioned. The Sea of Death is entered when Odysseus has left Cythèra.

	Death.	The Earthly Paradise.	The Return to the Land of the Living.
First Series	The Lotophagi (or sleep preceding death). The Cyclopes.	The Æolian Island.	Odysseus' voyage to within one day's sail of Ithaca. This is broken short in order that the subsequent adventures may be tacked on.
Second Series	Læstrygones. Ææa. Hadês.	This is the myth of the most gloomy sort. Here we only distinguish three stages in the journey of the soul to the land of shades. There is no Paradise beyond death.	
Third Series	Ææa. Sirens.	Thrinakia.	The voyage from Thrinakia should have been to the land of the living, but it takes a different direction for the same reason which altered the course of the voyage from Æolia.
Fourth Series	Calypso.	Phæacians.	Return to Ithaca.

These parts again coalesce somewhat, and the grand division remains where I have put it at the adventures with Circè and Calypso. Of those

We have but to translate the story of Homer into a simpler mythical language to detect the unreal character of its events, and to feel fully the imaginative region into which the poet has strayed. If the tale had been told by our Norse fore-elders it would have been clothed in such transparent language; and we may for the nonce rechristen the scenes of Odysseus' adventures with the names which a Northern bard would have given them.

First, then, we have the voyage to Sleep Home. The wind which bore him from Ilium carried the hero to the land of the Cicones, and thence to Cythera—historical places within the compass of the Ægean. After that he rounded Cape Malea, and burst into the sea of wonders where his course was to lie so long. The shore at which Odysseus next touched was the shore of the Lotophagi, who ate the lotus flower or fruit for food. 'And whoever partook of that pleasant fruit no more wished to tell of his coming home, nor to go back thither; but they choose rather to stay with the lotus-eaters and to forget their return.' This is Sleep Home.

And now on to Giant Land, where the Cyclopes dwell. The Norsemen, we know, had their Giant Home (Jötunheimar), on the borders of the world. Their gods ruled over Asgard and Man's Home; but the power of the Æsir did not stretch beyond the world of men. They had only so far shown their might that they were able to banish the jötun brood from the ordered world. Outside the limits of that the giants lived in defiance of them, and were for ever threatening to invade the home of gods and men. Something the same had been the history of the Titans

which follow one is essentially a story of the voyage to heaven, the other essentially a story of the journey to hell.

The recurrence of the number *nine* has been remarked upon in the adventures of Odysseus, and assigned as a reason for supposing it a sun myth. The hero is nine days after first leaving the known world, i.e. after rounding Cape Malea, before he sights land, the land of the Lotophagi; he is nine days again sailing homewards from the island of Æolus.

and giants of the Greek cosmology. Zeus had banished these to a Tartarean land, unvisited by sun or breath of winds, that land where Iapetus [1] and Kronos dwell for ever.

The essential picture in Greek and Norse mythology is the same; it is of a sunny world ruled by the gods, beyond it the dark Giant Land. To this region and to the Titan brood the Cyclopes belong. 'They care not for ægis-bearing Zeus, nor the blessed gods.' [2] They plough not, nor sow. They have no assemblages for council nor any public law; each is a law unto himself and to his household, and heeds not his neighbour. They live in caves upon the mountain-tops and through the windy promontories.[3]

Odysseus landed first upon an uninhabited island close by the island of the Cyclopes. There immense flocks of goats fed undisturbed, for the Cyclopes had never reached that near coast, because they had no art of ship-building and no 'crimson-prowed barks.' This is a little touch of reality, a reminiscence of some land where the ignorance of the inhabitants in matters of seamanship—displayed so clearly by such an instance of a neighbouring island unvisited—had struck the attention of mariners.

Next Odysseus and his comrades went on to the Cyclops' island, and while the rest stayed in the ship the hero and twelve others ascended from the shore to spy out the land. Here we have the first detailed picture of the Giant Land of Greek mythology. When they had gone but a little way inland they saw on the land's edge a cave near to the sea, but high up and hidden by laurel trees. Around were stalled much cattle, and sheep and goats. And a high wall was built there with deep-embedded stones and with tall pines and towering oaks. 'Twas the dwelling of a huge man who by himself was feeding his

---

[1] Father of Prometheus and of Atlas. (See Ch. IV.)
[2] *Od.* ix. 275.   [3] *Od.* ix. 105-106, 400.

x

flocks afar off. He did not fellow with his kind, but in solitude fed upon evil thoughts. A horrid monster he, not like food-eating men, but liker to the woody top of some great mountain standing alone.

The name of this giant was Polyphemus. Odysseus and his comrades hid themselves in the cavern to await Polyphemus' return.

'He came bearing a huge burden of dried wood to light his evening meal. Inside the cave he threw it down with a mighty noise, and we in terror hid ourselves in the recesses of the cave. Then drove he into the wide cavern of his fat flocks all those whom he would milk; the males, the rams and goats, he left outside that deep hall's door. Then he fixed up a barrier great and weighty. Two-and-twenty wains could not have moved that mighty rock. And he sat down and milked the sheep and goats duly, and to each one set its young.' And when he had lit his fire he saw the wanderers and spake to them.

'O strangers, who are ye, and whence have ye plied o'er the moist ways hither? Was it for barter, or come ye as pirates, who wander, their lives in their hands, bringing evil on all men?'

And Odysseus: 'We are strayed Greeks from Troy, driven by contrary winds over the sea's great deep. And now, in search of our homes, have we come another road by other ways. . . . But do thou, best one, revere the gods. We are suppliants to thee, and Zeus avenges the cause of strangers and suppliants.'

And he with savage mind replied, 'Foolish art thou, O wanderer, to tell me to fear or shun the wrath of the gods. The Cyclopes care not for ægis-bearing Zeus nor the blessed gods. . . .' Then he fell upon them and seized two of the comrades of Odysseus; seized them like whelps and dashed them down to the ground, and their brains flowed out and moistened the ground. 'In despair, weeping, we held up our hands to Zeus.'

In Saxon legend we shall hereafter meet with the

counterpart of this giant, the 'eotan' Grendel,[1] and see him snatching up his victims in the same manner and devouring them. The Cyclopes personify immediately the storm or the stormy sky, in which the sun, like an angry eye, glares through the clouds. As a part of the giant race the Cyclopes represent also the uncultivated and uncultivable tracts of country, the out-world region, that which was in the language of other times the *heathen* world—the world of heath and wild moor. To the Teutons the jötun or eotan race had the same meaning; wherefore is this Grendel's home 'among the moors and misty hills.'[2] First representing the outer regions of nature, the parts remotest from men and from the safety of towns and villages, the giant kind in all mythologies personify likewise the outer world or *other* world itself, the land of death. As we shall see in a future chapter, there is no distinct line of demarcation between the Norse Jötunheim and Helheim—Giant-home and Hel's Home. Many among the inhabitants of Jötunheim are by their names seen to be personifications of the funeral fire, or of the grave. The Cyclopes do not display their character so nakedly as do the giants of the North, but we easily admit that their home also must lie by the Sea of Death and near the borders of another world.

Or again, we may, merely looking upon the Cyclopes as monsters, take them for symbols of the all-devouring grave. We should then have to compare them with the man-eating ogre of mediæval European folk lore.

How Odysseus and his companions escaped from Polyphemus' cave does not need telling here. It is rather with the imagery of the strange regions into which the wanderers come, than with the details of their adventures, that we have to do. Everyone knows too in what way the wily Greek plotted revenge upon the giant, and his

---

[1] Chapter VII. And very similar to Grendel is the giant *Sushna* of the Rig Veda, 'who walks in darkness.'

[2] See Chap. VII.

own and his comrades' escape; how he produced his wine
skins with a beverage never before tasted by the Cyclops,
how Polyphemus became drunk with the wine, and how
Odysseus and his fellows, seizing an immense bar which
they had previously heated in the fire, bored with that
into the Cyclops' single eye and blinded him so; and,
finally, how, tied beneath the bellies of the sheep, they
eluded his vigilance and made their way into the open air.

They have been to Sleep Home, and thence to Giant
Land; their next stage is to Wind Home. I have said that
the details of the earlier adventures are often a faint fore-
shadowing of the later ones; and in the Æolian island I
see a sort of prediction of the earthly paradise which we
shall meet again in larger dimensions and brighter colours
when we come to the land of the Phæacians. On this
floating land dwelt Æolus, son of Hippotas, dear to the
immortals. All round the island was a brazen wall, irre-
fragible; and a smooth rock rose up to meet the wall.
To Æolus had been born in his palace twelve children, six
girls and six strong sons. And he gave his daughters for
wives to his sons. And these feasted together continually
about their dear father and honoured mother, and dainty
food they lacked not. And the sweet-scented hall echoed
to their voices by day, and by night they slept beside
their chaste wives on napery and bedsteads ornamented.

Are we not now getting nearer to the homes of Paradise? For, see, the charm of the land of sleep lay only in
the 'pleasant food' of flowers, which made men forget all
that they had suffered and what they had still to endure.
From this calm we awoke to find ourselves in the devouring cavern of death; and the place we come to now seems
certainly a kind of paradise beyond death. Dante, it is
true, placed his Wind Home at the outside of Hell. But
then he spoke the thoughts of mediæval Catholicism, which
darkened all the pictures of the future life. Wind Home
might quite as well lie on the borders of Paradise.

Of course this picture of the Æolian land is but as a

minor note anticipating the end of the piece. We have by no means yet passed out of the mortal sea; the giants will appear again, and more images of death than any we have yet encountered. Nevertheless it is true that in these its first three scenes—Sleep Home, Giant Home, and Wind Home—we get a faint picture of the whole drama of Odysseus' voyage. But to continue the story.

In friendly wise Æolus entertained Odysseus for a whole month, and enquired everything of him touching Ilium and the Grecian ships and the Greeks' return; 'and all things I related as they were. And when at length I asked for a journey and would have him send me away, he did not refuse, but prepared my voyage. Of a nine-year-old ox's skin he made a bag. And in it he tied the ways of blustering winds; for Kroniôn made him the keeper of the winds, to hush or raise whiche'er he would. . . . With a bright silver chord he bound it in the hollow ship, that not the smallest breath might escape. To me he gave West Wind, to waft our ships and us. But he was not fated to perform it: our own folly was our un-doing.'

The notion of a return home belongs not of right to the drama of the Sea of Death. But in the Odyssey the story has been rationalised; and as it now stands we read that Odysseus sailed for nine days, and was within one more day's journey of Ithaca.[1] They could even see men lighting fires upon the land. But unhappily upon Odysseus, who had been steering the ship for all those nine days, 'sweet sleep on a sudden fell;' and, as he slept, his comrades, deeming he bore away a treasure in his bag, undid it, and all the storms burst on them at

[1] The likeness between the place taken in this story respectively by the Æolian island and the land of the Phæacians is conspicuous in this fact, that the visit to each heralds a sail backwards to the east—to Ithaca, in fact. We can easily understand how, when various short myths were tacked together to form one long story, the episode of the journey to Ithaca from Æolus' island was made to take a quite different termination from that which it originally had.

the seventh came to Lamos' lofty city, Læstrygonia. This was only another land of giants. Perhaps this incident of the journey and the story of the Cyclops are two legends which have been woven together. The descriptions are slightly varied; and on that account their points of likeness are the. more instructive; for they must have a distinct reason and intention. It is generally characteristic of the giant to live in the earth; especially so if he be in a manner a representative of the grave itself. The Cyclops lives in a cave. But the Læstrygones are much more civilised : they have cities and agoræ.

'Behind the high promontory where we lay,' says Odysseus, continuing his narrative, 'I could see neither the signs of cattle nor of men; only smoke we saw issuing as from the ground. So I sent forward three of my companions to enquire what sort of men they were. And they went along the smooth road whereby waggons carry wood from the mountains to the city, and they met before the town a damsel bearing water, the strong daughter of Læstrygonian Antiphates. Then they stood by and spake to her, and asked her who was the king of these people and who were those he ruled. And she straightway showed to them her father's high-roofed house. When they had entered the illustrious dwelling, they found the mistress there lofty as a mountain-top; and they were afeared. And she called at once her husband, famous Antiphates, from the assembly.'

There is much less of the true jötun nature about these giants. They have houses and cities and assemblies. I

think it probable that in this part of the voyage we have
more to do with legend than with myth. Granting that
the myth had asserted that a giant race lived somewhere
in mid-sea, this special account of the giants may have
been taken from the actual experience of travellers. The
Læstrygones have, however, all the savageness of their
brethren the Cyclopes. Antiphates at once seized one of
the comrades to prepare his supper; the other two ran
back to the ship. And the giant raised a clamour through
all the town. The strong Læstrygonians came flocking
from every side in thousands—not men, but giants—who
hurled at them with stones torn from the rocks. And an
evil cry arose among the ships as the Greeks perished and
navies sank. . . 'At length, drawing my sword from my
thigh, I severed the rope of the blue-prowed ship. I
called on my comrades and bade them to throw themselves
upon the oars, that we might escape the evil. . . .'

Here for a moment let us pause. Far more important
and significant than any of the previous adventures is the
next which befalls the seafarers—that is to say, their
coming to the home of Circé. Circé and Calypso, I suppose, are the same; and each is very Death herself. Images
of mortality lie scattered throughout the history of the
voyage; but in these two only do we see the true personifications of the dreadful goddess. After the visits to their
homes the story changes somewhat. The latter part in
either case presents a picture of the destiny of the soul
—one future after the habitation with Circé, another
future after the habitation with Calypso; from Ææa to
Hadês, from Calypso's island, Ôgygia, to the earthly
Paradise.

Circé is Death first presented in the image of a hawk
or wolf. She is the child, as it seems, of the night sun, as
the Egyptians would have said of the dead Osiris; in the
language of Grecian fable, she is the daughter of Helios
and Perse (the destroyer), Perse herself being the daughter
of Oceanos, into which the days disappear. The name of

her island (it is also another name for Circé herself),[1] Æœa, means a land of such wailing (αἰαῖ) as men utter by a grave.[2] Circé's palace is buried deep in forest gloom, and over dense coppices of oak and underwood its smoke is seen ascending. Around the enchantress are wild beasts, mountain wolves and lions, which she herself has tamed. But her attendant maidens are the personifications of the simplest nature religion, the daughters of the fountains and the groves and holy rivers, which flow into the sea; for she belongs to an old-world order of things; before the gods were she is. She is fate; and, like all the fates, she weaves a thread, the thread of destiny.[3] It is a beautiful image which is repeated in the case of Calypso, that when this goddess of death is first discovered to us she is weaving her immortal web and singing over it with a lovely voice.

When the comrades of Odysseus have come to her palace, they stand without the gates, shouting aloud, and she comes forth and opens the shining doors and bids them in. They do not keep men standing at that door.[4]

---

[1] Her son is Æœus, her brother Æetes. This Æetes is a kind of king of death, for the labours of Jason and the Argonauts may be compared to the labours of Heracles in the other world. (See ante, Chap. IV.) It is noticeable, as witnessing to the likeness between Circé and Calypso, that one is sister of ὀλοόφρωνος Æetes, the other of ὀλοόφρωνος Atlas. Atlas is a being like Iapetus, a King of the West, a King of Death.

[2] Cf. what was said above concerning Cócytus and Gjöll.

[3] I doubt if the metaphorical notion of weaving the thread of destiny belongs to the earliest genesis of myth. It may be that the weaving or sewing goddess (like the Frau Holda of the Germans) is originally only an earth divinity; hence a mother goddess, and so a patroness of all housewifery. Athéné sometimes appears in this character. The earth goddess, from being very old (wralt), becomes the goddess of prophecy, and so of fate (see Chaps. II. and V.) With the notion of fate, again, may be connected the quite physical one of the navel chord which unites the new-born child to its mother. Man might be supposed in the same way united by an invisible thread to the mother of all, to the Earth. This at death is cut.

[4] See the fine lines of Christina Rossetti:—

'Shall I meet other wayfarers by night?
Those who have gone before.
Then must I knock or call when first in sight?
They will not keep you standing at that door.'

The lower road is not a hard one. *Sed revocare gradus.*
. . . She seats them upon thrones, and makes ready their
supper of cheese, and meal, and honey, and Pramnian
wine; but with the food she mingles the fatal narcotic
drug which makes them forget their native land. And
last she strikes them with her rod, and they are transformed into swine. 'They had the heads and voices and
hair and bodies of swine, but their understandings were
unshaken as before.' That turning the comrades into
swine is, however, a later addition; the original Circê had
only to touch them with her wand—which is one with the
sleepy rod of Hermês [1]—and they awoke no more.

By Odysseus, and through the council of Hermês,
the companions are freed from their enchantment. So
at least the story stands in Homer. But how freed?
Whither are they at liberty to go? To the house of
Hadês, that is all. Odysseus is warned by Circê herself
that he must go thither, and in the dialogue between them
we are once again taught the lesson of the *facilis descensus
Averno*. 'Who,' exclaims the hero, 'will guide me on
that way? None has yet sailed to Hadês' gate.' And she
answers, 'O wise Laertes' son, let the want of a pilot
on thy ship be cause of little care to thee. Raise but
your mast and let your white sails fly, and Boreas' breath
will bring you there.' Then she describes the unknown
land. 'And when at length thou hast crossed the stream
of Ocean, where is the shore, and where are the groves of
Persephonê, of towering poplars and fruitless willows,
there leave thy ship by Ocean's depths, and go thou thyself to Hadês' drear halls. . . .'

Then they went down to the sea, and awful Circê sent
behind them a kindly breeze, which filled their sails. And
the sails, as they passed over the sea, were full-stretched

[1] Him thought how that the wingèd god, Mercury,
Beforne him stood, and bad him to be mery.
His *slepy yerde* in hond he bare upright;
An hat he wered upon his heres bright. . . . *Knight's Tale.*

all that day. Then the sun set, and the ways were over-shadowed. And now they had come to the far limit of the deep-flowing Ocean, to the home in which live the Cimmerians, covered with darkness and mist. Them the sun never visits when at morning he climbs the starry heaven, or when he returns backwards towards the earth; but hateful night broods there. There they drew up the ship; and there they passed through the groves of Perse-phonê, with the towering poplars and fruitless willows, to the house of Hadês. There Phlegethôn and Côcytus, which is a stream of Styx, join the Acherôn; and where a rock marks the meeting of the *loud-sounding rivers* [1] Odysseus dug a trench and filled it with the blood of sheep, and made a sacrifice and a libation, and besought the unsubstantial dead to draw near. [2]

In the version of the story which has come down to us no valid reason is given for the journey of Odysseus to Hadês. He goes there only to invoke the shade of a prophet, who is to tell what further adventures lie ahead for him and his comrades. But Circê was herself a pro-phetess. And, besides, the best of auguries would have been to send him home; and Circê, who could give him a breeze to carry him to the west, could, one would have sup-posed, have given him one which would have borne him to Ithaca. We should suppose this, I mean, if we looked upon Odysseus as merely a common adventurer, and the wonders which he meets with as only the wonders inci-dental to distant travel. But when we strip from all the story its later dress, and see it in its original intention, we perceive that there is a meaning in each detail; we see

[1] Cf. Gjöll.

[2] This feeding with blood the unsubstantial shades (i.e. *images* of the dead such as are seen in dreams), in order that they may obtain something like human capabilities, is very remarkable, and is a test of the psychology of the time. The object of it is purely material, and it produces immediate material results: each one who has drunk of the blood gains a voice and also understanding (as in the case of Anticleia). The object is not senti-mental, as that of a sacrifice is. It is in no proper sense a sacrifice to the dead which Odysseus is making.

too how many points have been retained in the later and rationalised edition of the legend, when their full significance is forgotten. Odysseus is not a common traveller. He is either the soul escaped from life, or else he is the *one* living man who has been permitted to visit the halls of the dead, to sound the depths and shallows of the Sea of Death, and has survived to tell the tale. Odysseus' going to Hadês is merely the legitimate bourn of his journey. Circê can waft him there, but she cannot send him back to the world. The importance, therefore, of the visit to the Realm of Shades does not lie in the alleged object of Odysseus' coming, the prophecy which he hears from the mouth of the seer Teiresias, but in the whole picture of the dark land which he bears away with him.

Now, therefore, we behold the hero in the outer courts of Hadês' city :—

'Much I prayed to the empty figures of the dead for my return, vowing them a young heifer the best I had; and to Teiresias I promised a coal black sheep, excelling all the flock. And when I had called upon the nations of the dead, I cut the throats of the sheep over the ditch, and the black blood flowed out.

'And the souls of the dead came flocking forth from Erebus—brides and unmarried youths, and much-enduring old men, and tender girls, new-sorrowing souls, and men with many wounds, slain in battle and bearing their bloody arms; all these, with an immense clamour, were wandering round the ditch. Then pale fear seized me. . . .

'First came the soul of Elpenor, my comrade; he was yet unburied [1] beneath the broad earth, for we had left his corse in Circê's house, unwept, unburied, for another task was ours. . . .'

---

[1] Or unburned, Ου . . ἐτέθαπτο. According to Grimm (*Ueber das Verbrennen der Leichen*) θάπτειν means etymologically to 'burn.' It was used for any funeral rites. As we see by a later passage (v. 74) it was rather burning than burying that Elpenor wished for. Grimm's etymology for θάπτειν has been disputed.

'Elpenor,' cried Odysseus, 'how is it that to this murky darkness thou art come sooner on foot than I, who sailed in my black ship?' Then Elpenor gave an account of how he died, and asked for his funeral rites to be duly performed on Odysseus' return to Æœa. . . . All the while Odysseus kept guard over the blood. His mother, Anticleia, 'daughter of the noble-minded Autolycus,' passed by; but her he would not suffer to drink at first. 'At length the form of Theban Teiresias came by, grasping a golden sceptre; and it knew me and spake. "Why, unhappy one, hast thou left the sun's light, and come hither to see the shades and their drear abode? Go back from the ditch; put up your bright sword, and let me drink of the blood; then will I prophesy unto thee." . . .'

How dim this region is; how shadowy and unsubstantial the figures which haunt it. It is like to that outer circle of Dante's hell where the shades move for ever aimlessly and in a 'blind life devoid of hope.' There is no speculation in their eyes. Anticleia, Odysseus' mother, sits all the while silent by the trench of blood with looks askance; she dare not look straight at her son nor recognise him. Teiresias alone is possessed of his heart and mind as on earth, for he had been a prophet and was wiser than common men.

'Tell me, O king,' Odysseus, speaking of his mother, says to him, 'how can she know me for what I am?'

And Teiresias answers—

'Whomsoever among the departed dead you suffer to come to the blood, he will speak sensibly to you. But if you disallow it, silent will he wander back.'

'So spake he, and the soul of King Teiresias turned back to Hades' house. And I remained steadfast until my mother came forward and drank the black blood. At once she knew me, and wailing spake with winged words. . . .'

They conversed for awhile, and now follows a wonderful touch, showing the nature of these shades of the departed.

'I wished,' Odysseus goes on in his account of the scene,
'I wished to take hold of my mother's spirit. Thrice
my thoughts urged me to embrace her; but thrice from
my arms *like a shadow, or even a dream*, she flew away.
And sharper grief arose in my heart; and to compel her
I spake with winged words. "Mother! why stay you not
for me to lay hold on you? So might we two, folded in
each other's arms, have joy mid our sorrow even in Hadês.
Has Persephonê deluded me with a shadow only, that I
might grieve the more?"

'So I said, and my honoured mother straight answered.

'"Ah, woe, my son! Persephonê has not deceived you;
this is but the state of mortals when they are dead. They
have no more flesh, nor bones, nor sinews; [1] for the strong
force of fire consumed these when first the spirit left the
whitened bones. Then the soul itself flits aimlessly away
like a dream."'

This condition of the dead is exemplified in the case
of all the others whom Odysseus in turn encounters.
Agamemnon knows him not till he has drunk of the black
blood. Achilles would change his life below for that of a
mean hired labourer, but yet he can feel delight at hearing of the fame of his son, and after the dialogue with
Odysseus he passes on making great joyful strides through
the asphodel meadows. In some of the inner courts of
Pluto's palace the punishments of the dead are positive.
There Odysseus sees Minôs the judge; there is Tityus
stretched on the rocks while the vultures are dipping their
beaks in his liver; there Tantalus stands in the water
which flees from his touch; there too is the shade of
Orion perpetually hunting through the meadows; and the
shade of Heraclês (Heraclês himself being on Olympus [2]),
which moves darkly, seeming ever ready to let fly a shaft.

---

[1] Lit. 'Their sinews no longer hold the flesh and bones,' i.e. they no
longer have sinews holding the flesh and bones.

[2] See what is said in Chap. IV. concerning the double nature of
Heraclês, (1) as a mortal and (2) as a god.

We have lingered somewhat over this picture of the realm of Hadês, the first vivid presentation of the under world which meets us in the literature of the Aryan race. And the beauty and solemnity of the picture may well excuse this pause; for it is a beauty and a power which familiarity can scarcely lessen. We now retrace our steps, and return with Odysseus once more to the portal of Death, where he stood when he entered Circê's island. But in this case Death is represented not by Circê, but by Calypso.

First of all in the actual course of the poem we find the hero upon the island of Calypso, called Ogygia. Etymologists connect the word Ogygia with Oceanus, and this connection shows us that the name was not originally the name of an island so much as the general one of the sea.[1] Ogygia means, moreover, something primeval, so that it is also the name of Egypt, the oldest land of the world, and Ogygês is the name of the earliest Attic king; in this sense Ogygia is likewise chosen to be the home of Time, Kronos. On this island Odysseus sleeps perforce beside Calypso in her hollow cave; and hither, when he has been seven years in the embrace of the dreadful goddess, Hermês comes, by command of Zeus, to set him free.

It was, we remember, by the advice of the same messenger that Odysseus overcame the spells of Circe. Hermês in later times, partaking of the nature of Apollo and advancing as Greek civilisation advanced, became the god of merchandise and of the market as well as the patron of agonistic contests. But in Homer he has his primitive character; he is the god of the wind. His name is connected with those Vedic Sârameyas of whom we have lately spoken; it is also connected with the Greek ὁρμάω, to rush. We have seen why the Sârameyas, as winds, were the psychopomps or leaders of the soul over

---

[1] Ogygês was connected with the fabulous primeval deluges in Bœotia and in Attica.

the Bridge of Souls; and how they might also be the representatives of the morning and evening breezes. All these functions are united in the Greek messenger god. His rod has a twofold power: it closes the eyes of men in sleep and awakens them from sleeping. Or in a wider sense it either calls men from the sleep of death or drives them to the under world. Hermês is (like the Sârameyas) most present when we are *near* the other world. This last reason, perhaps, explains why he is the messenger of the Odyssey but not of the Iliad.[1]

As the wind of morning, the awakener, Hermês comes now over the sea to rouse Odysseus from his fatal slumber; he comes, in the beautiful language of the poet, like a gull fishing over the wide brine, now (so we fancy him) dipping down to the wave, now rising again.

> Windlike beneath, the immortal golden sandals
> Bare up his flight o'er the limitless earth and the sea;
> And in his hand that magic wand he carried
> Wherewith the eyes of men he closes in slumber
> Or wakens from sleeping.

The divine messenger finds Calypso within her cave, at the mouth of which burns a fire (we often meet with this fire at the entrance to the house of death),[2] a fire of cedar and frankincense, which wafts its scent over the island. She is singing, and as she sings she moves over the web a golden shuttle, and in the wood behind the birds are brooding.

Then Calypso, seeing that the commands of Zeus might not be disobeyed, instructed Odysseus how to make a raft, and sped him on his way. For seventeen days he sailed

---

[1] Hermês is always the messenger of the gods in the *Odyssey*; but in the *Iliad* this part is played by Iris, the *rainbow*. There is a natural connection between the rainbow, the Bridge of Souls (in the Vedas, &c.), and the wind (Sârameyas, Hermês), who is the leader of souls. In the *Odyssey* (xviii. beg.) we hear of an Irus, who may be the same as Hermês.

[2] Chaps. VII. VIII.

upon that raft over the trackless sea, and sleepless watched the constellations as they passed overhead, 'the Pleiads, and late-setting Boötes, and the Bear, which they also call the Wain.'[1] He was not fated yet to find his home. On the eighteenth day, as the shadowy mountains of the Phæacians began to appear, Poseidon, who still burned to revenge the death of his son Polyphemus, raised a storm, so that the raft was borne upon a rock and Odysseus was all but destroyed. But a sea goddess, Ino Leucothea, gave him her veil to buoy him up when he left the sinking raft, and Athênê stilled the waves. The appearance of Ino in this scene is appropriate. For we are now close to the Land of the Blessed, and she herself was once a mortal who found a home in this heaven.[2]

At length Odysseus, swimming, gained the shore. Before he reached this, his last haven, the troubles of Odysseus had attained their climax. He had lost all his comrades, his ships, his treasures, and now this last refuge, the raft, brake beneath his feet. *Nudus egressus, sic redibo,* 'All come into this world alone; all leave it alone.' Welcome, therefore (we may well believe), as is the father's life to his children when he has lain long in suffering and disease, and the Hateful Goddess has grazed close by him, such to the wanderer was the sight of this new land.

The name of the land on which he was cast was Scheria. The island of Ôgygia means literally the ocean; this land with the same etymological exactness signifies the shore—Σχερία, from σχερός.[3] The contrast of mean-

---

[1] We think of Dante's Ulysses.

> 'Tutte le stelle già dell' altro polo
> Vedea la notte, e il nostro tanto basso
> Che non suggeva fuor del marin suolo.'

[2] See Pindar, *Ol.* 2.

[3] It is in keeping with the principles of mythopoesis that Calypso's land embodying the notion of the Sea of Death, should be in the midst of the sea—that is to say, should be an island. Scheria means shore. There is nothing said of *its* being an island. Nevertheless the Greek paradise was generally thought to be one, e.g. the *Islands of the Blessed* of Pindar, &c.

ing takes us back to a time when the myth of the great
traveller was more simple than we find it in Homer, and
told only of his passing over the Sea of Death and arriving
at the coast beyond. This shore is the home of the god-
like Phæacians, and the king of it is Alcinoüs. In the
description of the people and of their country we easily
recognise a place such as is not in this world, and a race
not of mortal birth. Far away, says Alcinoüs—

Far away do we live, at the end of the watery plain,
Nor before now have ever had dealings with other mortals;
But now there comes this luckless wanderer hither.
Him it is right that we help, for all men fellows and strangers
Come from Zeus; in his sight the smallest gift is pleasing.[1]

This place is the due antithesis of Hadês. Like Hadês
it lies at the extreme limit of the watery plain. But it is
a land of everlasting sunlight and happiness, instead of
one of darkness and death. Remote from men, near to the
gods (ἀγχίθεοι), as Zeus himself declares,[2] the Phæacians
live, like the blameless Æthiopians, somewhere on the
confines of earth. Hither it was that yellow-haired
Rhadamanthus fled when persecuted and driven from
Crete by his brother Minôs—the just Rhadamanthus,
who, by some legends, is placed as ruler in the land of
the blessed. Hither was come the fainting Odysseus.

How the wanderer hid himself at the river mouth, and,
having fallen asleep, was awakened by Nausicaä, the king's
daughter, when at play with her maidens, and how he discovered himself to her, needs not to be retold. When
Odysseus had related his adventures to Nausicaä, she bade
him follow her to her father's house. This was a para-
disiacal palace, much like those which occur so often in
our Teutonic fairy tales. It is made as beautiful as the
Greek imagination of that time could paint it.[3] Built all

[1] *Od.* vi. 304 sqq.   [2] *Od.* v. 35.
[3] Mr. Pater, in his article on the ' Beginnings of Greek Art ' (*Fortnightly
Review*), has admirably followed out the exact artistic conceptions which
are implied in the descriptions by Homer of the palace of Alcinoüs.

of bronze, it had golden doors and silver pillars, and silver lintels with a golden ring. On either side the entrance were gold and silver dogs, 'which cunning-minded Hephæstus made to guard the house; they were immortal, and free from old age for ever.' We recognise in these descriptions the dawn of the Hellenic love of art. But the two dogs have, I fancy, a special meaning. I see in them the descendants of the Sârameyas, or whatever in early Aryan belief preceded those guardians of the house of death, who are own brothers to the two dogs of the Wild Huntsman, Hackelberg. The garden which surrounds the palace of Alcinoüs distinctly presents the picture of a home of the blessed; it is just like the Gardens of the Hesperides, and like all the pictures which before and after have been drawn of an earthly paradise. Here the trees and flowers do not grow old and disappear, winter does not succeed to summer, but all is one continued round of blossoming and bearing fruit; in one part of the garden the trees are all abloom, in another they are heavy with ripe clusters.[1]

Nevertheless the Western Land, though a place of Paradise, is also the land of sunset; and by their name the Phæacians appear as beings of the twilight—φαία⧣ strengthened from φαιός, dusky, dim. Their most wondrous possessions are their ships, which know the minds of men and sail swifter than a bird or than thought. 'No pilots have they, no rudders, no oarsmen, which other ships have, for they themselves know the thoughts and minds of men. The rich fields they know, and the cities among all men, and swiftly pass over the crests of the sea

---

[1] Compare Pindar's description of the Happy Isle:—

'Where round the Island of the Blessed
  Soft sea-winds blow continually;
  Where golden flowers on sward and tree
  Blossom, and on the water rest—
  There move the saints in garlands dressed
And intertwined wreaths of colours heavenly.'

shrouded in mist and gloom.' [1]   Yet the Phæacians themselves live remote from human habitation, unused to
strangers.[2]   It would seem, then, that the ships travel
alone on their dark voyages.   For what purpose?   It is
not difficult to guess.   Their part is to carry the souls of
dead men over to the Land of Paradise.

We can imagine these ships of the Phæacians sailing
into every human sea, calling at every port, familiar with
every city, though in their shroud of darkness they are
unseen by men.   They know all the rich lands; for every
land has its tribute to pay to the ships of Death.   They
are the counterparts of the 'grim ferryman which poets
write of;' [3] only that the last plies his business in the ancient underground Hadês, and that the Phæacian barks
have their harbours on the upper earth; albeit they can
pass from this life to the other.[4]

Their business with Odysseus is to bring him back to
the common world—to beloved Ithaca.   He has passed
to the cave of Hel and through the gates of Death;
he has emerged to visit the Land of Paradise.   Now he
returns that his adventures may be sung in the homes of
Greece.

> What reports
> Yield those jealous courts unseen ?

How could men ever tell tales of that strange country if
it really were a bourn from which *no* traveller returned?   So
when the hero has told all his tale in the hall of Alcinoüs,
the latter orders the sailors to prepare his homeward
voyage.

---

[1] *Od.* viii. 562.   [2] See ante, p. 321.

[3] Charon is not known to Homer.   It is not impossible that he may have
been imported from Egypt.   These Phæacian ferrymen are of true Aryan
birth, and have a native place in Greek belief.

[4] It seems to me that there is no ground for endorsing Welcker's theory
(*Rheinisches Museum für Philologie*, N.S. vol. i.) that the Phæacians were
imported from a Teutonic home.   That the Teutons had a parallel belief
concerning the soul's voyage is true enough (Ch. VIII.); but in this chapter
it has, I think, been made clear that the notion was an universal Aryan one.

mayst thou have joy here in thy children and in thy people, and in King Alcinoüs.'

So saying the godlike Odysseus crossed the threshold, and with him Alcinoüs sent a herald, to lead him to the swift ship and to the sea-shore. And Arêtê sent women servants with him to bear, one a clean robe and a tunic, another a heavy chest; and a third bare bread and wine. They came to the ship and to the sea; and his renowned guides received the things and stowed them in the hollow ship. And they made ready for Odysseus linen and a blanket, that he might sleep there at the stern, without waking. Then he embarked, and silently lay down; and they sat each one upon his bench; and they heaved the cable, loosened from the bored stone. Then leaning back, they threw up the sea with the oar; and as Odysseus lay, anon deep sleep weighed down his eyelids—a sweet, unwakeful sleep, most like to death. . . . Then as arose the one bright star, the messenger of dawn, the ship touched the shore of Ithaca.

Mythology cannot show, out of all the imagery which has grown up around the Sea of Death, a finer picture than this one of the wanderer who has been dead and is alive again—awakening, along with the day-heralding star, to find himself once more in the world of living men.

CHAPTER VII.

THE BELIEFS OF HEATHEN GERMANY.

§ 1. *The Gods of the Mark.*

WE have scattered notices of German heathenism extending over many centuries. There are the few facts which Tacitus collected, a passage here and there in other classic authors, then the later histories of the Teutonic peoples themselves—Procopius, Jornandes, Paulus Diaconus, Gregory of Tours, and lesser chroniclers—which shed some light upon the Germans' early belief; the 'Danish History' of Saxo, full of legendary history, which is but transformed myth; the 'Historia Ecclesiastica' of Adam of Bremen and such like works of men, Christians themselves, but yet in close proximity with the heathen; and finally we have the Eddas, the last voice of Teutonic paganism, rising up from the land which was the latest to give admittance to the creed of Christendom. These are as recent as the twelfth and thirteenth centuries. They have been, it is probable, handed down for many hundred years, but they speak directly only of the heathenism of the Norsemen. Despite all the diversities of time and place which these different sources imply, we can see that the belief is in essentials the belief of one people; a race whose life through all the centuries had little changed, which was united not by language alone, but was one in its institutions, in its civilisation, and in its barbarism, one even in the climatic influences to which it was subjected.

And this last is a great matter. The foregoing chapters must have made it plain that the creed of a

people is always greatly dependent upon their position on
this earth, upon the scenery amid which their life is
passed and the natural phenomena to which they have
become habituated; that the religion of men who live in
woods will not be the same as that of the dwellers in wide,
open plains; nor the creed of those who live under an
inclement sky, the sport of storms and floods, the same as
the religion of men who pass their lives in sunshine and
calm air.

The more sombre aspects of nature were revealed to
the German races from the Danube to the Baltic.   Tacitus
has left us a picture of the Germans he knew, the dwellers
in Central Europe, and of the land they inhabited.   He
describes their dark, lonely life under the perpetual gloom
of trees, and their country 'rugged with wood or dank
with marsh.'[1]   The Norsemen had their homes amid
mighty pine forests and on rocky heights looking over the
main—not such a sea as the Ægæan, but the sea of those
Northern regions, icy and threatening, not often tranquil.
Inland and sea-shore had their own beauties, but they
were of a wild kind.   The Eddas tell us of the marriage
between a god of the sea and a daughter of the hills;
each utters a complaint of the other's home.   'Of mountains I weary,' says one—[2]

> Of mountains I weary.
> Not long was I there—
> Nine nights only—
> But the howl of the wolf
> To my ears sounded ill
> By the song of the sea bird.[3]

And the hill goddess answers—

---

[1] Tac. *Germ.* 5.   And again, 'asperam cœlo, tristem cultu aspectuque
(c. 2).

[2] Edda Snorra, *Gylfaginning*, D. 23.

[3] Lit. swan (*svanr*).   Swan in Norse poetry seems constantly to be used
for a sea bird.   Etymologically of course it would be merely a bird that
could *swim*.   See also p. 341.

In my bed by the shore ;
For the scream of the wild birds,
The seamews, who came
From the wood ffying,
Awoke me each morning.

But the child of this union between the mountain and
the sea was the religion and the poetry of the Teutonic
race; beside the howl of the wolf and the scream of the
seamew it struggled into life.

As for the social condition of the Germans when first
described to us, to credit the accounts of classic authors,
the people seems to have been scarcely raised above the
earliest stage of society, the hunting state. They sowed
but little; when they were not engaged in war or in the
chase, the men sat idle;[1] usefuller occupations were
abandoned to the unwarlike classes—to old men, to
women, and to slaves. The Germans made very little
practice of agriculture, says Cæsar, or (in some places)
they did not use it at all.[2] They 'lived chiefly on meat,'
&c.[3] Tacitus says that the men in time of peace sat idle,
and gave over household management to the women
and to the infirm and old.[4] And from these descriptions
we learn how far apart had drifted the lives of the various
peoples of the Aryan race, who yet, when they separated
to begin their migrations, started from the same point on
the road to civilisation. The earliest recollections of
Rome and Greece pointed back to a time when men sub-
sisted altogether by the labours of agriculture, ere commerce with its attendant refinements and luxuries had
been introduced. In Rome the praisers of past days re-

---

[1] Nor were they much engaged even in the chase, according to Tacitus
(*Germ.* 15).

[2] 'Minime omnes Germani agriculturæ student.'—Cæsar, *B. G.* vi. 29 ;
'Agriculturæ non student,' 22.

[3] 'Neque multum frumento sed maximam partem lacte atque pecore
vivunt (Suevi).'—Cæsar, *B. G.* iv. 1.

[4] *Germ.* 16.

called the glories of the Republic when a Cincinnatus had to be dragged from the plough to become a leader of armies. Yet even those pictures were partly imaginary, for, as more recent historians have pointed out, Rome even in prehistoric days must have been possessed of an important commerce.[1] By the Greeks in the time of Homer the transition from a merely agricultural life to one which knew commerce and art had already been made. Yet hundreds of years after Homer or the early days of Rome the Teutons and the Celts had not fully accustomed themselves to the condition of a settled agricultural people; and they preserved in an almost unchanged form some of the institutions which characterised the life of the old Aryas.

It has been already hinted that before the separation of the nations the proto-Aryas had acquired a kind of embryo states, miniature republics which afterwards expanded into the states of Rome and Greece, of Germany and France and England. The germ of the *civitas* and of the πόλις is to be sought in the *village community* of the Aryas, of which the representatives still existing are, first, the village communities of India, and, at a farther distance, the Russian *mirs*. The same institution dictated the form of early German life with the division and the disposal of property among the Teutonic races; in a large measure it lay at the foundation of feudalism and the statecraft of mediæval Europe.

The village community consisted of a group of families in the possession of a certain space of land; and the principle of property was based upon the division of this land into three parts. First there was a tract immediately around each house, and belonging to it; there was another portion of land set apart specially for agricultural purposes;

[1] See the fourth chapter of Mommsen's *Röm. Gesch.*, wherein the historian shows that Rome must, even in prehistoric days, have been an emporium for the productions of central Italy, and probably possessed a mercantile navy. This was very likely afterwards destroyed by the growing power on the sea of the Etruscans (Tyrrheni).

and lastly, there was the surrounding open country, which was used for grazing. No one of any of these three divisions was possessed as an absolutely personal property, but over some parts the rights of individuals, over other parts the rights of the state, were paramount. The latter was the case with the agricultural portion; whereas the land immediately surrounding the homestead belonged to the household there.[1]

Of such a kind as this village must have been the *vicus* of which Tacitus speaks in describing the Germans. But though these people were thus joined together in a common society, it does not appear that even then they lived near one another. 'It is well known,' says our authority, 'that the Germans do not inhabit towns. They do not even suffer their dwellings to stand near together; but live apart and scattered, each choosing his own home by stream or grove or plot of open ground.'[2]

'By stream or grove or plot of open ground,' but most of all by grove and tree. Life beneath trees was the great feature of their existence, and tree worship the most important part of their primitive creed. The German's house was built about a tree. That form of architecture, of which we have some faint traces among more civilised Aryas, as in the description of the chamber of Odysseus,[3] was in full use among the Teutons down to historic days. The house of Völsung was supported by the tree Branstock, and the world itself was by imagination constructed in imitation of a common dwelling,[4] and had its central tree, Yggdrasill. The sacred trees and village trees long survived the introduction of Christianity; they survive in our Christmas trees of the present day. In every raid which the new faith made upon the old we read of the

---

[1] Concerning the constitution of the village community among the Germans see Von Maurer's *Mark- u. Dorf-Verfassung*; see also Kemble on the Mark (*Saxons in England*, i. ch. ii.)

[2] *Germ.* c. 16.

[3] See Chap. II.

[4] The world from the house, the earth (Erd) from the hearth (Herd).

felling of these sacred trees. Near Gudensberg in Hesse, formerly Wuodenesberg, stood the oak dedicated to Wuotan, the greatest of the gods, and this Boniface cut down.[1] In a deep forest recess stood the famous Irminsul, which Charlemagne destroyed.

But, beside the village trees which were in the midst of every clearing and the house trees which supported every house, there was the denser growth of untraversed forest land which lay around. This dreary and waste region, in which men might sometimes go to pasture their horses and cattle, or more often to hunt the wild animals who inhabited there, was called the *mark*. In after years, when these tiny embryos of commonwealths, the villages, had expanded into states, the marks grew in proportion, until they became great territorial divisions such as our Mercia (Myrcna); the *marches* between England and Wales; Denmark, the Danes' mark ; La Marque, which separated that country from Germany; the Wendisch-mark, which divided Germany from the Slavonic lands. And the guardians of the marks were turned into marquises, marchios, markgrafs. But at the beginning these last were only the chief warriors of the tribe ; they had their home in the waste, and stood as watchmen between the village and the outer world ; so that none might come into the village if they came to do it hurt. We know that it was a point of honour with each community to make this encircling belt as wide as possible : the greater the mark the greater was its power.

It would be scarcely safe for the stranger to venture across the solitudes; no doubt the peacefuller among the villagers rarely did so. The men who undertook some predatory excursion against a neighbouring community were avowedly entering a region which lay outside their customary life. The more primitive the state of any people, the narrower commonly is the space of earth

---

[1] Grimm, *Deutsche Mythologie*, i. 126. At Geismar also there was an oak which Boniface felled and used in making a Christian church.

within which they are imbound; their experiences are
more limited; and their genius, as we should say, more
confined. For what we call the genius of a people is, in
truth (at least it is in early days), very near indeed to what
the ancients understood by that word; it is, as the Greeks
would say, a *daimón epichórios*, a watcher of holy places,
which infuses into these places its spirit and partakes of
theirs. A genius of woods, that is forest-like; a genius of
wells and streams, that is watery.

> Kindly terrene guardians of mortal men,

Hesiod calls them.

So the genius of the German was narrowed within the
limits of his narrow world; his primitive home with its
surrounding mark became, and long remained, for him the
type of all existence; from this microcosm he painted his
cosmos; and then, having made a picture of the world in
space, he used the same outlines to represent the world
in time, and upon one model constructed his history and
his prophecy.

The Germans are described as building no fanes,
making no images for worship, but in their forest recesses
calling upon the unseen presence (*secretum illud*), which
they honoured by the names of various gods.[1] The word
'grove' is with the German races a convertible term with
'temple.'[2] 'Single gods may have had their dwellings in
mountain-tops, or in rocky caverns, or in streams; but
the universal worship of the people found its home in the
grove.'[3] Adam of Bremen has left us a description of a
holy grove, as it was to be seen in Sweden in the eleventh
century. It was at Upsala. 'Every ninth year,' he says,
'a festival is celebrated there by all the provinces of
Sweden, and from taking a part in this none is exempt.
King and people must all send their gifts; even those who

[1] *Germ*, 9.
[2] O. H. G. *wih*, grove; O. S. *wih*, temple; Norse *ve*, holy
[3] Grimm, *D. M.* p. 56.

presence, there can be no question that the creed of the Germans was largely founded upon a fetich worship of the trees themselves.

And what is here said of the Germans applies, in almost equal measure, to the Celts. Most classical writers, who have spoken of these people, have borne testimony to the large place which tree worship, or, at any rate, which a worship in the forest, occupied in the Celtic creed. Of one people, the Massilii, we know that, like the men of Upsala, they offered human sacrifices to the trees;[2] and of other Celts the very name bestowed on their priests, Druids (from δρύς, an 'oak'), is a proof of their addiction to tree worship. The mistletoe gained its sacredness from its being born in the bosom of the oak tree. Pliny has left on record a description of the ceremonies which accompanied the cutting of the sacred mistletoe from the oak; and this description is the best picture which remains to us of the ritual of Druidism. It is probable, therefore, that much of what we are about to unfold concerning the nature of the Teutonic beliefs would apply, with only some slight changes, to the creed of the predecessors of the Germans in Northern and Western Europe. Undoubtedly, in prehistoric days, the Germans

[1] Adam of Bremen, iv. 27.
[2] Cf. Lucan, B. C. iii. 405. 'Omnis . . . humanis lustrata cruoribus arbos.' Maximus Tyrius (Dissert. 38) tells us that 'the Celtic Zeus is a high oak.'

and Celts merged so much one into the other that their histories cannot well be distinguished. But no sure records of the Celtic religion have come down to us; so we must be content to draw our picture from the literature of the Teutonic folk alone.

The Germans of Tacitus' day had certainly got beyond fetichism and the direct worship of trees. But the influence of tree worship still remained with them; all that was most holy they associated with the forest, or, to use their own term, with the mark. Their greatest gods were the gods of the mark; these, therefore, are the deities whom we must first take into account.

Now the word 'mark,' which at first meant 'forest,'[1] came, in after years, to signify boundary. The mark was always the division between village and village. When the beginnings of commerce are set in motion among any nation, it is in the midst of neutral territories such as these, half-way between one community and another, that the exchange takes place. The *market* is held in the mark.[2] The Greeks and Romans, who had once their village communities, had once too, I suppose, their surrounding marks. And when we think of the origin of their markets—their agoræ, their fora—we must let our imaginations wander back to a time when these barter places were not in the midst of the city, but in wild spots far away. The god who among the Greeks presided over the agora, and over all which was connected with it— over buying and selling, over assemblies and public games —was Hermês. But Hermês did this because he was by rights a god of the wind. Far more true, therefore, was he to his real nature when he guarded the forest markets and haunted their solitudes, as the wind god must always do.

With the Germans, in the times whereof I speak, the mark had not lost its original character. It was the most

---

[1] Grimm, *D. M.* p. 56   [2] Cf. *mera, Mercury.*

important—because the least explored and most awe-inspiring—part of the German's world; wherefore the god of the mark, the god of winds and storms, was the greatest of his divinities. He was Odhinn (Wuotan). Tacitus said of the Germans of his day that they worshipped Mercury, Hercules, and Mars, and Mercury chief of all. There can be no doubt that by Mercury Wuotan is meant; by Hercules and Mars, Thorr (Donar) and Tyr (Zio). Wuotan stands in the centre, as Wodens-day stands between Tewes-day (Tyr's-day) and Thors-day [1]—in the centre and far above the other two. His name is not wanting from the pantheon of any Teutonic people. The Germans of Germany called him Wuotan; the Norsemen, Odhinn; the English, Woden (Vodan); the Lombards, Gwodan.[2] The tree and the forest are the central points of German life, and Odhinn is the spirit of the tree and the breath of the forest; for he is the wind.

We have followed out the process whereby the older god of the sky, common alike to all the members of the Indo-European family, gave place, in many cases, to a more active god; whereby Indra and Zeus, each in their spheres, supplanted Dyâus. And when we were following out that process something was said of how a similar change could be traced in the Teutonic creed. The new and active god is, in this case, Odhinn. The wind is a far more physical and less abstract conception than the sky or the heaven; it is also a more variable phenomenon; and by reason of both these recommendations the wind god superseded the older Dyâus, who reappears, in

---

[1] I shall, in future, use the Norse mode of spelling for the names of the gods whenever these are such as are mentioned in the Eddas. The reason for doing this is that the references to the Eddas are so much more frequent than references to any other authority for German belief.

[2] 'Wodan sane, quem adjectâ literâ Gwodan dixerunt, et ab universis gentibus ut deus adoratur' (Paulus Diaconus, i. 8). This *litera adjecta* is only in keeping with the Italian use in respect to German names—as Wilhelm, Guglelmo; Wishart, Guiscardo, &c. Warnefrid is naturally speaking of the Lombards after they were Italicised. Odhinn is from a verb vaða, to go violently, to *rush*; as Ἑρμῆς, from ὁρμάω.

was always far inferior in importance to both Wuotan and Donar. Among the Norsemen he was frequently supplanted by another god, Freyr, and the trilogy then stood thus: Odhinn, Thorr, and Freyr.

German religion, like most creeds, had its energetic and warlike and its placid and peaceful sides; the first one was here, as elsewhere, represented by the gods of air and heaven, the other by the gods (and goddesses) of earth. But, as we might guess from the character of the German people, with them the warlike part by far outweighed the peaceful. This side of their creed was represented by the gods of the mark. It seems especially to centre in Odhinn. Beside Odhinn stood Thorr, very like him in character, yet with a distinct individuality, bearing something the same relation to his father which Apollo bore to Zeus. Odhinn became so much the representative god of the Teutons that he could not remain wedded always to one aspect of nature; for he had to accommodate himself to the various moods of men's worship. Still we need never imagine him without some reference in our thoughts to the wind, which may be gentle, but in these Northern lands is generally violent; whose home is naturally far up in the heavens, but which loves too sometimes to wander over the earth.

Just as the chief god of Greece, having descended to be a divinity of storm, was not content to remain only that, but grew again to some likeness of the olden Dyâus,[1] so Odhinn came to absorb almost all the qualities which belong of right to a higher God. Yet he did this without putting off his proper nature. He was the heaven as well as the wind; he was the All-Father, embracing all the earth[2] and looking down upon mankind. His

[1] See Ch. IV.

[2] Alföőr; originally, no doubt, as Rangi in the Maori tale is the All-Father, because the Heaven begets all living things. But in the Norse belief this idea has become moralised.

seat was in heaven, and from heaven's window (Hlið-
skiálf[1]) he could see not only the Gods' City (the Æsirs'
burg, Asgard) and Man's Home (Mannheimar), but far
away over the earth-girdling sea to icy Jötunheimar,
where giants dwelt, and where was the Land of Death.[2]
In this way Odhinn was a perpetual watchman, who kept
the dwellings of gods and men free from alarms.

For the giants, like the Greek Titan race, were the
enemies of the gods and of men,[3] and were for ever
trying to make their way against the city of the gods.
Fate had decreed that one day a great final battle between
the gods and giants was to ensue; it was the Armageddon of the Norse religion; but till that day should come
Odhinn kept watch and ward, and kept the giants off.
Odhinn was the wisest of all the gods ('þu ert æ visastr
vera Oðinn—Thou art the wisest ever, Odhinn'); he alone
could look into futurity; and mythology told a tale of
how Odhinn had won this priceless gift of prophecy by
coming to the Well of Wisdom, guarded by a certain
Mimir,[4] of the race of the giants, and by obtaining a drink
therefrom. But the god could only obtain the draught
at the price of one of his eyes, which he was compelled to
throw into the water.[5] The story was, no doubt, originally

---

[1] 'Lid-shelf,' the window or seat of Odhinn. Grimnismál (prose); Hrafn.
Oð. 10; cf. with Gmml. l.c., Paulus Diac. i. 8.
[2] See Chaps. VI. and VIII.
[3] Much more so, in fact, than the Titans.
[4] Or Mimr.

[5]   All know I, Odhinn. Where thou thine eye didst loose,
        In wide-wondered Mimir's well,
        Each morn drinks Mimir, from Val-Father's pledge.
        Know ye what that means or no?— *Völuspá*, 22.

This Mimir is a curious being. Etymologically he is connected with
μιμνήσκω, *meminisce*, *memor*, &c., and hence with Minôs. Minôs is the first
man (all these words from root *mâ*, to measure), and much the same as
Yama and Yima. (See Ch. IV., and Benfey's *Hermes, Minos und Tartarus*.) Mimir seems also to be a personification of the sea, or earlier of
the earth-girding river, and therefore the same as Oceanus. (See Chs. II.
and VI. for Oceanus in character as parent of all—root *og*. Ogyges, &c.)
The sons of Mimir who dance at the end of the world (Völuspá, 47) are
the waves.

a nature myth. Odhinn's eye is the sun;[1] the well of Mimir is the river of rivers which runs round the earth, the father of all fetiches and of all wells of wisdom.[2] And as Odhinn's eye is here the sun, Odhinn must, in this his character of the Wise One, be the heaven.

Having become thus learned, Odhinn proceeded to impart his knowledge to mankind; and in this aspect of him he was the gentle breeze which visits men in their homesteads and sees them at their daily toil. Odhinn taught mankind the great art of runes, which means both writing and magic, and many other arts of life. He is represented as continually wandering over the earth and coming to visit human habitations. In most creeds it is too much the fault of the heaven god that he lives remote from human affairs; this fault does not lie at the door of Odhinn, who is the wind as well as the sky.

In this gentler aspect of his character—the visitor to human homes, the wise friend and counsellor of men— Odhinn was called Gagnrâd,[3] which means 'the giver of good counsel.' Indeed, the two chief by-names of Odhinn seem to express the wind in its two aspects—either when coming to men as the storm in which whole navies sink, or coming as the gentler wandering breeze. These two names are Yggr and Gagnrâd. Yggr is the 'Terrible.' It is as Yggr that Odhinn is the overseer and ruler of the world; for the world tree, Odhinn's ash, is called Yggdrasill.[4] As Gagnrâd Odhinn comes in a simpler fashion to teach arts and magic.

It is not generally as the gentle wind, nor as a messenger of peace, that the Northern god appears to us in myth and saga. His chief business with men was

---

[1] The sun is, as we have seen, called the eye of Mitra and Varuna in the Vedas. See Ch. III.　　　　[2] See Ch. II.

[3] Probably this god is also the Gangleri, 'the ganger,' of the Gylfaginning.

[4] Odhinn appears under the name of Ygg on those occasions especially when he undertakes to visit the other world and the realm of giants, &c. (cf. Vegtamskviða, 8; Vafþrúðnismál, 5). Ygg has those who fall by the sword (Grímnismál, 53). These facts, taken in connection with the name of Yggdrasill, show Yggr as the lord of life and death.

at the battle field; and his duty there was to collect the souls of all the brave who had fallen in battle, and to transport these to the heaven prepared for them. This home of dead heroes was called Valhöll, the Hall of the Chosen. In thus bearing souls away Odhinn was serving tho interests both of gods and men, for the more heroes that were collected in heaven the stronger would be the army of the gods when it sallied out to fight the great last fight against the giant powers. Odhinn, when he came among men, was seen generally in the guise of an old one-eyed man—one-eyed because he sank his eye in Mîmr's well—clad in a blue cloak (the mantle of the wind, the air, or cloud), and wearing a broad-brimmed hat. This last is the same as the cap of concealment, the *tarn-kappe*,[1] known to the Nibelungen lay and to many folk tales, and is in its physical aspect the dark cloud or the night. Odhinn's coming was rather to be dreaded than longed for; seeing that, like the raven, he scented slaughter from afar. He was, in this respect, like that Norse king described in one of Fouqué's tales, who, whenever he showed himself, was sure to be the forerunner of misfortune, so that men got to dread above all things the sight of his helmet with vulture wings. We have a picture of Odhinn coming to the house of Sigmund precisely in this guise of an old one-eyed man. In the back of the house-tree he left sticking the sword Gram as a prize to whosoever should be able to pluck it out; and that sword was the cause of strife and of bloodshed to the Völsungs and Giukungs.[2]

---

[1] Tarn-Kappe, cap of concealment, from *ternen*.

[2] The scene has been admirably pictured by Mr. Morris:—

Then into the Volsung dwelling a mighty man there strode,
One-eyed and seeming ancient, yet bright his visage glowed;
Cloud blue was the hood upon him, and his kirtle gleaming-grey,
As the latter-morning sun dog when the storm is on the way.

. . . . . .

So strode he to the branstock, nor greeted any lord,
But forth from his cloudy raiment he drew a gleaming sword
And smote it deep in the tree bole.'—*Sigurd the Volsung.*

When the battle has actually begun, Odhinn goes to
it not in this disguised manner, but in true wind-wise.
The picture we have is of him riding through the air on
his eight-footed horse Sleipnir, the swiftest of steeds.
Over sea and land he rushes, through mountain gorges
and through endless pine forests. He breathes into men
the battle fury, for which the North folk had a special
name—the berserksgangr, berserk's way.[1]

The greater part of the forests of Northern Europe are
black forests—that is to say, composed of pine trees—and in
such the coming of the storm is made the more wonderful
from the silence which has reigned there just before. Who
that has known it does not remember this strange stillness
of the pine forest? Anon the quiet is broken by a distant
sound, so like the sound of the sea that we can fancy
we distinctly hear the waves drawing backwards over a
pebbly beach. As it comes nearer the sound increases to a
roar: it is the rush of the wind among the boughs. Such
was the coming of Odhinn. And now see! far overhead
with the wind are riding the clouds. These are the misty
beings, born of the river or the sea, whom we have already
encountered in so many different mythologies. In India
they were Apsaras[2] (formless ones) or Gandharvas; in
Greece they were nymphs, nereids, Muses, Aphroditês,
Tritogeneias. In the Teutonic creeds they are the warlike,
fierce Valkyriur.[3]

The myth of the Valkyriur, as it was developed by the
Teutons, became one of the most beautiful, and likewise

[1] Zeus also did something of the kind. See the description of Hector
in *Il.* xv. 605, &c. :—

> Μαίνετο . . . .
> Ἀφλοισμὸς δὲ περὶ στόμα γίγνετο, τὼ δέ οἱ ὄσσε
> Λαμπέσθην βλοσυρῇσιν ὑπ' ὀφρύσιν· . . . .
> . . . αὐτὸς γάρ οἱ ἀπ' αἰθέρος ἦεν ἀμύντωρ
> Ζεύς. . . .

[2] On the nature of the Apsaras see Chap. II., and compare Weber's *Ind
Stud.* i. 398.

[3] Icl. sing. *Valkyria*, plur. *Valkyriur*, Germ. *Walchurium*.

the most characteristic, in all their mythic lore. In essential features, however, the Valkyriur resemble other beings of like birth in the Indo-European creeds; wherefore the germ of the Valkyriur myth may be discovered in the earlier creeds of India and of Greece.

In one of the later Vedas we are told a story concerning certain fairy maidens, Gandharvas, who can at will change themselves into the likeness of birds. One of these, who was called Urvasi, fell in love with a mortal, Pururavas, and for awhile they lived happily together; but the kindred of the fairy laid a plot against her joy, and contrived the separation of Urvasi and Pururavas. The wife left her husband, and he wandered about to all lands seeking her in vain. At length he came to a lake on which Urvasi was sitting with her kinsfolk; but they were transformed into *birds*, and he knew them not. . . .[1] The story, in its essential meaning, is the myth of the loves of the sun and of the dawn; and the dawn (Ushas-Urvasi) is here bodied forth to sense as a cloud. The Gandharvas are beings of the same kind as the Valkyriur, and in this particular tale they are the clouds of morning. The idea of such bird fairies is to be found in the mythologies of most races of the Indo-European family. Athênê and Hêra, as heaven goddesses, sometimes were seen as birds—that is to say, they sometimes became visible as clouds. In the Teuton myth of the Valkyriur these maidens of Odhinn can transform themselves into swans, and in this shape they fly through the air with the god. They are thus called 'Odhinn's swan maidens,' and also 'Odhinn's shield maidens' and 'helm maidens.'

Here is one description of these maidens from the Völuspâ. The wise woman who speaks in that poem tells us that—

[1] The story has been published and explained by Prof. Max Müller in his *Chips from a German Workshop*, vol. ii. It is from the Bráhmana of the Yajur Veda.

> She saw Valkyriur coming from afar,
> Ready to ride to the gods' gathering.
> Skuld held the shield; Skögull was another.
> Gunn, Hild, Göndul, and Geirskögull
> Now named are the Norns of Odhinn,
> Who as Valkyriur ride the earth over.[1]

And again—

> Three troops of maidens, though one maid foremost rode.
> Their horses shook themselves, and from their manes there fell
> Dew in the deep dales and on the high trees hail.

In which their origin from the clouds is very clearly shown.

Altogether we have a fine imaginative picture drawn from the study of the wind and its accompanying sights and sounds. By day, when the white clouds are sailing overhead like white swans, these are the Valkyriur shedding dew down into the dales. By night the scream of wild birds mingles with the screaming of the storm; and this again is the sound of Odhinn and the Valkyriur hurrying to the battle field, scenting the slaughter, hearing from afar the din of arms.

The Valkyriur were called, it has been said, 'swan maidens.' *Swan* is, etymologically, any bird that can *swim*; and though of course the word was never applied so promiscuously as that, it may have been used for sea fowl, which are like the swan in two particulars—first, in being white; secondly, in swimming. We find the sea called the swan's road (swan-râd) in Beowulf. So in our imaginary picture of the Valkyriur we may include sea birds such as those who woke the hill goddess Skadi in her bed upon the stormy Northern shore.

The Valkyriur were not always goddesses. They might be mortal maidens; and in fact there are many Northern tales in which they play the part of heroines. The story of Urvasi and Pururavas finds its closest counter-

[1] Völuspá, 24.

Svanhvit, and Völund Alvit. These Valkyriur lived █
their husbands seven years; but at the end of that █
they flew away, seeking battles, and did not return. █
went off on his snow-shoes to seek for Ölrun, and Sla
went in search of Svanhvit; but Völund abode in █
Dale.' [5]

This story bears in one or two points a resemblanc
the tales of bird maidens in other mythologies. The █
ing of the three by the water in the morning [6] is like
meeting of Pururavas and the Gandharvas in the V
tale. The marriage of Völund and Alvit is comparabl
the marriage of Hephæstus and Aphroditê or the attemp

---

[1] See Beowulf, 914, &c.
[2] Swan-white.
[3] All-white.
[4] Alrun (Aurinia, Tac.), the typical name of a prophetess.
[5] Völundarkviða, beginning.
[6] These three Valkyriur have some relationship to the three Nor
fates (see Völuspá, 24, just quoted, where the Valkyriur are called N
who spin like them, and, like the Valkyriur, generally know the fu
All are essentially stream goddesses; the connection between the █
and Urd's fount is unmistakable. The Valkyriur became clouds, h
been previously streams (see Chap. II.)

enforcement of Athênê. Both Aphroditê and Athênê belong to the order of cloud goddesses.[1]

More interesting still and more beautiful were the adventures of another Valkyria, the famous Brynhild. Of these it would take too long to tell the whole. But the beginning of her history is that in which she appears in her character of swan maiden, and this part is thus narrated in the Sigrdrifumâl and in the Fafnismâl. In the former of these lays Brynhild appears under the name of Sigrdrifa.[2] There were, it is said, two kings who had made war. One was named Hjâlmgunnar (War Helm), an old warrior befriended by Odhinn. The other was Agnar, whose cause no one had espoused. And we learn from this story that the Valkyriur were not always attached to the train of Odhinn; for Sigrdrifa ranged herself with Agnar and caused him to gain the victory. In revenge for this audacity Odhinn pricked the maiden with a sleep thorn and sent her into a slumber on Hindarfjöll. The sleep thorn, as we shall see in the next chapter, is a symbol of death; and therefore, as the myth was at first understood, the meaning of this pricking doubtless was that Odhinn had slain Brynhild. But in the form in which we read the story this incident has been softened down. Sigrdrifa only fell into a sound slumber. The ingenious reader has perhaps already detected in this adventure the germ of one of our most familiar nursery tales. Anon came the prince to awake the maiden from her sleep. He was the famous Sigurd, and it was the incident just related which was the prelude to his first meeting with Brynhild.

Sigurd had just returned from slaying the famous serpent Fafnir, who guarded the treasure of gold. When

---

[1] Aphrodité is not the wife of Hephæstus in the *Iliad*; but that probably only shows that the poet followed another tradition, not that her marriage with the Smith was unknown then.

[2] Victory-giver (lit. *driver*) = Gr. Nikê. I hope at another time to have an opportunity of tracing the relationship between the Greek *Niké*, the Norse *Valkyria*, and the mediæval conception of the *Angel*.

Fafnir had been killed, Sigurd took out his heart and roasted and ate it. At once he became possessed of prophetic gifts, and could understand the speech of birds. Then where he sat he heard the eagles speaking overhead. They told one another of his deeds, and they prophesied his meeting with Brynhild, which was presently to come about and cause his after dule. As he listened they told one another of the green paths which the Fates were making smooth to lead him to the house of Giuki, and of the fair maiden who there awaited him. An eagle said—[1]

> A hall is on high, Hindarfjöll ;
> With fire without 'tis all surrounded.
> Mighty lords that palace builded
> Of undimmed earth-flame.

And another eagle answered—

> I know that on the fell a war maiden sleeps.
> Around her flickers the lindens' bane.[2]
>
> . . . .
> Thou mayst gaze at the helmed maiden.
> She from the slaughter on Vingskomir rode.
> Sigrdrifa's sleep none awaken may
> Of the sons of princes, before the Norns appoint.

So Sigurd rode, as it was said, and found Brynhild lying asleep on Hindarfjöll. He opened her corselet with his sword Gram, and she awoke and raised herself, and said—

> Who has slit my byrnie?
> How has my sleep been broken ?
> Who has loosed from me the fallow bands ?

And he answered—

> Sigmund's son with Sigurd's sword
> But now has severed thy war weeds.

Then Sigurd besought her to teach him wisdom, and the rest of this poem is devoted to the runes and wise

[1] Fafnismál, 42–44.   [2] I.e. fire.

sayings which Sigrdrífa was supposed to have repeated.
Whence we see how large a part the Valkyriur had in the
wisdom and magic power which belonged to the Fates and
prophetesses.

These cloudy beings, remote as they may seem from
the things of nature and from the experience of life,
filled a considerable space in Teutonic thought. They
represented the ideal of womanhood to the rude chivalry
of the North. Their functions were twofold; they presided over battles, and foretold future events. Tacitus
and Cæsar have described how the German wives used to
urge their husbands forward in the day of the fight, and
how, on more than one occasion, an army which· had
actually turned to fly had been driven back against the
spears of their opponents by the exhortations or the jibes
of their womankind. The same writers have told us of
the prophetic powers ascribed to women by the Teutons—
of an Aurinia (a name which appears in the Ölrun of the
Völundarkviða), who is taken for a single individual by
Tacitus. The name is probably that of a whole class of
wise women. These Valkyriur had some influence upon
the Middle Age conceptions of angels, and a greater
influence· (as in a future chapter we shall show) upon the
conception of witches.

The German gods are—if I may make such a comparative—less immortal than those of Greece and Rome.
I do not know that the latter were really expected to live
for ever, seeing that there was a constant lurking expectation that the reign of Zeus would end as it had begun,
and make way for the restoration of the milder Kronos.
In the myth of Prometheus the notion is very clearly set
forth. Nevertheless to the Greek gods are constantly
applied such phrases as ἀθάνατοι, immortal, οἱ ἀεὶ ὄντες, the
ever-living. So it is evident that the idea of the Olympians
dying in a body, though it was not altogether extinguished,
was pushed quite into the background. In the Norse creed

this was not the case. The gloomy outer world of the
Teuton was so large as contrasted with the narrow limits
of his home and homestead that for him life itself seemed
to be surrounded by a veil of darkness, and at the end of
every avenue of hope there seemed to stand an immovable
shadow. The general idea of life in its relation to death,
and of the known in its relation to the unknown, which
appears throughout the Teutonic beliefs, has never been
more beautifully expressed than by that saying of a thane
of the Saxon king Eadwine, at the time when Paulinus
came to preach the Gospel to the Northumbrians. ' This
life,' said he, ' is like the passage of a bird from the
darkness without into a lighted room, where you, King,
are seated at supper, while storms of rain and snow rage
abroad. The sparrow, flying in at one door and straightway out at another, is, while within, safe from the storm;
but soon it vanishes into the darkness whence it came.' [1]

It was in the spirit of these words that the Norseman
saw gloom in the past and in the future; the world had
sprung out of chaos, and into chaos and darkness it was
to sink again. There was to be an end of the Æsir and
of Asgard, a ' Gods' Doom ' (Ragnarök [2]), when the Æsir
and the giant race were to meet in mutually destructive
battle, and chaos should come again. We have seen how
Odhinn, who knew most about the future, was for ever on
the watch against the coming of the giants; and how he
continually recruited his band of heroes. Of these more
than four hundred thousand would, it was said, go forth
to fight on the Last Day. [3]

[1] Beda, ii. 13. A saying often quoted, e.g., by Wordsworth in his Ecclesiastical Sonnets.

[2] The usual writing of this word in the Edda Snorra is Ragnarökr, i.e.
' Twilight of the Gods.' This is evidently, however, a corruption from an
earlier form, Ragnarök, ' Doom of the Gods.' See Vigfusson and Cleasby's
Icelandic Dictionary, s.v. ' Rökr.' This change of the word is, in my eyes,
a witness to the antiquity of the belief in Ragnarök. All modern writers
have (naturally enough) followed the corrupted form of the word made use
of in the Edda Snorra.

[3] In exact numbers 432,000—that is to say, 800 out of each of the 540
gates of Valhöll, as is said in Grimnismâl, 23—

Beside the duty of their keeping themselves armed and exercised against the day of trial, it would seem that the gods must ride every day to the Urdar fount beneath the roots of Yggdrasill, to take counsel about the future, and perhaps also about the present governance of the world. They rode together along the rainbow—Ashrû, the Æsir's bridge, as it is sometimes called, or otherwise Bifröst, the trembling mile.[1]

This, then, is the world of the Norseman. Asgard is far away, hidden in the clouds, or to be caught sight of, perhaps, *between* the clouds of sunset—a city glittering with bright gold, set upon a hill. Now and again, moreover, men may see, bright-shining and trembling between earth and heaven, the Æsir's bridge, the rainbow. This is the *Kinvad* or the Sirât[2] of the Northern world; and, that it may not be an easy ascent for mortals or for giants, fire is mingled with the substance and burns along all its length: and that is the red of the bow.[3] Bifröst is the best of bridges,[4] and will remain until the Last Day; but, strong though it be, it will break in pieces what time the sons of Mûspell (the Fire), who have crossed the great river, come riding over it.[5] At one end of the rainbow stands Heimdal, the Memnon of Norse mythology, who, at the approach of any danger, rouses the gods with his sounding horn.[6] Bifröst at night may have been confounded with the Milky Way;[7] it was imagined almost conterminous

> Five hundred gates and forty more, I ween,
> In Valhöll are;
> Eight hundred heroes shall from each gate together go,
> When they go thence the wolf to fight.'

[1] But on the meaning of these words see Chap. VI.
[2] See Chap. VI. [3] Edda Snorra, D. 15. [4] Grimnismál, 44.
[5] Edda Snorra, D. 13. Lit. 'who have crossed the great *rivers*.' What is meant is the great earth-girding river of which I have spoken so often.
[6] *Gjallar-horni*. This horn must originally, I think, have sounded at sunrise; while the sound itself is the thunder. Heimdal lives at the horizon of morning. He himself is the morning home of the sun (Home Dale). Whether the *Gjallar-horni* be itself the sun (like Baldur's *Hring-horni*) I leave the reader to determine as he pleases.
[7] See Chap. VI.

with the span of heaven's arch, and must, like the other
Bridges of Death spoken of in the sixth chapter, have
been thought of as overbridging the Midgard Sea.

That mighty tide which was for the Greek a ' shadowy
sea,' a ' sea calamitous,' was not less terrible here in the
North. The Norseman was at home upon common seas,
but this was no earthly one. ' Bold must he be,' says the
Edda, ' who strives to pass *those* waters.'[1] If anyone
should be journeying toward this Sea of Death, even while
he was still on Mannheimar (man's earth) he would become
aware, I suppose, of entering a region which was misty and
ghost-like and dangerous.

The Teuton needed not suppose himself to have reached
the confines of the habitable world, even though he had
strayed far from his village community and the protection
of his friendly gods. If the more or less known recesses
of the forest had their terrors, fearfuller still to the fancy
must the region have been which lay quite out of ken,
farther than any band of explorers had ever reached.
Wherefore in the imaginary world of the Norseman the
scene even on this side the Sea of Death grew dim and
threatening ; a wintry land stretched before the wanderer's
steps. These regions of cold lay especially toward the east
and the north, the coldest quarters. To the eastward of
Midgard stood the Iron Wood (Jârnviŏr), a gloomy place
with leaves and trees of iron, where chillness reigned.
' Here sitteth the old one '—a witch, called the Iron Witch,
emblematic of death—' and reareth the wolf's fell kindred.'[2]
These wolf-kin are a race of witches and were-wolves.

And now suppose the Iron Wood passed and the sea-
shore reached. We might call the leafless wood an
emblem of *approaching* winter ; that is, of late autumn.
Beyond the sea is full winter, a land of perpetual ice and
snow, and of frosty fog hanging over the ice, with all the
magic and all the sense illusions which could have their

---

[1] Edda Snorra, D. 8.   [2] Völuspá, 32.

birth in such a misty world. Here the sun never shone when he was climbing heaven in the morning or at evening returning earthward to rest, any more than he shone upon the gloomy Cimmerians' land. If any light was here in Jötunheim, it must come from Aurora Borealis, which shed sometimes a fitful gleam. This northern light was in the Eddaic stories imaged as a girdle of fire, a 'far-flickering flame'[1] which surrounded Jötunheim, and served it as a wall to keep men from venturing there. Jötunheim seems sometimes as if it only existed in the night and could not be visited by day; it is as it were born and cradled in gloom, having no part in the light of the sun. Wherefore when a messenger is sent thither from Asgard we find him speaking thus to the horse who is to carry him thither:—

> Dark it grows without. Time I deem it is
> To fare over the misty ways.
> We will both return, or that all-powerful Jötun
> Shall seize us both.[2]

Is it safe for us to venture further? Scarcely, seeing we are but mortal. If we desire to journey into Jötunheimar we must attach ourselves to the company of a god and go with him thither. Thorr is the one who is continually making these journeys, 'faring eastward,' as the Younger Edda has it, 'to fight trolls.'[3] While Odhinn stays in Asgard and keeps guard against the giants, Thorr the son, like those children of adventure who sally forth on their viking-goings, carries the war into the enemies' country.

The following is a history typical of these journeyings of Thorr to Jötunheimar:—

The god upon this occasion set out with the intention of discovering a certain giant, Útgarðloki, who was especially powerful and especially the enemy of the gods. In truth he was a sort of king of the under world, and

---

[1] Fiölsvinnsmál.   [2] För Skirnis, 10.   [3] Edda Snorra, D. 42.

Thorr's journey to his hall is comparable to the descent of Héraclês to the realm of Hadês.[1] After some travel the god arrived at the shore of a wide and deep sea. On the sea stood the bark of the ferryman, the Northern Charon, Harhar't by name.

> Steer hitherward thy bark : I will show thee the strand.
> But who owns the skiff that by the shore thou rowest ?[2]

Thorr was, on this occasion, travelling with Loki and two mortals, his servants, called Thialfi and Röska. They crossed the wide deep sea, and entered a boundless forest. No sooner had Thorr and his comrades thus got well into Jötunheim than they began to fall victims to its spells and enchantments; and the glamour increased the farther they went, till at last their adventure ended only in disastrous defeat. They came to what they took for a hall, with wide entrance, having one small chamber at the side; and while resting they were disturbed by a noise like an earthquake, which made all but Thorr run into the chamber to hide themselves. In the morning an immense man, who had been sleeping on the ground hard by, and whose snoring it was that had so frightened all, arose, and presently lifted up that which they had fancied was a hall, and which now proved to be his glove. Then Thorr and his companions and the giant, who was named Skrýmir, continued their journey together. But in the

---

[1] This, by the way, is the only one among Herakles' labours which finds a prominent place in Homer.

[2] Harbar'tsliö't, 7. I have combined this incident with the story of the Younger Edda, because I have no doubt that the Harbar't of the Harbar'tsliö't is really the ferryman across the wide and deep sea which Thorr crossed on his way to Útgar'tloki (Edda Snorra, D. 45). This ferryman will not bear the weight of living men in his boat. This is why Harbart refuses Thorr, and why the ferryman in the curious fragment the *Sinfjötlalok* refuses to carry Sigmund. The two instances are exactly parallel. Thorr, it is to be noticed, generally, in these matters of crossing the Sea of Death or of going over the Bridge of Souls, shares the disabilities of mortals. The twenty-ninth verse of the *Grimnismál* is usually explained as meaning that Thorr may not cross As-brú.

night Thorr, thinking to kill Skrýmir, hurled against the giant's head his death-dealing hammer, Mjölnir, the force of which none, it was thought, could resist. Yet, behold, Skrýmir only asked if a leaf had fallen upon him as he slept. A second time the god raised his hammer, and smote the giant with such force that he could see the weapon sticking in his forehead. Thereupon Skrýmir awoke and said, 'What is it? Did an acorn fall upon my head? How is it with you, Thorr?' Thorr stept quickly back and answered that he had just awoken, and added that it was midnight and there were still many hours for sleep. Presently he struck a third time, with such force that the hammer sank into the giant's cheek up to the handle. Then Skrýmir rose up and stroked his cheek, saying, 'Are there birds in this tree? It seems to me as if one of them had sent some moss down on my face.'

Anon Thorr and his companions came to the city of the giant Útgarðloki, in whose hall, and among the company of giants, feats of strength were performed, to match the new comers against the men of that place. First Loki vaunted his skill in eating, and was matched against Logi (Fire). A trough was placed between them, and, after each had seemed to eat voraciously, they met just in the middle. But it was found that Loki had eaten the flesh only; whereas Logi had devoured the bones and the wood of the trough as well. Then, again, Thialfi stood to run a race with anyone, and was set to try his speed against Hug (Thought), who, in three courses, vanquished him utterly. And now the turn came to Thorr. First he was challenged to drain a horn, 'which,' said Útgarðloki, 'a strong man can finish in a draught, but the weakest can empty in three.' Thorr made three pulls at the beaker, but at the end of the third had scarcely laid bare more than the brim. The next trial was to raise a cat from the ground. 'We have a very trifling game here,' said the giant, 'in which we exercise none but children. It consists in merely lifting my cat from the ground; nor should I have dared to mention it to thee, Thorr, but that I have already seen thou art not the man we took thee for.' As he finished speaking a large grey cat leapt upon the floor. Thorr advanced and laid his hand beneath the cat's belly, and did his best to lift him from the ground; but he bent his back, and, despite all Thorr's exertions, had but one foot raised up; and when Thorr saw this he made no further trial.

'The trial,' said the giant, 'has turned out as I expected. The cat is biggish, and Thorr is short and small beside our men.' Then spake Thorr: 'Small as ye call me, let anyone come near and wrestle with me now I am in wrath.' Útgardhloki looked round at the benches and answered, 'I see no man in here who would not esteem it child's play to wrestle with thee. But I bethink me,' he continued, 'there is the old woman now calling me, my nurse Elli (Age). With her let Thorr wrestle if he will.' Thereupon came an old dame into the hall, and to her Útgardbloki signified that she was to match herself against Thorr. We will not lengthen out the tale. The result of the contest was that the harder Thorr strove the firmer she stood. And now the old crone began to make her set at Thorr. He had one foot loosened, and a still harder struggle followed; but it did not last long, for Thorr was brought down on one knee. . . .

The next morning, at daybreak, Thorr arose with his following; they dressed and prepared to go their ways. Then came Útgardhloki and had a meal set before them, in which was no lack of good fare to eat and to drink. And when they had done their meal they took their road homewards. Útgardhloki accompanied them to the outside of the town; and, at parting, he asked Thorr whether he was satisfied with his journey, and if he had found anyone more mighty than himself. Thorr could not deny that the event had been little to his honour. 'And well I know,' he said, 'that you will hold me for a very insignificant fellow, at which I am ill pleased.' Then spoke

Útgardhloki: 'I will tell thee the truth now that I have got thee again outside our city, into which, so long as I live and bear rule there, thou shalt never enter again; and I trow that thou never shouldst have entered it had I known thee to be possessed of such great strength. I deceived thee by my illusions; for the first time I saw thee was in the wood; me it was thou mettest there. Three blows thou struckest with thy hammer; the first, the lightest, would have been enough to bring death had it reached me. Thou sawest by my hall a rocky mountain, and in it three square valleys, of which one was the deepest. These were the marks of thy hammer. It was the mountain which I placed in the way of thy blow; but thou didst not discover it. And it was the same in the contests in which ye measured yourselves against my people. The first was that in which Loki had a share. He was right hungry, and ate well. But he whom we called Logi was the fire itself, and he devoured the flesh and bowl alike. When Thialfi ran a race with another, that was my thought, and it was not to be looked for that Thialfi should match him in speed. When thou drankest out of the horn, and it seemed to thee so difficult to empty, a wonder was seen which I should not have deemed possible. The other end of the horn stretched out to the sea: that thou didst not perceive; but when thou comest to the shore thou mayest see what a drain thou hast made from it. And that shall men call the ebb.' He continued, 'Not less wonderful and mighty a feat didst thou when thou wast at lifting of the cat; and, to speak sooth, we were all in a fright when we saw that thou hadst raised one paw from the ground. For a cat it was not, as it seemed to thee. It was the Midgard worm, who lies encircling all lands; and when thou didst this he had scarce length enough left to keep head and tail together on the earth; for thou stretchedst him up so high that almost thou reachedst heaven. A great wonder it was at the wrestling bout

A A

which thou hadst with Elli; but no one was nor shall be whom, how long soever he live, Elli will not reach and *Aye* not bring to earth. Now that we are at parting thou hast the truth; and for both of us it were better that thou come not here again. For again I shall defend my castle with my deceptions, and thy might will avail nothing against me.' When Thorr heard these words he seized his hammer and raised it on high; but when he would have struck he could see Útgardhloki nowhere. He turned toward the city, and was for destroying it; but he saw a wide and beautiful plain before him, and no city.

Thus is the veil lifted for us for a moment, so that we may see into Giant Land. The picture held up before us · is not quite of the making of primitive belief. As we shall see in another chapter, there was, in this story of Thorr's visit to Útgardhloki, once a serious meaning, which has been here lost sight of; and the whole history is converted into something like a fairy tale. The myths of Scandinavia were beginning to seem like fairy tales in the thirteenth century—which was the time at which Snorri Sturlason composed his Edda; and while their old substance is retained in this compilation of legends they are dressed up in a new way and in a new spirit. Still the picture of Giant Land which we have been looking at is one which had been handed on from ancient days. This essential characteristic still clings to the place; it is a land of mystery and magic.

The full moon near its setting, gleaming through an icy fog, this is the giant Skrýmir,[1] or the mountain which Thorr took for him. In its face we still see the three deep gashes which Mjölnir once made. How completely do all

---

[1] I have little doubt that the incident of the three gashes or valleys is meant to refer to the face of the moon. Such a representation would be quite in the spirit of mythology. It would be in the spirit of mythology too that Skrýmir should have been first himself the moon, and that after-wards in this story the moon should be the mountain which was mistaken for him. Skrýmir is thus as the full moon a relation of the Gorgon. The name *Skrýmir* means simply a monster (cf. skrimsl).

Nature's forces seem upon the side of the giant race—fire, the sea, Jörmungandr, who is a personification of the sea!

Thorr is not always so unsuccessful as he was in this adventure. Indeed, we may fairly say that he can conquer all giants save Útgardhloki. And why he cannot overcome *him* will appear in the next chapter. Here is a more successful expedition.

In revenge for that disastrous journey to Útgardhloki, so the Younger Edda tells us,[1] Thorr once more sallied forth from Midgard, and came, *at dusk*, to the dwelling of the giant Hýmir, and persuaded that giant to go out a-fishing with him. For bait he wrung off the head of a gigantic bull, and this he fixed upon a string, and let down the line. The object of his fishing was the great Earth Serpent. Jörmungandr saw the bait and took it, so that the hook became firmly fixed in his jaw. Thorr began to draw up the prize, while Jörmungandr struggled so violently that he all but upset the boat. And now Thorr exerted all his divine strength, and pulled so hard that his feet went through the boat and reached the bottom of the sea. Then the Sea Serpent lifted up his head out of the water and spouted venom at Thorr. Thorr now raised his mallet to strike, and would, perhaps, have slain the enemy, had not Hýmir, who grew afeard, cut the line and let the serpent sink again into the water.

Or take this story—a rather better one—from the Elder Edda.[2] The giant Thrymr once stole the hammer of Thorr, and Loki was sent to find where he had hidden it. It had been buried deep in the ground, and Thrymr would restore it only on condition that the Æsir should give him the beautiful Freyja to wife. But at such a

---

[1] D. 48.

[2] Þrymskviða, or Hamarsheimt. Þrymr is a being of the same nature as Thorr, as his name means *Thunder*. Concerning the double character frequently given to a natural object see p. 130. Thrymr may, perhaps, be an older thunder god than Thorr.

proposal the goddess waxed wroth, and would in no wise
consent to it. So the gods took counsel, and, by the
advice of Heimdalr, one of the Æsir, they devised a plan
by which the giant could be cheated. The thunder god
dressed himself in Freyja's weeds, he adorned himself
with her necklace—the famed Brisinga necklace- he let
from his side keys rattle, and set a comely coif upon his
head.[1] Then he went to Jötunheim as though he were
the bride; Loki went with him as his serving maid. The
god could scarcely avoid raising some suspicions by his
unwomanly behaviour; he alone devoured an ox, eight
salmon, and all the sweetmeats women love, and he drank
three *salds* of mead. Thrymr exclaimed with wonder [2]—

> 'Who ever a bride saw sup so greedily?
> Never a bride saw I sup so greedily,
> Nor a maid drink such measures of mead.'
>
> Sat the all-cunning serving maid by,
> Ready her answer to the giant to give.
> 'Nought has Freyja eaten for eight nights,
> So eager was she for Jötunheim.'
>
> 'Neath the linen hood he looked, a kiss craving;
> But sprang back in terror across the hall.
> 'How fearfully flaming are Freyja's eyes!
> Their glance burneth like a brand!' ·
>
> There sat the all-cunning serving maid by,
> Ready with words the giant to answer.
> 'For eight nights she did not of sleep enjoy,
> So eager was she for Jötunheim.'
>
> In stepped the giant's fearful sister;
> For a bride's gift she dared to ask.
> 'Give me from thy hand red rings,
> If thou wilt gain my love,
> My love and favour.'
>
> Then said Heimdalr, of Æsir the brightest,
> 'Woman's weeds on Thorr let us lay;
> Let by his side keys rattle;
> And with a comely coif his head adorn.'—*Þrymskv.* 16, 17.

[2] Þrymskv. 25 sqq.

Then spake Thrymr, the giants' prince:
'The hammer bear in, the bride to consecrate;
Lay Mjölnir on the maiden's knee
And unite us mutually in marriage bonds.'

Laughed Hlórriði's [1] heart in his breast
When the fierce-hearted his hammer knew.
Thrymr first slew he, the thursar's lord,
And the race of jötuns all destroyed.

He slew the ancient jötun sister,
Who for a bride gift had dared to ask;
Hard blows she got instead of skillings,
And the hammer's weight in place of rings.

Finally, in another poem of the Elder Edda, we find Thorr engaging Alvis (All-wise), of the race of the thursar,[2] in a conversation upon the names which different natural objects bear among men, among gods (Æsir and Vanir), among giants, and among elves, so that he guilefully keeps him above the earth until after sunrise, where it is not possible for a dwarf or a jötun to be and live. So Alvis bursts asunder.[3]

These stories are somewhat childish, and do not bear all the characteristics of early belief; but we can look through the outer covering to something more serious within. How clearly, for instance, in this last story are Alvis and his fellows shown to be beings of darkness, and therefore their land to be a land of gloom. This aspect of Jötunheim and of the giant race would be more apparent if we were further to take into consideration all the stories which connect Jötunheim with the Land of Shades. But this is the subject for another chapter.

Let it suffice us in this to have gained some picture of the actual world of the Teuton. We will forbear, as yet, to pry into his land of death; and we will forbear,

---

[1] Thorr's.
[2] Giant does not translate *thurs*. Most of the *thursar* were giants, as opposed to the *dvergar*, dwarfs; but this Alvis is spoken of as a dwarf.
[3] Alvissmál.

likewise, to pry into the Future of the Teutoı
What we have been looking at hitherto has beeı
sent world, the actual living nature, in the light
the German saw it from beneath the dark shad
forest. Is not this view likely to have had its
upon his future creed, even at a time when he I
nally put off Odhinn (put off the 'old man,'
white-bearded, with his cap of concealment) an
Christ? In every feature of his belief, old oı
reflected the life of the mark—its gloom, its
uncertainty concerning all beyond. In every to
speaks his creed we hear the echo of the worɩ
thane comparing to the sparrow flying in for ɛ
from the storm the brief life of man. Life wı
Teuton in very truth the 'meeting-place betv
eternities,'[1] both unknown.

We have, fortunately for ourselves, the means ɩ
further the creed of the Teuton race. We can ɛ
the stories of the Edda, stories professedly
indeed, but breathed upon and partly witheree
breath of unbelief, born at a late time when the
spirit had been too long familiar to the world
the heathen doctrines to be any longer seriou
another story of a much earlier date, which, thɩ
fessedly Christian in tone, has about it far mo
ancient spirit of Teutonism. The Eddas give u
the actual facts of Northern belief; but Beowulf
the spirit of the belief. This poem, in the form
it now exists, belongs to the eighth century. Buı
was doubtless brought, in some shape or other, to ɑ
by early invaders from Jutland or Denmark, or
south of Sweden. It has no direct connection
English race; it recounts the deeds of a hero of ɑ
in South Sweden, and of a King of Denmark.]
it is only one of many such poems, which may l

[1] Carlyle.

sung by gleemen in the brilliant court of Offa, or even have cheered the sad heart of Eadwine when he ate an exile's food at the board of King Redwald. Other poems would tell of Hengist and Horsa, or of Ælli and Cissa, and such-like heroes, more genuinely English.

Even in Beowulf, a Christian poem, written for men who were not unacquainted with the Latin civilisation of their times, we must make allowance for the changed condition of men's lives between the old prehistoric German days and these more modern Christian ones. The fear of solitude, or perhaps I had better say the *sense of solitude*, which had become ingrained in the Teuton mind by centuries of forest life, did not at once fade away when the Germans had advanced a little in civilisation; probably at the first it increased somewhat. There was in old days a holiness as well as a terror about the woody groves, for Odhinn and his fellow gods inhabited there; only round the extreme outskirts of the mark (the Teuton's world) hovered the giants and evil spirits. And this notion was expressed in the Norse religion by placing the jötuns far away beyond the Midgard Sea. But when the Æsir were expelled by Christianity and the sacred groves cut down; when the old village Enclosure was replaced by the walled Town; [1] when men no longer dwelt *discreti ac diversi*, but congregated in strong places—then an added horror attached to the *outlands*, to the moors and fells, to their drear expanses, their dark valleys and their misty, stagnant pools.

The outland men, the dwellers on the heaths (heathens[2]), were henceforward regarded as the worshippers of fiends; Odhinn was driven forth and became the Wild Huntsman, or else Satan himself, the Prince of the Air.[3] The giants

---

[1] The different meanings of the German *Zaun* and English *town*, both etymologically the same, are very expressive of the change from German to English life, as experienced by our forefathers.

[2] The analogy is shown still more strongly in the German *Heide*.

[3] See Chap. X. The 'Prince of the Air,' which is one of the Biblical names for Satan, was that most often made use of in Middle Age descrip-

We hear of gold plates adorning it. The

when the plunder to be got from the Romar
lands was almost unlimited, and we have p
barbarians converted the wealth which the
the coarsest uses; so the story of a house
gold plates may not be altogether fabulou
had prepared Heort for himself and his th
night in the ' beer hall ' they held high revel
to the gleeman's song, which told the stories
doings in ancient days, and ' bow. the All-
framed the earth plain in its beauty, whic
girds round, and set in pride of victory the s
as beacons to light the dwellers on land.' -]
from all this joy and revelry, deep in the st
or among the windy moors, dwelt a terribl
natural being, named Grendel. He brooked
what was going on in the house of Hrothga
the foe of men.

tions of the Devil. It is evidently very appropriate to a w
turned fiend.
  ' The *Waldmann* or *Wilde Mann* was another popt
mediæval popular lore. We see him upon the arms of Br

Grueful and grim this stranger called Grendel,
This haunter of marshes, holder of moors.
In the Fifel-race' dwelling, the fen and the fastness,
The wretched one guarded his home for awhile;
Since by the Creator his doom had been spoken.

. . . . . .

Thence he departed at coming of nightfall
To visit the house-place and see how the Ring Danes
After their beer bout had ordered it.
On the floor found he of ethelings a throng
Full-feasted and sleeping. Care heeded they never,
No darkness of soul nor sorrow of men.
Grim now and greedy, the fiend was soon ready;
Savage and fierce, from sleep up he snatched then
Of those thanes thirty, and thence eft departed.

From that time Grendel waged wicked war against
Hrothgar and all his house. It was the old war of darkness against light—the darkness of misty moors against
the civilisation of those who dwelt in houses; of heathens
—only that this word got afterwards a special significance
—against town men. Or it was the war of the gods of
German mythology against the dwellers in that savage
far-off land across the ocean, Jötunheim. Here the race
of monsters, the Fifel Brood, seemed like to gain the victory. Hrothgar himself indeed, as the Lord's anointed,
Grendel could not touch; but the king and his men were
driven out of Heort, which, in place of its song and feasting, was given up to darkness and to Grendel. Nor would
this monster accept any truce with the Danes; but still
like a death shadow he roamed over the fens, and plotted
against the lives of warriors and youths.

The report of this was brought to Beowulf, the brother
of Higelac, king of the Geatas, or Goths. The heroes of
these stories are rarely at the outset kings themselves, for
it was the recognised duty of kings to stay at home among
their own peoples; but the hero, true precursor of the
knight errant, must first wander abroad in search of adventures; and very often he won a kingdom by his sword.

This was both the theory and practice of the Norsemen and the more warlike among the Germans. They could not all, it is true, find monsters and dragons to slay, but as a substitute they contented themselves with going on viking—that is to say, upon a pirate voyage. Beowulf, who had the fortune to live in quite prehistoric days, when 'eotens, elves, orkens, and such giants' (as Grendel) were still on earth, needed only to sail from Gothland to Denmark. So he made ready a good ship, and set out upon the 'swan's path'—the sea—to seek the good King Hrothgar. The Scylding's (Hrothgar's) warder, who kept the cliff, saw from the wall the gleam of arms upon the vessel's bulwarks, and rode down to the sea to meet the warriors ere they landed, brandishing his spear in his hand. 'What armour-bearing men are ye, in byrnies clad, who thus come with your foaming keel over the water-ways, over the sea-deeps hither? There at Land's End have I ever held seaward, that no foes might come with ship array to do us hurt,' he cried. And he was answered, 'We are of race Goths, Higelac's hearth friends. We have come in friendship to seek thy lord and to defend him. For soothly.we have heard say that among the Scyldings some wretch, I know not who, in the dark soweth with terror unknown malice and harm and havoc. And I may, in the depth of my mind, give Hrothgar counsel how he should in wisdom overcome the foe.'

Then Beowulf was allowed to proceed. He rode into the town; the men wondered at his kingly bearing, and the greatness of his followers, and Hrothgar sent to ask why he came, whether in peace or war. Great joy prevailed in Hrothgar's house when Beowulf disclosed his intention of himself meeting the foe face to face, and once more the sound of feasting was heard in the deserted palace; the Queen Waltheow bare round the drinking cup to the hero, and pledged him. At last night fell.

> After that darkening night over all,
> Men's shadow-covering, advancing came,

and Hrothgar knew the signal for retiring from the
haunted place, which was thus left to the Goths and
their leader. As for Beowulf, he had determined that he
would trust only to his own strength of arm, not to byrnie
or falchion—indeed, Grendel was impervious to weapons—
and he prepared for the death struggle in a speech just in
the character of all the poetry of this epoch. 'I ween
that he intends, should he prevail, to devour in safety the
people of the Goths, as he has often done the Danes.
Thou wilt have no need to bury me, for if I get my death
he will have eaten me all dashed with blood: he will bear
away my gory corpse; he will taste me, the night-stalker
will devour me without mercy: he will place my burial
mound upon the heath: thou wilt have no thought of
burning my body. Send to Higelac, if I fall, that best
of mail shirts which guards my breast, the choicest of
doublets; 'tis Hrædla's bequest and Weland's work.'

The finest passages, those wherein the poet seems
touched by the strongest inspiration, are always they
which paint the gloom and horror resting over Grendel
and all his actions: showing how the darkness and
mystery of the world about them laid hold on the imaginations of these Northern seers. The author of Beowulf
never tires of presenting and re-presenting the image of
this shadowy being and of the places wherein he dwells.
So here, so soon as night has come, the note of revelry is
changed to one of grim expectation or of horror.

Then from the moor came, the misty hills under,
Grendel stalking; God's anger he bare;
Meant the dread enemy some one of man's kin
Here to entangle within the high hall.
He went 'neath the welkin along, till the guest house,
Man's golden seat, he recognised well,
With the plates that adorned it. Not now for the first time
Sought the destroyer Hrothgar's homestead;
Yet never in life save now, after nor earlier,
Hardier men among hall thanes he found.
To the house door then the monster came prowling,

The house reft of joys ; soon flew the door wide
And wrought iron burst 'neath the strength of his hand.

. . . . . .

Sleeping together full many a warrior,
Peacefully sleeping upon the hall floor,
Beheld he the kinsmen : his heart laughed within him,
For the foul fiend was minded before break of day
The soul from the body of each one to sever,
And hope of full feasting on his spirit there fell.
Then straightway asleep he seized one of the warriors,
Bit deep in his body and drank of his blood,
And the flesh tore in fragments, in small morsels swallowed,
Till all was devoured to the feet and the hands.

Then stepping up nearer, he took at his resting
The mighty-souled warrior, Beowulf, there :
But *he* stretching forward, on his elbow half rising,
Seized all on a sudden the ill-minded foe.
Full soon then discovered this keeper of crimes
He never had met in the mid-earth's wide regions
Among strangers a hero so strong in his hand-gripe.
And now he is minded to flee to his cavern
To seek out his devil's crew. . . .
                    . . . . But Higelac's kinsman
Remembered his evening speech : up he stood
And tightened his clutch. . . .

The hall echoed with the shrieks of the wretch. So
fiercely they strove that it was a wonder the house did
not fall, though it was held firm with iron bands.   Over
the North Danes crept a ghastly horror when they heard
the cries of this hell's captive, and many of Beowulf's
earls drew their swords, but no steel had power over
Grendel's life.   And still the Goth held his enemy by, the
hand, tearing his arm : at last the sinews started in his
shoulder, which opened a gaping wound ; the flesh burst.

To Beowulf now was the fight's fury given.
Death-sick flies Grendel beneath the fen-banks,
Seeking his joyless home ; well must he know
That of his life's days the tale is o'ertold.

What were the rejoicings among the Ring Danes and in the house of Hrothgar we may partly picture. 'I have been told,' says the bard, 'that on the morrow many a warrior came from far and near to that gift hall. The clan-heads came over wide ways to see that wonder—the traces which the enemy had left behind. Grendel's death seemed not doubtful to any who saw the track of the miserable one, and how heavy-hearted, conquered, death-doomed, banished, he bare his death traces to the Nicker's Mere. There the water bubbled with blood, the waves surged and mingled with the hot clotted gore—after the outcast had rendered up his life, his heathen soul, in the fenny haunt. Joyfully and proudly old and young turned back from the pool and rode home. They sang the praises of Beowulf and of their good king Hrothgar. At times the young men ran races on their well-trained steeds; at another time some old bard would sing either in Beowulf's honour, or of deeds of prowess done long ago, of Sigmund the Wælsing, and how the ring hoard was guarded by the wondrous worm.

'Hrothgar went into the hall, and, standing on the daïs, surveyed the vaulted roof adorned with gold, where hung Grendel's hand. Then he spake: "For this sight to the Almighty thanks be given: ever can God, the Shield of Honour, work wonder after wonder. Not long ago I never guessed that though my best of houses stood stained with gore any revenge would be mine. Now this hero hath, through God's grace, done a deed which with all our wisdom we could not contrive. Henceforward, Beowulf, best of men, I will cherish thee in my heart like a son. Nor shalt thou have any want which it is in my power to satisfy. For to deeds of less prowess I have given great rewards and honour at my hearth." Then was Heort cleansed and adorned once more by human hands, and many men and women set to work upon the guest hall. For the bright place was shaken in the wall and door; only the roof had remained uninjured. Now wonders of

gold-varied webs shone along the walls. And the son of
Healfdene gave to Beowulf a golden banner as a sign of
victory, and a sword of great price was borne to the hero,
. . . . a helmet, and eight steeds, on one of which lay a
saddle of cunning work. And beside, the lord of warriors
(Hrothgar) gave a token to each of those who had travelled
the sea road with Beowulf.'

All, however, was not ended with Grendel's race. It
was soon seen that an avenger had survived the foe—
Grendel's mother. She came as her son had been wont to
come, when the thanes slumbered after their beer-drinking.
Wrathful and ravenous, she burst into Heort, where the
Ring Danes lay asleep. There was soon a terror among
them, but less than before. They seized their armour and
sharp swords, but she being discovered hastened to get
back. She hurried back to her pool one of the ethelings,
the best beloved of Hrothgar's warriors. Beowulf was not
there, for another dwelling had been assigned to him.
The witch took the well-known hand of Grendel, all bloody
as it was. Hrothgar was in a fierce mood when he heard
that his chief thane was slain, and quickly was Beowulf
sent for. Beowulf greeted the aged king, who spoke:
'Ask not of my welfare. Sorrow is renewed for the Danes
people. Æschere is dead, who knew my secrets, my
counsellor, my close comrade when we guarded our heads
in battle, in the crush of hosts. A wandering fiend has
been his undoer here in Heort. I know not whether the
ghoul has returned again. She has avenged the quarrel
in which thou slewest Grendel the other night.' And
he described the two fiends and the place where they
dwelt.

> A father they know not, nor if among ghosts
> Any spirit before was created. And secret
> The land they inhabit, dark wolf-haunted ways
> Of the windy hill-side by the treacherous tarn,
> Or where covered up in its mist the hill stream
> Downward flows.

To this pool Beowulf now went, and the king and
many warriors with him. The track of the destroyer was
soon found; through forest glades and across the gloomy
moor they followed it; into deep gorges, by steep head-
lands, led on the strait and lonely road, by the homes of
the nickers. Then Hrothgar went forward, accompanied
by a few, until they came to a joyless wood where trees
leaned over the hoar rock, and beneath stood water troubled
and bloody. Great was their grief when near it they
found the head of Æschere. The well bubbled red: their
horns sounded a funeral strain. Along this tank's edge
they saw many creatures of the worm kind, sea dragons
creeping along the deep, and nickers lying in the ness.
Beowulf did on him his warrior's weeds, a twisted mail-
shirt, and helmet begirt with many rings, and his biting
sword, which was named Hrunting. Then he plunged in,
and the whelming waters passed over his head. It was
some time ere he could discern what lay at the bottom,
but soon the old hag, who for fifty years had had her
home there, discovered that some one from the world
above was exploring the strange abode. She grappled
with Beowulf, seizing him in her devilish grip, but she did
not hurt him by that, for the mail shirt protected his body
against her hateful fingers; next she dragged the Ring
Prince into her den, yet could he not, despite his rage,
wield his sword. At last he perceived he was in a hall,
where the water could not harm him nor the fatal embrace
of the witch, and by the light of a distant fire he saw the
old were-wolf. He struck a ringing blow upon her head,
but the steel would not hurt her. Then the warrior, the
Goths' lord, threw away his weapon and seized Grendel's
mother, and shook her so that she sank down. But she,
paying him back, griped his hand, and he, over-reaching
himself, likewise fell down. Grendel's mother leaped
upon him and drew a knife, seeking to find a way under
his corselet, but that held firm, or he would have perished.

At last Beowulf saw among the rubbish a victorious

blade, an old sword of giant days, with keenest edge.
The Scylding's champion seized the hilt, and despairing of
his life he drew the blade and struck fiercely at her neck.
It broke the bone-joints and passed through her body.
She sank upon the floor. And he, rejoicing in his deed,
sprang up; a light stole down into the water as when the
lamp of heaven mildly shines, and he saw throughout the
house. Then he perceived Grendel's hated body lying there,
and swinging his sword around Beowulf cut off his head.

When the wise men, who with Hrothgar were watching
the pool from above, saw the water all dabbled and stained
with blood, they made no doubt but that the old she-wolf
had destroyed the noble earl.   Then came on noon-day, and
the Scyldings grew sick of heart; the king of men turned
to go homeward; but still they gazed upon the lake,
longing for their lord to appear.   And down below, behold!
in the hot blood of the giant all the sword had melted
away, like ice when the Father (He who hath power over
times and seasons—the true God) looseneth the bond of
frost and unwindeth the ropes which bind the waves.
Then Beowulf dived up through the water: soon he was
at the surface. And when Grendel died, the turbid waves,
the vast and gloomy tracts, grew calm and bright.

So, too, after her centuries of gloom, the mild light of
Christianity shone down into the deep waters of German
thought, and in time their tracts too grew calm and bright.
But this was not yet. We have still, in another chapter,
to try and see something of how the dark shadow which
was an inheritance of so many ages hung over the creed
of mediæval Christendom.   By virtue of this inheritance
mediæval Catholicism entered into the line of descent from
the creeds of heathen Germany.

§ 2. *The Gods of the Homestead.*

We have gained some insight into one side of Teutonic
belief; and that the most important side. We have been

standing with the warrior, who had his home in the mark and who spent his time in hunting there. His world and his gods are those who lie beyond the familiar ground of the village farm; still farther away, as the half-known changes into the wholly strange, awe and gloom merge into horror and darkness, and we pass from the homes of the warlike Odhinn, Thorr, and Tyr to hateful Jötunheim. The joys of Odhinn's heaven were for the warrior. He only who had died by the sword could gain entrance there. Every morning the heroes of Valhöll rode out to the field and fought till they had .hewn each other in pieces; but at even they were whole again, and they spent the night over their cups of mead. This perpetual fighting was, as we know, a preparation for Ragnarök.

A paradise such as this would ill have suited quiet folk: and even among the Germans there were some of these There was a simpler sort of religion which belonged to those who in after years became the peasantry.[1] They were averse from war, but fond of rustic life and its quiet pleasures. There must always be in the midst of a society, however warlike, a large class of those who have no taste for the favourite pursuit, who have no desire for adventure nor for change of home. These are the true children of the soil. We trace their influence in every creed; and their religion is the faith of worshippers to whom no mere change of creed is of vital importance. They have their poetry of nature, which asks no aid from anxious thought and aspiration. Whatever others may discover of the secrets of life, they can find out this at least, that there are still cakes and ale to be met with there, and open sunny meadows, and grasses and flowers, and silvery streams, and soft shy wood creatures, and fishes and innumerable

---

[1] The old Germans had not precisely slaves after the Roman fashion, but they had serfs, who cultivated the soil for them (Tac. *Germ.* c. 25, and Guizot, *Cours, &c., Hist. de France,* i. p. 265). These serfs may have been originally Slavonic by blood (slav = slave), but they spoke German, and made up the lower population of the Germans.

birds. For them, as the true bard of all this craft [1] in old days said, ' for them earth yields her increase; for them the oaks hold in their summits acorns and in their mid-most branches bees. The flocks bear for them their fleecy burdens, and their wives bring forth children like to their fathers. They live in unchanged happiness, and need not ply across the sea in impious ships.' There were such men and women as these among our own forefathers ; and the religion which they made their own was of necessity somewhat opposed to the creed of the Wodin-worshippers.

There are two gods who seem to belong to this faction : both gods of summer and the sun. One is Balder, the brightest and best beloved among the Æsir, who was the very sun himself, the day star in his mild aspect, as he would naturally appear in the North. Balder's house was called Breiðablik, Wide-Glance—that is to say, it was the bright upper air which is the sun's home. This palace was surrounded by a space called the *peace-stead*, in which no deed of violence could be done.[2] Balder appears to us like the son of Lêtô in his most benignant mood. When he died all things in heaven and earth, ' both living things and trees and stones and all metals,' wept to bring him back again : [3] as, indeed, all things must weep at the loss of the sun, chief nourisher at life's feast.

The other sun god, or summer god, was Freyr, who was connected with the spring and with all the growth of plants and animals ; he was a patron of agriculture, and, like Balder, a god of peace; 'to him must men pray for good harvests and for peace;'[4] a 'beauteous and mighty god' he was, like Apollo Chrysaôr, girt with a sword ; not so much for fight as because the sun's rays are ever likened to a sword. Freyr can fight upon occasion ; and he will engage in one of the three great combats of Ragnarök.[5]

---

[1] Hesiod, *Works and Days*, 232
[2] Edda Snorra, D. 49, and Friþiofssaga, beginning.
[3] E. S. l. c.   [4] E. S. D. 24   [5] See Chap. VIII.

The gentler side of the religion was in the North, as it always is, associated rather with the goddesses than with gods. Here, as among Greeks and Romans, the great patron of the peasant folk was the earth goddess.[1] In Tacitus the divinity appears under the name of Nerthus, which is perhaps Hertha.[2] A similar goddess among the Suevi is called by him Isis. Other German names which seem to belong more or less to the same divinity are Harke, Holda, Perchta, Bertha. We must class with these beings the Norse Frigg (German Freka). Her I have already taken as an example of the way in which the earth goddess may lose her distinctive character and put on that of the heaven god through becoming his wife. Hêra, we saw, did this in the Greek pantheon, and Frigg does the same in the Northern. She is not a conspicuous character in the Scandinavian mythology.

To Frigg Freyja bears the same relationship that Persephonê bears to Dêmêtêr; wherefore we may say that Frigg, Freyr, and Freyja correspond to Dêmêtêr, Dionysus, and Persephonê, and more closely still to the Ceres, Liber, and Libera of the Romans. After what was said in Chapter V. touching the relationship of these latter gods, no further explanation is needed of the character of Frigg, Freyr, and Freyja.

It is strange, however, to see how the tale of the wanderings and sorrows of the earth goddess in search of the spring reappears in the mythology of every land, and ends in every case in some form of mystery. There are two stories in the Eddas[3] which especially correspond to the myths commemorated in the *anodos* (up-coming) of Persephonê and her marriage with Dionysus and in her

[1] See Chap. V.

[2] The identity of Nerthus and Hertha is assumed by most writers who are not specialists upon the subject of German etymology; but, as it is not admitted by Grimm, I hesitate to assume it, probable as, at first sight, it appears (see Grimm, *D. M.* chap. xiii.) Nerthus, says Meyer, corresponds to the Skr. Nritus, *terra* (*Nachtrag* to Grimm's *D. M.* iii. 84). Nritus or Nirrtis became the Queen of the Dead (see p. 289).

[3] From E. S. D. 37, and Skirnismál.

kathodos (down-going) and the sorrows of Demeter for her
loss. The first is the history of the wooing of Gerd by
Freyr, and it is thus told :—

There was a man named Gýmir,[1] and his wife was
Örboža (Aurboža), of the mountain jötuns' race. Their
daughter was Gerd, fairest of all women. Once Freyr
mounted the seat of Odhinn, which was called Air Throne;
and looking northward into far Giant Land, he saw a light
flash forth. Looking again, he saw that the light was
made by the maiden Gerd, who had just opened her father's
door, and that it was her beauty which thus shone over the
snow. Then Freyr was smitten with love sadness, and
determined to woe the fair one to be his wife; and so he
sent his messenger, Skirnir, to whom he gave his horse and
magic sword. Skirnir went to Gerd, and he told her how
great Freyr was among the Æsir, and how noble and happy
a place was Asgard, the home of the gods; but for all his
pleading Gerd would give no ear to his suit. At last the
messenger drew his sword, and threatened to take her
life, unless she would grant to Freyr his desire. So Gerd
promised to visit the god nine nights thence, in Barri's
wood.

Here a very simple nature myth is told us. The
earth will not respond to the wooing of the sun unless he
draw his sharp sword, the rays. Freyr himself it must
have been who in the original myth undertook the journey
into dark Jötunheim.[2] In very northern lands we know
that the sun himself does actually disappear in the cold
North, the death region. When he is there the earth con-

---

[1] Gýmir is a name of the sea god Oegir = Oceanus etymologically and
actually. See Oegisdrekka, beg. The relationship between such a being and
the earth is not quite plain, though the explanation may certainly be
suggested by what has been said of the nature of Oceanus in Chapter II.
and in various places. Gýmir is by Simrock connected with Hýmir, who
is the winter sea (Hýmiskviða). (*Handbuch der deutschen Mythologie*, p.
64.) Simrock also says that Gýmir is an under-world god (p. 398).

[2] Skirnir is in fact only a by-name of Freyr (see *Lex. Mythol.* 706b).
The same authority says that Skirnir means the *air*, which somewhat com-
plicates the solution of the story. The Icl. *skirr* is our *sheer*.

sents to meet him again with love nine nights hence—that
is to say, after the nine winter months are over. They meet
in Barri's wood, which is the wood in its first greenness.[1]

We turn now to the Norse version of the κάθοδος of
Persephoné, which is shorter than the history of the
wooing of Gerd, and which, it will be seen, bears more
resemblance to the history of Isis, who lost her husband,
than to the history of Dêmêtêr, who lost her daughter.
The part of the earth is taken here by Freyja. Freyja,
we are told, had a husband, Odhur,[2] who left his wife to
travel in far countries and never returned. Freyja went
in search of him, and in that quest passed (like Dêmêtêr)
through many lands; so that she has many names, 'for
each people called her by a different one.'[3] But all her
journeyings were vain; 'and since then she weeps continually, and her tears are drops of gold.'[4]

We know that one of the essential parts of the mystery
of the earth goddess was that part which celebrated her
'coming' in the form of spring, and how this advent was
represented to the sense as a journey of the image—the
rude agalma or the statue—of the goddess from place to
place. For this reason was Isis carried in a car or in a
boat,[5] and in a car was drawn the Ephesian Artemis, like
many another earth goddess of Asiatic birth; for this
reason once was dragged Dêmêtêr in that car harnessed
with panthers and lions to which the chorus of Euripides
makes allusion; or the image of the spring god, Iacchos,

---

[1] *Barri* is 'green.'

[2] Odhur is really identical with Odhinn, as Freyja is (this tale among
others, and her name too, showing her to be so) with Frigg. It is worth
noting that whereas Frigg has generally to conform her nature to
that of her husband, in this particular story Odhinn (Odhur) takes upon
himself a character foreign to the heaven god, in order to complete the
myth of the earth.

[3] Edda Snorra, D. 35. See what was said on p. 49 and in Chap. V.
touching the different names of the earth goddess.

[4] The rains of autumn, so rich for future gain, yet which are shed by
the Earth as she looks upon the decay of summer and searches in vain for
the verdure of spring.

[5] Apuleius Met. xi.; Lactantius, i. 27.

was borne from Athens to Eleusis. In these forms of
mystery the mythic journey was translated into a real one.
We have the best reason for believing that as similar
ceremonies were observed in the case of the German earth
goddess, among the Germans also there existed a mystery.
This was not indeed a celebration of the highly developed
kind, such as the Eleusinia, but one of that primitive
rural order of mysteries such as are still traceable within
or behind the more elaborate ceremonial of the Greek
mysteria.[1]

Tacitus appears to mention two German earth goddesses, Nerthus and Isis; it is probable that the two names
really connote the same personality. When the historian
calls one of them, the divinity of the Suevi, Isis, he assuredly
bestows this name upon her on the same principle by
which he gives the names Mercury, Hercules, and Mars to
Wuotan, Donar, and Zio—namely, because there was that
in the character of the German goddess which recalled to
his mind the Isis known to the Romans. In truth, one of
these points of likeness he immediately afterwards men-
tions—the fact that the image of the German goddess was
carried from place to place in a boat. We may conclude
from these data that the Suevian goddess had her mysteries, which were not unlike those of the Roman Isis.[2]
Again, concerning the other earth goddess, Nerthus, Tacitus
is still more explicit. In the first place we learn that she
was recognised as a personification of the earth—*Nerthus
id est Terra Mater*. Some have thought that for Nerthus
in this passage we should read Hertha.

This Nerthus had, it seems, her home in an island of
the Northern Sea—Rügen, as is supposed, or Heligoland.[3]
Her secret shrine in the centre of the island was sur-

[1] See Chap. V.
[2] I use the term *Roman Isis*, because there can be no question that the
Isis as worshipped in Rome differed much from the goddess of the ancient
Egyptians. See Chap. V.
[3] Heligoland = *Heilige Land*. Rügen, however, is the most probable
conjecture for the identification of the island in question.

rounded by a dense thicket, which none but priests might
enter. Thence every year she was taken to be shown for
a season to the people, and in order that her wanderings,
like those of Dêmêtêr, should be made the subject of
dramatic representation. When brought to the mainland,
she was dragged from place to place in a closed waggon—
which was probably fashioned like a ship mounted on
wheels [1]—and wherever she came she brought gladness
and peace. ' Happy is the place, joyful the day, which is
honoured by the entertainment of such a guest; no war can
go on, no arms are borne, the sword rests in its scabbard.
This peace and rest continue till the priest takes back the
goddess, satiate of converse with mortals.'[2]

Evidently we have here the trace of mystic celebrations
not unlike the beginnings of the Greek Eleusinia; rites
of a simple kind such as are suited to the feelings of a
primitive race.

Now it is to be expected that the rustic side of
heathenism, the worship of the peasant class, should have
kept its observances more free from the destructive influence of Christianity than was possible to the fiercer part
of the creed, that side of it which was represented by the
great divinities Odhinn, Thorr,[3] and Tyr. The worship of
the gods of the mark might be called the Church militant
of heathenism. The votaries of these gods were the men
who first sallied forth to conquer in the territories of Rome,
and who, having been victorious in arms, were again themselves conquered by Christianity. Those who remained behind, when they had to submit to the new religion, quietly
fashioned it to suit their own ideas. They strove to make
Christianity a creed fit for rustic folk concerned with few
cares, unless to secure good harvests, and with offerings to

---

[1] The reasons for this supposition may be best studied in Grimm, *D. M.*
ch. xiii.   [2] Tac. *Germ.* c. 40.

[3] Thorr had a certain relationship to peasant life which Uhland has
brought prominently forward in his interesting and poetical *Mythus von
Thorr*. Nevertheless he belonged originally to the fighting gods. As a
god of the peasant folk he appeared later.

deity, whether we call her Nerthus, or Frigg, or Berchta, or Holda; and we find her rites surviving in popular religion from the Middle Ages down even to our own times.

One example, perhaps the most striking of which any record remains, of the appearance in the Middle Ages of a ritual observance allied to the ancient rites of Nerthus is worth quoting. The record of it is to be found in the chronicle of Rudolf, Abbot of St. Tron, a place between Liège and Louvain.[1] The ceremonial—for such we must call it—which in this passage the chronicler describes, arose out of the rivalry between the rustic population near Aachen and the weavers of the neighbourhood, and took the form of a distinctly heathen revival. Weavers have generally been noted for their piety, and not least so the weavers of the country of the Lower Rhine, who have counted among their ranks, on the one hand, some of the devoutest spirits of Catholicism, as Thomas of Kempen, and, on the other, some of the most zealous champions of the Reformed Creed. It is conceivable that the weavers of Abbot Rudolf's history combined with their attachment to Christianity no small contempt for the uncultured and half-heathen rustics who lived around. These last, who were in a numerical majority, determined to have their revenge. So in a neighbouring wood they constructed a *ship*, which they placed *on wheels*, and carried in procession from place to place. Multitudes joined the concourse, both men and women, and they proceeded with heathen

[1] The date of this chronicle is *circa* A.D. 1133. It is published by Pers, xii. 309, and is quoted by Grimm, *D. M.* i. 214.

and licentious songs and unrestrained gestures, until the
whole celebration must have assumed the aspect of a Dionysiac orgy. The weavers, willy nilly, were compelled to drag
the heathen thing about.[1] It was taken from the village
where it had first been made (Cornelimünster, near Aachen)
to Maestricht. There it was furnished with a mast and
sail, and thence dragged to Tongres, and from Tongres to
Loos. Some of the nobility favoured the movement,
which grew to the proportion of a small tumult and
could not be put down without bloodshed.

There are many other examples of rustic festivals of
a soberer kind, such as were approved by the Church. One
of these was the festival or fast of the death of Balder,
which has been preserved down to modern days in the
St. John's Days' fires, Johannisfeuer, feux de St.-Jean.
But of these I shall speak again in another chapter; for
the story of Balder's death has yet to be told. The
Midsummer fire of Balder, though the greatest among
Teutonic celebrations of this kind, is only one among
several which are preserved in the popular customs of
Teutonic and Celtic peoples. Three other seasons were
specially set apart for this sort of festivity. One was
Easter, now a Church festival and movable, originally a
stationary feast in honour of Ostara (*Sax. Eastre*), a goddess
of spring, who is scarcely distinguishable from Freyja.
Another was the first of May, now SS. Phillip and James,
in German Walpurgistag; the third was the festival of

---

[1] 'Pauper quidam rusticus ex villâ nomine Indâ hanc diabolicam ex-
cogitavit technam. Acceptâ a judicibus fiduciâ et a levibus hominibus
auxilio qui gaudent jocis et novitatibus, in proximâ silvâ navem com-
posuit, et eam rotis suppositis affigens vehibilem super terram effecit,
obtinuit quoque a potestatibus, ut injectis funibus textorum humeris ex
Indâ Aquisgranam (Aix) traheretur. . . .

'Textores interim occulto sed praecordiali gemitu deum justum judicem
super eos vindicem invocabant, qui ad hanc ignominiam eos detrudebant
. . . . Cumque haec et eorum similia secum, ut dixi, lacrymabiliter con-
quererentur concrepabant ante illud nescio cujus potius dicam, Bacchi an
Veneris, Neptuni sive Martis, sed ut verius dicam ante omnium malignorum
spirituum execrabile domicilium genera *diversorum musicorum turpia
cantica et religioni Christianae concinentium.* . . .'

is a time of new birth and of a sort of heathen baptism; to wash in May dew guards against bewitchment.[4] The Nativity of the Virgin Mary is another festival of the spring, of the anodos; the Virgin here standing in popular superstition for Persephonê or for Gerðr.

The way in which the maypole is or was honoured in our village festivals recalls to some extent the ancient tree worship, which preceded even the cult of Odhinn or of Nerthus; but the ceremonies are also specially connected with the worship of the earth goddess.

The author of the 'Anatomie of Abuses' has drawn for us a picture of the way in which Mayday Eve and May Morning were spent in the villages of England in

[1] It is hardly necessary to remind the reader that, until the change in the style, the civil year began on the 25th of March.

[2] So at least says Wuttke, *Deutsche Volksaberglaube*.

[3] Called in Germany *Freudentanz* and *Freudensprung*.

[4] Wuttke, l. c.

[5] May was also sacred to Thorr, and to the hammer of Thorr, the symbol of law. It was the time for *Folk-things*, the *Champs de Mai*, &c., the fore-runners of our *May Meetings*.

the sixteenth century; drawn it, doubtless, with an unfriendly pencil,[1] but, we may well believe, truly as to the
main details.

'They goe some to the woods and groves, some to the
hills and mountaines, when they spend the night in plea-
saunt pastime, and in the morning they return, bringing
with them birche boughes and branches of trees to deck
their assemblies withal. But their chiefest jewel they
bring thence is the maypoale, which they bring home with
great veneration as thus: they have twentie or fourtie
yoake of oxen, and everie oxe hath a sweet nosegaie of
flowers tied to the top of his hornes, and these oxen drawe
the maypoale, the *stinking idol* rather. . . . I have heard
it crediblie reported that of fourtie, three score, or an
hundred maides going to the wood, there have scarcely
the third part returned as they went.'

By the severity of this picture of the *stinking idol* and
its licentious abuses we are perhaps brought all the nearer
to the ancient rites out of which the May dances had their
rise; I mean to that primitive earth worship which begins
so far back and lasts so long. For orgiastic rites had no
small share in this primitive ritual.

In being present at such ceremonies nowadays, and in
watching the dance round the maypole — which might
rather be called a sort of rhythmic walking of interlacing
figures than an actual dance—I have had my thoughts
forcibly led to that mimic search for the lost Persephonê,
a search from side to side with lighted torches, which was
part of the dramatic celebration of the Eleusinia. The
simple music which accompanied the dances might have
been given forth by a choir of the Eumolpidæ, or by the
shepherd pipes which led the procession in the Roman
Lupercalia.

But again, to turn the picture a little, although the
midnight festival which formed part of the old Teutonic

---

[1] Stubbs, in his *Anatomie of Abuses*, 1595.

earth worship was still kept up in the 'pleasant pastimes' of Mayday Eve, yet in it we may likewise detect the germ out of which mediæval superstition was to foster its belief in the terrible Brocken dance of the *Walpurgismacht*.

Another among the customs which belong to spring time is that of dragging from place to place a *plough* upon wheels. This plough is the changed form of the ship which we have seen carrying the image of Nerthus, a form suitable to settled folk and to agricultural lives.[1] In some places where this festival of the plough takes place the young men who drag about the car compel any girl they meet (who has not previously furnished herself with a lover) to join their band. And in this custom we detect a faint shadow of ancient orgiastic rites. Shrove Tuesday is the day generally set apart in Germany for the dragging of the plough; in England it is the previous Monday, hence called *Plough Monday*.[2]

The tradition of the Wandering Jew—he is Odhinn transformed—is that he can rest one night in the year only—namely, on the night of Shrove Tuesday—and that then he rests upon a plough or upon a harrow. Shrove Tuesday is of course the day when all sins should be absolved (Shrive Tuesday); but, in addition to this notion, I cannot but see in the resting of this sinner (who is also the fierce war god) upon the plough a reminiscence, however faint, of the joyful and peaceful day when the earth goddess came round drawn in her car.

Where the image of this earth deity would once have been borne, that of the Virgin (the Marienbild) was in the Middle Ages, and is now, carried about to bless the fields.

---

[1] Our word *plough*, the German *Pflug*, is etymologically connected with the Greek πλοῦς, a sailing, or πλοῖον, a ship. Therefore *plough* probably originally meant a ship.

[2] 'They plough up the soil before any house whence they receive no reward' (Strutt, *Sports and Pastimes*, 260). This writer says that Plough Monday was the first Monday after Epiphany. My own recollections of the festival are associated with the day before Shrove Tuesday. We also read of a Fool Plough (Yule Plough?) dragged about at Christmas (p. 259).

The days set apart for this journey are the Rogation Days, corresponding, no doubt, very closely to the time of year in which Nerthus would' have appeared, bringing fruitfulness with her. During these Rogation Days, or upon Ascension Day, takes place that charming relic of old heathenism (Celtic, I should suppose, rather than German) called in England ' well-dressing.' In Brittany the choirs of the churches, headed by the priests, make (or used to make) solemn procession with flowers and chaunts to the fountain-head.[1] In England well-dressing is common chiefly in the midland counties or toward the west, in the districts which were once part of Mercia or of Strathclyde. At Lichfield well-dressing is celebrated with choral processions as in Brittany.

The task of tracing the remains of German heathenism in popular lore and popular customs is fascinating, but it is endless. We will therefore let our attention rest only on one other season beside those which have been already spoken of, the most important season of all. I mean the twelve days (*die Zwölfen*). With us this phrase ' twelve days' always means the days which follow Christmas. In Germany that is likewise the usual reckoning; but sometimes the days are all counted before Christmas, and made to end on Christmas Day. Sometimes they are the twelve days which precede the New Year (Yule)—that is to say, those extending from St. Thomas's Day till New Year's Day. Sometimes, again, they are the twelve days which follow New Year's Day. The Easter feast was in honour of Freyja or of Ostara; the Midsummer feast was in honour of Balder; but that of Midwinter, the Yule, was sacred to Odhinn, as such a season might well be to a god of storms. According to the most usual disposition of the days, therefore, this Odhinn festival of Yule fell in the very midst of the twelve days, and the season took its character from Odhinn.[2] Twelfth Day is, in Germany, dedicated to the

---

[1] Cambry, *Voyage dans le Finistère*. Ed. Souvestre.

[2] Winter and wind; an etymological significance which appears again in χειμών and χεῖμα, *hiems*, &c.

Three Kings of Cologne, and hence called *Dreikönigstag*. The Three Kings are, it is well known, supposed to be the three Magi, and their names Gaspar, Melchior, and Balthasar. Frederick Barbarossa is said to have brought their remains from Milan to Cologne.[1]

This is only a tradition, however, which the Italian historian has repeated. We have proof that the Three Kings were worshipped long before the days of Frederick,[2] and I have myself little doubt that the original Three Kings were Odhinn, Thorr, and Tyr, or, to give them their proper German names, Wuotan, Donar, Zio. This is why the Three Kings were so widely honoured in the Middle Ages, and why the superstitions which still attach to them are so many. They are still a great feature in the observances of Yule. The initials of their names, followed each by a cross (thus, G + M + B +), are placed at this season upon all the doors for a charm against evil spirits.[3] Thus may the twelve days be regarded as a season of contest between the Christian and the heathen powers, between the new creed and the old. Of old we know how Odhinn used sometimes to walk the earth, alone or in company with his brothers Hœnir and Loki; now it is Christ who is said to revisit earth at this season of the twelve days, alone or with one or more of His disciples, very often accompanied by Peter and Paul. The man who on Christmas Eve stands under an apple tree (but for this apple let our memories of an earlier belief supply *ash*) sees heaven open. At this time, too, witches dance and hold Sabbath, and the Wild Huntsman[4] goes his round. Then is all magic rife. The Wise Woman (Weise Frau) is seen at such times: she may be Frigg or Holda, for she often brings men good luck; or she may, in her evil aspect,

---

[1] Villani.

[2] They are mentioned in the *Chanson de Roland*, which is of the eleventh century, a hundred years before Frederick Barbarossa (1152-1190).

[3] Wuttke, l. c.

[4] Hackelberg. See also Chap. X.

be one of the witches. The beasts in the stall at this time speak and foretell the future. Dreams and all other signs of fate are more sought after, and they are more frequent at this season than at any other of the year. All that is dreamt in the twelve nights becomes true. And it is also said that the whole twelve days are a sort of epitome of the following twelve months; so that, whatever be the character of any individual day, fair or stormy, lucky or unlucky, of the same kind will be the corresponding month of the ensuing year. Wherefore the proverb says, 'The more fearfully the storm howls, so much the worse for the young year.' The Yule-tide storm is the last voice of Odhinn in men's ears.

THE shadow of death which we have seen in the German's outward world, his world in space, so closely surrounding all life, hemmed it in not less straitly in the world of time, even the gods themselves not being able to escape final destruction. There is a much closer relationship between Asgard and the Scandinavian nether kingdom than there is between Olympus and Hadês; so that, while among the Greeks only some few among the gods visited the lower world, and of those who went all came back victorious, having overcome death, several among the Æsir visited Hel's abode, and one conspicuous figure in their body went there not to return. Though we have already said much concerning the gloominess of the German mythology, much more remains to be said; for that mythology cannot be understood until we have passed in review the numerous images and myths of death which it contains. But we must remember, on the other hand, that the German could often win out of his saddest celebrations occasion for mirth and merriment, as an Irishman will do at a wake, and his very familiarity with sombre thoughts and images gave him a kind of desperate cheerfulness in the common affairs of life.

The very term funeral feast is, indeed, a kind of paradox: yet funeral feasts have existed among all nations. Among the Teutons not only were the private occasions of mourning turned into seasons of hilarity, but the very

funerals of the gods themselves—for some of the gods
had funerals—were so used. And this habit strikes
the key-note of much that is characteristic of Teutonic
heathenism.

In a former chapter we passed in review the principal
myths and figures whereby the Aryan races have represented to themselves the idea of death. Each one of
these is to be found in one or more shapes in the Teutonic
mythology. These people preserved all the legacy of
thought upon such matters which had been bequeathed
to them by their forefathers, and they further added
some which were their peculiar creation. The devouring
beast or dragon, the man-eating ogre, the pale Goddess of
Death with her Circê wand, the mortal river and the
mortal sea, the Bridge of Souls, the ghostly ferryman—all
these are to be found in the belief of the Teutons; all
these through the Teutons became afterwards part of the
mythology of the Middle Ages.

As the greater number of these creations are in a
certain degree familiar to us, it will not be necessary to
spend much time in pointing out their characteristics.
Rather we will let them appear in their proper places when,
in this or the other narrative, in company, as the case may
happen, of a human hero or of a god, we shall ourselves
make the journey to the Norseman's under world. But
there is a series of personifications of death which are
strange to other systems of belief beside the Teuton
system, and of which, therefore, we have had as yet no
occasion to speak. These we must first consider.

The images of mortality whereof I speak are those
which are personifications of the funeral fire, and which
therefore spring directly out of the custom of burning the
dead. We have seen how the rite of cremation very probably arose from the worship of the fire god and the
desire to commit the dead into his charge. It was, no
doubt, the sense of the special friendliness and human love
of this divinity—the Agni of the early Aryas—which

c c

induced men to entrust him with the care of the dead body rather than commit it to the care of the universal mother, the earth. But it is easy to understand that if the rite of corpse-burning had become an ancient one, and if its original meaning had become obscured by time, men's feelings toward that same Fire Divinity might come to be the very reverse of what they had once been. He might come to be for them a symbol of death, a genius of destruction, a hateful rather than a beneficent being. When the ordinary uses of fire had grown familiar through long possession, this peculiar aspect of the fire, that it was used for the consumption of the dead bodies, might still stand out in clear relief. And when the worship of the ordinary god of flame fell into abeyance, a sort of new being would rise up, who symbolised only the funeral fire. This seems to have happened among the German races, or at any rate among the Teutons of the North.

The personification of the funeral fire was Loki.[1] His name means simply fire (logi), and he was once doubtless a kind and friendly deity. Even in the Eddas he sometimes shows in this character. We read in the second chapter of the great creative trilogy who came from among the Æsir, and created man out of the stumps Ask and Embla, of how

---

[1] I have not thought it advisable, in speaking of the Norse mythology, to enter into any discussion of the views put forward upon the subject of the mythology of the Eddas by Prof. Bugge and by Dr. Bang. Anyone, however, who has read Prof. Bugge's paper will at the mention of Loki have his thoughts directed to the passage in that paper wherein the learned writer endeavours to derive Loki from the Biblical Lucifer. I have detailed elsewhere (*Trans. Roy. Soc. Lit.* vol. xii., ' The Mythology of the Eddas ') some of the chief points in which I am compelled to differ from Prof. Bugge's conclusions, and my reasons for these differences; and I hope, when the time comes, to continue the subject further. Altogether I see nothing which has yet been brought forward by Bugge which tends to shake materially the foundations of the Eddaic mythology. Nor, again, can I give much weight to the arguments by which Dr. Bang has endeavoured to prove that the whole of the Völuspá is an importation into the North from foreign sources. And in this opinion I am glad to have the support of so learned a writer as Dr. C. P. Tiele in a recent article in the *Revue de l'Hist. des Rel.* vol. ii.

From out of their assembly came there three
Mighty and merciful Æsir to ma 's home.
They found on earth, almost lifeless,
Ask and Embla, futureless.

The names of these three were Odhinn, Hœnir, and
Lodr, and Lodr is generally identified with Loki.[1] Nay,
if Loki had not once been a friendly power he could not
have been classed among the Æsir, as he generally is.

Nevertheless the more common appearances of this
being are in a precisely contrary character. In most of
his deeds he has quite forgotten his kindly office and
become an enemy to gods and men. The change which
the personification of fire underwent between the days of
Agni worship and the days of Loki worship is very remarkable, and can only be explained by the fact that the Norsemen looked with such gloomy thoughts upon the funeral
fire. Agni, the companion and friend of man, the
guardian of the house, the one who invited the gods
down to the feast, was the same who bore away the dead
man's soul from the pyre. But in this case his kindly
nature overrode his more terrible aspect. In the Norse
creed it was quite different. Loki was essentially a god of
death.

Loki is represented siding sometimes with the gods,[2]
more often with the giants.[3] He has a house in Asgard and
yet he is called a jötun.[4] There are, therefore, in reality
two Lokis. One is the As-Loki, who must once have been
friendly to men, as all the Æsir were; the other is the giant
Loki, who has a home in Giant Land. But in the account
which is preserved of Loki in the Eddas he appears almost
always as unfriendly to both gods and men. ' Loki,' says
the Younger Edda, 'never ceased to work evil among the

[1] Simrock, *Handbuch der deut. Myth.* 31; Thorpe's *Edda*, Index, &c.;
Grimm, *D. M.* i. 200.
[2] Þrymskviða, Thorr's journey to Jötunheim, &c.
[3] Völuspá, Œgisdrekka, &c., Death of Balder, Punishment of Loki,
Ragnarök, &c.
[4] Völuspá, 48, 54; see also 50.

Æsir.' Therefore the giant nature has overborne the Asa nature; but both exist in him. This duplicity of being marks him on every occasion. He had two wives, we are told. One was in Asgard, but the other was of giant kind. The name of this last was Angrboða (*Angst-bote*, pain messenger), and by her Loki begat the Fenris wolf (Fenrisûlfr), the Midgard serpent, and Hel.

Now of this family of Loki each member is a personification of death in one or other of its forms. The Fenrisûlfr, or wolf Fenrir, is a familiar image enough; he is the Cerberus of Greek mythology, the Sârameyas of Indian mythology; he is, in a word, the devouring tomb. Jörmungandr is his own brother, almost his counterpart. The name of Jörmungandr means the ravening monster; his nature as the earth serpent shows him to be nearly allied to the River of Death.[1] Angrboda is a personification of darkness and of death. We shall anon meet with her sitting at the entrance to the House of the Shades. Her daughter Hel, the very Queen of the Dead, asks the help of no commentary to explain her nature.

There are other ways in which the funeral fire came to take its place in the Teuton's eschatology, or belief concerning the way to the Land of Shades. Seeing that the dead man had to pass through the funeral fire to get there, it was natural that the place should be imagined surrounded by a circle of flame, a kind of hedge of fire. Indeed, a combination was effected between two ideas, the idea of the world-encircling Sea of Death and the notion of the hedge of fire through which men must pass to win

---

[1] Fenrir and Jörmungandr, like the man and the serpent whom Dante saw, seem to have joined their beings and then appeared apart clothed each with the other's proper nature. For while the second is recognised as the earth-girding river, the name of him is literally 'monstrous wolf.' On the other hand, Fenrir is shown by his name to be a watery being (fen); so that his name rather than Jörmungandr's is connected with the earth-girding river, which notwithstanding the other personifies. 'Fenrir' (Fenris) is, I believe, connected etymologically with the Sanskrit Panis. The Panis were water beings, perhaps originally not unlike Ahi and Vritra, the great Vedic serpents.

their way into another world. The former image came to be replaced by the latter; and men now imagined a belt of flame lying between them and Helheim. And as Jötunheim was in thought scarcely distinguishable from Helheim, the girdle of fire was made to surround that land.

We may combine this scattered imagery into one simple picture, and see thereby what an added gloom and marvel is imparted to the Teuton's world so soon as we have fully realised the shadow of death which lay upon every side of it.

The cold region of Jötunheim was all around. But to appreciate its horrors let us think of it as lying in the North, on the other side of an icy sea. We travel on and on; the air grows colder and the scene more desolate at every step. Anon, stretching its gaunt arms heavenward, we see the iron wood, which starts out in blackness from the surrounding snow. From its recesses come the dismal howls of the witches and were-wolves who have their home therein, the kindred of Fenrir and of Garm. Then on to the borders of the wintry sea—'Bold will be he who tries to cross those waters.' Its waves are made the blacker by the floes of ice which lie in it.

Somehow the region beyond, the true Land of Shades, cannot be reached in the day-time—for the same reason, doubtless, that in the belief of every people the sun himself had to travel through a twilight region before he quite withdrew from earth; for the same reason that the kingdom of Amenti, through which the soul of the Egyptian journeyed to Osiris' house, was a twilight land. For so it is here. Skirnir, the messenger of Freyr, had to journey to the Land of Shades, when he went to seek out Gerð (the winter earth), who had been carried thither.[1]

---

[1] Like Persephoné. See last chapter. This myth is, as was there said, the story of the *anodos* of Persephoné and of her marriage with Dionysus. The story of Freyja and Odhur was in the same place compared with the *kathodos* of Persephoné and the sorrows of Démétér for the loss of her daughter. This last is, of course, far more like the companion history of Isis and Osiris. There are also in classic mythology stories which in actual

He waited till it was nightfall before he set out. First, knowing that he had to ride through a hedge of flame, he had required that Freyr, the god who sent him on his message, should give him his own horse.

> Give me thy swift steed then, that he may bear me through
> The far flickering flame.

And afterwards in the beautiful passage before quoted he addressed the horse—

> Dark it grows without! Time I deem it is
> To fare over the misty ways.
> We will both return, or that all-powerful jötun
> Shall seize us both.

To mortal eyes, perhaps, this flame surrounding Jötunheimar appeared as the Aurora Borealis lighting up the wintry sky. Men gazed upon the shooting fires as they shone upon the horizon, and shuddering they thought of how their souls might need[1] one day to pass that awful barrier and wander into the dark, cheerless region beyond. According to the fancy of the moment, this hedge of flame could be pictured as surrounding all Jötunheimar, or only some particular giant's house. This latter notion is the one most commonly presented to us in the Eddas. But when this is the case the giant's house becomes *ipso facto* the House of Death, and the giant, whatever his name, is himself transformed into King Death. The mythic fire is recognised as the fire of the other world, or, as it is

form more nearly represent the myth of Freyja and Odhur than does the tale of the parting of Démêtêr and Persephonê—for example, the history of the loves and sorrows of Amor and Psyché, which again corresponds to the Indian myth of Urvasi and Pururavas (see last chapter), and in a remoter degree to that of Zeus and Semelé (see Liebricht in the *Zeitsch. f. v. Sp.* xviii. 56). All these stories, however, are less intimately connected with the chthonic divinities than are the histories of Démêtêr and Persephonê or of Freyja and Odhur.

[1] *Might need.* Whether they in reality would need to do this depended, as they deemed, upon their being elected among the band of Einheriar (heroes), who were after death translated to Valhöll.

generally called, the out-world or outward (ut-garð) fire. And when the flame is personified the proper name for the personification must be Útgarðloki, Out-world Loki.

Still onward, and we come to the very House of Death, guarded by the two dogs whom we know so well in Indian mythology. At the entrance to Helheim, at the 'eastern gate,' as it seems, sits in a cave Angrbodha, the wife of Loki and the mother of Hel; she sits there in a cave or in a *tomb*. Then past that gate we reach the court of Hel herself.

In the Eddas many, both of gods and men, make their way to these abodes of death. Some come back again; but some, both of gods and men, never return. We will take the chief among these in the order of their importance—that is, of the amount of knowledge which they impart to us concerning the other world.

The first story which I shall take leaves us even at the end still but at the entry of the tomb; but, at all events, it shows us one way by which the dead man went to another world, and it shows us, too, how the ghost might return to earth. The images which are presented to us in this lay—the Second Lay of Helgi Hundingsbane—are not those which have been dwelt upon just now, but those connected with the Bridge of Souls and the passage of the dead to Paradise by that road. Helgi, the hero of the poem, was a great warrior of the race of the Völsungs, and his wife was named Sigrûn. She was a Valkyria. She had been first betrothed against her will to Hödbrodd, prince of Svarinshaug; but not liking the match, she flew away to Helgi at Sevafjöll and married him. Helgi lived not to be old, for Dag, the brother of Sigrûn, slew him.[1] It happened that a woman slave passed one evening by

---

[1] This is in effect the story of Sigurd and of Siegfrit in the Nibelungen. Helgi seems to be the same as these two heroes. This poem proves, it seems to me, that the one-eyed Hagan of Troneg is Odhinn; for in this poem Odhinn lends Dag his spear to slay Helgi.

Helgi's tomb, and she saw his ghost ride into the mound
with many men.   Then she spake—

> Is it a delusion, that which I ween I see?
> Is it the Last Day?   Dead men ride.
> Ye goad the horses with your spurs.
> Is this the coming of heroes to earth?

And Helgi's ghost answered—

> It is not a delusion, that which you deem you see,
> Nor the world's ending,
> Although you see us our swift horses
> Goad with spurs.
> To the heroes is a home-going granted.

Then the woman went home and told Sigrûn—

> Go hence, Sigrûn, from Sevafjöll,
> If thou wouldst see the people's prince.
> The hill is open; out has come Helgi :
> Their spurs bleed.   The prince prays for thee,
> To stanch for him his bleeding wound.

Then Sigrûn went to the hill to Helgi, and spake—

> Now am I fain to find thee again,
> As Odhinn's hawks are to find their food,
> When they scent the smell of corpses and warm blood,
> Or, drenched with dew, the dawning day descry.

> Now will I kiss the lifeless king,
> Ere thou cast off thy bloody byrnie.
> Thy hair is clotted, Helgi, with sweat of death ;
> The chieftain is steeped in corpse dew.
> Ice cold are the hands of Högni's child ;
> Who shall for thee, king, the blood fine pay ?

Helgi speaks—

> Thou, Sigrûn of Sevafjöll,
> Now becomest the bane of Helgi ;
> Thou weepest, golden one, cruel tears,

Sunny one, southern one, ere to sleep thou goest;
Each one falls bloody on the hero's breast,
Ice cold, piercing, sorrow-laden.[1]

Well shall we drink a precious draught;
Together we have lost life-joy and lands.
No one shall sing o'er me a funeral song,
Though on my bosom wounds he may behold.
Here are brides in the hill hidden;
Kings' daughters beguile me, who am dead.

Sigrûn prepared a bed on the mound, and spake—

Here have I, Helgi, for thee a bed made,
A painless one, O son of Ylfing!
And I will sleep, prince, in thy arms,
As by my king while living I would lie.

Helgi—

No one now shall deem us hopeless,
Early or late in Sevafjöll;
For thou sleepest in my arms,
Fair one, Högni's daughter, .
In the hill;
For thou art quick [I dead], king's daughter!

Time it is for me to ride the ruddy road,
And my pale horse to tread the path of flight;
I to the west must go, o'er *Wind-helm's Bridge*,
Before Salgofnir[2] the heroes awakens.

Helgi rode his way, and the women went home.
Another night Sigrûn bade her maid keep watch by the
hill; and at sunset Sigrûn came to the hill, and spake—

Now would come, if he were minded,
Sigmund's son from Odhinn's hall;
Of the hero's return the hope I deem dwindles.
On the ash's boughs the eagles sit,
And to the dreaming-stead[3] all men betake them.

[1] That is to say, her tears were cruel because they pierced him like drops
of ice. A common belief this, that the tears of a wife give physical torture
to the beloved one in his grave.
[2] 'Hall-gaper,' a mythic cock; probably the cock who crows over Valhöll
before Ragnarök. See infra. [3] The place of dreams.

The maid—

> Be not so rash as to go,
> O king's daughter, to the dead men's house
> Stronger are at nightfall
> The ghosts of heroes than by day.

'Sigrûn was short-lived, from hurt and grief.   It was believed by our fore-elders that men were born again, but that they now call an old wives' tale.   He was Helgi, Hading's hero, and she Kara, Halfdan's daughter, as is sung in the lays of Kara.   She was a Valkyria.'

We have already seen Skirnir start out upon his mission to the flame-girt house in which the maiden Gerð lay imprisoned.   The house was the house of Gýmir. When Skirnir arrived there he found *fierce dogs* at the door within the hedge,[1] which protected Gerd's hall.   He rode to where a cowherd sat upon a hill, and spake to him—

> Tell me, cowherd, who on this hill sittest
> And watchest the ways,
> How may I come to speak with the fair maiden,
> Past these dogs of Gýmir?

The cowherd's answer is noticeable as expressing the nature of the place which Skirnir had come to—

> Art thou at death's door, or dead already?
> Ever shalt thou remain lacking of speech
> With Gýmir's godlike maiden.

Then Gerð heard Skirnir's voice.   She sent a maid forth to bid him enter the hall.   At first she refused to grant the prayer of Freyr, but at last she yielded to the instance of Skirnir.   The earth at length grew green before the heat of the sun's rays.

Another story which seems to enclose the same ger-

---

[1] Notice for future use the fact that Gýmir's house is surrounded by a hedge as well as by a circle of flame.

minal idea—in fact, the same nature myth as the story of Gerð—is that told in the Lay of Fiölsvith. Fiölsvith is a devil's porter like Gÿmir. The maiden whom he wards is called Menglöd.[1] By Fiölsvith's side are *two fierce dogs*, called Gifr and Geri. The lay tells how this giant porter, looking out into the night, saw approaching the lover of Menglöd, who came disguised under the name of Vind-kald.[2]

> From the *outer ward* he saw one ascending
> To the seat of the giant race.

And so he cried out—

> On the moist ways hie thee off hence;
> Here, wretch, it is no place for thee.

> What monster is it before the entrance standing,
> And hovering round the dangerous flame?

After awhile the wanderer and the warder fell into talk, and the former asked of the latter many things concerning the house before which he was standing. The significance of some of the things is quite lost to us; but there is enough left to show that there was some mysterious importance which attached to what they spoke of. Many of the names mentioned have connection with Ragnarök, the Gods' Doom;[3] and I should not wonder if all the things

---

[1] Menglöd means 'glad in a necklace' (men). It is evidently another name for Freyja, who wears the famous Brising necklace (Brisinga men). Freyja is Gerð (Chapter VII.) Menglöd may have been, like Persephonê, sometimes a Queen of Death. She is so, I think, in the Gróugaldr, where the son says to his mother (step-mother?), Gróa—

> 'A hateful snare thou, cunning one, didst lay
> .   .   .   .   .
> When thou badest me go Menglöd to meet,'

which is to be interpreted that this witch step-mother had sent her son to his death (to meet Menglöd), and afterwards finds him at her own tomb. See Gróugaldr.

[2] 'Wind cold.' I suppose as Vindkald he is the winter sun, which cannot get sight of Freyja (the germ). As Svipdag, 'Swoop of Day,' he is the summer sun. Originally this was a day myth.

[3] The things chiefly spoken of are: 1. The world tree, and what is to be

enumerated were associated with the under world. At last
it was made known that the wanderer was Svipdag, the
betrothed of Menglöd. The iron doors flew open and let
him in. This is like the 'swoop of day' after night has
passed.

These are but slight notices of the under world. More
vivid and more detailed is the history of Odhinn's descent
to Hel, to enquire of the wise Vala, whose tomb stood at
Hel's gate, touching the impending fate of Balder.[1] The
Æsir and the Asyniur (goddesses) were in council how
they might avert the evil which seemed to hang over the
beloved Balder, and which was forewarned to him in dreams.
So Odhinn determined to make this journey to the house
of Hel.[2]

Then the Allfather saddled his horse Sleipnir and rode
down to Niflhel (Mist-hell).

> He met a dog from Hel coming;
> Blood-stained it was upon its breast.
> Slaughter-seeking seemed its gullet and its lower jaw.
> It bayed and gapèd wide; .
> At the sire of magic song
> Long it howled.

> Onward he rode—the earth echoed—
> Till to the high Hel's house he came.
> Then rode the god to the eastern gate,
> Where he knew there was a Vala's grave.
> To the wise one began he his charms to chaunt,
> Till she uprose perforce, and death-like words she spake.

> 'Say, what man of men, to me unknown,
> Trouble has made for me, and my rest destroyed:
> Snow has snowed o'er me! rain has rained upon me!
> Dew has bedewed me! I have long been dead.'

its end. This will only happen at Ragnarök. 2. The golden cock Vidofnir,
which is, I imagine, the cock which crows at Ragnarök (Völuspá). 3. A
heavenly mountain, Hyfjaberg. 4. The maidens (Norns?) who sit by
Menglöd's knees.   [1] Vegtamskviða.

[2] This poem, the Vegtamskviða, is probably familiar to most readers in
the form in which it has been rendered by Grey under the title of the
'Descent of Odin.'

He answered—

I am named Vegtam, and am Valtam's son:
Tell thou me of Hel; I am from Mannheim.
For whom are the benches with rings bedecked,
And the glittering beds with gold adorned?

She spake again—

Here is for Balder the mead-cup brewed,
Over the bright beaker the cover is laid;
But all the Æsir are bereft of hope.
Perforce have I spoken; I will now be silent.

The dialogue continues upon matters relating to the approaching death of Balder, and ends thus. She said—

Not Vegtam art thou, as once I weened,
But rather Odhinn, the all-creator.

And he answered—

Thou art no Vala nor wise woman,
The mother rather of three thursar.

Who are these three thursar (giants)? Who else can they be than that mighty trinity Fenrir, Jörmungandr, and Hel? This supposed Vala must be Angrbodha, the wife of Loki.

We have now passed through all the stages which were necessary to show us the way to the Norseman's under world. We have seen the ghost come from out of the mouth of the grave, and then enter it again. We have ridden down the dark valley which leads from that grave-mouth to the nether kingdom; we have met the fierce hell-hound coming towards us, blood-stained on mouth and breast. Farther on we have ridden, and have found at the eastern gate of Mist-hell a Vala's grave, and in this Vala we have recognised the very mother of the Queen of the Dead. We shall have anon to penetrate Hel's own house.

But before we do this we will turn to a story of a

descent to the nether world, in which the characteristic features of that place are represented in rather a different guise from the ordinary one, and of which, on account of this variation, the true meaning has been obscured by time.

We have already told the incidents of this story; for it is the history of Thorr's journey to the house of Ût-gardhloki. But because we were not then concerned with the myths of death I did not stay to point out its full significance. It requires, however, no great penetration to discover that this Ûtgardhloki is nothing else than one of the forms of the god Loki, who we know generally personifies the funeral fire. The Ûtgardhloki of this myth is simply that fire expanded into a hedge of flame surrounding the world of death, and that again personified as a being, a King of Death. Ûtgardhloki is the personification of the fire which the porter in the Fiölsvinnsmâl had around him in his *outer ward*, or that 'far flickering flame' through which Skirnir rode.

It is for this reason that the journey of Thorr to Ûtgardhloki's hall is so much like the descent of Hêraklês to the house of Pluto; though there is this great difference between the two myths, that the Greek hero is always victorious, while the Norse god is by no means victorious. Each one among the feats which Thorr performs in Ûtgardhloki's palace is appropriate to the place and the occasion; each is in reality a contest with death in one of its forms, death represented by one among the children of Loki. The first attempt of Thorr was to drain a horn; but in doing that he was really draining the sea, and in fact the Sea or River of Death. Wherefore this was in reality a contest with Jörmungandr, who is the Sea or River of Death. The second was the endeavour to lift up Ûtgardhloki's cat, which turned out to be really Jörmun-gandr, the Midgard worm, himself. This scene reminds us of Hêraklês bringing Cerberus from the under world.[1]

---

[1] It should be remembered that this among the 'twelve labours' of Hêraclês is the only one known to Homer. It is evident that the descent

Cerberus corresponds most nearly to Fenrir; so we may imagine Thorr's struggle with this cat to have been originally a struggle with Fenrir. Fenrir and Jörmungandr are continually exchanging their natures.[1] Each one of these accounts has, as I imagine, been perverted from its original form by the fancy of an age to which all the deeper meaning of the myths had become obscured. But of all the three the story of the third contest has suffered the most vital change. In the story, as we now read it, a wrestling bout takes place between Thorr and an old woman called Elli—that is to say, Eld. But this is a fanciful idea; the personification of Old Age is not a notion characteristic of a period of genuine mythic creation. It is most probable that the old dame was at first Hel, the daughter of Loki (i.e. of Útgardhloki). So that the three battles of the god were with the three children of the death giant, to whose house he came. The wrestle of Thorr and Hel is exactly parallel to the fight of Héraclés and Thanatos, of which Euripides speaks.[2] This, it has been shown, is one form of an ancient legend.

The journey of Thorr to Útgardhloki is therefore the second story of the descent of one among the Æsir to the lower world, the first being the descent of Odhinn, commemorated in the Vegtamskviťa.

The third history is far more interesting and important than the other two, being the descent of Balder to Helheim. In this the gloom deepens greatly. The other two gods only went down for a time. Odhinn came back with a certain measure of success; for he had, at any rate, gained the information which he went to seek. Thorr

of the hero into the nether world was the incident in his history which was most essential to his character. We know too that Héraclés fought with Hadés himself, and 'brought grief into the realm of shades.' The struggle of Héraclés and Thanatos, which will be presently compared with one of the 'labours' of Thorr, is only another form of the same idea. Lastly, Homer knows of a fight between Héraclés and a sea monster. Therefore the three labours of the Norse god are represented by three of the oldest labours of the Greek hero.

[1] Supra, p. 388, note.   [2] *Alkestis.*

Balder went to Helheim and returned not.

The whole story is told in Snorri's Edda (Dæmisaga 49), and is briefly this. It happened that Balder the Good dreamt a heavy dream, which was told to the Æsir, whereon when they had taken the auguries the responses were that Balder was destined for death. Then went all the gods (Æsir) and goddesses (Asynior) to counsel how they might avert this calamity from gods and men. And Frigg took an oath from fire and water, from iron and all metals, from stones, from earths, and from diseases, from beasts, birds, poisons, and creeping things, that none of them would do any harm to Balder. And, when they had all given oath, it became a common pastime with the Æsir that Balder should stand in the midst of them, to serve as a mark, at whom they were wont some to hurl darts, some stones, whilst others hewed at him with swords or axes. Yet, do what they would, not one of them could harm him. And this was looked upon among the Æsir as a great honour shown to Balder.

But when Loki the son of Laufey saw this, it vexed him sore that Balder got no hurt. Wherefore he took the form of a woman and came to Fensalir, the house of Frigg. Then Frigg, when she saw the old dame, asked of her what the Æsir were doing at their meeting. And she said that they were throwing darts and stones at Balder, yet were unable to hurt him. 'Aye,' quoth Frigg, 'neither metal nor wood can hurt Balder, for I have taken an oath from all of them.'

'What,' said the dame, 'have then all things sworn to spare Balder?' 'All things,' answered Frigg, 'save a little tree which grows on the eastern side of Valhöll and is called *mistletoe*, which I thought too young and weak to ask an oath of it.'

When Loki heard this he went away, and, taking his own shape again, he cut off the mistletoe and repaired to the place where the gods were. There he found Höðer standing apart, not sharing in the sports on account of his blindness; and he went up to him and said, 'Why dost thou not also throw something at Balder?' 'Because I am blind,' said Höðer, 'and see not where Balder is, and have beside nothing to cast with.' 'Come then,' said Loki, 'do thou like the rest, and show honour to Balder by throwing this twig at him, and I will direct thine arm toward the place where he stands.'

Then Höðer took the mistletoe, and, under the guidance of Loki, darted it at Balder; and he, pierced through and through, dropped down dead. And never was seen among gods or men so fell a deed as that.

When Balder fell the Æsir were struck dumb with horror, and they were minded to lay hands on him who had done the deed, but they were obliged to stay their vengeance from respect to the Peace-stead where the deed was done. . . .

. . . . Then the Æsir took the body of Balder and bore it to the shore. There stood Balder's ship Hringhorni (the Disk of the Sun), which passed for the largest in the world. But when they would have launched it to set Balder's funeral pile thereon, they could not. Wherefore they called out of Jötunheim a giantess named Hyr‑rokkin (*Fire Smoke*),[1] who came riding upon a wolf, with serpents for reins. And as soon as she had alighted Odhinn ordered four *berserkir* to hold her steed fast, but this they could not do till they had thrown the animal upon the ground. Hyrrokkin then went to the prow of the ship, and with one push set it afloat, and with such force that fire sparkled from the rollers and the earth shook all around. Thorr, enraged at this sight, grasped his mallet, and, save for the Æsir, would have broken the woman's skull.

Then was Balder's body borne to the funeral pile, and when his wife Nanna, the daughter of Nep, saw it, her

---

[1] She is another embodiment of the funeral fire.

burning of Balder. First to name is Odhinn, with Frigg and the Valkyriur and his ravens. And Freyr came in his car yoked to the boar Gullinbursti or Slíðrugtanni. Heimdalr rode on his horse Gulltoppr, and Freyja came drawn by her cats. And many folk of the rime giants and hill giants came too. Odhinn laid on the pile the gold ring named Draupnir, which since that time has acquired the property of producing every ninth night eight rings of equal weight. Balder's horse was led to the pyre and burnt with all its trappings.

Meanwhile Odhinn had determined to send his messenger. Hermóðr to pray Hel to set Balder free from Helheim. For nine days and nine nights Hermóðr rode through valleys dark and deep, where he could see nought until he came to the river Gjöll, over which he rode by Gjöll's bridge, which was roofed with gold.[1] A maiden, called Módgudr,[2] kept that path. She enquired of him his name and kin, for she said that yestereve five bands of dead men rid over the bridge, yet did they not shake it so much as he had done. 'But,' said she, 'thou hast not death's hue on thee. Why then ridest thou here on Hel's way?'

'I ride to Hel,' answered Hermóðr, 'to seek Balder. Hast thou perchance seen him on this road of Death?'

'Balder,' answered she, 'hath ridden over Gjöll's bridge. But yonder northward lieth the way to Hel.' . . .

Hermóðhr then rode on to the palace, where he found his brother Balder filling the highest place in the hall, and in his company he passed the night. The next morning he besought Hel that she would let Balder ride home with

[1] Treasures of metal belong to the under world. So the Persian Yama is a god of treasure, and so is Ploutôn, who is not to be distinguished essentially from Ploutos (see Chap. V., also Preller, *G. M.*, Demeter, &c.)
[2] Soul's Fight.

him, assuring her how great the grief was among the gods.
Hel answered, 'It shall now be proved whether Balder be
so much loved as thou sayest. If therefore all things,
both living and lifeless, mourn for him, then shall he fare
back to the Æsir. But if *one* thing only refuse to weep,
he shall remain in Helheim.'

Then Hermôdhr rose, and Balder led him from the
hall and gave him the ring Draupnir, to give it as a
keepsake to Odhinn. Nanna sent Frigg a linen veil and
other gifts, and to Fulla a gold finger ring. Hermôôr
then rode back to Asgard and gave an account of all he
had seen and heard. And when Hermôdhr had delivered
Hel's answer, the gods sent off messengers throughout the
world to beg everything to weep, in order that Balder
might be delivered out of Helheim. All things freely
complied with this request, both men and every other
living being, and earths and stones and trees and metals,
'just as thou hast no doubt seen these things weep when
they are brought from a cold place into a hot one.' As
the messengers were returning, and deemed that their
mission had been successful, they found an old hag named
Thökk sitting in a cavern, and her they prayed to weep
Balder out of Helheim. But she said—

> Thökk will weep with dry tears
> Over Balder's bale.
> Nor quick nor dead for the carl's son care I;
> Let Hel hold her own.

The nature myth out of which this story has grown is
very easily traced. Balder is the sun; his ship Hringhorni is the sun's disk, and as it floats out into the west
it shows the picture of a burning sunset. After awhile
out of the day myth sprang the myth of the year.
Balder's Bale commemorates the death of the summer, or
the actual descent of the sun for some weeks' or months'
duration into the realm of darkness; a phenomenon
known only in Northern lands. The witch Thökk sitting

there in her cave is undoubtedly the same whom we have
met many times at the eastward entry of hell.   She was
originally simply the darkness—the same as Dökkr, dark.[1]
So Shelley sings—

> Swiftly walk over the western wave,
> Spirit of night,
> Out of the misty *eastern cave*.

Being originally no more than a nature myth, the story
of Balder's death came in time to exercise a most important influence upon men's beliefs concerning death and the
future.

In the story as it has just been related the hope which
was for a little while held out of Balder's again returning
to earth was defeated through the machinations of Loki.
But I do not fancy that it was by most people thought
that Balder stayed in Helheim for ever.   In the Völuspá,
as we shall presently see, there is the prophecy of a new
world which is to follow the destruction of the old world
at Ragnarök; and to that new world it is said Balder shall
return, to reign supreme in it.   True, it is likely that
these concluding verses of the Völupsá have been written
under the influence of Christian ideas; but even so they
point to some early foundation for the belief that Balder
would reign as the king of paradise.[2]   There must have
been some legend which made Balder, like others, sail
away to a land of the blessed beyond the western horizon
and the kingdom of shades.   It was, we may well suppose, in virtue of some such belief that there arose the
custom of burning the hero in a ship, in the same way
that Balder was burned in Hringhorni.   Before historic
times, however, the meaning of this rite had been generally
forgotten, and scattered remains of it only survived.

[1] That is to say, the name has probably been changed from Dökkr to
þökk, *thanks*, in obedience to an allegorising spirit like that which changed
Hel into Elli.
[2] See also next chapter.

Yet the very fragmentariness of these remains is the best witness we could wish for to the importance once attaching to rituals which commemorated the burial of Balder. For example, we find in historic times that men were often buried in a *ship*—that is to say, in a coffin made in the shape of a ship. Not many years ago was unearthed from a Norwegian burial ground a large vessel which had served as a resting-place for the dead. Of course to use the vessel in this way was to defeat the very purpose for which the ship had been at first called into requisition; for the body, when buried, could not sail away in the track which Balder had made. But the use of this form of coffin shows that men had once understood the meaning of laying the dead man in his ship. It shows incidentally this also: that the belief commemorated in the story of Balder's bale belongs to a date earlier than the date of this use of the ship as a coffin.

It is highly interesting to find, in the accounts of a traveller among certain Northern Teutons in the tenth century, the description of a funeral which is evidently a close copy of the funeral of Balder, with just such an omission or change of one or two features in it as may serve to show that the funeral rites in question had been long in use, and had had time to degenerate here and there into empty forms.

The account to which I refer is in the ' Kitâb el Meshâlik wa-l Memâlik' ('Book of Roads and Kingdoms') of the Arab traveller Ibn Haukal. The book was written during the tenth century: the Arab's travels, I believe, extend from A.D. 942 to 976. The people whom Ibn Haukal visited were the Russ or Varings, dwelling in the centre of Russia (near Kief), to which country they have bequeathed their name. For all that they were a Gothic and not a Slavonic race.

In his description of the funerals of these Russ, Ibn Haukal has first to tell us that the bodies even of the poor were *burned in a ship* made for that purpose; those of the slaves were abandoned to dogs and birds of prey; that the Russ were wont to burn their dead with the horses, arms, and precious metals which belonged to them; and that 'if the dead was married they burned alive with him his wives.' The women themselves desired to follow their husbands onto the pyre, thinking that they went with them to Paradise.'

The narrative then proceeds, 'As I had heard that at the deaths of their chiefs the Russ did even more than to burn them, I was anxious to see their funeral rites. I soon heard that they were going to render the last duties to a rich merchant, who had died not long before. The body of the defunct was first placed in a ditch, where it was left ten days. This interval was employed in making him new robes. His property was divided into three parts: one part passed to his family; the second was spent on his robes, and the third in the purchase of drink to be consumed at the funeral; for the Russ are very much given to strong drink, and some die with a flask in their hands. Then the family asked of the slaves of both sexes, "Which among you will die with him?" Whoever answers "I" cannot go back from his word. Generally the female slaves are those who thus devote themselves to death. In this case they asked the female slaves of the dead man which of them chose to follow him. One answered, "I." She was given into the charge of two females, who were bidden to follow her about everywhere and serve her, and who even washed her feet. This girl passed her days in pleasure, singing and drinking, while they were getting ready the garments destined for the dead and were making the other preparations for his obsequies.

'The day fixed for the funeral was Friday. I went to the bank of the stream on which was the vessel of the dead. I saw that they had drawn the ship to land, and men were engaged in fixing it upon four stakes, and had placed round it wooden statues. Onto the vessel they

---

¹ This statement is only partially confirmed by what follows.

bore a wooden platform, a mattress and cushions, covered
with a Roman material of golden cloth.   Then appeared
an old woman called the Angel of Death, who put all this
array in order.   She has the charge of getting made the
funeral garments and of the other preparations.   She, too,
kills the girl slaves who are devoted to death.   She had the
mien of a fury.

'When all was ready they went and took the dead from
his sepulchre; whence too they drew a vase of spirituous
drink, some fruits, and a lute, which had been placed beside
him.   He was clad in the robe which he had on at the
moment of his death.   I noticed that his skin was already
livid, owing to the cold of this place; otherwise he was not
at all changed.   They clad him now in drawers, trowsers,
boots and tunic, and a coat of cloth of gold; his head they
covered with a brocaded cap furred with sable, and then
they carried him to a tent which had been erected on the
ship.   He was seated on the couch and surrounded with
cushions.   Before him they placed some drink, some fruit
and odorous herbs, some bread, meat, and garlic; around
him were ranged all his weapons.   Then they brought a
dog, cut it in two, and threw the portions into the ship.
They made two horses gallop till they were covered with
sweat; then they cut them into pieces with their sabres,
and they threw the fragments onto the vessel; two oxen
were cut up, and their fragments thrown on in the same
manner.   Lastly they killed a cock and hen, which they
threw on in the same way.   Meanwhile the female slave
went and came.   I saw her enter a tent, where a man
said to her these words: "Say to thy master, I have done
this for love of thee."   Towards evening she was led to a
sort of pedestal, newly erected.   Onto this she climbed,
placing her feet in the hands of various men who stood
round, and said certain words.   Then they helped her
down.   They made her ascend a second time: she spoke
some more words, and came down again.   She mounted
a third time, and when she had said some more words

they made her descend once again. Then they gave her
a fowl, whose head she cut off, and this she threw down.
The men about cast the body into the ship. I asked my
interpreter for an explanation of what had passed. He
said, "The first time that she climbs up the pedestal she
speaks these words, 'I see my father and mother;' the
second time, 'I see all my dead relations seated;' and
the third time, 'I see my master in Paradise, who is most
fair and crowned with green, and beside him I see men
and slaves. He calls me; I will go and join him.'" Then
they brought her to the ship. She drew off two bracelets
and gave them to the woman called the Angel of Death.
She undid the two rings which she wore on her limbs and
gave them to the two slaves who attended her. Then they
made her ascend the ship, and thither she was followed by
men armed with shields and staves, who gave her a vase
of spirituous liquor. She began to sing and drink.
The interpreter said that she was bidding adieu to
those dear to her. They gave her a second cup; she
took it and began intoning a long chaunt; but the old
woman pressed her to drink and enter the tent where
her master was, and, as she hesitated, the old one
seized her by the hair and dragged her in. Thereupon
the men began to strike their staves upon their shields, to
drown the cries of the victim, fearing lest other women
slaves should be terrified thereat, which would prevent
them some day from asking to die with their masters.
At the same moment six men entered the tent, surrounded
the victim, and placed her lying beside the dead. Two
held her by the feet, two by the head; the old woman
passed a cord round her neck, and gave it to the two
remaining men who stood near, and these strangled her.
At the same moment the old woman, drawing a large
knife, struck it into the wretch's side.

'Then the nearest relative of the dead man came
forward quite naked, set fire to a fragment of wood, and
walking backwards towards the vessel, holding in one of

his hands the kindled wood and having the other hand placed behind him, set fire to the pile under the ship; then other Russ advanced, holding each a kindled staff, which they cast upon the pile. It took fire, and the ship was soon consumed with the tent, the dead man, and his woman slave. A terrible wind which had arisen stirred the fire and increased the flame.'

Not the least interesting part in Ibn Haukal's account of the Russ funeral is the incident with which it concludes. 'Hearing,' says the Arab, 'a Russ speaking to my interpreter, I asked what he said. "He says," was the answer, "that as for you Arabs, you are mad, for those who are the most dear to you and whom you honour most you place in the ground, where they will become a prey to worms; whereas with us they are burnt in an instant, and go straight to Paradise." He added, with laughter, "It is in favour to the dead that God has raised this great wind: He wished to see him come to Him the sooner." And in truth an hour had not passed before the ship was reduced to ashes.'

Observe that in the creed of these people burning is the necessary gate from earth to heaven; if a man is buried he falls a prey to worms and perishes utterly.

We see in this ritual all the concomitants of the great drama of Balder's death. The old woman who is called by Ibn Haukal the Angel of Death is certainly either Hel herself or else she is the witch Thökk (or Angrbodha), who sits at the entrance of the nether kingdom. In the death of the slave we have a poor substitute (no doubt the best attainable) for the beautiful incident of the death of Nanna, the wife of Balder. 'And when Nanna the daughter of Nep saw it' (i.e. the funeral pile prepared) 'her heart brake with grief and she too was placed upon the pyre.'[1] The theory doubtless was that the slave wife's heart too brake just when she saw her husband placed

---

[1] Edda Snorra, D. 49.

upon his bier; but, as the fact could not be made to hold
pace with the theory, the girl had to be strangled before
she was burned.

But there are some points in which the ritual has
decayed. The funeral fire lighted in the ship has here
sunk to be an unmeaning rite; for not only were these
Russ not settled by the sea—*no longer* by the sea, we may
say, for they had migrated inland from the Baltic shores
—so that there could be no drifting westward to the
setting sun, but the ship was not even launched in a river.
It was dragged up upon the bank and then made firm with
stakes before lighting. We may believe that the Russ
had carried their old custom inland when they left the
coast. The very senselessness of the rite in this its later
form bears witness to the potency of the associations which
had given it birth and of the myth out of which it sprang.

The relics of Balder's bale are not to be looked for
only in funeral rites. We have said that with the Teutons
more than with any other people the saddest occasions
seemed to exchange places with times of festivity and
joy. In festivals which lingered long after the worship
of Balder had been forgotten we can recognise the remains
of this great funeral feast of the sun god. The later
commemorations were the St. John's fires, of which something has already been said.

The celebration of Balder's bale was to some extent
confounded with a feast of a different origin, a feast held
in honour of the sun; but that the two should have thus
mingled shows that Balder's bale fires must very early
have been made occasions of festivity. These bale fires
were lighted at Midsummer, taking the moment at which
the sun began his decline to commemorate the story of the
sun's death.[1] On the same principle the Teutons chose
the time of the year's shortest days to announce the advent
of the new spring. Wherefore the same season was fixed
upon by the Church to celebrate the advent of Christ.

[1] See p. 227.

Though Balder's bale fires were at first occasions of mourning, they very early took an opposite character. The
festival still survives; it has lived on all through the
Middle Ages to our own times; only, after Christianity
supplanted heathenism, the fires, instead of being Balder's
fires, changed their name into the St. John's fires, feux
de St. Jean, Johannisfeuer, which are known in the
principal countries of Europe.

'On this day,' says a writer of the twelfth century,[1]
describing the St. John's fires, 'they carry brands and
torches for the lighting of great fires, which typify the
Saint John, who was a light and a burning fire and the
forerunner of the True Light. In some places they roll
wheels, which signifieth that, as the sun riseth to the
height of his arc and can then rise no higher, so the fame
of St. John, who was at first thought to be the Christ,
lessened; according to the testimony of his own words
when he said, "He shall increase, but I shall decrease."'
Rather a strained analogy, as one must allow; and yet if
we were to put Balder back again in the place that had
been usurped by St. John, these words would express, not
inaccurately, the place which their ancient sun-god held
in the hearts of men who were Christians but who still
kept a kindly memory for their old creed. 'Balder,' they
might have said, 'seemed to us like a Christ before we
knew Christ; but as the other increased so his fame de-
creased.' The rolling of the wheel which did really, as
this twelfth-century writer sees, typify the rolling of the
sun up to its highest arc, and its descent through heaven,
was far more appropriate to Balder than to the Scriptural
St. John the Baptist.

Not very different from this description of the twelfth
century is one of the nineteenth. It is of the St. John's
fire at Konz,[2] on the Mosel, in the year 1823. Here the

[1] Johannes Beleth, *Summa de Divinis Officiis* (circa. 1162), cap. 137,
quoted by Grimm, *D. M.* 516.
[2] Not far from Thionville, and then in French Lorraine; but a German-
speaking place then as now.

custom was that every house should furnish a bundle of
straw, which was carried to the summit of a neighbouring
hill, the Stromberg, where in the evening the men, old
and young, assembled, while the women and girls stayed
below by a stream called Burbach.   With the straw an
immense wheel was made, with a strong stake running
through the axle and standing out three feet on either
side. What remained of the straw was twisted into brands.
The mayor of Sierck gave the signal, and the wheel was
lighted, and with much shouting was then set rolling.
All threw their brands into the air. Some of the men
remained on the top; some followed the burning wheel
down the hill to the Mosel. The wheel might go out before
it reached the river; if it did not, then men augured a
good year for the vines.

In accounts such as these we are naturally brought to
think of the Eleusinian and Dionysiac festivals, or of the
mystery of Isis accompanied by a 'throwing of brands.'
Unquestionably, in the ceremony above described, there
does lurk some element of earth worship and of Dionysus
or wine-god worship, as the prediction about the vintage
testifies.   Interesting, too, is it to see in this case, as in
so many others, the *magical* element of the myth lingering
when the meaning of it has been forgotten.   Though men
have quite, or almost altogether, lost sight of the connection
between their fiery wheel and the sun, they still keep hold
on the notion that the length of time during which the
former burns will affect their vine harvest.   The length of
time during which the sun continues to give out his heat,
before he sinks into his winter sleep, of course *is* a matter
of importance.

In Finistère the feux de St. Jean present, or did present—for the writer from whom I quote[1] complains that,
even at that time, 1835, the old customs of Brittany were
rapidly on the wane—a unique sight. 'Cries of joy are

---

[1] Souvestre in his edition of Cambry's *Voyage dans le Finistère*.

heard from every side. Every promontory, every rock, every mountain, is alight. A thousand fires are burning in the open air, and from afar off you may descry the shadow-like figures moving round the fire in their dance : one might fancy it a dance of *courils.*[1] The fires are often lighted by the priests, who make processions through the villages with consecrated tapers. At St.-Jean du Doigt an angel is made to descend from the church tower, bearing a torch in his hand. He sets alight the principal fire, which burns in the churchyard. On every road you meet companies of maidens coming out to dance round the fires. They must not return until they have danced round nine of these, if they wish to be married within the twelve-month.' At Brest, again, as at the Johannisfeuer at Konz, 'people whirled round torches, to look like wheels. . . .'

'On the vigil of St. John the Baptist, commonly called Midsummer Eve,' says Strutt,[2] 'it was usual in most country places for the inhabitants, both old and young, to meet together and make merry by the side of a large fire, made in the middle of the street or in some open and convenient place, over which the younger men *frequently leapt by way of frolic,* and also exercised themselves with various sports and pastimes.' And he quotes from a rhymed English version, made in the sixteenth century, of the 'Pope's Kingdom,' by Tho. Neogeorgius, wherein the same festivities are described.

Then doth the joyful feast of John the Baptist take his turne ;
When bonfires great, with lofty flame, in every street do burne,
And younge men round about with maides doe daunce in everie
    street,
With garlands wrought of mother wort, or else of vervaine sweet.

The leaping over the flame recalls the leap of Skirnir (or of Sigurd, as we shall presently see) through the death fire. It is a sort of vaunt on the part of the youth that

---

[1] A race of fairies native in Brittany.
[2] *Sports and Pastimes.*

Loki has not yet gotten them.   At Burford, in Oxfordshire,
they used in these ceremonies of Midsummer's Day to carry
a dragon through the town, to which was added the image
of a giant.[1]   In these we see Loki and Jörmuungandr.

On popular tales, from the great epics of the German
race, the tales of Sigurd and Siegfrid downwards, the
imagery of death, drawn from the funeral. fire, has left a
peculiarly vivid impress; and in these stories, as in many
of the rites above described, the true meaning of the myth
has been forgotten, and therefore the incidents which
should have expressed that meaning exist in garbled forms,
as survivals only.   This is markedly the case with the
Völsung saga.   The story must once have been in part
at least a nature myth, being, as it is in parts, almost
identical with the story of Freyr's (or Skirnir's) ride to
Jötunheim to seek out Gerð.   In its present shape there
is this difference between it and the Gerð myth, that in the
latter the meaning of each element of the tale is brought
very plainly forward, whereas in the Völsung legend a
great portion of the meaning has been obscured by time,
so that the narrator only records incidents without understanding their special significance.   By comparison of the
two myths—not forgetting the story of the Fiölsvinnsmál,
which we spoke of above, and which furnishes, in some
matters, a link between the legends of Skirnir and Sigurd
—we can recast the history of Sigurd and Brynhild in its
original form.   We have seen how Freyr or Skirnir had
to ride through the flickering flame into the courtyard of
Gýmir, in whose house Gerð was for the time imprisoned;
and how in the Fiölsvinnsmál Svipdag had to pass through
the same circle of flame to come to Menglöd; and we
know that without question this fiery barrier is symbolical
of the funeral fire—that is, of death.[2]
Now read the description of Sigrdrifa asleep on the
hill:—

[1] Strutt, 270.   [2] Fafnismál, 42_4.

A hall is on high Hindarfjöll ;
With fire without 'tis all surrounded.
Mighty lords that palace builded
Of dire undimmed *flame.*

I know that on the fell a war maiden sleeps ;
Around her flickers the *linden's bane.*[1]
With his thorn-thrust Odhinn through her weeds has
    pierced her,
The weed of the maid who for heroes contended.

The pricking by Odhinn with a sleep thorn is really a
sending into mortal sleep; for the thorn had become an
image of death from its connection with the funeral pyre.
Therefore the death of Brynhild is doubly expressed in the
above passage. Sigurd eventually found Brynhild as he
had been directed. He rode up the Hindarfjöll and thence
into Frankland. On the fells he saw a great light, as if a
fire were burning and casting its light high up into the
sky. He found there a ' shield-burg '[2] and entered it, and
there he saw one whom he took for a warrior lying asleep
in complete armour. It was Brynhild or Sigrdrífa. Her
corselet had grown quite tight upon her body.[3] Sigurd
ripped it open, and so awoke her. After Sigurd had
plighted his faith to Brynhild he went to the court of
King Giuki, whose wife was Grimhild and his daughter
Godrûn. Grimhild gave Sigurd a draught which made
him forget his love and all his promises. He then married
Godrûn, the daughter of Giuki and Grimhild. Grimhild
now counselled her son Gunnar to woo Brynhild. Brynhild
had vowed to wed him only who could ride *over the blazing
fire* which lay around her hall. Gunnar could not make
his way through the fire; so Sigurd changed forms with
him and then rode through. The description of this flame
might stand for a description of the great Muspilli, the

[1] Fire
[2] *Skjaldborg,* which generally means an array of battle; here, perhaps,
used for some palisaded place full of slain, among which lay Brynhild.
[3] Sigrdrífumal, Introd. See also Sigurþakv. Ffnb. I., 16.

earth-consuming fire.[1] 'Sigurd rode, having in his hand
his sword Gram; his horse Grani plunged forward, feeling
the spur. Now was there a great noise, as it says—

> The fire began to rage, the earth to shake;
> The flame rose high as heaven itself;
> Few of the people's princes ventured forth
> The fire to ride through or to overleap.

> Sigurd with his sword compelled Grani,
> And the fire quenched before the hero;
> The flame was dimmed before the glory-lover,
> On the bright saddle that Rök[2] had known.'

Brynhild was compelled to receive him, but Sigurd
gave himself the name of Gunnar. When the marriage
bed was prepared, he laid his sword between himself and
the bride, and when Brynhild asked why he did this he
answered that he had been enjoined so to do. But they
exchanged rings. Then Sigurd rode back through the
fire, and he and Gunnar took their right forms again.

Notable are the likenesses and the points of difference
between this story and the Nibelungen-Lied. In the latter
Siegfried, who has made himself Gunther's *man* for love
of Criemhild, sister to Gunther, performs an office for the
bridegroom almost the same as that which Sigurd did for
Gunnar. That is to say, he overcomes the unwillingness
of Brunhild to receive the embraces of her husband, and
then he gives place to Gunther without dishonouring his
bed. But there is nothing said of the feat of riding through
the flame. For at the time at which the Nibelungen was
composed all shadow of meaning had been taken away
from this incident.

Yet the same incident still lingers on in popular lore,
though in a form different from that which it wears in the
Norse poems, and in one which without some previous
explanation would be scarcely recognisable.

---

[1] See infra.
[2] Rök is Doom. The meaning of this passage is not, however, quite
clear to me.

We owe to the researches of Grimm the proof that some among the common thorn trees were by the Teuton races so intimately associated with their use for lighting fires that they received names from this use.[1] They were sufficiently identified as 'burning plants.' The Gothic word *aihvatundi*, which generally means simply white-thorn, has etymologically the signification of the 'burner.' If, then, the ideas of thorn and fire were so intimately associated in the German's mind, it is not wonderful that a hedge of fire should sometimes have been replaced by a hedge of thorn. This we find has happened in many myths. The circle of flame which in earlier legends was seen surrounding the house of death becomes converted, in later German *märchen*, into a thorn hedge. When this transformation has taken place the true meaning of the hedge has, however, been forgotten. It is by this process of change that even in the Brynhild myth the thorn makes its appearance. The maiden was pricked by Odhinn with a sleep thorn. This means that she was sent to the house of death. Accordingly, when we next see her on the Hindarfjöll, she is lying on a mound surrounded by a circle of fire.

This story reappears in a household guise which is familiar enough to us. The maiden whom we call the Sleeping Beauty,[2] and the Germans *Dornröschen, Thorn-rose Bud*, harmless and childlike as she seems, is in reality no other than the Valkyria of the North, Brynhild herself. This we easily see by examining the details of her history.

---

[1] *Ueber das Verbrennen der Leichen.*

[2] Grimm, *Kinder- u. Haus-Mährchen.* In the same mediæval poem, *Notre Dame Ste. Marie,* from which, in Chap. II., I quoted a passage which showed the vitality of the belief in the *parent tree* and in descent from a tree, we find another incident which seems to have arisen in the same way as the hedge of briar in Dornröschen. Part of this history relates how the mother of St. Anne, while a virgin, became with child only by smelling the fruit of the life-giving tree (see Chap. II. p. 64). She was accused of immorality by the Jews, and to prove her innocence she consented to walk through the fire. As she passed, the flames *turned into roses.*

E E

The angry fairy, who had not been invited to the christening, foretold that when the Rose Maiden had reached her fifteenth birthday she would be pricked with a spindle and fall down dead; but this terrible sentence the other fairies were able to commute to a sleep of one hundred years. All happened as it was foretold, although, to escape from fate, the king had, after the decree of the fairies, ordered every spinning-wheel throughout the land to be destroyed. The king and queen chanced to go out upon the very day on which the maiden attained her fifteenth year, and she, wandering about alone, came to an unused tower of the castle, and there found an old dame sitting alone and spinning. This dame is Fate.[1] 'What are you doing there?' said the king's daughter. 'Spinning,' said the old crone, and nodded her head. 'How prettily the wheel turns round.' Then the princess took the wheel and began to spin; but scarcely had she done so than the prophecy was fulfilled. She pricked her hand and fell down in a deep sleep. And all the court fell asleep too, and at last a thick thorn hedge grew up about the palace and quite hid it from view. But still the tale lived on in the neighbourhood of how there was a beautiful maiden sleeping behind the hedge. At last, when her fate was accomplished, came the prince, the Sigurd of this fairy story, and broke through the hedge of thorn and kissed the maiden back into life.

So much for the visits of gods and men to the world of death. We have now to look on a still more awful picture, which we might call the visit of the World of Death to Mannheimar and Asgard. This is, in fact, the long-foreseen, long vainly guarded against *Last Day*, when the powers of darkness and chaos are to rise against order and light, and bring destruction on the whole earth.

[1] But she is also the same as Angrbodha. See what was said in Chap. VI. of the spinning of Circé and of Calypso.

§ 2. *Ragnarök.*

A gaping gap and nowhere grass. This is the primal condition of things whereof the Edda speaks; or of *no-*things, for the gaping gap (Ginnungagap) is a translation almost exactly of the Greek chaos,[1] and means but void space. But imagination cannot dwell with mere negation, so that the picture of Ginnungagap actually given us is of a deep pit in the midst of which welled up, 'at once and ever,' a mighty spring called Hvergelmir. From Hvergelmir flowed many streams, which rolled venom in their course, and anon these hardened into ice, and the vapour which rose from them hardened into rime. Thus on one side of Hvergelmir were peaks of snow and ice; but on the other side was a fiery region called Mûspell's-heim, old as the great gap itself, and old as Niflhel (Mist-hell), which lay beneath the earth. This Mûspell's-heim was a land too glowing to be entered by any save those who were native there. 'He who sits on the land's end to guard Mûspell's-heim is called Surtr (Swart). He bears a flaming sword in his hand, and one day he shall come forth to fight and vanquish all the gods, and consume the world with fire.'[2]

Fire and ice, which are thus shown as earlier than the ordered world, were destined to outlive that world, and be the chief agents in its destruction. Fire and cold were to the Norseman the two great symbols of death—one the funeral fire through which men passed to the other world, and the other the chill of the tomb. It was from the meeting of the heated air from Mûspell's-heim with the icy vapour from Hvergelmir that the giant race came into being; and that *swart* god Surtr, who was the leader of the sons of Mûspell, was himself a king of death. In the account of Ragnarök we see ranged under the leadership

---

[1] χάω, aor. ἔχαδον, to gape. Thus Simrock derives 'ginnung.' Vigfusson, however, prefers to connect it with the A. S. *beginnan*, Eng. *begin*. Vigfusson and Cleasby's *Icl. Dict.* s. v. *ginn.*

[2] Edda Snorra, 4.

Three cocks, it is said, are to proclaim to the world the dawning of the Last Day: over the Æsir shall crow the gold-bright Gullinkambi;[3] in the bird wood over Mannheimr, a bright red cock; and beneath the earth, to rouse the troops of ghosts, a cock of sooty red. When he hears these, the giantesses' watch, the eagle, makes reply.[4]

> There on a hill sat, and his harp struck,
> The giantesses' watch, glad Egdir.[5]
> Before him crowed, in the bird wood,
> The blood red cock, Fiallar called.

The giant race rejoices and the central tree takes fire. Heimdal, who had been set to guard the rainbow, now blows loud his gjallar-horn[6] to warn the gods that danger is near; for in truth Surtr is hastening with his fiery bands from Mûspell's home towards the Æsirs' bridge. Then the gods take counsel together, and ride down to meet the foe on Vigrid's plain. Odhinn consults Mim's head. Can the danger yet be averted? Time is drawing to an end.

[1] Curiously enough, the same tradition of the awful winter which was to herald the Last Day existed among the Persians.
[3] Völuspá, 46 (Lüning).   [3] Gold-combed.
[4] Völuspá, 34.   [5] The storm eagle.
[6] Loud-sounding horn. Heimdal is a kind of Memnon.

Yggdrasill trembles ; though the ash still stands,
Yet groans that ancient tree.   The jötun [1] is loosened ;
Loud bowls Garm [2] from the Gnûpa cave ;
The fetter breaks and the wolf [3] runs free.[4]

Now from the east comes sailing a ship; Hrym (Rime) steers it, and all the frost giants are within.   Another ship, Naglfar, made of the nails of dead men, brings the troops of ghosts, and that Loki steers.[5]   Surtr rides over Ashrû, which takes fire beneath his tread and is burnt up ; men tread hell's way, and heaven itself is cloven in twain.

Surt from the south fares, the giant with the sword ;
The gods' sun shines, reflected from his shield.
Rocks are shaken, and giantesses totter.
Heroes fare to hell, and heaven is cleft atwain.[6]

The opposing powers meet in middle earth.   On the one side are Odhinn with the other Æsir and the Einheriar—that is to say, the heroes who have been taken to Valhöll—on the other side are the giants and the ghosts with Loki and his progeny, and with Surtr and his band of fire.   The field of battle is Vigrid's plain.

How fares it with the Æsir ? how with the Alfar ?
Jötunheim roars ; the Æsir come to council ;
And the dwarfs are moaning before their stony doors.
Know ye what that betokens ? [7]

The three great combats of Ragnarök are between Odhinn and the wolf Fenrir, between Thorr and the Midgard serpent, and between Freyr and Surtr.

---

[1] Loki.
[2] Garm, a hound who will devour the moon, and who is in nature comparable to Fenrir.
[3] Fenrir.   [4] Völ. 48 (Lüning).
[5] The two Eddas give different accounts of the sailing of Naglfar. The Younger Edda confuses this ship with the one steered by Hrim, the King of Frost Giants, the power of cold.
[6] Völ. 51   [7] Ibid. 52.

> Now arises Hlin's second grief,
> When Odhinn goes with the wolf to fight
> And the bright slayer of Beli with Surt.
> Then shall Frigg's beloved one fall.[1]

Hlin is Frigg; the bright slayer of Beli is Freyr. In each of these battles there is a fitness. Fenrir is the type not so much of destruction as of emptiness and the wide mouth of the tomb, and so he is the natural antagonist of Odhinn, the fount of all existence. Thorr is a kind of sun god, analogous to Apollo or Hèraclès, and like them he combats the great sea or river serpent. Still more appropriate is it that Freyr, god of the spring-time and of the newness of life, should be opposed to Surt, the god of death.[2] 'Freyr,' says the Younger Edda, 'would have been victorious had he not given away his sword to Skirnir what time he was a-wooing Gerð;' and the nature myth underlying this saying is not difficult to interpret. To these three combats recorded in the Völuspá the Younger Edda adds a fourth—namely, of Tyr with Garm—and in this instance, as in so many others, Tyr is but a pale shadow of Odhinn, for Garm cannot be essentially different from Fenrir.

When Odhinn has been killed by Fenrir he is revenged by Vidar, who strikes his sword into the heart of the wolf. Thorr kills Jörmungandr; but, suffocated by the dragon's poisonous breath, he recoils nine paces and falls dead. Tyr and Garm slay one another. Last of all Loki and Heimdall fight; each kills the other. And now Death (Surtr) stalks unhindered over earth and, spreading flame on every side, consumes it all.

> The sun darkens; the earth sinks in the sea.
> From heaven fall the bright stars.
> The fire-wind storms round the all-nourishing tree;
> The flame assails high heaven itself.[3]

---

[1] Völ. 53.

[2] Surtr is scarcely to be distinguished from Loki; each of them conducts the sons of Múspell (Völ. 50; Edda Snorra, 4).   [3] Völ. 56.

The original myth of Ragnarök perhaps ended here, drawing a veil over all things, plunging the earth again into darkness, as out of darkness it had emerged. As the old proverb said, 'Few can see farther forth than when Odhinn meets the wolf.' But the Eddas do pass beyond this picture, and, influenced thereto perhaps by Christianity, they lift the veil again upon a new world, which rises out of the ocean of chaos, peopled by a new race of mankind and a younger generation of Æsir. In a passage of the Völuspá, of unrivalled beauty, we are told how the prophetess, with an eye which pierces beyond Ragnarök,[1]

> Sees arise, a second time,
> Earth from ocean, green again;
> Waters fall once more; the eagle flies over,
> And from the fell fishes for his prey.

> The Æsir come together on Ida's plain;
> Of the earth-encircler, the mighty one, they speak.
> Then to the mind are brought ancient words[2]
> And the runes by Fimbultyr[3] found.

> Then will once more the wondrous
> Golden tablets in the grass be found,
> Which in the ancient days the Æsir had,
> The folk-ruling gods, and Fiolnir's race.

> Unsown shall the fields bear fruit.
> Evil shall depart, Balder come back again;
> In Hropt's[4] high hall dwell Balder and Höder,
> The happy gods.

> . . . . . .

> A hall I see brighter than the sun,
> With gold adorned, on Gimil;
> There shall noble princes dwell,
> And without end the earth possess.

> Then rides the Mighty One, to the gods' doom going,
> The Strong One from above who all things governs.
> He strifes shall stay and dooms shall utter,
> Holiness establish which shall ever be.

---

[1] Völ. 57 sqq.   [2] Or perhaps 'deeds of might.'
[3] The great Tyr, i.e. the great god.   [4] Odhinn's.

Yet even now *all* is not well[1]—

> Then comes the dark Dragon[2] flying,
> The serpent from below, from Niflhel.
> Nidhögg bears upon his wings that fly
> Earth's fields over,
> A corpse. . . .

Nidhhög, serpent of death, is still not dead. Is, then, the old course of life and death to be repeated for ever? We cannot say.

The impression of this great myth remained in Germany, but it was in Christian times overshadowed by other more distinctly Biblical pictures of the Day of Judgment. Nevertheless some of the names and incidents were preserved. Ragnarök was by the Germans called Muspilli. This word, in the sense of the fire of doom, has been preserved in many different dialects of the German language, notably in Saxon and in Bavarian.

We have a long poem in Bavarian bearing the name Muspilli. The personages of the poem have undergone the same kind of transformation which turned Balder into St. John the Baptist; but the character of the old battle and the combats recorded in it are to a great extent the same as those of the Eddaic Ragnarök. The place of Loki is taken by the old fiend; that of Surtr is taken by Antichrist, with whom fights Elias, a veritable sun god, though not a Northern one.[3]

'This have I heard the wise ones declare. Elias shall

---

[1] Völ. 64.

[2] *Drrki*, an unusual word, the presence of which affords one reason for supposing this passage of late insertion.

[3] In Greek popular tradition the deeds of the sun god (Apollo, Hélios) are transferred to Elias. The chief motive for the choice of this Old Testament prophet lies in the likeness of his name to that of Hélios. Besides that Elias drives in a chariot up to heaven. I take Elias here to be Freyr; Simrock, however, says he must be Thorr (l. c. p. 130; see also Grimm, s. v. *Elias*). Elias is undoubtedly the thunderer, and has a chariot. Still Antichrist must be Surtr, the antagonist of Freyr.

strive with Antichrist. The *wolf* is prepared; a battle there shall be. Mighty the combat; mighty the reward. Elias strives for everlasting life; of the righteous will he the kingdom establish; wherefore all heavenly powers to his help shall come. Antichrist upholds the old fiend, Satan. . . .' Both Antichrist and Elias will fall. The blood of the latter is to set the world afire. 'The hills burn; no tree in all the world remains. The seas dry up; the heaven is consumed in flame. The moon falls from heaven; Mittelgard burns. No rock stands firm; the day of vengeance is at hand. . . .'

We might fairly say that the old heathen hell or Helheim lived on in men's belief in the form of purgatory; while the gloomy thought of Catholicism added a hell which was infinitely more terrible than Helheim. Purgatory formed a middle term, which helped men to measure the horrors of eternal punishment. But, as a fact, it happened that the gloomy teaching of the Church overreached itself; the most terrible picture was beyond the capacity of imagination, and men recoiled from it and kept their eyes fixed upon purgatory. I doubt if the notion of eternal punishment was really very often present to men's thoughts in the Middle Ages; for we find that the indulgences were always offered in the profession of saving men from a longer durance in purgatory; they were offered even to the living on that plea; whereas it might have been supposed that men's first thought would have been how to escape the place of eternal pain. We find too—a thing most significant—that mediæval legend is full of visions of purgatory; but that, before the time of Dante, we hear little of visions of hell.

It is in the purgatory legends, therefore, that we must search, if we wish to discover traces of the beliefs of heathenism touching the nether world in the Middle Ages. And it may be added that it is in visions of journeys to the earthly Paradise that we must look for like information concerning the survival of the old heathen Paradise. We do find many traces of both these orders of belief. It is certain that the essential features of the heathen underworld reappear in the Christian purgatory legends; but it is not so easy to say that these have been handed down directly from the beliefs of *German* heathenism. Many images taken from classic antiquity, and many drawn from the Bible, are to be found mingled in the picture. Nevertheless there are some elements which are especially characteristic of German thought, as we shall presently see.

At first the visions are meagre in details, because, as I suppose, the marriage between Christian and heathen belief was not yet completed; gradually they expand in variety, until they reach their perfect form in the vision of the Florentine.

The heathen belief in hell cannot be kept altogether apart from the belief in heaven; and no more can the purgatory legends be kept quite apart from those of the Earthly Paradise. Nevertheless we must leave to speak of the latter in any detail until the next chapter. We shall in that chapter see more fully the reasons which made Ireland (the most western island known to mediæval Europe) a home for all myths connected with the future of the soul. We shall see how that the great Middle Age legend of the Earthly Paradise was the legend of the voyage of St. Brandan, an Irish monk. The great Middle Age legend of purgatory was that of the purgatory of St. Patrick; and of the lesser visions which prepared the way for the myth of St. Patrick's purgatory, or for the still more awful vision of Dante, a very large number indeed had their origin in Ireland.

One of the earliest visions of the other world vouchsafed to a Christian monk was that of St. Fursey, an Irish monk, said to have been the nephew of St. Brandan; his story is mentioned by Bæda, and reported at length in the 'Acta Sanctorum.'[1]

---

[1] *Acta SS. Jan.* ii. 36.

Once it happened that Fursey was sick nigh to death. He was being borne back to his monastery, wishing to die there. Upon the journey they began to sing a vesper hymn, and suddenly while he was singing a darkness seemed to surround him; he felt four hands placed beneath him to lift up his body, and he could discern that four white wings bore him along. As he grew more accustomed to the darkness he saw that two angels were carrying him, and that before them went a third, armed with a white shield and flaming sword. The angels, as they flew, sweetly chaunted 'Ibunt sancti de virtute in virtutem; videbitur Deus deorum in Sion;'[1] and he heard the choir of angels answering in song from above. This was all he knew. Another time the same two angels bare him to the mouth of hell, where he saw nothing but heard the howling of demons. Afterwards he saw the four fires of purgatory, at the four corners of the earth.

There is scarcely any link, saving the fact that the vision was seen in Ireland, which connects this story with the older notions of heathen mythology. It is pure Christian throughout, and of great beauty in its simplicity. Yet may we not say that the two white-winged angels of this vision are not greatly different from those other two, Hypnos and Thanatos, who bore Sarpedon to his tomb in Lycia?[2] who in their turn only present in a fairer form the belief in the two dogs, 'the four-eyed guardians of the path, guardians of men.'

Another vision recorded by Bæda is the vision of Drihthelm, a Northumbrian monk. This story too came from Ireland.[3] First we have the appearance of the *dark valley* which we know so well in all visions of the under

---

[1] Ps. lxxxii. 8, Vulg.

[2] *Il.* xvi. 681, &c.; see also Chap. VI.

[3] See Wright, *St. Patrick's Purgatory*, p. 18. The story was said to have been told by Drihthelm to Hæmgils, a monk of Ireland, and by him to Bæda. Wright says, 'The vision of Drihthelm, like that of Furseus, was the subject of a homily in the Saxon Church, of which a copy is preserved in a MS. of the public library' (University Library) 'of Cambridge, Ti, 133.'

ice. This combination of heat and cold is
Norse belief, which placed hell in the Nort
Loki, the god of fire, come from icy Jötunhe
the swart King of Death, fare from Mûs
jötuns themselves were born of the mingli
ice.[1] St. Brandan found hell in the Nort
for his sight of purgatory travelled north-e
is in accord with the tradition of Norse m
the end of the valley of heat and cold Drih
the mouth of a pit from which arose an into
and thence came a wailing and a laughter
devils dragging souls into the pit. In both
as in almost all which follow, purgatory is im
earth, but hell *beneath* it. The latter is in a
far down, of which the visionary sees the
Purgatory we might liken to Jötunheimar,
heimar.

In the vision of Charles the Fat, Kin
which is a couple of centuries at least late
Drihthelm,[2] more details have grown into
the other world, as, for instance, a labyrint
death, along which the soul, like Theseus in
labyrinth, must guide itself by a thread. In
Emperor saw giants, serpents, rivers of molt

---

[1] Edda Snorra, 5.
[2] It was first published by William of Malmesbury
be no earlier than the twelfth century. Charles ascend
884.

many pits in which the wicked were punished; but there is nothing very distinctive in the picture.

The great era for the record of journeys to the land of shades was the twelfth century, and in these all the belongings of purgatory and of hell which we have become familiar with from studying mediæval art or from reading Dante begin to appear. There are at least half a dozen accounts, more or less detailed, of visions of purgatory; and these culminate in the legend of Henry of Saltrey touching the visit of a certain knight to St. Patrick's Purgatory in Lough Derg, Ireland. From the tenth to the fourteenth century constitutes an important era in the history of Catholicism; for during that time the conceptions both of this world and of the next grow steadily darker, until the mythology of that age is consummated in the 'Divine Comedy.' From the time of Henry of Saltrey to the time of Dante (1153–1300) the ruling influence which moulded the popular conception of the nether world is to be looked for in the legend of St. Patrick's Purgatory. There is moreover one point of marked difference between this narrative and the purgatory legends which preceded it. The earlier stories were founded on mere visions; the spirit was believed to have been snatched away during an illness of the visionary or in his sleep. But the legend of Henry of Saltrey relates the descent of a living man. This man was Sir Owayne, who went down in the body, remained, like Dante, in the nether kingdom during *one night*, and returned unscathed the following day. There can be no question that the ground ideas which went to the shaping of the 'Comedy' are to be traced to the legend of Owayne Miles.

The idea of the descent of the living man is a very important element in the belief, because this descent itself is recognised as a sort of expiatory act. Wherefore Sir Owayne is not in the place so much of one who (as in a vision) sees the punishments of others, as of one who shares in those punishments. He has, in fact, actually been to

the nether world—in every sense—just as Odysseus in the
earlier legend concerning him must have been imagined
actually undergoing death and not merely visiting Hades'
kingdom.   Such is the idea which lies concealed in the
notion of St. Patrick's purgatory and in the promise
which Jesus made to the saint that this purgatory should
be for anyone to go down into who would, and whosoever
dared to go there it should be for him as if he had passed
through purgatory after death.

> 'What mon,' he sayde, 'that wylle bereyn wende,
>   And dwelle theryn a day and a nygth
>   And holde his bylve and rygth,
>
>   .   .   .   .
>
>   Whether he be sqwyer or knave,
>   Other purgatorye shalle be non have.'[1]

The journey of Owayne, therefore, may fairly be compared with journeys of the old Norse heroes and gods to
the nether world, such as those which we traced in the
earlier part of this chapter.

The purgatory of St. Patrick received its name because
the entrance to it had been revealed by Christ to St. Patrick,
with that promise attached which I have just quoted. The
saint built a monastery about the entrance, and secured
the way with a strong iron gate. One day came the knight
Owayne and obtained leave for penance' sake to make the
journey into that purgatory. The door which the prior
opened for him led to the long dark Valley of Death, and
at 'the deep ditch's end' Owayne emerged from pitch
darkness to a sort of twilight. This dim region, which we
might call the land of the setting sun, was the fore-court
to the place of punishment. It corresponds well enough
to the limbo in which Dante met the poets and philosophers
of Greece and Rome; as these lived in a 'blind life' bereft
of hope, so was the first place to which Owayne came a

---

[1] *Owayne Miles*, Cotton MS. Calig. A. ii. f. 89. See *St. Patrick's Purgatory*, p. 66. This is a metrical version of the legend of Henry of Saltrey.

desert, a 'wildernesse, for ther grewe nother tre ner gresse.'
And, somewhat as Dante met in limbo the comrades of
Virgil, did Owayne meet in this place fifteen men in white
garments, who warned him of all that he would have to
undergo. After that there broke upon the knight's ears
the *din* of hell, which, hinted at long before in the names
of the infernal rivers *Côcytus* and *Gjöll*, became from this
time forth a very conspicuous feature in the mediæval
visions of the under world. We know how that din broke
upon the ears of the Florentine.

> Diverse lingue, orribili favelle,
> Parole di dolore, accenti d' ira,
> Voci alte e fioche, e suon di man con elle,
> Facevano un tumulto, il qual s' aggira
> Sempre in quell' aria, senza tempo tinta,
> Come la rena quando il turbo spira.

In Owayne's case it is

> As alle the layte [1] and alle the thonder
> That ever was herde heven under,
> And as alle the tree and alle the stones
> Shulde smyte togedyr rygth at oones.

And now farther on into the region of Jötunheim; for
it became presently 'derke and wonther colde,' where a
man

> Hadde he never so mony clothes on
> But he wolde be colde as ony stone.

Anon the fiends led him into another field of punishment,
where the pains were all from burning fire and where were
many pits full of molten metal, in which men stood. Some
were in up to the chin, some to the paps, some to the
middle, some only to the knees. This imagery too has
been of service to Dante.[2] The journey still continued
till the knight reached the mouth of hell. He came, says
the narrative, to a great water, broad and black as pitch.

[1] Lightning.
[2] As in his description of the River of Blood, *Inferno*, canto xii.

> Over the *water* a *brygge* there was,
> Forsoothe kenere than ony glasse:
> Hyt was narrowe and hit was hyge.

And that made the bourne of his journey in that direction. Afterwards he had a sight of Paradise.

Contemporary with this history of Sir Owayne is the vision of Tundale, also an Irishman and a monk. This is not a journey, but a vision. The same concomitants to the orthodox under-world appear here—a dark valley, a stinking *river*, and a *lake*, and over these a *bridge*. One side of the valley was burning, the other side frozen. In this case, moreover, there was a windy place which was a kind of fore-court to purgatory, and which in a certain sense corresponds to the second circle of Dante's hell, where the souls of carnal sinners are whirled round in a perpetual storm of wind and hail.[1]

Dante once more brought hell, and with it the notion of eternal punishment, prominently before men's eyes. But in doing this he had considerably to lighten the colours in which purgatory had been depicted by other hands. For all the purposes which concern our enquiry—that is, for everything which concerns the picture of the under-world presented to the thoughts of men—the train of association runs as we have traced it, from the heathen Helheim to the mediæval purgatory and from that to the hell of Dante. I have said that in this matter the connection between German heathenism and Christianity is not very close; but yet in certain points it has been clearly traceable.

CHAPTER IX.

THE EARTHLY PARADISE.

WHEN Christianity drew a curtain in front of the past creeds of heathen Europe, a veil through which many an old belief was left still faintly visible, she succeeded more than with most things in blotting out the images which in former days had gathered round the idea of a future state. It is as if the new religion were content to leave this world under much the same governance as before, provided only she were secured the undisputed possession of the world beyond the grave. So the heathen gods were not altogether ousted from their seats. The cloak of Odhinn—that blue mantle, the air, of which the sagas tell us—fell upon the shoulders of St. Martin; his sword descended to St. Michael or St. George : Elias or Nicholas drove the chariot of Hélios or wielded the thunders of Thorr.[1] They changed their names, but not their characters, passing for awhile behind the scene to be refurnished for fresh parts : just as when the breath of the new creed blew over the fields, the old familiar plants and flowers died down—Apollo's narcissus, Aphrodité's lilies, Njord's glove, or Freyja's fern—to grow up again as the flowers of Mary, Our Lady's hand, the Virgin's hair.[2] But it was different with the beliefs which passed beyond this life. The whole doctrine of a future state, which for the European races had formerly belonged to the region of languid half-belief,[3] now suddenly became a stern reality.

[1] Wuttke, *Deutsche Volksaberglaube*, p. 19, and Grimm, *Deut. Myth.* pp. 127, 946, and 68 n., 371, 4th ed. Elias, id. p. 144.

[2] Cf. Johannis Bauhini, *De plantis a divis sanctisve nomina habentibus*, Basiliæ, 1521. Cf. also Grimm, *D. M.* 4th ed. p. 184 (Balders brâr).

[3] *European races.* Among the Indo-European nationalities the Persians

This doctrine grew greater while earthly things grew less, until at last it seemed to take a complete hold upon the imagination, and to gather round itself all that was greatest in the poetical conception of the time. Then, from having been so impressive, the idea of eternity became familiar by constant use. At last it took, in the hands of dull unimaginative men, a ghastly prosaic character, whereby we see the infinities of pleasure and pain, of happiness or woe, mapped out and measured in the scales.

It is on this account not easy to trace back the belief of Northern and Western Europe on such matters to that state in which it was while yet untouched by the doctrines of Christianity. Beside the dreadful earnestness of the two great pictures of Catholic mythology, the mediæval heaven, and the mediæval hell, the less obtrusive notions of earlier days fell into the background. The older idea of a future state was not of a place for rewards or punishments so much as for a quiet resting after the toils of life, as the sun rests at the end of day. If such a creed were to live on at all in the Middle Ages, it must do so in defiance of the dominant religion. It must survive in virtue of the Old Adam of pagan days, not yet rooted out. It must find its home in the breasts of those who had not really been won over to the dominant creed; who resented as something new and intrusive the presence of a restraining moral code, or who would fain believe that the neglected gods were not really dead; that they were, peradventure, asleep, or upon a journey and had not for ever given up their rule. It was through such influences as these that the pagan notions concerning a future state survived in the mediæval pictures of an Earthly Paradise. This was a home of sensuous ease, unblessed perhaps with the keenest enjoyments of life, but untouched also with the fear by which these pleasures are always attended—that they will

raised the doctrine of heaven and hell to supreme importance, and in so doing greatly, though indirectly, affected the creed of Christendom.

soon be snatched away. The saints and confessors might have their heaven and welcome. Their rapturous holy joys were not suited to the heroes of chivalry. There must therefore be, men thought, another home set apart for them, for Arthur and his knights, for Charlemagne and his paladins; where, untroubled by turbulent emotions, they should enjoy the fruit of their labours in a perpetual calm.

Catholicism of course made some concession to this spirit. A way for doing this was opened by the Biblical account of the garden of Eden; for though the Mosaic record says that man was turned out of the garden, it says nothing about the destruction of Paradise. And accordingly we find lay and clerical writers alike speculating upon the nature of this place and the road by which it was to be reached : and presently we find accounts of both real and mythical voyages to the east in search of the desired land. But there still remained a question in dispute between orthodoxy and ancient heathenism. The former naturally insisted upon the fact that Eden was in the east, but heathenism had an obstinate prejudice that its Paradise lay westward ; so on this point there was a battle between the two faiths.

In truth, we find that, like the needle when a neighbouring magnet has been withdrawn, popular belief on the matter of the Earthly Paradise, when not subject to the influence of ecclesiastical teaching, tends constantly to veer round from the orthodox tradition. And this fact would alone be enough to convince us that the myth which we traced in the story of the voyage of Odysseus has had its echo in other lands. But we are not left to this inferential proof. We have seen how the notion of the earth-girding Sea of Death permeated the beliefs of heathen Germany; and though, because of the gloomy character of that creed, the darker side of the conception seems always to lie uppermost, we have no reason to question that there was another and a brighter side.

Whether even in the case of the story of the death of
Balder some picture of a paradise did not follow after the
scene of death I am much inclined to doubt. We know
how universal among the Norse people was the desire
for a funeral which should imitate as closely as possible
the funeral of Balder ; and I cannot but believe that the
Norsemen fancied that in this way they went to join the
sun god in a far-off happy land. And the vision which
succeeds the Vala's account of the destruction of all things
at Ragnarök, the vision of a new and better earth arising
once more from the sea, and Balder coming again from
Helheim to rule there, seems to express the hope in which
men went to death.[1]

But, as we well know, the belief in an earth-encircling
Sea of Death was not confined to the Teutons of the North,
nor even to the German race. There are visible traces of
it among all the nations of Europe ; it and the belief in
the soul's passage over that sea have been the property of
all the Aryas. With some among the races of our stock
these myths existed only as parts of a vague and general
belief. But among all those who lived near the Western
Sea—that is, beside the Atlantic or the Mediterranean—
the belief grew to be a precise one. Most of these peoples
could have pointed out some spot in their country whence
the ghostly cargo set out upon its voyage, and most had
some special tradition of the locus of their home for the
departed spirits. One among such resting-places for the
shades was the little island of Heligoland. This was the
belief current among Germans of the north of Continental
Germany. To the Germans of the Rhine mouth, the
Ripuarians or the Frisians, our own island at one time
occupied the same place in popular mythology, and from
being Angel-land became Engel-land, wherein no living
man dwelt. It was this, too, to still nearer neighbours of

---

[1] Though the colours of this picture have been much deepened through
the influence of Christianity, I doubt not but that the belief was grounded
upon heathen tradition.

ourselves. Procopius gives us a picture of the belief which by the sixth century had grown up among the peasants of northern Gaul concerning Britain. Britain in his narrative has become changed into a fabulous island, Brittia; one half of which was thought to be habitable by living men, while the other half was set apart to be the home of ghosts. Between the two regions stretched a wall, which none could pass and live; whoever did cross it instantly fell dead upon the other side, so pestilential was the air. But serpents and all venomous things dwelt on that other side, and there the air was dark and spirit-haunted. It was said that the fishermen upon the northern coast of Gaul were made the ferrymen of the dead. To them was assigned the office of carrying the souls across the Channel to the opposite island of Brittia, and on account of this strange duty Procopius declares they were excused from the ordinary incidence of taxation. Their task fell upon them by rotation, and those villagers whose turn had come round were awakened at dead of night by a gentle tap upon the door and a whispering breath calling them to the beach. There lay vessels to all appearance empty and yet weighed down as if by a heavy freight. Pushing off, the fishermen performed in one night the voyage which else they could hardly accomplish, rowing and sailing, in six days and nights. When they had arrived at the strange coast, they heard names called over and voices answering as if by rota, while they felt their vessels gradually growing light; at last, when all the ghosts had landed, they were wafted back to the habitable world.[1]

Claudian makes allusion to the same myth, referring it to the same locality and connecting it with the journey of Odysseus to Hades.

Est locus extremum pandit quâ Gallia littus
Oceani prætentus aquis, ubi fertur Ulixes
Sanguine libato populum movisse silentem.

[1] Procopius, *Bell. Goth.* iv. c. 20, pp. 620–5, ed. Paris; ii. p. 559 sqq. ed. Bonn.

Illic umbrarum tenui stridore volantum,
Flebilis auditur questus. Simulacra coloni
Pallida, defunctasque vident migrare figuras.[1]

And I cannot help associating with the same superstition a story which we find in Paulus Diaconus.[2]   When
Pertaric, the dethroned King of the Lombards, was fleeing
from the power of Grimvald the Usurper, he went first to
France; but finding that Dagobert. II., the Merovingian
king, was friendly to Grimvald, and fearing lest he should
be delivered over to his enemy, he took ship to pass over
to Britain. He had been but a little while upon the sea,
when a voice came from the hither shore, asking whether
Pertaric were in that ship; and the answer was given,
' Pertaric is here.'   Then the voice cried, ' Tell him he may
return to his own land, for Grimvald departed from this
life three days ago.' Surely this must have been the
ghost of Grimvald himself, arrived at the point of his sea
transit. Perhaps he could not pass over until he had
made this reparation for the injury done.

It must, one would suppose, be in memory of these
legends of the dead crossing the Channel that the men of
Cape Raz in Finistère still call the bay below this point,
the most westerly in France, ' la Baie des Trépassés,' the
Bay of the Dead.[3]

Here again is a variation upon the same myth, taken
from the mouth of a peasant of modern Brittany. The
difference is that a certain river in Brittany has replaced
the British Channel, and that the shores of the departed
now lie along that river's banks. Saving that change we
have the essential parts of the older legend; we have the
souls snatched away in a boat by the grim ferryman, just
such an one as he who plied across the Styx or across the
Northern Midgard Sea. I reproduce the story here not
because it is considered as a story specially curious—for

[1] *In Rufin*. i. 123.   [2] *Gest. Long*. v. 32, 33.
[3] Cambry, *Voyage dans le Finistère*, ii. 240.

there are similar legends of the Rhine; and the Erl König himself is a kind of King of Death—but because of the interest which belongs to the locality where the legend is found lingering. All sorts of people have had their myths of the Mortal River; but those Bretons who live upon the borders of what was once deemed the Sea of Death have a special right to treasure this myth in their familiar folk lore.[1]

'Many years ago there lived in the village of Clohars a young couple called Guern and Mabarit; they were betrothed, and were to be married two days after the "Pardon of the Birds," which, as everyone knows, happens every year in the month of June at the forest of Carnoët.

'One evening after sunset the lovers came home from a visit to some relatives in the parish of Guidel. When they reached the ferry of Carnoët, Guern shouted for the ferryman.

'"Wait for me, Maharit," he said, "while I go and light my pipe at my godfather's cottage: it is close by."

'The boatman of the ferry was a mysterious being, who lived alone in a hut beside the river. . . . He soon appeared. He was tall and wild-looking, and long grey hair floated over his shoulders.

'"Who wants me?" he growled. "It is too late. Are you alone, maiden?"

'"Loïk Guern is coming; he has only gone to light his pipe."

'"He must be quick, then. Get into the boat," said the ferryman impatiently.

'The girl obeyed mechanically. But she was surprised and frightened to see the ferryman jump and push the boat off from the bank without a moment's delay.

'"What are you doing, my friend?" she cried. "We must wait for Loïk Guern, I tell you."

---

[1] *Pictures and Legends from Normandy and Brittany*, by Thomas and Katherine Macquoid, p. 19 sqq. For a similar German legend see Kuhn, *Sagen, Geb. u. Märchen*, i. 9.

'There was no answer, and now the boat reached the current, and, instead of passing across to the opposite shore, they shot rapidly down the river.

'"Stop, stop, my friend, for pity's sake!" cried Maharit in an agonised voice. . . . She clasped her hands imploringly; but the ferryman neither spoke nor looked at her, and the boat, still impelled forward, descended the river more and more rapidly.

'Maharit bent towards the shore. "Loïk! Loïk!" she cried. The words died away on her lips, for she saw shadowy forms standing on the gloomy banks; they stretched their arms towards her with menacing gestures, and she drew back shuddering. She knew they were the spirits of the murdered wives of Commore. . . .

'Loïk Guern lit his pipe, said a few words to his godfather, and hastened back to the ferry. But Maharit was gone, and the boat was gone too! He gazed anxiously across the river and up and down its banks, now cold and sombre in the gathering darkness. There was no sound or sight of living thing.

'"Maharit! Maharit!" he cried, "where art thou?" From far away a cry came to him on the night breeze. . . .

'Suddenly, from amidst the tall weeds and rushes, rose up the gaunt figure of *an old beggar woman.*[1]

'"You waste your breath, young man," she said. "The boat and those in it are already far from here;" and she pointed down the river.

'"What do you mean, mother? What has happened to Maharit?"

'"*The young girl has gone to the shores of the departed.* She forgot to make the sign of the cross when she got into the boat, and she also looked behind her. . . ."

'He set off running like a madman along the river banks in the direction the old woman had pointed out,

---

[1] The counterpart of the Norse Thökk, &c.

waking the silence of the night with cries for his beloved Maharit.

'" Come back to me ! " he cried, " come back ! " but all in vain.'[1]

Ireland, more westerly still, inherited in still larger measure the glamour which popular superstition in the dark ages shed over Britain. Ireland was thought to be the very Earthly Paradise itself, and was therefore christened with a name the exact counterpart of Pindar's μακάρων νῆσοι; it was the ' Island of Saints.' But then, according to other legends, it was likewise the home of the damned. Here was the entry to St. Patrick's purgatory, the most famous mouth of hell known in the Middle Ages ; and in this island it was that Bridget saw in a vision a place where souls were falling down into hell as thick as hail.

But the Irish themselves supposed the Island of the Blessed lay to the west of their land ; and they told how a monk of their own country, a descendant of St. Patrick, having set out to make the voyage to Paradise, had lighted upon this happy island, which henceforward went by the name of St. Brandan's isle. Though the legend itself—the priestly version of it at least, which has alone come down to us—represents the saint as sailing eastward, tradition insisted upon believing his land lay in the west. Sometimes it was to the west of Ireland ; it could be seen in certain weathers from the coast, but when an expedition was fitted out to go and land there, the island somehow seemed to disappear. Or it was localised in the Canaries. It was, as the Spanish and Portuguese declared, an island which had been sometimes lighted upon by accident, but when sought for could not be found (*quando se busca no se halla*). A king of Portugal is said to have made a conditional surrender of it to another when it should be found ; and when the kingdom of Portugal ceded to the Castilian crown its rights over the Canaries, the treaty

---

[1] For the rest of the story I refer the reader to the delightful book from which I have made this extract.

included the is'and of St. Brandan, described as 'the island which had not yet been found.' [1]

Dante, we know, did not accept the Greek story of Odysseus' return from the Phæacians. In the eighth chasm of Malebolge it is that the poet meets Ulysses, and learns from him the narrative of his death. The same motive influenced this Ulysses—and this is the fact of supreme importance to us—to venture into the Atlantic which doubtless Dante knew had influenced many sailors of his time—the hope to find a new land away in the west.

'When I left Circe,' the much-enduring Greek says, 'when I left Circe, who held me a year or more near Gaëta—before Æneas had given that place its name— neither my fondness for my son, nor piety towards my aged father, nor the love with which I should have lightened the heart of Penelope, could conquer the strong desire which swayed me to gain knowledge of the world and of human wickedness and worth. So I set forth upon the open sea with one ship and with that small band by whom I had never been deserted. One shore and the other I saw, as far as Spain and Morocco, and the Island of Sardinia, and other islands which that sea washes round. I and my companions were old and slow when we gained the narrow strait where Hercules has set up his sign-posts, that men should not venture beyond. On the right I passed Seville; I had already passed Ceuta on the left. "Oh! my brothers," I cried, "who through a hundred thousand dangers have reached the West, refuse not to this brief vigil of your senses which is left the knowledge of the unpeopled world beyond the sun. Consider your descent; ye were not made to live the life of brutes, but to follow virtue and knowledge." I made my comrades with this short speech so eager for the voyage, that had I wished it I could scarce have held them back; and turning our backs upon the morning and bearing always towards the left we

---

[1] Wright, *The Voyage of St. Brandan*. Percy Soc. Pub., vol. xiv.

made our oars wings for our foolish flight. Night saw already the other pole and all its stars, and our pole so low that it did not rise above the ocean floor. Five times relit and quenched as often had been the light which the moon sheds below, since we entered on the steep way, when there appeared before us a mountain, dim with distance, which seemed so high as I had never seen mountain before. We rejoice;· but our joy was soon turned to grieving ; for from the land came a tempest which struck the fore part of our vessel. Thrice it whirled her round with all its waters, and the fourth time the poop rose up and the prow turned downwards—such was the will of God—and the sea closed over us.'

Dante, we see, had no sympathy with the hopes of those who thought to win by mortal means to the Earthly Paradise. He calls the west 'the unpeopled land beyond the sun ; ' for he was upon the side of orthodoxy, and in his confession of Ulysses doubtless meant to cast reproach upon those obstinate ones who, against the teaching of Scripture, still hoped to find a place where they could avoid death. The mountain which he places in the Atlantic, the high mountain, *bruna per la distanza*, which Ulysses sees, is the Mountain of Purgatory ; and only by ascending that could men reach the Earthly Paradise. Other land he recognises none there. But he bears witness to the belief that the west was not unpeopled. How without such a belief could the traveller have been urged to seek the west by a desire of knowing more of human wickedness and worth ?

Columbus, it is well known, was not uninfluenced by the purely mythic stories of a western world. These tales had in his day been so long repeated and so much changed that they often wore the face of commonplace fact; and numerous were the successors as well as the predecessors of Columbus who fancied they were going to find an Atlantis or other fabulous place more wonderful than any they really lighted upon. Fancy and superstition here, as in the researches of astrologers and alchemists, commanded the aid of more exertion and of greater enthusiasm than would have been at the service of sober truth. Thousands of voyagers perished before any end was reached. But the journeys did at last end happily in the discovery, if not of a deathless land, at any rate of a new world.

Another story of a voyage over the Sea of Death is the one recorded by Saxo Grammaticus to have been made by Gorm the Wise, King of Denmark. In many particulars the legend as it has come to us in the pages of Saxo and in its Latin dress is clearly copied from the great Greek epic. But there are other incidents for which no originals could be discovered in the Odyssey; and the picture of the other world which it presents is on the whole quite in accordance with that which from other Northern sources we traced in the last chapter. It might, perhaps, be said that the history of the voyage of Gorm belongs rather to descriptions of hell than to accounts of the earthly Paradise. It records a journey undertaken rather to the Land of Death than to any heaven. But because we have had so much to say here concerning the passage of the soul over seas, and had so much less to say on this head in the last chapter, and because the feature of the sea voyage is put forward very distinctly in the Gorm legend—it cannot be amiss if we give one glance at this history.[1]

One of Gorm's subjects, a certain Jarl Thorkill, was reported to have previously made a voyage of the same kind as that which on this occasion Gorm proposed to himself— that is to say, a voyage to farther Biarmia, beyond any known region of land, to one where many giants dwelt, and as king of these giants Utgarthilocus. Thorkill, then, we may take to be in reality the god Thorr, and it is interesting to see that in changing the god into a man the name should have been changed into a not unusual proper name.[2] Gorm set sail with three ships, holding

---

[1] Saxo Grammaticus, *Historia Danica*, ed. Müller and Velsobow, 1839-58, p. 420.

[2] Thorkill is a very common Norse name for men. What the etymology

three hundred men, under the command of Thorkill. Their first adventure is evidently a plagiarism from the Odyssey. They landed on a certain island covered with flocks and herds, but, as these last were under the protection of the gods, Thorkill forbade the men to take more than was needful to satisfy their immediate wants. They were not to store away in the ships. This order the sailors disobeyed; and, in consequence, when night came on, a band of fearful monsters came flying round the ships, and the terrified sailors had to expiate their crime by sacrificing three men, one for each ship. When this had been done the expedition sailed away.

And now with favourable breezes they reached the coasts of farther Biarmia,[1] a land where constant cold reigned and where the ground was buried deep in ancient snow. It had thick untraversable woods, not abounding in fruit, but in wild beasts of strange kinds. There they drew up their boats ashore[2] and went forward afoot. As evening came on, a man of huge stature suddenly appeared before them. He was Gunthmund, the brother of Geruth, to whose palace they were faring. Anon they reached a river which was traversed by a golden bridge.[3] But when they would have gone over, Gunthmund showed them that this river separated the world of men from the world of monsters, and that no living man might traverse it. . . . It is curious to trace in these descriptions the admixture of ancient Norse belief and classical myth. The bridge is the Gjallar-brû, and could not have been borrowed from the Odyssey. But soon we get back again to the Odyssean legend. If they partook of food at the table of King Gunthmund the same fate would overtake

of it is I do not know—possibly Thor-ketill. It is curious that one of the monkish visions of purgatory current in the twelfth century was the visit of Thurcill.

[1] A sort of Ûtgard, as we shall see.

[2] Like Odysseus when he came to the shore of Ocean and to the groves of Persephoné.

[3] Gjallar-brû (see Chap. VIII.)

them which fell upon the feasters in Circê's hall. They would, as Thorkill told them, become as brutes, losing all memory. Thorkill was not wanting in excuses when the giant complained of the discourtesy of him and his comrades in not partaking of the meal. 'The food is strange to them; they cannot eat,' &c. Some, however, could not resist the delights offered, and fell victims to the enchantment. The rest journeyed further still to the dwelling of King Geruth,[1] and came to a black, barbarous-looking town, which seemed to them 'like a vaporous cloud.' *Two dogs* exceeding fierce guarded the entrance. Within the gates were horrible black spectres, and they were oppressed with the putrid stench with which the air was heavy. Thorkill made for a stone fortress, which was the palace of Geruth, but ere they reached it he warned his comrades to keep from their minds all avaricious longings; for if they took aught away they would fall into the power of the king. Then is reference made to the visit of the god Thorr to the same place, and to some of the feats which he performed while there. . . .

This picture is almost the same as that given us of the ancient Jötunheim, but it is re-dressed in a later form and furnished with some images borrowed from Homer. There is no need to follow further the adventures of Gorm and his comrades, many of whom, of course, perished as the comrades of Odysseus did, while the leader of the expedition and Thorkill got back home.

The story which was up to the end of the thirteenth century the most influential in sending men upon Odyssean voyages was probably that to which allusion has been already made—the legend of St. Brandan.[2] The account must be classed among the legends of the saints; it was told by priests, and has been committed to writing by a

---

[1] The Geirröd of the Edda Geirröd is a sort of giant and an enemy of Odhinn. *Grímnismál.*

[2] The name Brandan is probably allied to Bran, the Celtic hero—and sun god? For him see Matthew Arnold, *Celt. Lit.* The word means chief or head: it is the same as Brennus.

priost. It offers, in fact, a happy mixture of heathen fable and Biblical legend. It should be remembered that the cycle of the legends of the saints made up a literature more distinctly *popular* than even the stories of the legendary heroes of early chivalry, such as the paladins of Charlemagne and the knights of the Round Table.

These last were the theme of minstrels; they were told in the castle hall and bower to knights and ladies. The lives of the saints were repeated by the priests, who were of the peasaut class, and by them spread abroad among the peasantry. They formed the great popular literature of the Middle Ages. In them many of the old gods came to life again, and walked more easily in the garb of peasant saints than in the armour of knights and paladins. Therefore it is no exaggeration to say that the great legend of the Earthly Paradise from the eighth century to the fourteenth is the story of the voyage of St. Brandan. This is true, as that before the time of Dante the *locus classicus* among the purgatory myths was the story of St. Patrick's purgatory. Both these legends arose, as we have noticed, in Ireland, the legitimate 'Home of Souls.'

We have already seen how in the case of the story of St. Brandan's voyage popular prejudice was more powerful than the ecclesiastical tradition; and how even after it had become the accepted history of the journey to Paradise the same popular belief quietly garbled the text and modified the legend to suit its theories. The myth did not originally speak of a journey to the west, but of one to the east; yet common tradition succeeded in making the island of St. Brandan veer round from its eastern site to lie off the west coast of Ireland or off Portugal. It is evident that there will be some portions of the legend which express better than do others the popular belief concerning the Western Paradise. To find these, we must, therefore, read a little between the lines of the ecclesiastical story. It is not the eastern land to which St. Brandan finally attained which could have represented to men's imaginations their western ' St. Brandan's Isle,' but some one among the islands which the saint met with in the course of his long voyage. There were many of these islands : each one, no doubt, possessed some features which were thought to distinguish the home of the blessed.

One was the ' Ylonde of Shepe '—we think of Odysseus on Thrinakia—' where is never cold weder, but ever sommer, and that causeth the shepe to be so grete and whyte.' Another island contained an abbey of twenty-four monks, ' and in this londe,' the monks told St. Brandan, ' was ever fayre weder, and none of us hath been seke syth we came byther.' But I take the following to be one of the best descriptions of an earthly Paradise to be found in Middle Age romance. It is the Paradise of Birds :—[1]

' But soone after, as God wold, they saw a fayre ylonde, full of floures and herbes and trees, whereof they thanked God of His good grace, and anone they went on londe. And when they had gone longe in this, they founde a full fayre well, and thereby stode a tree full of bowes, and on every bow sate a fayre byrde; and they sate so thycke on the tree that unneath ony lefe of the tree myght be seen, the nombre of them was so grete; and they sange so meryly that it was an heavenly noyse to here. . . . And than anone one of the byrdes fledde fro the tree to Saynt Brandan, and he with flyckerynge of his wynges made a full merye noyse lyke a fydle, that hym semed he herde never so joyfull a melodye. And than Saynt Brandan commaunded the byrde to tell him the cause why they sate so thycke on the tree and sange so meryly. And than the byrde sayd, " Sometyme we were aungels in heven, but whan our mayster Lucyfer fell down into hell for his high

---

[1] The notion of the soul entering into the shape of a bird is of course one among the most common in mythology. The wings of the bird naturally express the freedom and spiritual condition of the soul (see Chap. II.) In Lithuanian tradition the soul escapes along the *Milky Way* in the form of a bird. Hence the Milky Way is by the Lithuanians called ' the Way of Birds.'

pryde, we fell with hym for our offences, some byther and some lower, after the qualité of theyr trespace." [1]

This might be a fall from heaven, but it was a rise from earth. A place suited to the character of any who were, like these angels, of a temporising nature. For such the Earthly Paradise existed, for it was the creation of their own brains. They did not judge themselves so severely as Dante judges them. He, too, shows us the same angels who fell 'for no great trespace,' but he calls them

Il cattivo coro
Degli angeli,

'the caitiff choir of angels, who were neither rebellious nor faithful to God, but were for themselves'

A Dio spiacenti et a nemici sui,

'hateful to God and to His enemies.' . . . . As the mediæval purgatory was nothing else than a survival of the Greek Hades or Norse Helheim into the creed of Christendom, to the thought of which the terrors of the heathen place of punishment seemed to offer but an inadequate representation of hell, so this probationary Paradise of Birds is the truer survival of the heathen heaven than is the Eastern Paradise to which St. Brandan at last attained.

This legend I take to be one of the lingering footprints of a past Celtic mythology; other traces of it in this matter of the Earthly Paradise and of the Sea of Death are those stories which we gathered from Procopius and Claudian of a journey made by the souls from the west of France over sea to our island. It is fortunate that though the Celtic mythology as a whole is lost to us, some gleanings can still be had therefrom.

One other relic of Celtic belief survives in the account of the death of Arthur in the Arthurian Romance; for

[1] *The Legend of St. Brandan*, by T. Wright. Percy Soc. Trs., vol. xiv.

herein appears the name of the old Celtic Paradise, Avalon, which means the 'Isle of Apples.'[1] There is a shade of sadness thrown over the story; the loss of the hero from earth is too great to allow the poet much thought of Arthur's joys in the future state. Still he is going to Avalon, and Avalon is certainly the Celtic Paradise. h is the island of Hesperides, or the land of Phæaceans, under another name, distinguished not less specially than the Greek Paradises were by its wealth in fruits. For this is implied by the term 'Isle of Apples.' The battle in which Arthur was mortally wounded was Camelot, which Malory describes as 'on the downs by Salisbury, not far from the sea-shore.' Sir Bedivere bore Arthur from the field, and laid him in a chapel by the sea. Then Arthur sent his knight to give a signal to the fairy powers that they were to take him away to Avalon.

'My time bieth fast,' said the king. 'Therefore take thou Excalibur, my good sword, and go with it to yonder water-side, and when thou comest there I charge thee throw my sword in that water, and come again and tell me what thou there hast seen. . . .' When Excalibur was thrown into the sea, 'there came an arm and a hand above the water and met it and caught it, and so shook it thrice and brandished, and then vanished away the hand with the sword in the water. . . . Then Sir Bedivere took the king upon his back, and so went with him to that water-side. And when they were at the water-side, even fast by the bank hoved a little barge, with many faire ladies in it, and among them all a queene, and all they had black hoods, and all they wept and shrieked when they saw the King Arthur. "Now put me into the barge," said the king; and so did he softly. And there received him three queenes[2] with great mourning, and so these three queenes set him down, and in one of their laps King Arthur laid his head, and then that queene said, "Ah, dear

---

Therefore it corresponds to the Garden of Hesperides.
[2] The Nornir (= Valkyriur)?

brother, why have ye tarried so long from me? Alas! this wound on your head hath caught over much cold." And so they rowed from the land; and Sir Bedivere beheld all those ladies go from him. . . . And he then said, "I will to the vale of Avalion to be healed of my grievous wound. And if thou hear never more of me, pray for my soul." But ever the queens and ladies wept and shrieked that it was pity to hear.'[1]

Afterwards Malory says—

'Thus of Arthur I find never more written in books that be authorised, nor more of the certainty of his death herd I never tell, but thus was he led away in a ship wherein were three queenes: that one was King Arthur's sister, Queen Morgan le Fay; the other was Queen of North Gales;[2] the third was the Queen of the Waste Lands. . . . But some men yet say in many parts of England that King Arthur is not dead, but had by the will of our Lord Jesus Christ into another place. And men say that he shall come again, and he shall win the holy cross.'

The story of Arthur's going to Avalon is told here in no high key of triumph; but a little hope lingers about it. The circumstances in which arose the Arthur legend were not suitable to notes of exultation. The story is the epic of a defeated race; it was the inheritance of the Britons after the Saxon conquest. But if every myth is beautiful which tells of the dying hero going to the Happy Land of the Sunset, and which promises his return when his people are at its sorest need, twice as touching is the form which the legend takes in the mouth of a people whose hopes are dying out, and whose sun itself is sinking towards its western eclipse.

Much more full is the account of the visit of Oger le Dannois (Holger Danske) to the same Paradise of Avalon. The account which I here translate is only a sixteenth-

---

[1] Sir T. Malory, *Morte d'Arthure*, c. 168.　　　[2] North Wales.

-century version of the tale, but it is copied directly from the poetic version of the well-known troubadour Adenes, chief minstrel at the court of Henry III. of Bavaria (1248-1261), and for his excellence in his art called Le Roy or king of all.[1] There can be no doubt that in its chief particulars the story is far older than the days of Adenes. It is thus that the prose version from which I have translated tells the history of the adventure of Oger at Avalon:—

Caraheu and Gloriande were in a boat with a fair company, and Oger had with him a thousand men-at-arms. When they were a certain way on, there arose so mighty a tempest that they knew not what to do, only to commit their souls to God. So great was the storm that the mast of Oger's ship brake, and he was constrained to embark in a little vessel with a few of his comrades; and the wind struck them with such fury that they lost sight of Caraheu. Caraheu was so sore troubled that he was like to die, and he began to mourn the noble Oger; for he wist not what was become of the boat. And Oger in like manner lamented Caraheu. Thus grieved Caraheu and the Christians in his company, saying, 'Alas! Oger, what is become of thee? This is, I ween, the most sudden departure that I heard of ever.' 'Nay, but cease, my beloved,' said Gloriande; 'he will not fail to come again when God wills, for he cannot be far away.' 'Ah, lady,' said Caraheu, 'you know not the dangers of the sea; and I pray God to take him into His keeping. . . .'

Now I will leave speaking of Caraheu, and return to Oger, who was in peril, yet was ever grieving for his friend and saying, 'Ah, Caraheu, hope of the remaining days of my life, thou whom I loved next to God! How has God allowed me to loose so soon you and your lady?' At that moment the great ship, in which Oger had left his men-at-arms, struck against a rock, and he saw them all

---

[1] He is likewise the author of the *Cleomenes*, which is by some supposed to be the original of Chaucer's incomplete *Squire's Tale*.

perish, at which sight he was like to die of grief. And presently a loadstone rock began to draw towards it the boat in which Oger was. Oger, seeing himself thus taken, recommended his· soul to God, saying, 'My God, my Father and Creator, who hast made me in Thine image and semblance, have pity on me now, and leave me not here to die; for that I have used my power as was best to the increase of the Catholic faith. But if it must be that Thou take me, I commit to Thy care my brother Guyon, and all my relatives and friends, especially my nephew Gautier, who is minded to serve Thee and bring the paynim within Holy Church. . . . Ah, my God! had I known the peril of this adventure, I should never have abandoned the beauty, sense, and honour of Clarice, Queen of England. Had I but gone back to her I should have seen too my redoubted sovereign, Charlemagne, with all the princes who surround him.'

Meanwhile the boat continued to float upon the water till it reached the loadstone castle, which they call the Château d'Avalon, which is but a little way from the Earthly Paradise whither were snatched in a beam of fire Elias and Enoch, and where was Morgue la Fée, who at his birth had given him such great gifts. Then the mariners saw well that they were drawing near to the loadstone rock, and they said to Oger, 'My lord, commend thyself to God, for it is certain that at this moment we are come to our voyage's end;' and as they spake the bark with a swing attached itself to the rock, as though it were cemented there.

That night Oger thought over the case in which he was, but he scarce could tell of what sort it might be. And the sailors came and said to Oger, 'My lord, we are held here without remedy; wherefore let us look to our having, for we are here for the remainder of our lives.' To which Oger made answer, 'If this be so, then will I make consideration of our case, for I would assign to each one his share, to the least as to the greatest.' For

himself Oger kept a double portion, for it is the law of the
sea that the master of the ship has as much as two
others. But if that rule had not been he would still have
needed a double quantity, for he ate as much as two
common men.

When Oger had apportioned his share to each he said,
'Masters, be sparing, I pray you, of your food as much as you
may; for so soon as ye have no more be sure that I myself
will throw you into the sea.' The skipper answered him,
'My lord, thou wilt escape no better than we.' Their
food failed them all, one after another, and Oger cast them
into the sea, and he remained alone. Then he was so
troubled that he knew not what to do. 'Alas! my God,
my Creator,' said he, 'hast Thou at this hour forsaken
me? I have now no one to comfort me in my misfortune.'
Thereupon, whether it were his fantasy or no, it seemed
to him that a voice replied, ' God orders that so soon as it
be night thou go to a castle after thou hast come to an
island which thou wilt presently find. And when thou art
on the island thou wilt find a small path leading to the
castle. And whatsoever thing thou seest there, let not
that affray thee.' And Oger looked, but wist not who had
spoken.

Oger waited the return of night to learn the truth of
that which the voice foretold, and he was so amazed that
he wist not what to do, but set himself to the trial. And
when night came he committed himself to God, praying
Him for mercy; and straightway he looked and beheld the
Castle of Avalon, which shone wondrously. Many nights
before he had seen it, but by day it was not visible.
Howbeit, so soon as Oger saw the castle he set about to
get there. He saw before him the ships that were
fastened to the loadstone rock, and now he walked from
ship to ship, and so gained the island; and when there he
at once set himself to scale the hill by a path which he
found. When he reached the gate of the castle, and
sought to enter, there came before him *two great lions,*

who stopped him and cast him to the ground. But Oger sprang up and drew his sword Curtain, and straightway cleft one of them in twain; then the other sprang and seized Oger by the neck, and Oger turned round and struck off his head.

When Oger had performed this deed he gave thanks to our Lord, and then he entered the hall of the castle, where he found many viands, and a table set as if one should dine there; but no prince nor lord could he see. Now he was amazed to find no one, save only a horse which sat at the table as if it had been a human being.

We need not follow the adventure in full detail. This horse, which was called Papillon (Psyche?), waited upon Oger, gave him to drink from a golden goblet, and at length conducted him to his chamber, and to a bed whose fairy-made coverlet of cloth of gold and ermine was *la plus mignonne chose qui fut jamais vue.*

When Oger awoke he thought to see Papillôn again, but could see neither him, nor man, nor woman, to show him the way from the room. He saw a door, and, having made the sign of the cross, sought to pass out that way; but as he tried to do this he encountered *a serpent,* so hideous that the like has scarce been seen. It would have thrown itself upon Oger, but that the knight drew his sword and made the creature recoil more than ten feet; but it returned with a bound, for it was very mighty, and the twain fell to fight. And now, as Oger saw that the serpent pressed hard upon him, he struck at it so doughtily with his sword that he severed it in twain. After that Oger went along a path which led him to a garden, so beauteous that it was in truth a little paradise, and within were fair trees, bearing fruit of every kind, of tastes divers, and of such sweet odours that never smelt trees like them before.

Oger, seeing these fruits so fine, desired to eat some, and presently he lighted upon a fine *apple tree, whose fruit was like gold,* and of these apples he took one and ate.

But no sooner had he thus eaten than he became so sick and weak that he had no power nor manhood left. And now again he commended his soul to God and prepared to die. . . . But at this moment turning round, he was aware of a fair dame, clothed in white, and so richly adorned that she was a glory to behold. Now as Oger looked upon the lady without moving from his place, he deemed that she was Mary the Virgin, and said 'Ave Maria' and saluted her. But she said, 'Oger, think not that I am she whom you fancy; I am she who was at your birth,[1] and my name is Morgue la Fée, and I allotted you a gift which was destined to increase your fame eternally through all lands. But now you have left your deeds of war to take with ladies your solace; for as soon as I have taken you from here I will bring you to Avalon, where you will see the fairest noblesse in the world.'

And anon she gave him a ring, which had such virtue that Oger, who was near a hundred years old, returned to the age of thirty. Then said Oger, 'Lady, I am more beholden to thee than to any other in the world. Blessed be the hour of thy birth; for, without having done aught to deserve at your hands, you have given me countless gifts, and this gift of new life above them all. Ah, lady, that I were before Charlemagne, that he might see the condition in which I now stand; for I feel in me greater strength than I have ever known. Dearest, how can I make return for the honour and great good you have done me? But I swear that I am at your service all the days of my life.' Then Morgue took him by the hand and said, 'My loyal friend, the goal of all my happiness, I will now lead you to my palace in Avalon, where you will see of noblesse the greatest and of damosels the fairest.'

---

[1] The fairies were, like the Parcæ or Mœræ, especially frequent attendants at births. This fact our fairy tales have made sufficiently familiar to all. Among the instances of the attendance of the classic fates at birth we have the births of Iamos (Pindar, *Olym.* vi.) and of Meleagros (Ovid, *Met.* viii. 454), &c.

And she took Oger by the hand and led him to the Castle
of Avalon, where was King Artus, and Auberon, and
Malambron, who was a sea fairy.

As Oger approached the castle the fairies came to meet
him, dancing and singing marvellous sweetly. And he saw
many fairy dames, richly crowned and apparelled. And
presently came Arthur, and Morgue called to him and said,.
'Come hither, my lord and brother, and salute the fair
flower of chivalry, the honour of the French noblesse, him
in whom all generosity and honour and every virtue are
lodged, Oger le Dannois, my loyal love, my only pleasure,
in whom lies for me all hope of happiness.' Then Morgue
gave Oger a crown to wear, which was so rich that none
here could count its value; and it had beside a wondrous
virtue, for every man who bore it on his brow forgot all
sorrow and sadness and melancholy, and he thought no
more of his country nor of his kin that he had left behind
him in the world.

We leave Oger thus 'bien assis et entretenu des
dames que c'était merveilles,' and return to the earth,
where things were not going so well; for while Oger was
in Fairie the paynim assembled all their forces and took
Jerusalem and proceeded to lay siege to Babylon (i.e.
Cairo). Then the most valiant knights who were left on
earth—Moysant, and Florian, and Caraheu, and Gautier
(Oger's nephew)—assembled all their powers to defend this
place. But they lamented greatly because Oger was no
more. And a great battle took place without the walls
of Babylon, in which the Saracens, assisted by a renegade,
the Admiral Gandice, gained the victory.

Oger had been long in the Castle of Avalon, and had
begotten a son by Morgue, when she, having heard of
these doings and of the danger to Christendom, deemed it
needful to awake Oger from his blissful forgetfulness of all
earthly things and tell him that his presence was needed
in this world once more. Thereupon follows an account of
Oger's returning to earth, where no one knew him, and

all were astonished at his strange garb and bearing. He
enquired for Charlemagne, who had been long since dead ;
the generation below Oger had grown to be old men, yet
he still had the habit of a man of thirty. We need not
wonder that his talk excited suspicion. But at length he
made himself known to the King of France, joined his
army, and put the paynim to flight. He had now forgotten
his life in Fairie, he was beloved by the Queen of France
(the King having been killed) and was about to marry
her, when Morgue again appeared and carried him off to
Avalon.

It need not be said that this story of the *return* of the
hero to earth is an essential in the legend of the Earthly
Paradise.   In this way among others found expression
that favourite myth of the Middle Age of the sleeping hero
who, though withdrawn for awhile from the world and its
combats, was yet to come back again some day, and at the
hour of his country's supreme need stand in irresistible
might at the side of her warriors, ready to strike a final
blow for her deliverance.   This myth, I say, was universal
and fondly cherished.   Probably the sleeping hero was at
first the old national god, still dear to peasants' hearts.
That old god might serve for a symbol of the time when
these peasants themselves were freer and more warlike
than they had become.   For gradually arms were taken
from the hands of the freemen and the bonders, and they
sank to the condition of serfs.   They were buried, like
Thorr and Wuotan, beneath a mountain of new laws which
they could not shake off.

When the national god was forgotten a national hero
became the symbol of the sleeping past.   Where Wuotan
had once slumbered there now lay Charlemagne or Frederick Redbeard ; and on his heart weighed the mass of an
immense mountain, which yet moved with his breathing.
Or otherwise it was said that the hero had gone, like
Oger, to the far-off Earthly Paradise, and would return
again when most needed, as Oger did.

From the legends of this class are to be derived some of those bright but misty figures the *Paradise Knights*, who move across the field of popular lore, coming no one knows from whence and when their work is done going away no one knows whither. But there is another order of these half-celestial beings—the knights who are *born* in Paradise. Of Oger himself it is recorded that he became by Morgue the father of Mervain, and that this Mervain was a valiant knight in the days of Hugh Capet.

Indeed, as human beings, knights and dames, may be transported to the deathless land without undergoing death or changing their earthly nature, taking their *soulas* and all the enjoyments of our world, children, it is clear, may be born in that place; and these Paradise children, though they have powers above the range of common mortality, yet are in no way separated in interests from their fellow men. They may long to come to the common earth and perform here deeds of knight-errantry, and then to go back again if their work is over or they themselves unthankfully treated, as such celestial messengers often are. . Hence we have that beautiful and universal German myth of the child who comes *earthward* *from* the immortal land. As the hero goes away to Avalon in a boat, so this child comes wafted in a boat to some shore, or down some river. The child is sleeping; no one knows whence it has fared.[1]

In the introduction to Beowulf it is said that his father, Scyld, was after his death borne to a ship and placed in it 'with no less gifts provided than they gave him who at the beginning sent him forth over the wave, being a child.' The legend here alluded to is that this child had been borne in a boat without sail or oar to the

---

[1] In certain legends of saints a ship floats against stream, bearing their remains to a fit resting-place. The remains of St. Marternus were in this way carried up the Rhine in a rudderless boat and deposited at Rodenkirchen. The remains of St. Emmeranus were carried from the Iser to the Danube, and thence up stream to Ratisbon. See Simrock, *Handbuch der D. M.*, 285

shore of Scandinavia,[1] and that he was afterwards chosen
to be king of that land. There is a mistake made by the
author of Beowulf when he attributes this history to Scyld,
for the name should be Sceaf, the father of Scyld; but this
is of no consequence. The outlines of the legend stand
clear; and this legend gives the normal form of the myth.
The child born in Paradise is wafted by an unknown bark
from that unknown shore; he becomes king of the people
of his adoption. After death (or before it, when his work
is done) he is again carried away in a boat to Paradise.
Among the many mediæval forms of this myth one is
the legend of the Swan Knight, of which one special form
is the story of Lohengrin of Brabant.[2]

Lohengrin was son of Sir Percival, who, having been
while in the world long in search for the Holy Grail, had
been snatched up to a Fellowship of the Holy Grail in
another world. In this Paradise Lohengrin was born.
Then, at the prayer of Else of Brabant, he was sent into
the world to be her champion and to prove her innocence.
He married her and became Duke of Brabant. But the
condition of his staying by her side was that she should
never ask his name, and this condition she disregarded.
So once again the mystic boat came sailing down the
Rhine; and Lohengrin entered it once more, and was then
lost for ever to the world of men. But there is no need to
retell this tale to-day. Since this swan knight left the
world of popular lore he had slept in men's remembrance
till yesterday, when the wand of the magician again called
him back from the Paradise or Limbo of forgotten legends.
And now he has been reborn for us ' with no less gifts provided,' surrounded with a no less splendid halo of poetry
and beauty than they gave him who first sent him to
wander through the seas of human thought.

[1] ' *Insula* oceani quæ dicitur Scania.'—*Chron. Ethilw.* iii. 3.
' In quamdam *insulam* Scanzam, de qua Jornandes historiographus
Gothorum loquitur.'— *Wm. of Malmesbury.*
[2] See Grimm's *Deutsche Sagen*, ii. 256 sqq., for this legend, and several
others of the same kind.

CHAPTER X.

HEATHENISM IN THE MIDDLE AGES.

THE heathenism of Northern Europe cannot fully be studied if we confine ourselves to heathen literature and to heathen times alone ; for its beliefs are to be detected lurking in many secret places of the Catholicism of the Middle Ages ; nay, for that matter, they are to be discovered in contemporary creeds. We have already seen this in part, for while tracing out some special phases of belief—those, namely, which were concerned with the future state—we found ourselves insensibly being carried on from the mythology of the ancient Germans and Celts and of the Norsemen to similar myths which were current during the Middle Ages. We found ourselves passing, almost without intermission, from Helheim to the mediæval purgatory, and from the heathen notions touching the Earthly Paradise to the notions concerning the same place which were in vogue in the tenth and twelfth centuries.

What we have thus done in part and for particular elements of belief we ought to try and do for the whole. In a rough way we ought to try and discover what strain of heathenism still lingered in the Christianity of the Middle Ages, and how far the life and thought of the men of those days was a legacy from the past life and thought of the heathen days which had been before them. But this subject is an immense one, and cannot possibly be duly dealt with in one chapter. It can, at the very best, only be sketched in merest outline, and presented in a most fragmentary form. Wherefore what is set down in

the concluding pages of this volume is meant as a help to
the reader to recover for himself the threads of heathen
beliefs which run through mediæval Catholicism rather
than an attempt to draw out these threads in due order or
to trace their various interlacings.   Be it remembered,
too, that it is not into the ethical parts of Catholicism
that we are going to make enquiry.   It were far too great
a task to attempt to decide what elements in the moral
creed of the Middle Ages can be traced back to heathenism, and truly affiliated to the beliefs of heathen Europe,
and what elements are really Christian.   Moreover, though
our space were unlimited, that enquiry would always be
beyond the sphere of this work.   At the very outset of
this volume all intention was disclaimed of wandering
into the domain of morals.   The kind of belief which has
throughout been our study is that which is in its essentials independent of the moral code.   If ethics have entered here and there, they have come in, as we said they
would do, only by the way.

But another thing which was laid down at the outset
of the volume was this : that very early phases of belief
may subsist side by side with phases of much higher
development ; and that we are quite at liberty, if we
choose, to stray into these later fields in search of the
early 'formations' and nothing more.   Much, no doubt,
of mediæval Catholicism—nay, by far the greater part of
it—shows an advanced stage of religious growth.   As a
whole the creed lies far beyond that initial phase of monotheism which elsewhere we posed as the limits of our
special field of enquiry ; but there is yet something left in
Catholicism as a legacy from early days.   It is in quest
of these elements only that we turn to the study of it
now.

To say that we abandon the ethical parts of the creed
is the same thing as to say that we turn to search in
mediæval Christianity for those parts of it which spring
most directly from the contact of man with outward

nature. For it is by contact with outward nature that primitive phases of belief are formed. It is essential to the existence of these early strata of creeds that man should be still in a direct communion with external things, just as it is necessary to the growth of the later and ethical strata that man should be, to some extent at least, withdrawn from outside nature into himself; that he should have become, in a certain degree, self-conscious and introspective. Wherefore we must look to the outer regions of belief only. We must neglect all the higher aspects of Catholicism in neglecting all its ethical and reflective side. But this is the only way to bring the creed within the sphere of our present enquiry.

It is a thing to be remembered that the Middle, or, as we call them, the *dark*, Ages are essentially ages of mythology and not of history. To this they owe their character of *darkness*. They are dim to the historian, or, at any rate, to that historian who goes to them in the quest of naked fact. In the chronicles of these times we search in vain for anything which will help to form a complete or a true picture of the Catholic world—of society in those days, of its life and thought and aspirations. Each separate chronicle has been written in a corner by one who had no conception of the world beyond his own horizon. His outlook was generally that of a priest confined to a narrow cell. Few as are the actual facts which have come down to us, even these are robbed of the best part of their significance from appearing so disjointed as they do and without perspective. For we need to see not single objects but a succession of things before we can form a conception of the size or the distance of any one thing among them. In the histories of this time isolated occurrences loom for a moment out of the mist and then disappear into it again. There is no grand panorama of events. And all the characters who figure in these dramas are dim and shadowy, like the creations of a dream.

In place, however, of what we can fairly call history, there was, during all the dark ages, a copious growth of myth; and mythology is itself a kind of history. In the mythology of the Middle Ages we are allowed to see much of what the chroniclers keep from us. The myths hold up before us the world picture of the time. It is certainly an ideal and not an actual world which they present, but then the most ideal creations have somewhere a foundation in actuality and fact. The legend and the belief of this age is of more value than its naked history, for legend and belief then formed almost the greater part of men's lives; out of legend and myth their world was constructed. The dark ages of mediæval history are, in reality, prehistoric ages, though it may seem paradoxical to say so much. And the time before history begins, the time when men are less engaged in noting what does happen than in fancying what might happen, this is the golden age for myth and legend.

German folk tales delight above all things in that portrait of the youngest son of the house—he is the youngest of three—who is left behind despised and neglected when his brothers go forth to seek their fortunes. He is too childish or too lazy to be trusted with the magic wallet or staff which the father has bequeathed as their sole fortune among his sons. So the other two go forth. Each in turn tries his luck, and each returns with failure. Then it comes to the turn of the youngest. He tries and does not fail. In English stories we call this hero Boots. 'There he sits, idle whilst all work; there he lies, with that deep irony of conscious power which knows that its time must one day come and till then can afford to wait. When that day comes he girds himself to the fight amidst the scoff and scorn of his flesh and blood; but even then, after he has done some great deed, he conceals it, and again sits idly by the kitchen fire, dirty, lazy, despised, until the time for final recognition comes, and then his dirt and rags fall off—he stands out in all the majesty of his royal robes, and is acknowledged once for all a king.'[1]

The Germans of Germany, who, in their folk tales, have made this character so especially their own, might well have been led to do this by a lingering memory of their own history. They are the 'Boots' of Teutonic history during the era of the fall of Rome and of the barbarian invasions of Roman territory. The elder brothers—that is to say, the grown-up sons of the tribe—first went forth. Behind, in the ancestral village, beneath the immemorial shade of the village trees, they left the old and the very young, the father of the family and the 'hearth child,' as the youngest son is still described in our law of *Borough English.* That youngest son was to have a destiny of his own, different from theirs. From his loins were to spring the modern Germans of· Germany. But this Boots and his doings we will, as the stories do, for the present leave, and go forth with the elder brothers upon their travels. The stalwart sons of the house collect under their leaders (heretogas), throw up into the air a lance or a feather, and let Fate, in directing its fall or flight, show them the way they are to go.

At the time when the era of invasion first dawned the German people had so long led a settled life that their gods must have seemed to grow settled too, and even Odhinn, the wandering wind, must have been by each tribe narrowed into the wind which haunted its special corner of the forest. It must, therefore, have been that the Germans who quitted their homes and made their way southward or westward into Italy, or Gaul, or Spain, felt that they were leaving their ancient deities behind, and were migrating into the territory of new gods.[2] They fared forth much as Thorr had fared into Jötunheim, unknowing what magic spells might be weaving for them there.

[1] Dasent, *Norse Tales,* introd. p. cliv.
[2] See Milman, *Hist. Lat. Christ.* i. 338.

It happened ill with their ancient gods, as it had happened with Thorr; for though the German invaders overthrew the power of the Roman Empire, they were in their turn overthrown by the God of the country into which they came; they all, one after another, abjured the faith of Odhinn and adopted that of Christ. More than that, they were, to a certain extent, subdued by the nations whom they conquered; they became denationalised and ceased to be Germans, exchanging their rough Teutonic speech for the softer language of the Latins. It was by these conversions that the foundations of mediæval history were laid.

Between the beginning of the Teutonic invasions of Roman territory and the actual dawn of mediæval history occurred a long dark period of transition, which was occupied in the gradual and complete destruction of the Roman Empire by the barbarian hordes. At one time in many simultaneous streams from different quarters, and anon in successive waves of invasion from one direction, the sea of barbarism submerged the ancient fabric of the Roman Empire. From Mœsia came the Visigoths under Alaric, who thrice invaded Italy and laid siege to Rome, and who at last took the imperial city and sacked it. To their invasion, which did eventually flow away in a side stream without completing the destruction of the Western Empire, succeeded the more permanent conquests of the Ostrogoths, to be in their turn succeeded by those of the Lombards. And in the meantime to the north of the Alps there first came, from beyond the Rhine into Gaul, the miscellaneous army of the Suevi, Alani, Burgundians, and Vandals. Some (the Burgundians) settled in Gaul; the others passed on into Spain, and some from Spain to Africa. Then followed the stronger power of the Franks, who eventually overcame all their kindred German peoples, and wrested from them the whole of Gaul, with the exception of a small district in the south.[1]

[1] Narbonne, which long remained in the possession of the Visigoths.

The details of the contemporary conquest of our own island by the Angles and Saxons do not need to be recalled. The history of this era must needs seem to the student little less than a shifting of scenes or a pageant of players. By most writers it has been passed over as if it were no more than this. It is not an attractive epoch of history. It would be difficult, as Hallam says,[1] to find anywhere more vice or less virtue than in the records of this time. Along with the tragic dramas of these days there mingles sometimes a ghastly air of comedy, which suggests the idea of beings with the intellects of children inflamed by the fury of fiends.[2] But, despite the meanness and the horror which meet together in the history of this age, it was an epoch of great importance in the development of the German race. Out of it was born at least one great thing—namely, the greatest surviving epic in the German tongue.[3]

For I hold that the foundations of the Nibelungen poem were undoubtedly laid at this time. Nor, if we consider what a time of stir and excitement it was for the invading nations, will it appear strange that anything so considerable as a national epic should have been the result. Myths arise at many periods of a nation's life, and these myths weave themselves into the nation's early history and belief. But an epic springs up only occasionally, and in times which, whatever else they may be, are not ordinary ones.

We can hardly assign any period which seems so

[1] Echoing the words of Gibbon.

[2] Take for an example the account which Gregory of Tours gives us of how Theodoric, the son of Clovis, sought to compass the death of his brother Clotaire. He invited Clotaire to a conference in a room wherein he had meant to conceal behind a curtain a band of assassins. But the curtain was too short, and the men's legs were visible; so Clotaire got wind of the matter and came armed with a great company of his own people.—*Greg. Tur.* iii. 7.

[3] The conversion of the Germans to Christianity might be deemed the great event of this era. So in one sense it was. But no fruits of it were visible until the succeeding age.

appropriate to the growth of the Nibelungen epic—or
let me say the Nibelungen cycle of epics, for there are
many poems which belong to this class—as the era of the
Teutonic conquests. Some relics of the traditions of that
day may be traced in the events and the characters of the
drama. And we must confess that while, on the one hand,
no time was so likely to give birth to a great German epic
as the time I speak of, so also there is no other creation of
the German genius which can with reasonable probability
be held to have sprung up at that time. When a national
epic has begun to take shape, it inevitably follows that
many ancient myths, which were when alone comparatively
commonplace, group themselves about the hero or the
circumstance which the epic commemorates; like common
people wanting a leader, who range themselves under the
standard of a renowned chieftain. I do not say that no
songs and no stories like the Nibelungen had been sung in
earlier days than these great days of invasion and conquest;
but I say that it needed some mighty and sudden movement of society before these fragments could crystallise
into a single epic poem. Tacitus has left on record the
Germans' inveterate habit of composing war songs to
celebrate the deeds of ancient days. Some of these stories
may have gone to form a part of the Nibelungen. But
we may fairly suppose that at the time of which we are
speaking—the era of the barbarian invasions—the greater
number of the old legends gave place to new ones, suggested
by the fresh life into which the Germans entered.

The actual poem which has come down to us with the
name of the Nibelungen-Lied, or Nibelunge-Not (Slaughter
of the Nibelungs), is of quite a late period in mediæval
history. It belongs almost to the era of the *Revival of
Paganism* in the Renaissance. It is of the time of the
Hohenstaufen Emperors of Germany. The main object of
the story seems to have been to a great extent lost sight
of in the more modern extant poem, and subsidiary events
to have been enlarged so as to occupy the chief space in

the canvas. It is only by comparing this poem with
others which contain similar actions that we can recognise
the features of the original story. The incidents common
to all are of course the most antique. The other poems
beside which I place the Nibelungen are those of the
Völsung Saga in the North, including lays which have
found a place in the Edda, and the English poem Beowulf.
These together we may call the Nibelungen cycle of epic
poems.[1]

Of these three the earliest in date is Beowulf. The
portion of this poem which is akin to the stories of the
Völsungs and of the Nibelungs is not that of which a
sketch was given in the Seventh Chapter, but the concluding part which tells of the fight between Beowulf
and a great dragon which infested his land. The dragon
was the guardian of an ancient 'heathen hoard' of gold,

---

[1] It has been maintained by some writers that the Völsung Saga is
nothing else than a plagiarism from the Nibelungen. But the arguments
in controversion of this view are of overwhelming force. In the first place
a story of the Völsungs was known to the author of Beowulf.

> . . . . Hwylc geowæð þæt he fram Sigemunde
> Seogan hýrde; ellen-dædum;
> Uncuþes fela, Wælsinges gewin.
>
> .   .   .   .   .   .
> Sigemonde gesprong, æfter deáð-dæge
> Dóm unlytel; syðan wiges heard
> Wyrm acwealde. . . .   . . . l. 1758, &c.

> He told all that of Sigmund
> He had heard say; of deeds renounded;
> Of strange things many; the Wælsing's victories.
>
> .   .   .   .   .   .
> To Sigmond ensued after his death-day
> No little glory, when the fierce in fight
> The worm had slain.

The hero of the adventure was at first Sigmund—at least this was so in
the North. It is possible that the name of Sigurd is taken from Siegfried.
This evidence is alone, I should have supposed, tolerably decisive. But
even without the aid of the passage just quoted the elements of the
Völsung tale in Beowulf, the *intermediate condition* of the Völsunga Saga
between Beowulf and the Nibelungen, the remains of ancient heathen
belief in it which have been entirely forgotten in the Nibelungen-Lied
(see Chaps. VII. and VIII.), are tolerably decisive evidence of the antiquity
and originality of the Northern epic.

and Beowulf in killing the worm set free that treasure. But he could not himself enjoy it—or could for a brief moment only—for he had received a mortal hurt in the combat, and almost immediately after it was over he died. This is a very short and a very simple incident. But it contains what is, I suspect, the most germain matter of the original epic of this cycle. In the Völsung lays [1] the story is considerably expanded. We have first the history of Sigurd's fight with the worm Fafnir, which reproduces the distinctive characteristics of Beowulf's fight with his dragon, only with this difference, that Sigurd was not killed in the encounter.[2] He died from a different immediate cause. But still the slaying of Fafnir was the final cause of his death; for it seems to have been through greed of the gold of Fafnir, as much as from any other motive, that Sigurd was treacherously slain by Gunnar and Högni.[3] In these Völsung poems many fresh elements are introduced into the story. As the tale now goes we have first the finding of Brynhild by Sigurd and the vows which these exchange; then the oblivious potion administered to Sigurd and his marriage with Godrûn; then Brynhild's revenge, the death of Sigurd, and Brynhild's own suicide; and last of all Godrûn's vengeance on the murderers of Sigurd and the ensuing slaughter of the Niflungs.

In the actual Nibelungen-Lied, which I take to be the latest of all the forms of the epic, the finding of the

---

[1] It is hardly necessary to say that the *lays* of the Völsunga Saga are the oldest portions of it.

[2] Not at least in the story in its present form. But I have little doubt that in an earlier account Sigurd, after the fight with Fafnir, did descend into the House of Death; for the next thing which he did was to go through the fire at Hindarfjöll to wake Brynhild from her sleep of death. This fire, as was shown in Chap. VIII., is a symbol of death. Thus the myth has been obscured by time in the same way in which came to be obscured Apollo's descent to Admetus-Hades after *his* serpent fight.

[3] According to one account Sigurd was actually done to death by Guthorm, the younger brother of these two. But (as is said in the *Drap Niflunga*) Gunnar and Högni divided between them Fafnir's gold.

treasure has been almost left out of account, and now the whole history is of the jealousies of Brynhild and Godrûn and of the murders which ensue therefrom. Yet even in this latest poem the possession by Sigurd of the treasure of the Nibelungs, otherwise called the Rhine gold, is alluded to again and again in a way which shows that this must once have constituted an integral portion of the story.

Taking, then, the two essential features in the history of Sigurd to be his slaying the worm Fafnir and his own death by treachery, the first thing we notice is that the hero combines in himself the characteristics of two among the old Teuton divinities—of those two, in fact, whose characters have received most from the epic spirit of the Norsemen. These divinities are Thorr and Balder. The longest stories which the Younger Edda tells us are those which relate to these two gods, who were, moreover, each of them originally sun gods. The most important among the deeds of Thorr are his contests with the mid-earth serpent, combats which are, as I have said, reproduced in most of the mediæval dragon fights of Europe. The essential part of the myth of Balder is his premature death at the hand of his blind brother Höör. These two elements have been united to form the story of Sigurd or Siegfried; and here the worm Fafnir has replaced Jörmungandr, while in the place of Höör we have Högni or Hagen.[1]

This is enough to show us that Sigurd and Siegfried are true descendants from the heroes of ancient heathen days, and that the tradition of the heroic character had not been essentially changed from one epoch to another. Other remnants of heathen belief are visible in the Völsung

---

[1] Odhinn has come to be confounded with Höör in this later epic; for there can be no question that Hagen is meant for Odhinn. (See supra p. 391, note.) In the Völsung epic Odhinn has altogether sunk from the high position which he holds in the poems of the religious part of the Edda. He has ceased to be so much the friend of man and he has ceased also to be so powerful as he once was. See what is said in the next paragraph.

lays- -whereof in former chapters we have already noted
the most conspicuous—and in Beowulf. But in the latest
poem of the cycle, the Nibelungen, these minor traces
are not to be found. Perhaps the most noticeable thing
in the poem (and this applies in no small degree to the
Völsung Saga also) is the absence of religious feeling
from it. It is little affected by the beliefs of heathen
Germany, but still less is it affected by the creed of
Christendom. Yet this very absence of religious feeling
is expressive of the time during which the Nibelungen
epic sprang into existence. It belongs precisely to that
era of transition when a great part of the German nation
had left behind them their old gods and had, as yet, found
no new divinity.

In the Nibelungen the names of some few among the
actors of the drama are historical, as, for example, Etzel,
who is Attila, and Dietrich of Bern, who is the Ostrogothic
king Theodoric.[1] These names are enough to suggest the
time at which the Nibelungen epic had its birth. And
though the motive of the poem has insensibly shifted from
what it was at first, and has been presented in a form more
intelligible to the readers of the thirteenth century than it
would have had if it told only of disputes for the possession of a treasure, still the epic has preserved in a wonderful degree the spirit of the time which gave it birth.

I am insensibly led to speak of the ethic characteristics
of the Nibelungen, contrary to the principle which I laid
down anon that the ethics of the Middle Ages were not a
part of our concern, because the spirit and *morale* of this
great poem are so peculiar and so typical of the time in
which the Nibelungen legend first sprang up. It is the
spirit of that special period of transition from heathenism
to Christianity and from the total barbarism of the old
Teutonic life to the semi-barbarism of the Middle Ages. In
tone and in ethic the poem must be called heathen, in that

---

[1] Dietrich of Bern = Theodoric of Verona.

there is nothing in it at all suggestive of Christianity. But it does not suggest either the heathenism of the old days. It belongs only to that epoch during which the German invaders had abandoned Odhinn, for they had left him behind in their ancestral villages, but had not yet adopted Christ. The picture which the lay holds up before us is a horrible one, a tissue of aimless slaughter, a history almost altogether foul and bloody, in which if some noble figures for a time appear they are sure to be the first to perish.[1] It is not to be supposed that the picture here drawn, so different from those drawn by Tacitus and from those presented in more Christian epics, is true for all time; but it is undoubtedly true for the exact era to which it refers. The people were caught with the delirium of conquest and by the fatal enchantment of wealth. All their thought was now concentrated on heaps of gold, such as those for which their heroes are described as fighting. This desire for the possession of a hoard of buried treasure is the one motive force of the whole drama. While from the fiercer Völsung and Nibelungen poems the cruelty and greed look out in all their native horror, even in the milder Beowulf the importance attaching to the gaining of such a hoard is shown as conspicuously, though less repulsively. The killing of the dragon was the crowning act of the hero's glorious career. All his adventures were consummated in the gaining of the 'heathen hoard,' and a heroic life was thought to reach its due ending in such a deed. As Beowulf was dying he bade his comrade bring forth the treasure, to feast his eyes therewith. Then he gave thanks.

Ic ðára frætwa	For this treasure I
Freán ealles þanc,	Thanks to the Lord of all,
Wuldur cyninge,	To the King of Renown,
Wordum secge.	Do now express.

. . . .

[1] Siegfried, though he is the hero of the Nibelungen, and is besides the only fine character in the piece, is slain in the sixteenth *Aventiure,* and the poem contains thirty-nine of these cantos.

Ǽr swylt dæge, Ere my death day,
Swylc gestrýnan.[1] Such acquire.

That this fever should have seized upon the German races during the era of their first conquests in Roman territory will not seem strange to us when we think of all the enchantments which were woven for them in the lands to which they came. Little did they guess what powers lay in ambush there, powers not less intoxicating to the sense, and not less deceitful to the mind, than were the spells of those giants who, to Teutonic fancy, held all regions remote from the German's native home.

The enchantment which first fell upon the invaders came from that wonder of Roman civilisation of which they had before only heard. The Goths in Mæsia, to whom the apostle Ulfilas preached in the fourth century,[2] were living a life not greatly different from the life of their Aryan forefathers two thousand years before. Like the Aryas, who counted everything by their herds, these Goths had no wealth but in their cattle, and when Ulfilas desired to translate into their tongue any of the words for money in the New Testament he could find no equivalent but the Gothic *faihu*, which means cattle. Yet, before a generation had passed away, the same Goths had been transplanted into the midst of the teeming luxury of Italy and Southern Gaul. All the stored wealth of these countries lay before them to make their own. It is true that to them money, for the uses to which it is now put, had little value; and they probably never understood how coined metal could be made subservient to the gratification of civilised tastes and appetites. They had no need of and no care for the real beauties which adorned the life of a rich Roman citizen—his stately villas, his statues, his gardens —but his more portable wealth they could seize upon and

---

[1] Beowulf, l. 5580 sqq. [2] Circ. 340–388.

cherish, as though it held some charm which might convert their rough lives into lives capable of the enjoyments which they saw and envied and could not reach. We know what kind of useless use they *did* make of the treasures which they gained. One picture of their method of employing the precious metals is given to us in the inventory of the marriage presents which were brought to the Visigoth Ataulf when he espoused the sister of Honorius. Gibbon [1] tells of the hundred bowls full of gold and jewels which were brought by the Goths as a present to the bride Placidia; of the fifty cups and sixteen patens of gold; of the immense *missorium* or dish of the same metal, in weight 500 pounds, which was discovered in the treasure-house of Narbonne when that city was taken by the Franks. But a better notion of the rude use of treasure among the Teuton peoples is given by the roughly-made utensils—bowls, jars, and platters—all in solid gold, which, under the name of viking treasures, are preserved in the Museum of Copenhagen. Such witnesses as these from the historic past take away their utterly fabulous character from accounts of treasure contained in the ballad poetry of the same age; as, for example, the description in Beowulf of the palace of Hrothgar, King of the Ring Danes, which was roofed with pure gold. We may gather from these examples how the Germans actually employed the hoards that they won; but we can never learn the full effect which the vision of this wealth had upon their imaginations. Why the sight of treasure in the precious metals begets in men a wolfish craving and more than wolfish cruelty it were hard to say. It was so with the Spaniards of the sixteenth century, as with these Germans of the sixth. The whole nation had now, like their national hero, Sigurd, eaten of the serpent's heart—a dreadful sacrament of cruelty and desire. They had grown wiser, but they had grown to have, like Athênê, ' untender hearts.'

---

[1] Chap. xxxi.

We shall the better appreciate this characteristic of the Nibelungen epics when we have been able to compare them with another cycle of poems which are as essentially Christian as the Nibelungen are un-Christian. To find a true antithesis to the great epic of conquest and spoliation, such an antithesis as may show the change in men's thoughts and lives after the Middle Ages had really dawned, we shall have to pass on to that series of poems which are called the ' Chansons de Geste,' the great Karling epic of the eleventh and twelfth centuries. These poems are as completely informed by the spirit of mediæval Catholicism as the Nibelungen is informed by the spirit of the Teutonic conquests. But before we look at the ' Chansons de Geste ' let us turn aside for a moment to trace some of the lower currents of popular mythology, which existed during these ages—from the time of the Teutonic conquests to the time of the rise of the Karling poems.

Epics, it has been said, belong to an age in which some great emotion is stirring the hearts of the people, giving a unity to their national life and making them march together in a rhythmic motion as to the tune of a war song. Of this order of creations were, whatever their faults, the Nibelungen-Lied and the other poems of that cycle; of such an order was the Carlovingian epic, of which we shall have occasion to speak presently, and which arose when men's thoughts were being turned toward the great contest between the East and the West, between Mohammadanism and Christianity. But in quieter times or in places remote from the stir of excitement and adventure the stream of popular mythology keeps almost unchanged its tranquil, languid course.

The literature of the kind which the Nibelungen represents belongs to the warlike classes. Those who first chaunted the stanzas of the German epic were they who had been the votaries of Odhinn, the Wind, who had kept the mark and guarded the village. They went forth to become the ruling races in the countries which they conquered. In these lands they found the older inhabitants more civilised than themselves, but without national spirit or national coherence, who were destined soon to sink to the class of serfs and peasants. Thus for awhile these conquering Germans stood apart, forming a nationality of their own, belonging neither to their native country, which they abandoned, nor to the land into which they came. They lived still a life of camps; they were ever on the move and had no sense of property nor of a settled home.[1] Therefore the national epic which represents their deeds and thoughts is in many ways peculiar and can scarcely be taken for an episode in the regular development of belief. But with the peaceful brethren whom they left behind, and among the peasant folk whom they conquered, the old creeds, the religion of the Germans by the one and the beliefs of the Celts by the other, were cherished more persistently. But as the common people in both regions were for the present deprived of their natural leaders and of the more eager and adventurous minds among them, their creeds threw off the finer portions of them and sank down to be essentially the beliefs of peasants.

There is in every religious system a popular mythology which lies like a soft alluvial bed all round the more striking elevations of religious thought; and which, easily as it seems to take impressions, is sometimes found to form the most immutable portion of the creed. The earthquakes, the sudden cataclasms which overwhelm the heights, leave these parts uninjured. They become most noticeable when the striking features of the religion have been for a time annihilated; but they have pre-existed in days long anterior to these changes, and are not by such revolutions called into being. We have seen how, while

---

[1] This character attaching to the Merovingian Franks has been very well pointed out by Guizot (*Cours de l'Histoire de France*, 8ᵐᵉ leçon) and after him by Michelet (*Hist. de France*, livre ii.)

those elements of a creed which may be called national are always the grander ones, there may remain among separate fragments of the people many beliefs which are little removed from a primitive fetich worship. If the nation is for awhile denationalised, and transformed into a congeries of units, these primitive elements of belief will again come to the front. It was through this kind of separation between the different elements of society that opportunity was given for the mythology of the lower people to rise to the surface, and to take its place as it eventually did in the literary history of the Middle Ages.

There are, it seems to me, three distinctly traceable streams of folk belief which must be taken to have flowed side by side with the more important epics of the Middle Ages—side by side with the Nibelungen and side by side with the Karling poems. Each stream bears the character of a mythology sprung up among a conquered race or at any rate among the inferior orders of society.

First of all, there was among the Celts in England itself, and probably in other lands, a large body of ancient heroic myth which celebrated the deeds of the gods or heroes of the Celtic creed, and out of which the portion which has survived for us eventually took the shape of the legend of Arthur. This legend only became generally popular toward the very end of the Middle Ages. Having for centuries lived on in neglect, and passed from mouth to mouth among the peasantry, it suddenly grew into favour just at the time at which the more famous 'Chansons de Geste' were falling out of notice. This legend of Arthur contained in it many elements peculiar to the Celtic mytho- logy, elements of that mythology which are also noticeable in another popular tradition of which we shall presently speak. In a former chapter we saw how this legend pre- served the true Celtic form of the myth of the Earthly Paradise. But the Arthur legend could not have been in any wide sense a popular mythology. It was cherished by the Britons, but the Celts of Continental Europe had been too long Romanised, and were too thoroughly Christian, to remember the histories of their fabulous heroes. Therefore the legend belongs of right only to a small section of this race, and takes no important place in the mythology of mediæval Europe.[1]

Much more truly popular among the mass of the Celtic people—the inhabitants of Gaul, for example, in the days of Merovingian rule—must have been a parallel series of legends—those of the saints. These were to some extent examples of pre-Christian mythology, though clothed in the garb of Christianity.

The time at which these legends began to circulate was the century which followed the epoch of Merovingian conquest; it was after the beginning of the seventh century that men first began to collect the legends and write them down. The age of persecution had now ceased, and time was beginning to grow its moss and lichen over the memories of the martyrs of the preceding age, men who had been dear in every way to the subjugated people, as fellow-countrymen and as champions of Christianity. Then there arose a race of pious priests, who went about collecting the oral traditions and graving again, like Old Mortality at the tombs of the Covenanters,[2] the inscriptions which had once been written in men's hearts, but were now in too much danger of becoming effaced.

In morality the stories of the saints are as complete a contrast as could be looked for to the morality of the ruling races—as that was portrayed to and by themselves in their epic poems, or as it is portrayed to us by the contemporary chroniclers. The saint legend is childish in that innocent and simple fashion which bespeaks the mythology of peasant folk in every age. Where we are not face to face with the Christian element of the story,

---

[1] At the date when the Arthur legend became widely known the true mythic age of Europe had come to an end.

[2] This simile is Guizot's. See his fine essay, *Cours d'Hist. Mod.—Hist. de France*, leçon 17.

its morality, we have got back to the very primitive groundwork of mythology, the folk tale. These stories must have grown up side by side with the fairy legends which are so common in old France, tales of the courils, the corrigans[1] and lutins of Brittany and of the fays and dracs of the South. Such beings as these and the tales that are devoted to them are earlier than the great creations of mythology and the more serious parts of belief; and they are also much longer lived than these are.

> Perch' una fata non può mai morire
> Fin al di del giudicio universale.[2]

In days when the German races, despite their pretended conversion, would have little to do with Christianity, and it was ' a thing unheard of for a Merovingian to become a clerk,'[3] Christianity must needs have been in every way a religion for the peasantry. Even the rulers of the Church were in those days chosen from among the conquered race, from among such Romans[4] as had gained influence over the barbarians; the lower orders of the priesthood and the monks were drawn from the peasant and the slavish classes.[5] It was for this reason that the legends of the saints were so deeply imbued with the thoughts and beliefs of rustic life; the same kind of ad-

---

[1] The corrigans were probably, like the fays, originally women. The name comes from *corrig*, little, and *gwynn*, woman, or else *gwenn*, genie. Perhaps these two were originally the same word. See Leroux de Lincy, *Introduction au Livre des Légendes.* The presence of the fairy element in the Arthurian legend is also very noticeable, and makes a strong contrast between these myths and those of the Carlovingian era. The last were much more German than Celtic.

[2] Bojardo, *Orlando Inamorato*, li. 26. 15.

[3] See the story of St. Columba and Theodebert II.; also the story of Clotilda, who said that she would rather see her grandchildren dead than tonsured.—*Greg. Tur.* iii.

[4] Romanised Gauls or Goths.

[5] It was quite otherwise in the days of Charlemagne; for in the capitularies of that king slaves are expressly forbidden to become monks; this contrast is typical of the change which passed over Christendom during the eighth century.

venture runs through the saint legend and the popular tale. The intervention in one case is that of Providence or of some saint; in the other case it is that of the little familiar, the corrigan or fairy. The deeds of the two orders of heroes are different in detail, but they are the same in spirit and intention. In one set of stories the hero conquers his enemies by his fairy gifts, and gains the princess at the end; in the other he works the same wonders by his miraculous powers. overcoming all his foes, avowed and secret, and becoming the confidant of kings. That he afterwards falls into trouble and ends by suffering martyrdom is the result due as much to a canon of fitness external to the storyteller as to any predilection of his own.

The third current was, originally, a pure stream of popular mythology. It was unmixed either with religion or with any legends of that higher kind, such as are necessary to complete a religious system. The stream of which I speak was the great Beast Epic of mediæval Europe, of which we have some scattered remnants in the histories of Reineke the Fox and Isengrim the Wolf. Yet these tales are doubtless but fragments of an ancient apologue, which was current throughout Northern Europe.

The traces of the Reinhart legend in many different lands prove the wide distribution and the early origin of the story. Among extant editions of the fable, however, the greater number belong to the borderland between Northern France and Germany; they have generally come from Upper or Lower Flanders. All these extant forms of the Beast Epic are of too modern a date to give us a trustworthy clue to the nature of this epic at the time at which it sprang up among the peasantry of Northern Europe.[1]

---

[1] Grimm (*Reinhart Fuchs*) has published a number of the earliest extant forms of the fable of Reinhart and Isengrim. The first of these is a Latin poem of 688 lines, called *Isengrimus*. It belongs to the first half of the twelfth century. Of nearly the same date are the *Reinardus*, another Latin poem of 6,596 lines; the *Reinhart* (Old High German), of

I I

It is difficult to settle the claim to its authorship of the
two nationalities—French and German. For while, on the
one hand, the French has so completely adopted the story
that the name of the hero, Renard, has come in that language to stand for the generic name for fox, to the total
exclusion of the older word, *vulpe*, this name itself, as well
as those of the other chief actors in the story, Isengrim
and Bruin, are apparently words of German and not of
French origin.[1] That which we can distinguish in the
epic is that it was the possession of the lower strata of
society. The hero, Renard, is the representative of a subject race, while Isengrim, the wolf, represents the conquerors ; and the whole history of the poem is of the
wiles by which Renard gets the better of his stronger
cousin.

But though Renard represented the peasant class
wherever the legend was current, I am on the whole disposed to look upon him as standing rather for the lower
orders of the German race than for the subject Celtic
population. There is a close relationship between Renard
and Isengrim ; they are not of alien blood, though their
interests are ever opposed.[2] In truth, the character of
Renard is precisely the character of the men of the

2,266 lines ; and the *Reinaert de Vos*, of 2,350 lines.   The third of these
four poems comes from Alsace, the other three from Flanders.

The three great poems of the epic cycle are *Reinardus* (twelfth century), *Roman de Renart* (thirteenth or fourteenth century), *Reineke Fuchs*
(end of fifteenth century).

[1] 'Noble' (the Lion) is, on the other hand, a distinctly French gloss.
Otherwise the name would have been Adel. But, as Grimm says, the
Bear probably originally performed the office of king (*Reinhart Fuchs*,
Introd. xlvii. liii.) This office was, in course of time, transferred to the
Lion.

The essential characters of the drama are, says Grimm, the conqueror,
the conquered, and the judge—Wolf, Fox, and Bear or Lion.   For 'conqueror' and 'conquered' we may perhaps substitute 'ruling' and 'subject'
races.

[2] Throughout the poems they constantly call each other *cousin*, or *uncle*
and *nephew*. The nearness of kinship between the fox and the wolf in
popular belief is well shown by the etymology of the names for them, *wolf*
being etymologically allied to *vulpes*.

country to which '·Reinhart Fuchs' seems especially to belong, the inhabitants of the almost independent but yet physically weak trading cities of Flanders. These men were still essentially German, but their sympathies were not with German conquerors, with the nobility of France or Germany, but with the peasant class.[1]

The Thorr of Scandinavian or the Donar of Teuton belief became in time the patron god of the peasantry, and instead of being a warrior he grew to be a promoter of agriculture, and of that kind of war only which agriculture wages against the rude waste tracts of a country.[2] As Odhinn (Wuotan) remained the warlike god, and so the god of the ruling classes, there would naturally grow up some rivalry between the two chief Teuton divinities. A trace of this enmity is shown in one of the Eddaic poems, the 'Harbarðsljóð,' at least in the latest acceptation of its intention; for though Harbarð began by being a giant, there can be no question that he was eventually confounded with Odhinn. Without meaning it to be supposed that the original story of the 'Reineke Fuchs' was in any way founded upon the myth system of Asgard and the Teuton divinities, I can imagine that in its actual shape it does bear some traces of this mythology as it appeared during its latter years. It may well be that the red Reineke has inherited something from the red Thorr and the grey Isengrim, something from the grey Odhinn.[3] In Iceland the fox is still sometimes called holtaþórr (wood-Thorr).[4] Odhinn was generally the grey-headed and grey-bearded

---

[1] It is only in the later forms of the Reineke legend that the hero is converted into a knight possessing a castle Malepertus.

[2] See Simrock, *Handbuch* passim, and Uhland, *Der Mythus von Thor.*

[3] Thorr, as the Thunderer, was always the red God. He was imagined to have a red beard (Forn. Sög. ii. 182, x. 329). Odhinn is sometimes a red god, though more generally a grey. Reinhart is constantly addressed as the 'red,' as is indeed natural. See *Reinardus*, 284, 1463; *Reinaert*, 4394; *Rom. de Renart*, 463, 502, 4557, 6088, 6674, 6689, 8251, 8815, 9683. Isengrim is almost as often styled the 'grey,' *canus, cano,* &c.

[4] Grimm, *D. M.* i. 148.

god; and the wolf was especially sacred to him.   Wherefore Isengrim would be an appropriate representative of Odhinn.   And it is very probable that beside the element of primitive belief in this Beast Epic, a species of mythology which is probably earlier than the construction of any Asgard or ordered pantheon of gods, and which may have belonged as much to Celts as to Germans, there is likewise some reminiscence of the peculiar religious system of the Teutonic people.

Such fragments of pristine belief as these which we have enumerated I place about the period during which the German conquerors were settling into their new homes, and Europe was entering upon its mediæval life. I do this not because this kind of popular belief does in itself belong to any peculiar age, but because it is especially in times of transition, and we may say of deuationalisation, that primitive myths take an important place in the world's creed.   It is only under such circumstances that they rise to the surface and assume something of the dignity of national epics.

But the German race was not destined to remain for ever so little like a nation, so much like a house divided against itself, as it was during the age which immediately succeeded its conquests of Roman territory, during the rule of the Merovingian kings in France, of the Lombards in Italy, during the days of the Suevi and Visigoths in Spain and of our Heptarchy in England.   A new influence of German thought began to make itself felt when the Karling dynasty supplanted the Merovingian dynasty in France, and when through the strength of the eastern Franks that dynasty became in the person of Charles the supreme ruler in Europe.

Though a thousand unrecorded Christmas Days have passed away since then, history will not soo~ ~~~ ~~~~~~~ that Christmas Day of the year 800, whe was kneeling before the altar of S

Leo III. (so Eginhard tells the story [1]) came behind him unperceived, and placing a diadem upon his head cried out, ' Hail to Charles the Augustus, the great and peaceful Emperor of the Romans ! ' The vision which floated before the minds of the statesmen of those days was the revival of the old effete Western Empire under better conditions, with a strong orthodox Emperor at its head, and of a renewal with all its ancient glories of the Roman civilisation. But it was not this that the ceremony of that Christmas Day did really solemnise. The Roman nation was not galvanised into new life ; in place thereof the power of the barbarians was established and the era of their influence on European history was inaugurated. In the person of their king the crown was placed upon the head of the Germans.

Now for the first time for many hundred years some order and fixed law began to appear in the governance of society; for now all the nations, save those in the far North and in the East, had been converted to Christianity. Now, too, all the conquests of the Germans over the Romans and Celts had come to an end.[2] No longer a thought remained of migration or of further change. The life of camps was abandoned, and that complete settlement of the Germans in their new lands took place which directly led to the institution of feudalism, and hence to the petrified, unvarying life of the Middle Ages.

The literature which speaks most eloquently of the beliefs and feelings of the age which followed this establishment of the Carlovingian dynasty is that immense cycle of epic poems which has gathered round the name of the great emperor, and which is hence called the Karling epic. But the name by which they were distinguished in their own day was ' Chansons de Geste.' The stories which are told in these songs, almost without exception, revolve round the traditional figure of Charlemagne. But this

---

[1] *Vita Kar. Magni*, 100 ; *Annal.* 215.
[2] Save in the far West—Wales, Ireland, Scotland.

Charlemagne is not the historical king of the Franks; he is the mythic being which a couple of centuries of legendary hero worship have made him. The motive of the poems—the spirit, that is to say, which moves and animates them—is the spirit of the crusader, for they arose at the beginning of the great contest between the East and the West; they faded away when the enthusiasm of the crusades died down. In these poems Charlemagne is transformed into the ideal crusader. His deeds of arms are wrought for the discomfiture of the Saracen, and nearly all the actions of the other heroes of the songs have the same intent.

Though Christian in tone, the 'Chansons' are not Celtic; on the contrary, they are essentially Germanic. They are Teutonic in the spirit that animates them, in the tramp of battle to which they seem to keep time, in the forms of love and hate which they chronicle; they are Teutonic even in lesser details, as in the actual method of fighting which they describe and the mode of arranging an army, or in the system of administering justice.[1] There can be no doubt that the 'Chansons de Geste' are, not less than the Nibelungen, the offspring of the chaunts by which from time immemorial the German line of battle used to go encouraged into action, and in which, when the battle was over, the soldiers used to find their voice again by the fireside. Tradition, therefore, was never quite broken through between the days of the old heathen war songs and those of the birth of the newer Christian epic. And it could hardly be but that many of the legends of heathenism were handed on from one era to the other.

True the religion of the people had been utterly changed between the two epochs; and, so far as regards either the formal belief or the morality of the 'Chansons,' these afford as great a contrast as could be imagined to the thoughts of heathenism upon the same subjects. The Christian theory of morals, in the form in which that was

---

[1] See Léon Gautier, *Epopée française*, vol. i. p. 28.

understood in the tenth and eleventh centuries, shines brightly in these poems, and at once divides them by an impassable gulf from the poems of the Nibelungen cycle. But as regards the outer region of belief, that part which does not touch closely upon morality, and does not come in contact with the Biblical teaching concerning this world or the next, the barrier between the Christian epic and the older literature of heathen times is far less conspicuous. It was to a great extent upon the pattern of Odhinn, of Thorr, or of other gods and heroes of Asgard and Walhalla that the legendary characters of Charlemagné and his paladins were formed.

The emperor himself is in many ways the counterpart of Odhinn (Wuotan), and seems to perform the same duties in the midst of his twelve peers which Odhinn exercised among the twelve gods of Asgard. The part which Odhinn played in Valhöll the same part did Charles play at Aix. The former was, as we saw, essentially the counsellor and the wise one among the gods. Though he was a god of battle and mighty in the combat, he was less distinctively a fighter than a deliberator. Thorr and Tyr could do battle as well as he; but none possessed the wisdom of Odhinn. Now this is just the character which attaches to Charles. Roland or Oliver can do the fighting, but Charles is always the one who takes and gives counsel, who settles upon the occasion and the place of war. In the 'Chanson de Roland' there is a fine picture of Charles seated to receive the ambassadors from a certain Saracen king. We see him on a golden throne, with hair and long beard all white—

Blanche ad la barbe o tut florit le chief—

with head bent down, eyes cast upon the ground, long pondering before he gave his answer; 'for,' says the poet, 'Charles never spake in haste.'

Moreover the likeness between Odhinn and Charles appear peculiarly strong in one respect, viz. in the aspect of great age which each wears. It is as strange to endow a chief god as to endow a popular hero with the appearance of eld. Although the former might be supposed to have existed through all time, one could not have expected that men would have fancied him bearing on his person any impress of the flight of years; and one would have expected it least of all with a people who set so much value upon physical strength as did the Germans. Yet it is a fact that wherever Odhinn makes his appearance in later German tradition it is as a quite old, grey-headed, grey-bearded man. He is, in the language of Mr. Morris's 'Sigurd the Völsung,' 'one-eyed, and seeming ancient.' I do not know whether this had always been the conception of Odhinn, but it certainly was the image of him which existed in the latter days of paganism. And now in the dawning of the Christian epic we see the same conception embodied in Charles. There are some 'Chansons' which tell of Charlemagne's boyhood and early youth, though these are not among the earliest of the collection. In any case the minute this early youth is passed Charlemagne seems to have become suddenly a very old man. There is no intermediate stage between twenty and sixty or more. Charlemagne is nearly always called, as in the passage just quoted, him 'of the white beard.' In the 'Chanson de Roland,' the oldest and the most truly epic of all the collection, Charlemagne is made to be two hundred years old and more—*mien escient dous cens ans ad passet.*

Again, Charles has still somewhat the character of the tempest god; he seems to wield, like Odhinn, the powers of the storm, and the thunder like Zeus or Thorr; the glance of his eyes can strike men to the ground as if they had been struck by the bolt. Odhinn had for ever flying round his head two ravens, Hugin and Munin (Thought and Memory), who were his counsellors. In place of these Charles has two heavenly guides—namely, two angels—who never leave him.

Another thing which draws close the link between

the god and the epic hero is that in popular German tradition Charles the Great is made to lie asleep beneath a mountain, where, without question, Odhinn had once slept before.[1] In other traditions a still later national hero, Frederick Redbeard (Barbarossa), takes the place of the god. He sleeps at Kaiserlautern or at Kiffhäuser. Everyone knows the story of the shepherd youth who, by an underground passage, found his way into the midst of the hill, and there saw Frederick with his head upon a table, through which the beard of the king had grown. Frederick awoke at the sound of the strange footsteps, and demanded of the shepherd, 'Are the *ravens* still flying round the hill?' 'Yes,' he answered. 'Then must I sleep another hundred years.' In this tale the birds of Odhinn still linger to mark the place where he sleeps and the true individuality of the sleeper.

The Valkyriur too are not wanting from the legend of Charlemagne, for they are represented by the daughters of the emperor. These women are ever described as viragoes. They were said to ride with their father to battle; one of them, Emma, actually carried off by force a hesitating lover.[2]

One antique Teuton goddess, reappearing in these tales, does so while keeping her proper name. This is Berchta (Perchta), whom in a former chapter we spoke of as the counterpart in Germany proper of the Norse goddess Frigg, the wife of Odhinn. Berchta seems, in fact, to have been one of the names of this consort of Wuotan, and the goddess herself to have been a sort of Queen of Heaven.[3] The same name recurs continually in the 'Chansons de Geste.' There is *Berte aus grans piès* (Bertha Broadfoot), the mother of Charles; and another Bertha,

---

[1] In one instance, at all events, the mountain is called Wodansberg.

[2] Grimm, *Deutsche Sagen*, ii. 115, &c.

[3] See Grimm, *D. M.* i. 226 sqq.; Simrock, *Handb. der deut. Myth.* 293. 357, 364, 409, 548; also Wuttke, *Deutsch. Volksab.* ch. i.; Kuhn, *S. G. M.* &c. Berchta is something of an earth goddess, as is Frigg.

the sister of Charles and the mother of Roland. The first
of these two partook of the Valkyria nature. The name
of Broadfoot came to her from her having one foot webbed
like the foot of a swan. This was all that remained of the
power which once belonged to the Valkyriur of changing
themselves into birds. To such mean dimensions had
shrunk the beautiful myth of Odhinn's swan maidens.

As Charles was the due representative of Allfather
Odhinn, so was Roland, the great hero of this epic, a
representative of his son Thorr. We may perhaps say
that, like Siegfried of the Nibelungen, he combines in
himself traits taken from the two principal divinities of
the second generation among the Æsir. He, quite con-
trariwise to his uncle, is always young. He is evidently
meant to be in the glow of youth at the very day of his
death.

Amis Rollanz, prozdom, juvente bele! [1]

exclaimed Charles in his lament over him after Ron-
cesvaux. Roland was at the end still unmarried, though
affianced to the lovely Aude. Yet he was own nephew to
Charlemagne, who at the same time was two hundred
years old.

Roland was the bearer of the great horn or olifant of
Charlemagne's army. At Roncesvalles, when the rear-
guard of the French under Roland had been surprised and
nearly cut to pieces by the army of the Saracen, Roland
put the horn to his lips and blew a blast, in the hope of
recalling the main body of the army. He blew with such
force that the sound was heard thirty leagues away, and
reached the ears of Charles and of his army, who had
already returned to France. All the host of Charles stood
listening, and three times this distant echo came to their
ears. 'That horn had a long breath,' said the king. But ere
the main body of the French could get back to the battle
field the rear-guard had almost all been slain, and Roland

---

[1] Ami Roland, vaillant homme, belle jeunesse !

himself was wounded to death. Then he sounded the olifant once more—this time, alas ! but faintly—and when Charles heard it, in sorrow he turned to his barons and said, ' It is going ill. We shall lose my nephew Roland. I know by the sound of his horn that he hath not long to live.' This description is very suggestive of the thunder, first loud and presently spent and faintly rumbling. It should be remembered that, at the very time when this horn of Roland reached the ears of Charlemagne from far away, a tempest of thunder and lightning was raging over France. Roland may well have inherited his olifant from Thorr.

The history of Roncesvalles may have about it some lingering echoes of the prophecy of Ragnarök. We know that one of the tokens of the coming of the giants was to be the sound of the *Gjallar-horn*, blown by the god Heimdal, he who had been posted to hold the bridge Bifröst against the coming of Surtr. When the overwhelming host of the fire king comes upon him Heimdal is to sound that Gjallar-horn. Now this horn is undoubtedly the thunder. The peal belongs both to Heimdal and to Thorr; therefore the olifant of Roland may be the thunder too.

Literature of the kind represented by the Carlovingian epics belonged chiefly to the upper classes. These songs were sung by wandering minstrels not so often in the market-place as in the castle hall or bower. Half the barons of France traced descent in one way or another from the paladins, much as the petty Ionian kings to whom Homer sang deemed themselves the representatives of the chieftains who had joined in the conquest of Troy. The earlier songs from which the ' Chansons de Geste ' were a compilation were probably of a more popular character, but they are lost to us.

While these stories were being repeated in the lord's castle what sort of tales were passing current in the farm-house and the village, among vassals and serfs ? what

kind especially in those German lands where Wootan and
Donar had once swayed the popular creed?

There is in Germany a certain range of highlands
which, standing upon Switzerland as upon a base, stretches
up diagonally by the Black Forest and the Palatinate to
the Harz and Saxon Switzerland.   It corresponds to that
other series of elevations in eastern France or in Alsace
and Lorraine from the Vosges to the Ardennes.   Between
these ranges the broad Rhine wanders through fruitful
plains down to the Northern Sea.   The hills are two
opposing camps: the plain is the battle ground between
them.   Here has often been fought out the issue between
different nationalities and different creeds.   The eastern-
most of these two camps was once the stronghold of
German heathenism;   it is now the favourite home of
popular lore.   From this eastern range the Saxon or the
Thuringian once looked out upon his great river—his free
German Rhine and national god—and he saw it gradually
passing over to the new faith.   Cathedrals were rising all
along its banks: the great archbishoprics · founded by
Charles at Cologne and Mainz and Worms—Mainz, the
see of St. Boniface; Cologne, the most sacred and most
influential of the Middle Age towns of Germany; [1]—and
then beyond the Rhine, like the outposts of the advancing
army of Christendom, he saw other foundations spring up;
first among these the seven lesser sees established by
Charlemagne—Osnabrück, Minden, Paderborn, Werden,
Halberstadt, and Hildersheim, and the famous abbey of
Fulda.   As he beheld these churches rise, the heathen
German fled and hid himself in his mountain fastnesses.
How long his creed lingered there we cannot say, but when
it had finally departed it left the recollection of its presence
in the popular tradition.

The transformations which the German deities underwent when the people became Christianised took place

---

[1] The laws of the *hansa* were founded by the merchants of Cologne who
were resident in foreign lands.

more recently here than elsewhere, and therefore the recollection of the old gods is the clearer. It is here that
we must enquire if we wish to discover what became of
Wuotan and Donar, Freka and Holda. It is not in this
case as it is with the folk tales of the type of the 'Reineke
Fuchs,' or even with that popular mythology which peeps
from behind the legends of the saints. Both these kinds of
popular lore are chiefly of the universal folk-tale type, and
the beings which they introduce are such as would find
their counterparts in any land; as likely in the popular
tales of the Arabs or the Persians as in those of Europe.
A great proportion of the German folk tales are also of
this universal character; but there is another series which
contains certain tokens of the special German belief, and
which has much to tell us of the lingering effects of that
belief upon popular fancy.

First to notice is the legend of Hackelbärend, or
Hackelberg, or Herod, as he is variously called, the Wild
Huntsman, who is known to us in England as Herne the
Hunter. He is found all over North Germany and in
Denmark; he is well known in the Jura, and in the
Vosges, and in Switzerland; better known still in the
Harz. Hackelberg, the legend saith, was a wicked noble
who was wont to hunt upon Sundays as upon week days,
without distinction. One particular Easter Sunday he
had not only gone hunting himself, but had forced all his
peasantry to take a part in beating up the game. Presently
he was met by two horsemen: one was mild of aspect and
rode a white horse; the other was grim and fierce, seated
upon a coal-black steed, which from its mouth and nostrils
seemed to breathe fire. The one sought to dissuade him
from his enterprise, the other urged him on; but Hackelberg turned from his good angel and continued his wild
chase. So now, in company with the fiend, he hunts, and
will hunt to the Judgment Day. Men call him *Hel-jäger*,[1]

---

[1] In Low German also Dammjäger (Kuhn, *Sagen*, &c. ii. No. 9),
Bodenjäger (= Wodenjäger), Buddejäger, Woenjäger, Ewiger Jäger, &c.
(id. ii. 24-28).

hunter of hell. According to one tradition he seduced a nun, and she now rides by his side: some say she is transformed into the white owl Totosel; others call her Ursula[1]—a significant name.

Woe to the peasant who hears the wild chase sweeping towards him through some lonely mountain pass, and amid the din the cry of the Hel-jäger, '*Hoto! hutu!*' The barking of dogs may be distinguished from mid air, and yet nothing seen; or a rain of bloody drops may come down from above with a limb of one of the victims. One peasant boldly jeered at the Huntsman as he went by, and Hackelberg threw him down the arm of a man; 'for the Wild Huntsman,' says this legend, 'hunts only men.'[2]

There can be no doubt that the awful apparition is Odhinn himself transformed. Hakelbärend seems to have been the earliest name of the Huntsman; it means simply cloak-bearer, and we know how constantly Odhinn is represented travelling abroad clad in a long blue cloak, which is in fact the air or the cloud.[3] She who rides with the Wild Huntsman is the German goddess Hörsel (hence called Ursula), probably the same as Freyja,[4] and more remotely the same as Frigg. Odhinn and Freyja rode together to the field of battle to share in the division of the slain; in other words, they were the two psychopomps, or leaders of ghosts to the nether kingdom. Hackelberg performed a similar office; he was a hunter of men.

Hackelberg is, again, connected with some of the notions concerning the other world which in a former chapter we traced in Vedic mythology. We saw that in the Vedas the Milky Way was fancied to be the Bridge of Souls.

---

[1] Kuhn, ii. p. 10.

[2] Kuhn, ii. No. 21.

[3] Though of course the names given above render such testimony unnecessary.

[4] Hörsel, who seems sometimes to have represented the moon (hence Ursula and her ten thousand virgins, the stars), was also a goddess of love, as Freyja was. Thus in the various versions of the Tannhäuser legend we have sometimes a Hörselberg, sometimes a Venusberg, beneath which the enchantress is supposed to dwell.

Now Hackelberg is said to hunt all the year round along the Milky Way, save during the *twelve nights*[1]—those which intervene between Christmas and Twelfth Night—during this period he hunts on earth. He is accompanied by two dogs, who must be identical with the Sârameyas, the dogs of Yama.[2] All doors and windows should be kept shut when Hackelberg goes by; for if they are not, one of the dog fiends will rush into the house and will lie down on the hearth, whence no power will be able to make him move. There he will stay for a year, and during all that time there will be trouble in the house; but when the hunt comes round again he will rush wildly forth and join it.

Let us compare with this universal legend of Hackelberg another one which we find in Kuhn's collection.[3] Between the inhabitants of Epe and those of Engter there had existed for many years a dispute concerning their common boundary, or *mark*. Then came a man from Epe and swore that the boundary was so and so. But the oath was a false one; wherefore to this day that man forsworn comes at dusk to the boundary stone and sits upon it, crying 'Hoho! hoho!' and this he must do for ever. He is called Strêtmann (Streitmann, man of war?) This being is also, I suppose, the transformed Odhinn, who was once, we know, the arbiter of the *mark*, inasmuch as he was the impersonation of the storm.[4] The punishment here recorded was inflicted on him when he was dismissed from Asgard to hell, and from a god was changed into a fiend. Afterwards the crime was invented to account for the punishment. The same course was, no doubt, followed in the case of the Wild Huntsman, as well as in that more modern counterpart of him (evidently also a being of the

---

[1] On some of the beliefs concerning the 'twelve days' see Chap. VII. end.

[2] The 'wish hounds' that are heard in some parts of England are clearly these same dogs. 'Wish' is one of the names of Odhinn.—Grimm, *D. M*

[3] No. 34, p. 40. The story was orally communicated to Kuhn.

[4] See Chap. VII.

storm) Van der Dekken (the Man of the *Cloak*[1]), the Flying Dutchman. Herod, Hackelberg, Herne, Van der Dekken, Strètmann—these are all the counterparts of the great German god.

Two other stories must also be noticed. One is the 'Pied Piper of Hamelin,' which a great contemporary poet has rewritten with so much beauty, and has at the same time made so familiar to us, that the details need not be repeated here. The rats are symbolical of human souls. The Piper is the wind—that is, Odhinn—and the wind, again, in its character as the soul leader, like Hermês Psychopompos. The Piper's lute is the same as the lyre of Hermês; both have a music which none can disobey, for it is the whisper of death. First the Piper piped away the rats from the houses; but the townsfolk, freed from their burden, refused him his promised reward, and scornfully chased him from the town. On June 26 he was seen again, but this time (Mr. Browning has not incorporated this little fact) fierce of mien and dressed *like a huntsman*, yet still blowing upon the magic pipe. Now it was not the rats that followed, but the children. . . .

The symbolism of the soul by a mouse or rat, whatever may have been its origin and original meaning, seems to be a Slavonic idea.[2] Wherefore in this particular Hameln myth we can almost trace a history of the meeting of the two peoples German and Slavonic, and the uniting of their legends into one story. Let us suppose there had been some great and long-remembered epidemic which had proved particularly fatal to the children of Hameln and the country round about. The Slavonic dwellers there—and in early days Slavonians were to be found as far west as the Weser—would speak of these deaths mythically as the departure of the mice or rats

---

[1] Dutch *dek, deken*, is a 'cloak' as well as a 'deck;' *dekken*, 'to cover.'

[2] Ralston, *Songs of the Russian People*. Much has been said, and by many writers, of the connection between this story and the name of Apollo Smintheus (see Cox, *Aryan Myth.* &c.), but nothing which sheds any real light upon the place of rats or mice in either legend.

(i.e. the souls), and perhaps, keeping the tradition which
we know to be universally Aryan [1] of a water-crossing,
might tell of the souls having gone to the river; further,
they might deem that the souls had been led thither
by a piping wind god, for he is the property of Slavs
and Germans alike. Then the German inhabitants, wishing to express the legend in their mythical form, would
tell how the same Piper had piped away all the *children*
from the town; so a double story grew up about the
same event. The Weser represents the River of Death,
and might have served for the children as well as for the
rats; to make the legend fuller, another image of death
was chosen for the former, the mound or tomb. That
same mountain within which Charlemagne and Frederick
Redbeard sit, waiting for the Last Day, opened to let the
children pass, [2]

> And when all were in to the very last,
> The door in the mountain-side shut fast;

not to unclose again, we may believe, till the trumpets
shall sound at the Day of Doom. One more story—one of
universal extension—which bears a special relation to the
old idea of Odhinn is the story of the Wandering Jew.
This wretched man, as the legend goes, had mocked at Jesus
on His way to the Cross, and his doom was never to die
and never to rest, but to wander from land to land until
the Day of Judgment. His fate and the fate of Hackelberg and of Van der Dekken are therefore essentially the
same. In this case, and in that of Hackelberg or the
Flying Dutchman, nay, in the case of nearly all the heroes
of folk tales, the idea of sin and punishment is either
invented later than the original legend or introduced by a
side-wind of reflection into a pure nature myth. In every
instance cited the criminal is really none other than the
wind, who must perforce be the wanderer, who must be

---

[1] See Chap. VI.   [2] Ibid.

K K

the *Streitmann* or blusterous battle-goer, who must sit
for ever in the *mark* and whistle 'Hoho! hoto!'

The Wandering Jew, says the legend, may rest for one
night in the year, and that is the night of Shrove
Tuesday, or of Plough Monday, the day before. Tradition
varies on this point. Then, if anyone will leave a harrow
in the field, he will sit upon it and (this is not said in
every version) bring the man good luck. Others say that
he sits upon the plough.[1] This part of the myth makes
some confusion between the wind god and the earth
goddess; for it is Frigg or Nerthus who is connected with
the plough and whose rites (dragging her from place to
place upon a car) are still preserved on Shrove Tuesday
or on our Plough Monday.[2]

The stories which I have here cited are such as are
preserved in the present day; they are doubtless but inconsiderable fragments out of the great mass of Middle
Age legendary lore. Yet, such as they are, they will
serve, like chippings from a rock, to help us to guess at the
formations of thought which we cannot actually see. The
story of Hackelberg is by far the most important. It is,
in the first place, purely Teutonic; it is spread wherever a
German race has dwelt,[3] and it approaches most nearly
to the representation of Odhinn in the genuinely heathen
mythology. We have seen the Wild Huntsman riding
through the air, accompanied by Ursula, just as Odhinn
rode to battle accompanied by Freyja or by his Valkyriur.
Yet there is a difference between the two characters—a
vast one. Hackelberg is no god, but more than half a
fiend. There are some stories of benefits wrought by the
Wild Huntsman, but in most tales he and his dogs work
only ill. Wuotan was still remembered when this story
grew current, remembered by all the German-speaking

[1] Sometimes the *Ewige Jude* rests under two *oaks* grown *across*, i.e. the
oaks of Wuotan Christianised.—*Kuhn*, ii. No. 89.

[2] Chap. VII. § 2.

[3] Not always under the same *name*; but that fact makes the wide extension of the *story* more significant.

races, but he was remembered with fear and abhorrence.
This change will prepare us for the completer change
which we shall have to note anon when Odhinn became the
Prince of Darkness, and his swan maidens, the Valkyriur,
were transformed into witches.

From the two standpoints of the knightly epic and
the popular tale, we may form our estimate of the imaginative world of mediæval Europe. If we choose to raise
our eyes and study the actual world, we· shall see how
well it fitted into the ideal creation which clothed it round.
From the time of Charlemagne onwards, during all those
ages in which the Karling epic and the mediæval popular
tale were growing to their maturity, society had been
visibly settling down into a single fixed condition; it was
stiffening into that unchangeable though beautiful shape
of which the words Feudalism and Catholicism convey
some faint picture, and which is shown in a sort of allegory
by the architecture of the Gothic cathedral.

No sooner had the conquests of the Teuton races been
secured and their external enemies been put to silence,
than the people began again to turn their arms against
one another. Once each lesser leader had been like the
subordinate officer of an army, in strict dependence upon
the chief of the whole; but no sooner did they begin to
establish themselves permanently in the new lands than
they set up claims of independence, and erected their own
tribes or followings into miniature principalities. Then
arose the same rivalry and the same slumbering or active
war between barony and barony which had in old Teutonic
days existed between village and village. We see this
state of feeling plainly reflected in the ' Chansons de
Geste;' for even in the earliest among them, the ' Chanson
de Roland,' Ganelon and Roland make no scruple of defy-
ing one another while in the presence of Charles, in whose
army they are both officers. Ganelon's great act of
treachery, whereby the whole of Charles's rear-guard,

with Roland at the head, perished in the pass of Roncesvalles, was chiefly brought about by his desire to
revenge himself for the insult which he had received from
Roland. The incident shows us how much stronger might
be the influence of a private feud than of public duty.
In other 'Chansons' the same feelings are expressed much
more openly. In very many of them we see a powerful
baron bidding defiance to Charles and to all his army;
as, for example, did Girard de Viane, one of the great
heroes of these lays. One poem, 'Garin le Loherin,' is
entirely devoted to the description of feudal wars, and
contains nothing else but the history of a long vendetta
feud between two houses.

The growth of such a feeling must have made men
look to the security of their homes. Wherefore the result
was that in the age of Charlemagne and in the ages which
succeeded him we see the gradual rise of more and more
castles and the steady abandonment of the open villas in
which the chief notables had before lived. The Teutons,
when they came into new lands, took away the villas from
their possessors and adopted them for their own homes.
As these fell into decay, in their place strongholds began
to rise on every side. The villas had stood in open sunny
plains by river banks; but the castles perched themselves
on barren rocks or in steep mountain passes, and, like the
spirit of mediæval Christianity itself, they became at once
dark and aspiring.

The convents followed the example of the castles.
They too had once stood unenclosed, unguarded, in the
plain and by the river. A type of that earlier convent
was the one built by St. Eligius [1] (Eloi) near Liége, of
which St. Ouen, the biographer of Eligius, gives us a
delightful picture. It was merely a country villa converted by the saint to his pious purpose. It stood in the
midst of beautiful woods and bounded on one side by a

---

[1] A contemporary of the Merovingian king Dagobert I.

stream. The convent grounds were enclosed by no wall, only by a bank of earth surmounted by a hedge. An orchard immediately surrounded the monastery. 'And in the midst of this delightful retreat,' exclaims St. Ouen, 'the saddest mind is invigorated and enjoys its share of the blessings of a terrestrial paradise.'[1]

In the Carlovingian age the religious houses gradually changed their appearance and their sites. They, like the castles, sought to place themselves upon elevated spots, 'to be nearer heaven,' and they too became gloomy and armed. This change involved a change in the internal life of the convents. Constant work in the fields and in the open air had been one of the rules of St. Benedict. This was first set aside by the great founder of Western monastic institutions, St. Columba. It fell more and more into disuse. Instead of such healthy exercise the monks gave themselves up to sedentary pursuits; and when not engaged in religious exercises they were copying and illuminating MSS., writing down the 'Lives of the Saints,' or what not. It is easy to guess what effect the change of occupation had upon the thoughts of the cenobites and upon the development of the monastic system of theology.

The church architecture was affected by this new taste for building. Violet-le-Duc says that the seeds of that architecture which afterwards grew into the Gothic were implanted in the days of Charlemagne,[2] although men were yet many centuries ahead of the perfecting of that wondrous growth. While the church remained still in the basilica form, the first change was introduced at this time by the adding of the apse, the roof of which apse was generally arched. In this way men first passed from the flat roof to the round one. A more important novelty still was the building of church towers, which likewise began in the days of Charlemagne. The towers were not attached to the churches, but stood beside them, as we still

[1] *Vita S. Elig.* c. xvi.
[2] *Dict. de l'Arch.*, art. 'Architecture.'

commonly see them standing beside the churches of North Italy; and from these heights the bells now sent out their new music over the plain.[1] To us they are the voices from a bygone world.

The symbolism of Christianity—its white robes of baptism, its curtains, its bell tones, its lighted candles and incense—must have told more upon the imaginative spirit of heathenism than any mere preaching could have done. Take the picture which Bæda draws for us of the first landing of St. Augustine on the shores of Kent—of the procession which the Apostle and his brother missionaries formed with their crosses and tapers; of their white robes, their chaunting.[2] More wondrous even than the church bells was the church organ. Organs were said to have been first introduced in the West by Charles, and to have been brought to him by an embassy from the Byzantine Emperor; and tradition tells us of a woman who, in the reign of Charlemagne's successor, Louis, entered the cathedral at Metz, and there suddenly heard an organ for the first time. She was so overcome with emotion at the sound that she fell down and died there. Is the event an impossibility? I scarcely think so.

From this time forth mediæval life and society began to take their permanent shapes. And mediæval life and society rested, as we know, upon two pillars, each mighty but not of equal strength. The weaker of the two pillars was feudalism, the stronger and the more durable was Catholicism. Now, as regards feudalism; modern research and our more accurate knowledge concerning the growth of human institutions has tended greatly to modify the views which were once held concerning it. Feudalism was once thought to have been an entirely new birth in the Middle Ages, a pure invention of those times; but this theory is not now generally maintained. On the contrary,

---

[1] *New music.* Bells are not mentioned in any legends of the *Acta Sanctorum*, which are of an earlier date than the seventh century.

[2] See also Grimm, *D. M.* i. 4; Greg. Tur. ii. 31.

it is recognised that feudalism is a descendant—in a remote degree indeed, and with many features unknown to
the parent—of the German society of prehistoric times,
of that ancient constitution of the *village community* concerning which in a former chapter something was said.
Feudalism is a return to as near an imitation of the
village community as the changed conditions of surrounding things would allow. During their era of invasion the
German races had exchanged their primæval social or-
ganisation for the constitution of an army. In place
of their old tribal headmen or petty kings they had
ranged themselves under elected military leaders, duces,
heretogas.[1] This camp life lasted very many years, and
during their revolution some of the invading nations forgot
altogether their past, and when they came to settle down
adopted or imitated the civilisation of the Gauls and
Romans. This was the case with the Goths of Italy, of
Southern Gaul, and of Spain; in a less degree it was the
case with the Lombards. With the Franks and the other
invaders of the North—and these were the races who gave
the tone to the civilisation on this side of the Alps and
Pyrenees—it was not so. When they settled down they
fell back upon a social state which does recall the Teutonic
society of prehistoric days. They did this not in conscious

---

[1] The rex (i.e. *riks* or *kununc*) is distinguished from the dux (i.e.
heretoga, herzog) by Tacitus (*Germ*. c. 7). We must for historic Germany
(i.e. the Teuton race after the era of invasion began) distinguish two kinds
of society—(1) the peaceful, which implies the *village community* and the
king, (2) the warlike, which implies the *camp* and the *herzog*. Of course
this is not a fixed rule, and applies only to those places where part of the
nation remained behind as a kind of depôt. When a whole nation took to
conquest or migration the king was general also and leader. The two
types of society are reflected in the legends of this time of invasion: the
typical hero, Beowulf or Siegfried, who

' Durch seines Leibes Stärke ritt in manche Land'
(*Nibelungen*, 87, Busching),

being the representative of the young blood, is the herzog; Higelac, Sieg-
mund, Gunther, are the kings. See also some remarks of M. Guizot on the
camp life and comparatively small numbers of the invaders, *Cours de
l'Histoire de France*, i. 279; and Michelet, *Hist. de France*, i. 300.

imitation or even in recollection of their past, but because the national character tends always to form around itself the same social atmosphere. Feudalism was the nearest compromise they could make with the new sort of civilisation into which they had been forced. The English on the one side, and the Christianised Germans beyond the Rhine upon the other side, accepted in time this compact and adopted feudalism.

This, then, was in matters of social governance the compromise effected between ancient German prejudices and a changed outer world. Not less was mediæval Christianity also, and in an especial sense the Christianity north of the Alps, a compromise in matters of belief and of thought with bygone times. Mediæval Christianity likewise had its roots in prehistoric German heathenism. Some of these roots at least were there; for, like the tree Yggdrasill, Catholicism had many different roots in many different places; some were in heaven, but some were, we cannot question it, on earth, and some perchance in hell.

Religion may extend its sway over many regions of man's thought. It may chiefly affect his political feelings, or his social morality, or his artistic sense. It may give new dignity to man, and impart to him added pleasure in life and in the works of life. These were not the aims of mediæval Christianity. The essential lesson which it strove to teach was a profound sense of the supernatural, of a spiritual world enclosing this sensible world, as our earth is surrounded by its atmosphere, and of the little span of our life bounded by two eternities. This sense of mystery and of spiritual dominion found its nourishment in the thoughts which through centuries of gloomy forest life had grown familiar to the Teutonic mind, and which we know had left a deep impression on Teutonic belief. And although the creed of heathen Germany was in itself sensuous and material and concerned only in questioning the aspects of external nature, yet it had

of that immaterial perception of the Infinite which so
characterises mediæval Catholicism. It gave a training to
the imagination such as was destined afterwards to bear
abundant fruit. Awe and mystery were as the nourishing
rain and dew to the belief of the heathen German. Wherefore this belief developed afterwards into Catholicism
almost as necessarily as the society of the village commune
grew into the system of feudalism. But in the case of
feudalism and Catholicism alike, although there is a
resemblance to the earlier life and thought of pre-Christian
days, there is also a strange difference. It seems as if in
either case a living organism had been suddenly petrified
by some gorgon glance. The thing is fixed in its highest
development truly, a growth of wondrous dimensions and
of multiform delicate interlacings, but it has not the power
of further growth. Though made up of the fairest shapes,
it is of stone.

By gentle stages the Gothic cathedral grew to its
perfect form, and became the best expression of the
thought, the belief, the whole world-philosophy of the
Middle Ages. Gradually the Roman basilica changed into
the Romanesque church; slowly the Romanesque church
raised its roof and narrowed its aisles and multiplied
its pillars, until what had once been a house four-square,
visible from one end to the other, grew into a very forest
of stony trees, with glades and by-paths and dark recesses
as numerous and as bewildering as in the forest itself.
What had once been a common dwelling-house became
the seat of a mysterious, unseen, and awful Presence.
But we cannot say that this cathedral was altogether a
new creation of mankind, or that it had no relationship
to those forest fastnesses in which through so many ages
the ancestors of all the nations of Northern Europe—the
Teutons and the Celts alike [1]—had paid their vows to the
Wind God. And if the Gothic cathedral do own some

[1] See p. 332.

distant cousinhood to the forest temple of prehistoric
days, then certainly mediæval Christianity cannot refuse
to acknowledge a relationship to ancient Northern heathenism.

It was a belief of the Middle Ages that cunning Satan,
in order to gain sway over men's souls, would sometimes
enter the grass of the field, which in this way, when eaten
by the ox, transferred his devilish nature to the flesh of
that animal; then when the ox beef was consumed by man
his being became thereby corrupted and an entry was made
for sin.   It was a sort of sacrament reversed.   We might
suppose some such transfer of spirit to have taken place
when the shrines of German heathendom were made the
sites of temples to the new faith.   Boniface and Willibrod
went forth cutting down the sacred trees of Odhinn and
Thorr, and making out of them timber for Christian
churches.   They might well have taken warning from the
story of Satan in the grass.   For in very truth there was
a spirit lurking in those old shrines who refused to be
exorcised and driven away; the ancients would have called
him the δαίμων ἐπιχώριος, the *genius loci*, the genius of the
place; what we more prosaically name the association of
ideas.   Christianity found nothing so hard to drive away
as these genii of the soil; indeed, she never succeeded in
driving them away utterly, but had to make compromises
with them and to allow some at least (some formal changes
made in outward guise) to retain their homes.

In the German tongues we find that a word which in
one dialect means holy or temple means in another forest.
And this is as much as to say that the forest was ever
holy to the Teutons, and their sacred places were ever
their forest glades.   When Catholicism had attained its
full growth, and had by successive changes mo
holy place to express in the fullest way its
it once more worshipped in a grove—
In place of the trunks and branching t
along endless aisles of pillars and up

roof. This expresses in sum the difference between the old life and the new. The village community of ancient days had been stiffened into the immutable society of feudalism, and the old creed with its ancient shrine had been petrified into Catholicism and its cathedral. The trees were in a fashion still there. But they no longer put on fresh forms with the changing seasons. The branches no longer moved, swayed by the wind. No glimpses of a higher heaven could be seen above them; no stars shone down through their interstices. Yet here the old associations of solemnity and gloom remained. Here now dwelt *secretum illud* the Sacred Presence which the Teutons had so long worshipped.

Let us enter this temple of Catholicism. . In the centre we see a lighted altar, the rays from which are soon lost among the clusters of pillars and in the vaulted roof. Where this light reaches it shines upon beatified saints or angels, who spread their protecting wings and look down upon the worshipper. Here we are safe, within the charmed circle, close to the sacred relics or to the Body of Christ; but wherever pillar or groin throws a shadow, there may be detected, flying from the light and cherishing the darkness, images of the damned in hideous pain, or it may be devils in wait for the erring soul. And now those bat-like creatures which had once flitted about the outer trees of the grove, uttering mournful cries, are within the sacred aisles, themselves turned to stone. The organ sends forth its solemn, appealing sounds, the host is lifted up, the chaunt arises, and the powers of darkness are for awhile defeated. Yet this organ tone is but the wind of the forest made melodious; it is Odhinn himself transformed and brought into obedience to the new faith. The organ's music puts to flight the powers of darkness; but they are still there. Even if they are driven from the church they are still without the walls.[1] What if the

---

[1] Throughout the France of the Middle Ages, and in Germany and England likewise, it was the custom on certain days to make procession

worshipper, passing alone in the night, forget to cross himself, to bow before the altar or to dip his hand into the holy water?

For all around the Christian, nearer than he could tell, lay that dreadful world of spirits. Jötunheimar had drawn its coasts closer than they had been in heathen times. This was the case even in the days when the poem of Beowulf was written. Only the *heathen* might venture to live far away from human habitations. And it was this dread of the outer world which kept men fixed to one spot, and made them bear the burden of that feudal system which pressed with terrible weight on lord and tenant alike. The vassal was attached to the soil, and the lord too was rooted to the rock from which his castle sprang. '*No land without its lord,* also *no lord without his land* Man belongs to a single place. He is judged according as men can say he is of high and low place. There he is localised, immovable, held down under the weight of his heavy castle and his heavy armour.'[1]

This is the picture which is held up to us when we try and look into the Europe of the Middle Ages. The baron in his castle alone, unneighboured save for purposes of war. All without his own domain was strange, and in great measure under the governance of spirits. The distant sounds he heard, like those bells which 'from Langdale Pike and Witches' Lair' gave answer to the bells of Sir Leoline,'[2] were the sound of sinful spirits compelled by the Prince of Darkness. These tales of fear grew from age to age since the castle first rose upon the rock. The

through the town, carrying the image of Satan portrayed as a dragon. The procession knocked down everyone who crossed its path, and came at last to the church door, where the evil one was exercised. The image, we see, though it cannot enter the church, triumphs everywhere else. In the South they called the image *drac* or *tarasque*; in the North he was called *gargouille*, and under this latter name we still see him outside our churches.

[1] Michelet, *Hist. de France*, ii. 392.
[2] *Christabel.*

intense gloom which follows in the track of *ennui* deepened
the natural sombreness of all men's thoughts. The gloom
crept round them like a fog, around the baron and his
men-at-arms in the castle, around the villagers beneath
the castle hill, and thence it infected those men—growing
fewer from year to year—who lived away in the outlands.
This was the time when the old popular mythology of
Wuotan and the gods of Walhalla changed its guise,
when, passing through the characters of the Wild Huntsman and the Wandering Jew, the god was gradually transformed into the likeness of a fiend. Then grew up that
new system of mythology, or we may say that new worship,
which we call witchcraft.

The splendour of the Gothic cathedral shows us one
side of the belief of the Middle Ages. But there is
another side very different from that. The true antithesis, and yet in a manner the counterpart, to mediæval
Catholicism is the mediæval belief concerning witchcraft.

The partial transformation, which we noted just now,
of the chief god of ancient heathenism into Hackelberg
must prepare us for his total change into the Prince of
Darkness, the 'Prince of the Powers of the Air;' for this
last, out of all the Biblical names for Satan, was the one
most commonly used in the Middle Ages, and the one
which suited him best in his Odinic character. The most
striking and characteristic of all the Odhinn myths was
that which told of the god and the Valkyriur riding
together to the battle field; this in its transformed condition became the great Satan myth of the *Sabbath*. Hence
it is that we find the metropolis of mediæval Satan worship
to have been the last stronghold of Odinism. This lay in
the mountainous land of Saxony, the Harz.

We can in some instances trace the process which has
transformed lovely shield maidens, the companions of a
god, once the ideal of womanhood to the rude chivalry of
the North, into wretched hags, riding upon broomsticks,

upon trusses of hay, or upon sieves,[1] to join the Prince of Darkness in his midnight orgies.

In the story of Balderus and Hotherus in Saxo Grammaticus, which tells in a form more nearly resembling the form of mediæval legends the history of the death of Balder, we meet with some wood-women in a transition state between Valkyriur and witches. It was the part of the Valkyria to chaunt runes over her *Liebling*, her chosen warrior, and to bless his arms against hurt; she, as much as her later representative, was a professor of magic. But the Valkyriur had no need to conceal their powers; they were beings of the air and sunlight, not of caves and darkness. The wood-women to whom Hotherus goes do for him just what the Valkyriur always did for their heroes, just what, for example, Sigrdrífa (Brynhild) had done for Agnar; but they are only to be found in darkness; they have to be sought out in the thickest parts of the forest or in caves.

Balderus and Hotherus are in the story rivals for the love of Nanna, and are at war. And Saxo relates how, when Hotherus was hard pressed by his enemy, it fell out that one day, when hunting, having lost his way in a fog, he came unawares upon a conclave of young maidens, who saluted him and of whom he enquired their name. 'They affirmed that it was under their guidance and countenance that the fortune of a battle was determined, for they were often present at battles, when no one beheld them, and brought a wished for victory by their friendly aid.' They promised help to Hotherus, but good fortune did not always attend him, and afterwards we find him again in Denmark, beaten and hard pressed by Balderus. In this condition he was one day wandering in a vast and trackless

---

[1]   'In a sieve I'll hither sail' (i.e. corn sieve).—*Macbeth.*
The use of this means of locomotion is common among witches in folk tales. Moreover tradition says that a witch can be detected by any person who looks through a corn sieve (Kuhn, ii. No. 77, and Castrén, *F. M.* p. 68). Is this because the witches are sometimes earth goddesses transformed?

wood, when he found by chance the *cave* inhabited by his friends the maidens, whom he knew for those who had formerly presented him with an invulnerable garment. They enquired of him the cause of his coming, and he narrated to them the unlucky course which events had taken, and, complaining of the misfortune which had attended his endeavour and of the non-fulfilment of their promises, he declared that he would give up his designs. But the nymphs assured him that he had also inflicted great damage upon his opponent; moreover that the fortune of war would be his, if he could obtain possession of some magic food which was effective in renewing the strength of Balderus. Hotherus obtained this food, which was made of the spittle of serpents, and on his way back met Balderus, whom he wounded so severely that he died in the next day's battle.[1]

I have kept the names which Saxo employs; he calls these Valkyriur nymphs. But, recalling first what we remember of the nature of the shield maidens of Odhinn, and turning from them to contemplate the mediæval witch, do not these nymphs of Saxo seem to be in the actual course of change from one to the other? They preside over all battles and determine the issue of them; but they have their dwellings in caves of the wood, and their magic food made with the spittle of serpents. This last reminds us forcibly of the witches' cauldron in ' Macbeth ' or in ' Faust.'

We have seen that witchcraft was not only a form of belief, but likewise, to some extent, a form of *worship*.

Some suppose the sieve to typify the whirlwind, which is, of course, a very suitable accompaniment to Odhinn-Satan and to his band, and which also constitutes a recognised form of punishment in hell (see *Inferno*, canto 5).

[1] This part of the narrative, the climax, as one would have thought, is told with a brevity which reminds us of some passages in the idylls of a great contemporary poet. 'Qui cum pristinum iter remetiendo calle quo venerat repedaret, obvii sibi Balderi latus hausit eumque seminecem prostravit.'— *Historia Danica*, lib. iii.

We should be wrong if we imagined that it was the mere horror of magic which made up the dread and the detestation with which witchcraft came to be regarded in the Middle Ages. Magic was an idea so familiar to the minds of men at that time that it had scarce the power of alone exciting any very strong feeling. Magic was practised as much in causes accounted good as in bad ones. Did the witch cut off the hair from a corpse, and use that to raise the wind; why then Christianity too used the hair of a corpse (of a saint [1]), the paring of his nails, as talismans against shipwreck. The magic wand or the dead man's hand could make bolts fly back and locks open, and point to treasure hidden deep in the ground. So could the bones of a martyr, the nail or arrow, or spear, which had pierced him and drunk his blood, his dress, or even a fragment of any of these relics. We have in the Kalewala, and more sparsely in the Sagas, wonderful descriptions of the way in which the *steel*—sword or axe—was gifted with its power to hurt. Had Roland been a Norse hero instead of a champion of Christianity, we should have had the account of the runes said over his sword Durendal by some Valkyria maid. As it is we find it owed its indestructibility to more material, and therefore lower, kinds of magic. There was in the guard of Durendal a tooth of St. Peter, some of the blood of St. Basil, of the hair of St. Denis, of the weeds of the Virgin; [2] and, as a further example of the pure materialism that appears in the conception of magic at this time, we find that the power which the relics bestowed would be as useful to a Saracen if he gained possession of the sword as they were to Roland.

The Church therefore did not condemn witchcraft on

---

[1] A hair of St. Peter was sent to Norman William by the Pope to aid him in his invasion of England.

[2] *Chanson de Roland*, l. 2346 sqq. On this account, because Durendal would be as effective in the hands of a Saracen as in that of a Christian, Roland just before his death makes every effort to break the steel, but cannot. See also what was said in Chap. II. p. 89.

account of its material and superstitious character. In earlier and more enlightened days that had been the accusation brought against it. ' *Our* miracles,' Augustine had said, ' are worked by simple faith and the assurance which comes of trust in God, not by auguries or sacrilegious enchantments.' [1] But this was not the feeling of a later age. The real distinction between the witch and the priest was that the one was the practiser of a black art, the other of a white one ; one was the votary of Satan, the other of Christ. This was quite well understood on both sides ; the sorcerer introduced into his cult of Satan [2] a ritual the distinct antithesis of the Catholic ritual ; a black mass was opposed to the white mass. In this way witchcraft grew to be distinctly a *craft*. It became, that is to say, a social body, and had a *mystery* (of the religious sort) uniting its members. This cult was, in all probability, originally a mere survival of heathenism, and the mystery, like all other mysteries, at first of a simple kind, developing afterwards into more elaborate rites.

This mystery is known to us as the Witches' Sabbath. It would be a mistake to think of the celebration as a purely imaginary one created by popular superstition, and existing only in the minds of brain-sick old women who *fancied* they had attended it. The *Walpurgis-nacht* meeting on the Brocken may have been fancy, but, if so, it was only the imaginary consummation of a hundred, a thousand, a hundred thousand Sabbaths which were really celebrated in different parts of Europe. They were not confined to a few, nor were they everywhere regarded with the horror which priestly chroniclers feel and would have

[1] *De Civ. Dei*, viii. 9.

[2] Some popular tales witness in a curious way to the affection which the peasantry felt for Satan, i.e. for Satan-Odhinn. They try to save him by making him turn Christian. Compare, for example, the stories in Kuhn's collection (No. 220), *The Devil's Longing for God, Woking becomes a Christian, Woking's Baptism*, &c. (294, &c.)

us feel. In some places they were openly practised and commonly recognised. In the Basque province, for instance, all went, nobles included. 'Once none but the insensate were seen there; now people of position openly attend,' exclaims an inquisitor.[1] Priests even went, celebrating the white mass in the morning and the black mass at night. No doubt but that the celebration of the Sabbath —whatever name it might first have received—had at one time a more innocent guise than under the pressure of persecution it afterwards wore. But there was always in it a certain protest in favour of the old times, a protest both against Catholicism and against the twin brother of Catholicism, the social system of feudalism. It expressed a kind of communism; nobles, burghers, peasants, shepherds, were mingled in the feast with which the evening began; contributions were exacted by force, and fines were imposed for non-attendance. Such a strange inverted system of Catholicism would be especially likely to arise among a people who were in a degree alienated from their neighbours, the dwellers in some corner of a country, such as the inhabitants of the Jura, the Bretons, the men of the Basque Provinces. I imagine this initiatory feast to have been the earliest and most essential part of the Sabbath celebrations; afterwards followed other ceremonials, copied from the ritual of the Church— that ritual which in the tenth and eleventh centuries, from the final disappearance of spoken Latin, had become unmeaning to all; and in darker days of persecution the Sabbath ended in blasphemous defiance of the Head and Founder of Christianity.[2]

In the darkness which hides from our eyes the mediæval practice of witchcraft the last remains of the cult of the

---

[1] Lancre, quoted by Michelet, *Sorcière*.
[2] For a detailed description of the rites of the Sabbath see Michelet's *Sorcière*, ch. x.

heathen gods disappear. Long before witchcraft had reached its culminating point[1] a rumour of change made itself heard. In the midst of the intense stillness of the Middle Ages a faint movement began, a gentle rustling which betokened rather a coming than an actual wind. The first apostle of change was Peter the Hermit, who, in preaching the deliverance of Jerusalem, preached too the deliverance of many from the *ennui* which stifled them, and in pointing the way to the Holy Land showed men likewise a way to escape from the monotony of life. Immense must have been the relief to thousands. A road was opened to them to the unknown East; an impulse was imparted to them strong enough to break through the stifling laws of custom, and to give play again to the nomadic instincts which can never be killed in human nature. All the better that this new expedition was blessed by the Pope and approved of Holy Church. In thousands and tens of thousands men joined the standard of Walter the Penniless, careless many of them about the differences between Saracen and Christian, but longing only for some relief from the *ennui* of their dreary existence.

It was this mere transition from stillness to movement which awoke the world and heralded the Renaissance. In the train of this one great motive power followed other lesser ones, which are more easily distinguishable as the immediate forerunners of the Renaissance era. One of these was the growth of the burgher spirit, incidental partly to the absence of the seigneurs. The nobles flocked to the Holy Land; some few settled and many more died there. At home there followed an age of regencies or of weak younger princes sitting in a brother's seat, such as was our John. To obtain the means to emigrate the king and the nobleman alike needed money, and for the first time since the fall of the Roman Empire the want of a medium

---

[1] This we must take to have been at the beginning of the fourteenth century. See Lecky, *Rationalism*, p. 47.

of exchange came to be strongly felt.
of demon of change, inherently and f
slow, fixed, conservative life, such as w
Money, like writing, brings far thing
thoughts of another kind of life fro
moment we are leading. It was easi
demon than to lay it again. Liter
time little to tell us of the burgher cl
was the very arms and armour, or w
who in the peasant tale puts into
born swain the means to conquer a
Christendom. Still less has it to
forgers underground, the very mine
the treasure, who were hidden ben
knightly and literary society, but
selves to their old task of throwi
world in the shape of coined gold. T
the Rhine gold of the Nibelungen, w
the *Hardi d'or*.[1]

With money the burghers bough
the cities arose to rival the seigne
another novelty appeared, the ver
currency, of portentous significance t
knights—I mean the mercenary sold
a new sort of military science, a n
honour and courage, born of a new d
instinct of communalism.

Perhaps it was during this time
legend of the ' Reineke Fuchs ' took
expressed the feelings of the burgh
became more pointed and more consp

---

[1] Struck by Philip le Hardi, son of St. Lou
Fair. The issue of this coin may be reckoned
currency in Europe north of the Alps. St. Lou
gold coins, but probably very few only, as the
mann, *Monnaies royales de France*, p. 19). The
and of our Edward III. are the eras of a large g

instead of being a representative of the lower people,
became a knight, and as such a living satire upon the
knightly class. At this time too sprang up the form of
literature which was especially created for the burgher
class. That was the *fabliau*. What the 'Chansons de
Geste' at first, and later on the romances of chivalry or
the love songs of the troubadours, were for the highest
class, what the original forms of the Beast Epic and the
Legend of the Saints were for the lowest, such were the
fabliaux for the burgher middle class.

It was in deference to the same spirit of change, the
love of movement which was passing over Europe, that
Francis and Dominic instituted in the thirteenth century
their orders of begging friars. The rule of this new class
of monk was the exact converse of the rule of Benedict of
Nursia, the organiser and almost the founder of western
monasticism, and of the great revivers of that monasticism,
Columba and Bernard. In the ordinances of all these
strictest measures were taken to prevent the monk from
wandering from his home. He was absolutely forbidden
to partake of food outside the walls of the monastery;
and if a brother were obliged to be absent from it for a
whole day he was enjoined to fast. The Dominicans and
Franciscans, on the contrary, were to have no fixed home
and were never to rest for long in one place.[1] One cannot
but see that the rise of the begging friars was a direct
outcome of the spirit of the age, and unconsciously one
of the death blows to that very Catholicism which it
sought to revive. This is perhaps why these orders
degenerated sooner than did any other. What they had
become in the course of a century and a half from the
time of their institution we may judge from the pages of
Chaucer.

It is not our business here to trace the decline of the

---

[1] This at least was the original institution. It was not long observed.

mediæval spirit. The period at which w
arrived is important to the subject in hand fo
only, that Mediævalism did at this hour of dea
her greatest fruits. It was at this time—tl
during the thirteenth century—that the Gothic
attained the perfection of its form. And it
of this century or the early years of the suc
which gave birth to the second great pro
Middle Ages, the 'Divine Comedy' of Dante.
of these and of its gradual development sol
been said. Unlike the Gothic architecture,
Dante was a sudden growth. Nothing forete
literature of the preceding age. That from v
drew his inspiration was the legend of the
the thoughts concerning the other world witl
men of the cloister were chiefly concerned. T
and the heathen elements in them we have j
in a former chapter. They were couched in p
the greater part were prose of the dreariest cha
their dull literalness helped Dante to weave
tissue of imaginative creation. Just as in it
harmonious metre the 'Comedy' is allied not
alliterative Northern lay, nor to the uncertaii
the ballad, nor the faint assonance of the '
Geste,' but to the measured music of the cat
and the rhyming Latin hymn, so in matter th
been born of the musings and dreams of the
of the experience of the outer world. To tl
lived in such reveries the history of Europe re
changed. The world had passed from the j
Karling epic to the license of the troubadoui
the simplicity of the saint legends to the ci
the *fabliaux* or the pungent satire of the '
Vos.' But they remarked it not. The hyn
music which had been invented by Pope Grei
still suitable to the worship of the thirteen

and they and the thoughts which they uttered were still suitable to Dante. The 'Divine Comedy' is little else than an expanded *Dies iræ*—expanded truly and purified, and with a *Dies beatitudinis* added. It is because he is imbued with the beliefs of an era that had passed that Dante is so perfect a mirror of the highest thought of the Middle Ages.

In our ideal picture of the poet we are wont to fancy him marching ahead of his age, anticipating by his divine prophetic insight thoughts which are but beginning to stir faintly the rest of mankind, and discovering new truths which the slow course of enquiry will reveal to future generations. Is this theory justified by the history of genius? What shall we say of Shakespeare? Is there more of feudalism and of old aristocratic chivalry in him than of modern love of freedom and free opinion? Is it not true what Carlyle says of Shakespeare, that in him Catholicism was still alive, albeit it had been declared by Act of Parliament to be defunct? What, again, shall we say of Carlyle himself, to whom the modern theory of evolution is only another among many instances of the whimsical folly of mankind? In the same way to Dante the new outlook westward which was beginning to dawn upon mariners was impious merely; and the new outlook which was dawning upon men's spirits was not less impious and strange. When he wrote, for Italy at least, feudalism was already a past thing, and everywhere Catholicism was dying or in its death throes. But in statecraft Dante had always before his imagination that vision of the Holy Roman Empire, the ultimate source of all earthly power, which was of the very essence of feudalism. And he alone among his contemporaries looked into the other world with the eyes and in the spirit of Catholicism.

Thus outwardly his life was a failure. All things were taking a bent different from the direction Dante would have given them. But coming thus, as one born out of

time, to him it fell to accomplish a task which to no one else in the world at that time would have been possible. Many were the heralds of morning celebrating the rise of new beliefs and of new principles of life. To Dante it was given only to sit and lament over a darkening world, to assist at the obsequies of a dead creed, and for its enshrinement to prepare a costly and splendid tomb.

INDEX.